THE PUBLIC SECTOR IN AN AGE OF AUSTERITY

The Public Sector in an Age of Austerity

Perspectives from Canada's Provinces and Territories

Edited by

BRYAN EVANS AND CARLO FANELLI

McGill-Queen's University Press
Montreal & Kingston • London • Chicago

ISBN 978-0-7735-5334-7 (cloth)
ISBN 978-0-7735-5335-4 (paper)
ISBN 978-0-7735-5418-4 (ePDF)
ISBN 978-0-7735-5419-1 (ePUB)

Legal deposit second quarter 2018
Bibliothèque nationale du Québec

Printed in Canada on acid-free paper that is 100% ancient forest free (100% post-consumer recycled), processed chlorine free

This book has been published with the help of a grant from the Canadian Federation for the Humanities and Social Sciences, through the Awards to Scholarly Publications Program, using funds provided by the Social Sciences and Humanities Research Council of Canada. Funding was also received from the Office of the Dean of Arts, Ryerson University.

Funded by the Government of Canada | Financé par le gouvernement du Canada | Canada

Canada Council for the Arts | Conseil des arts du Canada

We acknowledge the support of the Canada Council for the Arts, which last year invested $153 million to bring the arts to Canadians throughout the country.

Nous remercions le Conseil des arts du Canada de son soutien. L'an dernier, le Conseil a investi 153 millions de dollars pour mettre de l'art dans la vie des Canadiennes et des Canadiens de tout le pays.

Library and Archives Canada Cataloguing in Publication

The public sector in an age of austerity: perspectives from Canada's provinces and territories/edited by Bryan Evans and Carlo Fanelli.

Includes bibliographical references and index.
Issued in print and electronic formats.
ISBN 978-0-7735-5334-7 (cloth) – ISBN 978-0-7735-5335-4 (paper) – ISBN 978-0-7735-5418-4 (ePDF) – ISBN 978-0-7735-5419-1 (ePUB)

1. Finance, Public – Canada – Provinces. 2. Fiscal policy – Canada – Provinces. 3. Civil service – Canada – Provinces. 4. Neoliberalism – Canada – Provinces. 5. Global Financial Crisis, 2008–2009 – Government policy – Canada – Provinces. 6. Canada – Appropriations and expenditures, Provincial. I. Evans, Bryan M., 1960–, editor II. Fanelli, Carlo, 1984–, editor

JL198.P83 2018 336'.01371 C2018-901384-2
C2018-901385-0

This book was typeset by Marquis Interscript in 10.5/13 Sabon.

Contents

Tables and Figures

TABLES

FIGURES

THE PUBLIC SECTOR IN AN AGE OF AUSTERITY

INTRODUCTION

The Permanent Unequal Union: Canada's Provinces and Territories in an Era of Neoliberalism

BRYAN EVANS AND CARLO FANELLI

The decades following the end of the Second World War witnessed the high-water mark in the construction of the Canadian welfare state. As the chapters that follow make clear, the provinces – often through federal cost-sharing arrangements – led this transformation in the public economy. The resulting expansion in public goods and services saw total provincial government spending rise from 6.4% of gross national product (GNP) in 1955 to 16% in 1974 (Stevenson 1989, 80). Canada's postwar federalism reflected a path of policy innovation and province building that emerged from an economy characterized by deep regionalization and the increasingly ambitious provincial states with responsibility over key accumulation policy domains such as natural resources, labour, transportation, and education. A significant fiscal policy role can be added to this mix. Obviously, other important policy areas not necessarily tied to accumulation strategies fell, in whole or in part, under provincial jurisdiction owing to the makeup of the Canadian constitution. For instance, the provinces and – initially excluding but slowly expanding to largely include – the territories were granted responsibility for social welfare, health care, and education, as well as jurisdiction over natural resources and employment standards legislation. On the other hand, the federal government oversaw concerns related to the national interest, equal treatment and opportunity, equalization payments, international trade (which brought resources under federal jurisdiction), and Indigenous concerns.

The three decades following the Second World War were formative to the creation of the Canadian version of the golden age of Keynesian-inspired capitalism. That paradigm began to unravel in the 1970s as the accumulation of capital stumbled and entered into a prolonged period of transformation. The provinces in particular, given the policy and program areas for which they were responsible, would by necessity become critical sites of struggle and contestation over the rolling out of what would eventually come to be called neoliberalism. At a basic theoretical level, neoliberalism can be understood as a policy framework characterized by strong private property rights, free trade, and unfettered markets backed by a state that creates and preserves the institutional arrangements conducive to such practices. The federal structure of Canada, together with the highly regional differentiation of the provinces' political economies, meant that this process would be uneven and fragmented.

While the provinces share certain institutional similarities as a result of their common Westminster parliamentary tradition and are allocated the same responsibilities by the constitution, each is also distinctive. Each jurisdiction has been shaped by formative political events, class structures and relations, demography, and economy. Of course, the territories are most distinctive as a consequence of their constitutional status as creations of the Government of Canada. This constitutional reality places significant constraints on their capacity to act autonomously, while the presence of comparatively large Inuit, Métis, and First Nations populations and their quest for autonomy and the settlement of land claims are central political and economic drivers. Thus, the existence of two levels of government in Canada, characterized by a generally distinct division of responsibilities in which the provinces – though much less so for the territories – possess considerable autonomy over politically and economically important policy domains, provides the structural basis for a variety of inter-regional, inter-sectoral, and inter-class conflicts.

It is in this context that the ascent of neoliberalism across Canada can, in historical perspective, be characterized as an uneven process. Canada was hardly immune from the economic crisis of the 1970s, which rattled both Keynesian economic policies and the more general political and ideological arrangements that composed the postwar capital-labour accord. The federal construct of the Canadian state meant that there were then ten provincial and two territorial political systems expressing regional differences in party competition and along ideological fault lines. Moreover, in the struggle for national unity, social policy innovations were a potent "political and ideological weapon ... in the struggle for 'national unity'" as they were a means of making a remote Ottawa relevant to the people of Quebec (Béland and Lecours 2007, 410). Social programs, whether purely the domain of the federal government or significantly funded through transfer payments to the provinces (and later, the territories), became the policy ties that bound the federation together. Through the 1970s and 1980s, consequently, more or less explicitly neoliberal governments came to power in various provinces (Manitoba, Saskatchewan, British Columbia), and the Trudeau and Mulroney federal governments wobbled, albeit during distinctly different moments and issues, with respect to their fidelity to the Canadian welfare state and the Keynesian paradigm.

There was, however, no coherent, pan-Canadian consensus on proceeding with a wholesale dismantling of the more popular and politically valuable programs. Both Progressive Conservative prime ministers Joe Clark (1979–80) and Brian Mulroney (1984–92), for example, declared their support for state-financed health care, although the approach to social policy shifted through the Mulroney era "from a more or less cooperative style in intergovernmental relations to one marked by a climate of contested and coercive federalism in which the federal government, often unilaterally, 'off loaded' programs and withdrew support from provincial initiatives in health and social services" (Prince and Rice 2007, 164). Compared to the Chretien cuts of 1995, though, the Mulroney government appeared generous (Prince and Rice 2007, 176). From a global perspective, the decade of the 1980s saw a major reconsideration of the postwar social contract, and Canada was in no way immune from that. In fact, in some respects Canada's provinces led the punctuated and uneven transition to neoliberal rule having moved from the margins of political practice to new orthodoxy across the provinces and party lines by the mid-1990s.

Initially, the Great Recession mobilized an unprecedented intervention by major governments across the globe. "While Canada's federal Conservative government engaged in stimulus measures in its 2009 and 2010 budgets to bring the economy out of the financial and economic crisis, most of these measures were time-limited to two years only"; however, during the years of Prime Minister Harper, the government "strongly promoted contractionary fiscal policies both domestically and internationally, with successive spending cuts at the federal level and advocacy of fiscal austerity through the G20" (Sanger 2013, 61). Canada's then-minority federal Conservative government was an outlier in this regard, having first refused to ramp up public expenditures before being forced by threat of being replaced by a Liberal–New Democratic coalition to make some policy changes. The intense and unexpected recovery of Keynesianesque countercyclical measures caused one academic commentator to declare that "Neoliberalism and monetarism are dead" (Collignon 2008, 8). But this was a vast overstatement. Instead, a financial crisis located primarily within the banking sector was reframed as a problem of public spending. Countercyclical fiscal policy was rapidly replaced, as the predominant "exit strategy" of expansionary austerity came to dominate the policy arena (Albo and Fanelli 2014). And so, the Great Recession has become not the graveyard of neoliberalism but rather the relaunch of a more aggressive version of the neoliberal project characterized by a "political strategy of class war undertaken by the financial and political elite to hold on to the wealth and power they accumulated during the decades of market liberalism" (Quiggin 2010, 233).

In the years following the Great Recession, the Canadian narrative has been dominated by the thesis of Canadian exceptionalism: the belief that Canada fared much better than other countries and that the damage done from the recession was shortly thereafter repaired. When stacked up against the empirical evidence, however, we see this exposed as a massive canard. As research by Jim Stanford (2012) has shown, when adjusting for population growth, Canada has yet to recoup the pace of employment creation and GDP loss experienced between 2008 and 2010. Moreover, when comparing key indicators of Canada's economic performance with its industrialized peers in the Organisation for Economic Co-operation and Development (OECD), Canada ranked sixteenth in real GDP growth and seventeenth in terms of the change in the employment rate out of thirty-three reporting countries. Far from being a world leader, then, Canada's national performance can at best be described as mediocre. And now that neoliberal orthodoxy has been restored at the federal plane, a simultaneous deepening of this process has often been occurring at the subnational level.

SUBNATIONAL STATES: THEORETICAL CONSIDERATIONS

A subnational state is defined as "the arena of political activity concerned with the relations between central political institutions in the capital city and those sub-central political organizations and governmental bodies within the accepted boundaries of the state" (Tarrow 1978, 1–2). Over the past several decades this "second tier" of government has emerged as a site of significant activity and policy innovation that has given rise to various considerations seeking to explain the phenomenon of "multi-level governance" (Bache and Flinders 2004), the "entrepreneurial state" (Eisinger 1988), and the "region state" (Ohmae 1993). Perhaps more specifically for the purposes of this volume, we can also refer to "meso-government," which is to say, "an intermediate level of government between the centre and the basic municipal or communal level" (Sharpe 1993, 1).

The devolution and decentralization of roles and functions from the central to subnational states figures prominently in the playbook of neoliberal state structuring. This is about the offloading of central government responsibilities, but it also situates subnational units as "important partners in promoting exports and attracting foreign direct investment. Multinational corporations have also taken notice of the ability of subnational states to affect global flows of goods, services and capital. Subnational states have been explicitly incorporated into international economic agreements" (Paul 2002, 468). There are two important elements here. First, subnational states are acknowledged as providing a strategic role in attracting investment capital. Second, on the other side of this coin is a recognition of the need to constrain the legal and policy capacity of the subnational state to regulate capital and limit state agency and autonomy to engage in policy innovations that constrain market actors. In other words, subnational states have at times demonstrated the will and capacity to present a certain degree of resistance to neoliberalism (Darel 2002, 484). The World Trade Organization and the US Supreme Court, among others, have exercised their power to address concerns of both national states and capital by reining in the latitude of subnational states to exercise autonomy (Paul 2001, 484). In this respect, the two predominant state-rescaling theses present a paradox. One contends that the state is shrinking or is in the process of being "hollowed out" as powers, functions and resources are transferred to supranational and subnational institutions and states. The second thesis, in contrast, contends that "government authority is being eroded at the subnational level, while the national level is being reformed to accommodate global economic interests" (Warner and Gerbasi 2004, 858). In actuality, what we observe are elements of both working in parallel. And given that Canada is among the most decentralized federal states in existence, such developments hold significant implications in the Canadian context where the federal structure allows a cascading down of restructuring and constraint as well as allowing for endogenous political forces within each province to respond and adapt to the constraints imposed upon them.

This "resurgence of regions" perspective is theoretically housed within the "New Regionalism" school of economic geography, which is primarily concerned with "the significance of the region as an effective arena for situating the institutions of post-Fordist economic governance" (MacLeod 2001, 807). The term "post-Fordist" refers to the nationally based regimes of production characterized by manufacturing, a significant and legitimized trade union presence particularly in industrial production, and a significant state role in regulation. These more locally scaled innovations and interventions are where class alliances and hegemonic social blocs are formed as "the contemporary subnational state is involved in the promotion of transnational liberal production and circulation as well as perpetuating the remnants of Fordist consumption policies ... This 'entrepreneurial state' ... is much more an autonomous agent than it ever was during the Fordist period" (Paul 2002, 470). This subnational resurgence can be understood as an intellectual/theoretical veneer to what is essentially an ideological movement serving to deepen a "culture of austerity." The growing intellectual influence of New Regionalism can be less attributed to any genuinely explanatory power that it may possess; rather, its value is in fronting as an "instrumental utility to powerful industrial, state and social constituencies" (Lovering 1999, 389). Through the 1970s and 1980s, particularly in Western Europe and the United States, the emergence of a "meso" level of subnational government as a significant policy actor required some explanation. The period since 1970 has been one of significant change in subnational state institutions including "territorial reorganization, changes in function, changes in money-raising and spending powers, and the expansion of local economic development activity" (Pickvance and Preteceille 1991, 1). These were decades coterminous with the end of postwar prosperity and the Keynesian state shell, which "housed" the paradigm as the period witnessed a "return of mass unemployment ... accompanied by new ideologies, specifically neoliberalism, regarding the role of the state" that brought into question the "use of public spending to run the economy at full employment, and to finance a welfare state" (ibid.).

Neoliberalism provides the "ideological software" necessary for states to construct globalization and in doing so imposes processes for state restructuring and rescaling (Peck and Tickell 2002, 380). This is not, to be clear, a "hollowing out" of the state leading toward a diminished state either in terms of capacity or size. Rather, it is an expression of a simultaneous, and paradoxical, roll back (constraint) and roll out (embedding and creation of new institutions) of state functions as a means of reorganizing the state apparatus as it adapts to the context of neoliberalizing globalization. This process of restructuring "involves complex changes in the relations between different levels/scales and branches/departments of the state apparatus, such that the relationship between the form and functions of the state is often altered in quite fundamental ways" (Peck 2001, 447). As an example, devolution/decentralization of power, functions, and resources from the central national state to subnational states is not simply a matter of "resiting" or "relocating" but involves a qualitative dimension of changes in "regulatory responsibilities, administrative capacities, financial control, political power" (ibid.). What is at work is the construction of "the neoliberal constitution of competitive relations between localities and regions" (Peck and Tickell 2002, 386) where responsibility but not power is effectively "dumped" upon subnational states.

A neo-Schumpeterian frame, first suggested by Ohmae, where the economy is characterized by a process through which firms – and now also state institutions and regulatory regimes – are created through innovation in technology or management and die as those same innovations become obsolete as the context changes, views the nation-state as an increasingly dysfunctional actor. "On the global economic map," Ohmae (1993, 78) writes, "the lines that now matter are those defining what may be called 'region states'" and it is at this level where linkages to the global economy are being forged and in so doing surpassing the national state. Wolfe (1996, 220) suggests that the emergence of the region state is a function not solely of "the sheer need to fill the policy gap left by the withdrawal of national levels of government" but also "the capacity of regional levels of government to foster both the industrial and policy climate hospitable to innovation in the emerging paradigm." Various American scholars have attempted to explain "the rise of the entrepreneurial state," that is, the expanding role of state-level governments in economic development strategies in the wake of the macro-crisis of the 1970s and the consequent retrenchment of the federal government vis-à-vis transfers to the state governments, resulting in an era of austerity captured under the rubric of the "New Federalism" (O'Bowman and Kearney 1986; Eisinger 1988; Fosler 1988).

It is indisputable that in the postwar era the production and delivery of the range and scope of public services associated with the welfare state (social, health, education, and welfare services) could not be easily addressed within the duality of local and national states. Coordination and production of such public services required decentralization. With the advent of the welfare state, government is "no longer an institution concerned solely with high politics, suitable for decision at the centre. It is now a state primarily concerned with matters of low politics," or the delivery of "everyday things" (Meny and Wright 1985, 16). In comparative terms, these services are for the vast part delivered through subnational states where most public employees are indeed located (ibid., 19). In an era of permanent austerity, where public expenditures are to be controlled and the role of the state is limited and/or transformed, the subnational state has a pivotal role to play in the marketization of public goods and services and in creating the conditions necessary for the construction of labour-capital alliances and the weakening of trade union and working-class means to resist such transformations.

RESTRUCTURING AND RESISTANCE: AUSTERITY IN THE PROVINCES AND TERRITORIES

The ultimate paradox of Canadian politics in the second decade of the twenty-first century is how much has changed profoundly, yet the fault lines remain so familiar. Brodie (1990, 5) summed it up elegantly, writing that "Canadian politics revolves around persistent and divisive conflicts about the spatial distribution of economic development, state activity, living standards, government services, and political power ... Our politics, in other words, has been dominated by the question of where economic activity has and will be located." Canada's subnational states are, of course, not coterminous with the various regions, but they are situated within geographic regions and shape those regions in particular economic and political terms. Brodie is concerned that the constitutional and political arrangements that compose federalism be kept distinct from the concept of regionalism. The ten provinces have been and still are "prominent actors in spatial politics" and particularly so through the province-building years marking the postwar era, but that does not correspond into "ten distinct regions whose boundaries overlap with provincial ones" (ibid., 15). For Brodie (ibid., 16), the historical/political point is that over the 1970s and 1980s, conflicts were constructed around divisions "between groups of provinces, especially resource-producing and consuming provinces." Moreover, Brodie rejects the argument that provincial governments are the only mechanism through which regional protest and agency can be expressed. That the federal party system was "the first vehicle for regional movements" – particularly farmers' movements but also, to a lesser degree, workers' movements and sectoral business interests (hydrocarbons, manufacturing) and linguistic movements (Quebec) – illustrates the point (ibid.). However, federal states are characterized by a greater incidence of "spatially based conflicts" than are unitary states (ibid., 70).

The problem here is that the spatial aspect of region is reified. While it is patently obvious that provinces and regions are not interchangeable, it is also equally obvious that rather robust provincial and territorial states have emerged that give regions political agency. It is around and through these highly autonomous subnational states that significant localized class, linguistic, and other struggles for representation and redistribution take place. And in this respect, it is not just that "the linkages between the state and the dominant class have been, and remain, not general and abstract but particularly close and intimate" (Panitch 1977, 9); it is because of this that the provinces and territories in particular have been and are still important sites of contestation. The very process of province building required significant institutional innovation entailing the acquisition of new and robust policy development and program delivery capacities, demonstrable competence in economic development and diversification, and the establishment of political and economic conditions conducive to social cohesion. This is the terrain upon which local/regional elites competed with one another as well as with other classes and sectional interests over the control and management of the institutions and state apparatus through which to exercise political power (Brownsey and Howlett 2001, 15).

The Public Sector in an Age of Austerity was conceived in this context. By bringing together leading experts from across the country, the book explores how public finances, services, and employment relations have been transformed in an alleged "post-recession" era. Contributors address a range of interrelated questions: To what extent have social program expenditures like health care, education, and social assistance been remade? How have these changes impacted different social and employment groups? Have provincial and territorial governments implemented new forms of expenditure restraint or revenue generation? In which ways have austerity measures led to confrontations with public-sector workers and community-based groups more generally? Which political and economic obstacles have been encountered along the way? What might alternative public policies emphasize? And what have (and, potentially, what could) forms of resistance look like? The following chapters each seek to grapple with these questions in various ways.

In chapter 1, Heather Whiteside shows how recent austerity measures in British Columbia parallel earlier periods of fiscal restraint and social program spending retrenchment, particularly the policies of Social Credit governments in the 1980s, the New Democratic Party (NDP) government in the 1990s and the Liberals through the 2000s. She shows how, contrary to the argument that austerity was/is necessary to create budgetary stability and economic prosperity, it has been a recurrent feature of neoliberal governance used to dismantle existing public services and public-sector trade-union militancy along more individualized, flexibilized, and market-oriented lines. In chapter 2, Keith Brownsey examines how revenue generation and public spending has been impacted since the 2008 recession in what has historically been Canada's most socially and fiscally conservative province, Alberta. Brownsey shows how former premier Ralph Klein used the deficit to make the case that Alberta had a spending problem and not a revenue problem. Tracing the focus on deficit and debt elimination from Klein to Ed Stelmach, he argues that the privatization of public services, austere public spending, reductions to public-sector workers' wages, deregulatory changes to electricity generation, and reductions to corporate income taxes became part and parcel of consecutive Alberta governments, known euphemistically as "the Alberta advantage."

Charles Smith turns our attention to Saskatchewan in chapter 3. While the election of the Saskatchewan Party in 2007 represented a turn toward incremental austerity, he shows how a neoliberalized political and economic context was inherited from both its Conservative and New Democratic predecessors. With reference to the privatization of public assets and services, Smith vividly details how the election of the Saskatchewan Party has intensified neoliberal social policy reforms, at times precipitating labour strife in the public and private sectors. In the context of the province's weakening labour movement, the government also tied individual workers more closely to the compulsions of the market, further constraining trade unions' political capacities to organize and bargain collectively. Next, David Camfield's chapter on Manitoba argues that neoliberalism in the province first found expression in the Progressive Conservative (PC) government of the late 1980s. Through the course of the 1990s, the PCs worked to implement core neoliberal policies, including the privatization of public assets and services, changes to labour legislation that made it more difficult for workers to unionize, and balanced budget legislation that constrained public services spending. In 1999, the NDP formed government and would go on to win the next three elections. However, Camfield contends that rather than retreating from neoliberalism, the NDP extended the hallmarks of marketization, most notably in the form of cuts to personal and corporate taxes. Although the provincial government did not turn to the harsh austerity measures adopted in other jurisdictions during the 2008 recession, Camfield shows how the "austerity-lite" measures of this period nevertheless negatively affected public-sector workers and access to public services.

In what follows, Bryan Evans and Carlo Fanelli shift focus to central Canada with an exploration of how the Great Recession has impacted the public finances of Ontario. They make the case that the policies emerging from the recession have pushed the ideological spectrum further to the right that evermore deploys anti-labour, anti-social welfare, and anti-democratic practices. With a focus on the development of labour legislation and social welfare policies over the postwar period, Evans and Fanelli show how McGuinty's and Wynne's Liberal governments of the 2000s have deepened and normalized the policies of the Common Sense Revolution left over from the Mike Harris Conservatives of the mid-1990s. Rather than repudiating neoliberalism, the Liberals further integrated the institutions of the provincial state with private capital and efforts to contain public-sector workers' right to free collective bargaining. Although Quebecers came into the crisis with a far more robust and redistributive welfare state, as Peter Graefe and Hubert Rioux Ouimet write in chapter 6, the ebb and flow of partisan politics seems to have made austerity a powerful card for conservative forces that have long sought to restructure the provincial state. They situate contemporary austerity measures in a historical light, drawing attention to how restructuring has been met by resistance and efforts to craft a more egalitarian and redistributive society, as illustrated by the Maple Spring of 2012. Graefe and Ouimet draw attention to how Quebec social and union movements have mobilized impressive opposition to austerity programmes, concluding with an examination of how the limited ability to form relays in institutional politics with the aim of blocking neoliberal initiatives has resembled these conditions elsewhere.

Moving east, in chapter 7 Jamie Gillies turns our attention to New Brunswick. He shows how the period from the 1960s to the end of the 1990s coincided with a range of new investments into the public sector, including infrastructure, health services and education in line with the rest of Canada. The last two decades, however, have been marked by growing uncertainty in New Brunswick over the ability to continue investing in the social and physical infrastructures of the province. Gillies makes the argument that federal offloading through the 1990s has resulted in a chronic structural deficit, which continues to hamstring provincial governments. If New Brunswick is to find its way out of the social and economic malaise, he argues, it needs to address fiscal pressures and grow the revenue side of public finance through economic development that is sustainable in the long run and not subject to volatile natural resources swings. Peter Clancy turns our attention to Nova Scotia in chapter 8 and shows how since the 1990s the province has experimented with a range of parties and policies, including everything from toll roads to planned tax cuts and mandated balanced budgets. In this respect, Nova Scotia offers a rich and varied site of neoliberal policy experimentation, some imported from elsewhere and some provincially conceived. Nevertheless, Clancy argues that considering both the structural and cyclical downturns in the provincial political economy, Nova Scotia governments have displayed moderation in the intensity of fiscal policies, notwithstanding at times fierce labour confrontations, as well as experimentation with a range of policy tools.

In chapter 9, Patricia Conrad turns to Prince Edward Island (PEI). She shows how PEI's largely rural setting, weak industrial base, and reliance on natural resources have contributed to the province's historically anaemic economic performance and dependence on federal transfers like equalization payments. At the same time, PEI has among the highest proportions of elderly residents and unhealthy populations, which has made a reliance on universal and accessible public services all the more necessary. Conrad carefully charts changes to PEI's health care system since the 1990s, which has moved from centralized to decentralized planning and, later, the formation of a single health authority that is arm's length from government and treats the Island as one large region. In focusing on changes to PEI's health systems management, Conrad shows how the context of austerity and retrenchment still lingering from the 2008 downturn has impacted Island budgeting and explores the implications it has had for the delivery of public services. In his discussion of Newfoundland and Labrador in chapter 10, Robert Sweeney shows how the province remains an outlier of sorts. While most provincial governments faced challenging political economic conditions brought on by the Great Recession, between 2005 and 2011 the province underwent perhaps its greatest transformation in Canadian history, with median incomes rising more than 40%. Over this time, the redistributive function of the provincial state was quite literally turned on its head as provincial policies generated marked increases in after-tax inequality. Sweeny shows how national-populist appeal in the province transcended divisions of class and gender by privileging race and ethnicity. It is this national-populist context, rooted in historical experiences not unlike Quebec, wherein a range of socially regressive cutbacks to welfare, particularly revenue-raising capacities, has characterized the last decade of neoliberal dominance.

Jack Hicks shifts our attention north where the Nunavut Act was passed in 1993, paving the way for the territory to come into existence in 1999. Although austerity is often thought of as something introduced in the 1980s and 1990s, Hicks shows how the Eastern and Central Arctic never had a period of "normal" Keynesian welfare state development prior to the period of fiscal restraint introduced by the Chretien/Martin Liberals in the mid-1990s. While it could be said that Nunavut has followed a fiscally conservative path, more fundamentally, argues Hicks, it has followed a politically conservative path – with conservative economic and social policies. He makes the case that so great is the desire of the political/managerial elite to be seen as a "normal" government running a "normal" jurisdiction that it has not found the courage to tackle the social suffering that continues to limit its future. In chapter 12, Ken Coates and Greg Poelzer show how, more than anywhere else in Canada, Aboriginal Peoples and politics matter, as Aboriginal Peoples constitute 25% of the population in Yukon, 50% in the Northwest Territories, and 85% in Nunavut. Focusing on the Northwest Territories (NWT), Coates and Poelzer argue that the politics of austerity characteristic in many of Canada's largest provinces did not occur in parallel ways across the NWT. They contend that greater regional autonomy and Aboriginal self-determination, as well as the federal government's response to these demands, is central to understanding fiscal relations, service delivery, and employment in the territorial North. Despite being heavily reliant on federal government subsidies and still in the process of securing control of their resources, the NWT followed a fiscally conservative path, eschewing major stimulus programs, rejecting a major expansion in territorial services, and maintaining small territorial surpluses through the recession. Jerald Sabin follows this analysis by showing how the Yukon continues to operate a high-cost, high-wage, and low-demand environment dominated by both the public sector and resource-extractive industries. As Sabin shows, despite its reliance on public-sector spending, Yukon has managed to double its revenues, post only one budget deficit in the past decade, and have no public debt. In this respect, the territory has largely avoided the divisive politics of austerity that has marred other jurisdictions. In contrast, the Yukon's political discourse has been dominated by debates over new capital and service investments, rather than public service cuts and privatization.

Together, these chapters provide original and timely analyses of public services, finances, and employment in an era of austerity. Some concepts and terms will be familiar to readers, while others will be new. As will become clear in the chapters that follow, Keynesianism refers to a series of policies inspired by the writings of John Maynard Keynes, notably in his book *The General Theory of Employment, Interest and Money*. Keynesian principles, dominant over the three decades following the Second World War, promoted active fiscal and monetary policies (even if that meant running temporary budget deficits), state-led planning and in some instances outright ownership of key economic sectors, progressive taxation, expanded employment standards and union rights, as well as a basic commitment to universal social programs, capital controls, and domestic reinvestment. Key among the gains made by labour over this period is what has come to be known as the Rand formula, named after Justice Ivan Rand's landmark 1945 ruling in a dispute between General Motors and striking workers, which institutionalized compulsory union dues checkoff for all employees in a bargaining unit whether they were members or not, since all workers in the workplace benefitted in some form from unionism. The Rand formula also prohibited all strikes during the term of a collective agreement and instituted a system of financial penalties, to be drawn from union dues, which would be levied against the union in the event of an illegal strike.

However, by the 1970s Keynesianism had reached an impasse. This was rooted in stagnant economic growth, rising inflation, the relative weakening of capital vis-à-vis labour, an end to historically exceptional profitability and a return to moderate rates of growth, unstable exchange rates, industrial strife, high unemployment, rising public debts, and weak capital investment. Keynesian policies were thus replaced by neoliberal strategies, which included social policies oriented toward fiscal restraint, trade policies designed to promote competitiveness and capital mobility, and labour relations that both individuated economic risks and sought to weaken the collective power of labour (Fanelli 2015). In Canada, as across many North American and European countries, union density (the proportion of unionized workers as a percentage of all paid workers) declined significantly, leading to a sharp rise in inequality (Schmitt and Mitukiewicz 2011; Jaumotte and Buitron 2015).

As noted above, governments also promoted a range of tax cuts that eroded public finances, services and employment, in some cases creating a fundamental imbalance between revenues and expenditures, otherwise known as a structural deficit, which resulted in the sale of public assets and reductions to the universality of social programs. Neoliberalism sought to radically transform the public sector in line with private sector practices, which included the implementation of "new public management" policies. This theory asserted "that government, and more broadly, the public sector should function more like the private sector and should look to the market for inspiration and, whenever possible, emulate it" (Shields and Evans 1998, 56). A policy manual materialized for public-sector management, which included the privatization of public goods and services, a greater reliance on short-term labour, outsourcing and contracting out, and commercialization of state services such as user-pay provisions, monetization of public assets, and competition between public agencies. All things considered, in the neoliberal "lean" state the privatization and commercialization of public services and assets has steadily usurped any counter-mechanisms – ombudsman offices, freedom of information, citizen participation and review panels, new forms of democracy, and so forth – for democratic accountability and social provision in what can otherwise be characterized as a period of "permanent austerity" (Albo and Fanelli 2014).

THE PLACE-BASED PARADOX OF AUSTERITY

In Canada, the vertical fiscal imbalance between the provinces/territories and the federal government, in addition to the horizontal fiscal imbalance between the provinces and territories, has been exacerbated by a shift in fiscal federalism from one informed by a nation-building imperative to one that sought to re-establish a sound money orthodoxy as the underpinning of federal fiscal policy. In addition, the resources boom of the latter half of the first decade of the twenty-first century was felt unevenly, with oil-producing provinces (Alberta, Newfoundland and Labrador, Saskatchewan) in particular reaping significant benefits while the manufacturing provinces (Ontario and Quebec) endured relatively stagnant economic growth combined with growing public deficits and debts. As a result, the Canadian dollar appreciated markedly, moving the modest Canbuck into the folio of petro currencies. Federal economic policy encouraged foreign investment in the hydrocarbon sector, some argued, introducing "Dutch disease" to Canada. Since the turn of the century, the once again ascendant resource industries, and oil in particular, returned Canada to its staples-economy roots (Stanford 2012, 1). The gravity of the resources boom drew in capital investment at the expense of more lucrative value-added export sectors. A similar phenomenon occurred in the Netherlands in the 1960s as that country embarked on the exploitation of North Sea oil, where the term "Dutch disease" was coined.

As the public finances of Alberta, Saskatchewan, and Newfoundland improved markedly, those of Manitoba, Ontario, Quebec, and other oil-less provinces languished. The collapse of commodity prices generally, and oil in particular, resulted in a 25% decline in the value of the Canadian dollar relative to the US dollar though the course of

2015. Searching for the silver lining, the expectation was that the benefit of a lower dollar would kick-start the ailing manufacturing sector. This failed to materialize in any substantial way, to the chagrin of Ontario and Quebec governments. Canada's return to a resources-driven, boom-and-bust economic dynamic was not entirely a result of emerging economies' demand for commodities. It was a policy choice that the federal government made, and it also resulted from the failure of the provinces to design and implement successful alternative economic development strategies. It was as if the debates of the 1960s and 1970s regarding Canadian economic sovereignty and value-added production had never taken place. The ideational dominance of neoliberalism within public-policy circles is locked in as much as alternative thinking about industrial policy is locked out.

Historically, the study of Canadian political economy has played an essential role in unpacking how divided societies were able to construct policies that sustained long-term capital accumulation within the rubric of a single state (Whitaker 1977). The regional dimensions of these policies are to be understood as "an expression of and a response to phases of capitalist accumulation and class conflict and they imprint themselves on the geographic landscape in the character of economic activity and in political conflict" (Brodie 1990, 4). When the federal government moved to restructure the economic and financial commitments associated with Canada's version of postwar Keynesian capitalism in the 1980s and 1990s, it effectively downloaded responsibility for curtailing redistributive policies and public expenditures onto the provinces and territories. As the chapters that follow make clear, the period since 2006, and in particular since the onset of the global economic crisis, can be understood as an intensive period of neoliberal restructuring wherein a particular vision of federalism understood in strict constitutionalist terms was rolled out, with important consequences across the provinces and territories.

REFERENCES

Albo, Greg, and Carlo Fanelli. 2014. "Austerity Against Democracy: An Authoritarian Phase of Neoliberalism?" *Teoria Politica: An International Journal of Theory and Politics*: 65–88.

Bache, Ian, and Matthew Flinders. 2004. *Multi-Level Governance*. Oxford: Oxford University Press.

Béland, Daniel, and André Lecours. 2007. "Federalism, Nationalism, and Social Policy Decentralisation in Canada and Belgium." *Regional and Federal Studies* 17 (4): 405–19.

Brodie, Janine. 1990. *The Political Economy of Canadian Regionalism*. Toronto: Harcourt Brace Jovanovich.

Brownsey, Keith, and Michael Howlett. 2001. "Introduction: The Provincial State in Canada." In *The Provincial State in Canada: Politics in the Provinces and Territories*, edited by Keith Brownsey and Michael Howlett, 13–22. Peterborough: Broadview Press.

Collignon, Stefan. 2008. "The Dawn of a New Era: Social Democracy after the Financial Crisis." *Social Europe* 4 (1): 9–13.

Eisinger, Peter. 1988. *The Rise of the Entrepreneurial State: State and Local Economic Development Policy in the United States*. Madison: University of Wisconsin Press.

Evans, Bryan, and John Shields. 1998. *Shrinking the State: Globalization and Public Administration "Reform."* Halifax: Fernwood Publishing.

Fanelli, Carlo. 2015. "The Radical Keynes: An Appraisal." *Workplace* 25: 69–81.

– 2016. *Megacity Malaise: Neoliberalism, Public Services and Labour in Toronto*. Winnipeg: Fernwood Publishing.

Fosler, R. Scott. 1988. *The New Economic Role of American States: Strategies in a Competitive World Economy*. Oxford: Oxford University Press.

Jaumotte, Florence, and Carolina Osorio Buitron. 2015. *Inequality and Labour Market Institutions*. International Monetary Fund. https://www.imf.org/external/pubs/ft/sdn/2015/sdn1514.pdf.

Keynes, John Maynard. 1936. *The General Theory of Employment, Interest, and Money*. New York: Harcourt, Brace & World.

Lovering, John. 1999. "Theory Led by Policy: The Inadequacies of the 'New Regionalism.'" *International Journal of Urban and Regional Research* 23 (2): 379–95.

MacLeod, Gordon. 2001. "New Regionalism Reconsidered: Globalization and the Re-making of Political Economic Space." *International Journal of Urban and Regional Research* 25 (4): 804–29.

Macleod, Gordon, and Mark Goodwin. 1999. "Space, Scale and State Strategy: Rethinking Urban and Regional Governance." *Progress in Human Geography* 23 (4): 503–27.

Meny, Yves, and Vincent Wright. 1985. "From Government at the Centre to Nationwide Government." In *Centre-Periphery Relations in Western Europe*, edited by Yves Meny and Vincent Wright, 13–32. London: Allen and Unwin.

O'Bowman, Ann, and Richard Kearney. 1986. *The Resurgence of the States*. New Jersey: Englewood Cliffs.
Ohmae, Kenichi. 1993. "The Rise of the Region State." *Foreign Affairs* 72: 78–87.
Panitch, Leo. 1977. "The Role and Nature of the Canadian State." In *The Canadian State: Political Economy and Political Power*, edited by Leo Panitch, 3–27. Toronto: University of Toronto Press.
Paul, Darel. 2002. "Re-scaling IPE: Subnational States and the Regulation of the Global Political Economy." *Review of International Political Economy* 9 (3): 465–89.
Peck, Jamie. 2001. "Neoliberalizing States: Thin Policies, Hard Outcomes." *Progress in Human Geography* 25 (3): 445–55.
Peck, Jamie, and Adam Tickell. 2002. "Neoliberalizing Space." *Antipode* 34 (3): 380–404.
Pickvance, Chris, and Edmond Preteceille. 1991. "Introduction: The Significance of Local Power in Theory and Practice." In *State Restructuring and Local Power*, edited by Chris Pickvance and Edmond Preteceille, 1–17. London and New York: Pinter Publishers.
Prince, Michael, and James Rice. 2007. "Governing through Shifting Social-Policy Regimes: Brian Mulroney and Canada's Welfare State." In *Transforming the Nation: Canada and Brian Mulroney*, edited by Raymond B. Blake, 164–77. Montreal and Kingston: McGill-Queen's University Press.
Quiggin, John. 2010. *Zombie Economics: How Dead Ideas Still Walk among Us*. Princeton and Oxford: Princeton University Press.
Sanger, Toby. 2013. "Canada's Conservative Class War: Using Austerity to Squeeze Labour at the Expense of Economic Growth." *Alternate Routes: A Journal of Critical Social Research* 24: 59–84.
Schmidt, John, and Alexandra Mitukiewicz. 2011. *Politics Matter: Changes in Unionization Rates in Rich Countries, 1960–2010*. Center for Economic and Policy Research. http://cepr.net/documents/publications/unions-oecd-2011-11.pdf.
Sharpe, L.J., ed. 1993. *The Rise of Meso Government in Europe*. London: Sage Publications.
Stanford, Jim. 2012. *A Cure for Dutch Disease: Active Sector Strategies for Canada's Economy.* Ottawa: Canadian Centre for Policy Alternatives. http://policyalternatives.ca/sites/default/files/uploads/publications/National%20Office/2012/04/Cure%20For%20Dutch%20Disease.pdf.
Stevenson, Garth. 1977. "Federalism and the Political Economy of the Canadian State." In *The Canadian State: Political Economy and*

Political Power, edited by Leo Panitch, 71–100. Toronto: University of Toronto Press.

– 1989. *Unfulfilled Union: Canadian Federalism and National Unity*. 3rd ed. Toronto: Gage Publishing.

– 2009. *Unfulfilled Union: Canadian Federalism and National Unity*. 5th ed. Montreal and Kingston: McGill-Queen's University Press.

Tarrow, Sidney. 1978. "Introduction." In *Territorial Politics in Industrial Nations*, edited by Sidney Tarrow, Peter Katzenstein, and Luigi Graziano, 1–27. London: Praeger.

Warner, Mildred, and Jennifer Gerbasi. 2004. "Rescaling and Reforming the State under NAFTA: Implications for Subnational Authority." *International Journal of Urban and Regional Research* 28 (4): 858–73.

Whitaker, Reg. 1977. "Images of the State." In *The Canadian State: Political Economy and Political Power*, edited by Leo Panitch, 28–68. Toronto: University of Toronto Press.

Wolfe, David. 1996. "The Emergence of the Region State." In *The Nation State in a Global/Information Era: Policy Challenges*, edited by Thomas Courchene, 205–40. Kingston: John Deutsch Institute for the Study of Economic Policy.

CHAPTER ONE

BC's Recurrent Austerity: Victory Unfettered from Success

HEATHER WHITESIDE

Austerity budgets are those that cut deficits by raising revenue through asset sales and higher taxes and/or by reducing government expenditures through cuts to program spending. The resurgence of austerity today across the countries in the Organisation for Economic Co-operation and Development (OECD) is unique to its context – the 2008 global financial crisis and its aftermath – but is equally part of a longer historical trend. Mark Blyth (2013a; see also 2013b) has traced the "love of parsimony over prodigality" in economic thought back to Adam Smith and finds examples of fiscal austerity over the past century.

In this vein, BC's austerity story does not begin in the wake of the 2008 crisis; instead, contemporary examples of austerity budgeting (particularly fiscal year [FY] 2013 and 2014) ought to be considered as recent episodes that follow earlier, and more significant, forays into austerity first in the 1980s under the Social Credit government and then again in the early 2000s under the Liberals. Though cast as "restraint" and "fiscal prudence," implications of austerity budgeting have extended beyond fiscal policy. Austerity initiatives over the past thirty years have fundamentally restructured state–society relations and have shifted (privatized, downloaded) risk, responsibilities, and burdens onto the shoulders of groups and individuals that were seldom, if ever, the agents responsible for provincial budget woes. Economic fluctuations creating cyclical deficits and voluntarily forgone government revenue through tax cuts have more often been the underlying causes of budget imbalances since the 1980s, not public-sector extravagance. This constitutes a victory for the austerity project unfettered from what would be its ostensible yardsticks of success: stable budgets and economic prosperity.

The use and impact of austerity budgeting in BC will be explored here in three sections. The opening two sections contextualize the recent round of austerity in the province. The first discusses the politics and economics of fiscal policy and government budgeting, including the theory and practice of fiscal austerity since the 1970s and the role of taxation in society. It historicizes the global return of austerity in 2010 as an idea, form of budgeting, and fiscal policy practice. The second section identifies the long run austerity trend in BC through an examination of its political economy since the 1970s. The final section details BC provincial government budgets since 2006. Set within its wider historical context, policy changes introduced since 2001 are of greater significance than the austerity implemented more recently. This suggests that the 2008 crisis was not the watershed moment for BC finances and state retrenchment that it may have been elsewhere in Canada and around the world.

THE POLITICS AND ECONOMICS OF PUBLIC-SECTOR BUDGETING AND FISCAL AUSTERITY

> Public finances are one of the best starting points for an investigation of society, especially though not exclusively of its political life. The full fruitfulness of this approach [fiscal sociology] is seen particularly at those turning points, or better epochs, during which existing forms begin to die off and to change into something new, and which always involve a crisis of the old fiscal methods. This is true both of the causal importance of fiscal policy (insofar as fiscal events are an important element in the causation of all change) and of the symptomatic significance (insofar as everything that happens has its fiscal reflection). (Schumpeter [1918] 1954, 101)

Analyzing changes in a public-sector budget requires first asking: who are budgets for? Examining alterations to state expenditures, particularly budgetary reductions or reallocations, can provide an answer to this question and reveal the highly political (though often invisible) activity that is public-sector budgeting. As the preceding quote by Joseph Schumpeter indicates, turning points in fiscal policy – involving both (real or perceived) crises and solutions – bears significant impact on other areas of public policy. Some 95% of spending in most Canadian public budgets consists of existing programs and statutory commitments made in previous years (and even by previous governments) (Doern et al. 2013, 4, 86). Thus, the new decisions, flashpoints, and hotly debated changes in the budget often revolve around new money or the lack thereof.

No matter the economic climate or ideology of government, budgetary instruments seek to achieve three objectives: allocation, distribution, and stabilization (Cutt 1989, 151). Allocation and distribution speak to the ways that state budgeting alters the enjoyment of resources in society and claims to wealth. By providing services to the general public through taxation or borrowing, redistribution and reallocation occur, often favouring those who might not be able to access such services through labour market earnings alone. Similarly, when user fees go up, when taxes become more regressive, and when public-service spending is cut or frozen, these changes signal new claims on wealth in society. In a related process, budgetary reductions also frequently entail the expansion of market-based allocation and distribution of relevant services.

From a technical perspective, austerity budgeting refers narrowly to reductions made in the cyclically adjusted fiscal deficit (accounting for macroeconomic ups and downs); from a wider perspective, changes in fiscal policy can greatly influence state-society relations. Austerity is, as Jamie Peck (2014, 4) suggests, a strategy of redistribution that pushes "the costs, risks, and burdens of economic failure onto subordinate classes, social groups and branches of government." The concomitant impacts of austerity on health and social services program financing, infrastructure and government procurement, and public-sector workers mean budget balancing and state retrenchment are often synonymous.

The shifting of social risks and responsibilities away from the state (eroding a collective bearing of risk) did not begin with this recent round of austerity. The past thirty years of neoliberalism are marked by various episodes of fiscal restraint. Consider the following quotes in reference to the Canadian federal government's plans:

> The Government will exercise restraint in its own expenditures with particular emphasis on improving effectiveness and efficiency in its existing operations while controlling expansion of new activities.

> To create the climate necessary for [recovery] the Government will continue to practice fiscal restraint ... the Government remains committed to a reduction in the growth of the public sector ... All federal programmes will be reviewed to identify those government activities which could be transferred to the private sector.

> The objectives of imposing more severe restraint on government spending are ... to encourage a more vigorous expansion of the private sector by reducing government's share of the nation's wealth ... to create a leaner and more efficient government ... The government is committed to reducing the size of the federal public service ... (and) to continued wage restraint in the public sector.

One could easily assume these are declarations made since 2010. Instead, they are taken from Canadian federal government budget speeches (Speeches from the Throne) dated, respectively, 30 September 1974, 12 October 1976, and 11 October 1978 (see table 4.5 in McBride 1992, 87). Despite their vintage, they easily fit with the tenor of the federal government's 2012 budget speech:

> Canadians need to be confident in our prospects for economic growth. This is the key not only to creating good jobs but also to sustaining our social programs and improving our quality of life ... To provide this confidence, we must ensure that Canada's finances are sustainable over the long term. To that end, we will fulfill the commitment ... to return to balanced budgets in the medium term ... We will implement moderate restraint in government spending. The vast majority of the savings will come from eliminating waste in the internal operations of government, making it leaner and more efficient. (Government of Canada 2012)

Note the striking similarities here, across time: government excess is cast as a bulwark against improvements in consumer confidence and investment climate, dampening economic growth and capital accumulation. By reallocating and redistributing roles and responsibilities in society, austerity is cast as antidote.

Cutt (1989, 152) writes that the third objective of budgeting – stabilization – is enacted when "governments use revenue and expenditure instruments to affect employment and price stability." During the postwar Keynesian era, countercyclical government spending was widely held to be an important tool of aggregate demand stimulation during economic downturns. These ideas were replaced in the 1970s with the notion that fiscal restraint can be a driver of economic growth and prosperity. Austerity was presented as a solution to the problem of "stagflation" (rising prices simultaneous to economic stagnation), which vexed the established Philips curve–derived policy orthodoxy at the time[1] by providing a simple explanation: government spending on the welfare state in the Global North was hurting growth by "crowding out" private spending and creating inflation through excess government borrowing to finance budget deficits.

In the 1990s, the rationale was further refined by neoclassical economists. Under the "expansionary fiscal consolidation thesis" it was argued that austerity was not only a solution to macroeconomic problems but also had a positive impact on expectations, which generated its own virtuous cycle. The elimination of public-sector deficits, though potentially painful in the short run, would boost investor confidence, reduce borrowing costs, stimulate private-sector growth and lead to lower unemployment (e.g., Alesina and Perotti 1995; Alesina et al. 1998; Alesina and Ardagana 1998; Giavazzi and Pagano 1990).

Whereas Keynesian theory dealt a critical blow to Say's Law (the notion that supply produces its own demand) and supported several decades of demand-driven growth policy formulation, fiscal consolidation supplies an argument in favour of austerity: supply creates demand and investor confidence is what drives growth. Controlling and reducing government spending is thus aimed at taming inflation and improving investor confidence. Yet, as Doern et al. (2013, 63–4) point out, despite the now decades-old shift away from Keynesian demand management a social obligation of public policy–makers remains, which they dub "structural fundamentalism" to reflect the widespread expectation that state actors will address the fundamentals of unemployment and effective demand. Consistent with the market-oriented nature of the neoliberal era more generally, an increasingly common way of addressing these fundamentals is now the tax system.

As a subset of public-sector budgeting, taxation likewise redistributes wealth in society through incentives and benefits (exemptions, deductions, credits, refundable credits, and preferential tax rates) (Block and Maslove 1994, 169–70).[2] The tax system is therefore an important component of social policy – directly, given that changes in taxation affect government revenue and hence the ability of government to pay for social programs, and indirectly when changes in taxation impact disposable income. Tax deductions, credits, deferrals, exclusion of income from taxation, known collectively as "tax expenditures," appear to be distinct from direct government spending, but the fact remains that tax deductions or credits are, *ipso facto*, forgone state revenue. The effects of this are described by Harder (2003, 62) in the following way:

> The demise of directly funded programs and the rise in tax expenditures appear as tax cuts and incentives to pursue our particular needs through the market. It is not immediately evident that, in enabling market provision, tax expenditures not only represent public spending but also redistribute foregone public revenues in the service of private profit.

In addition, not all taxes are created equal. Deductions tend to benefit those with higher incomes if the wealthy pay a relatively smaller proportion of their income (a regressive taxation system); tax credits might be more helpful for those with less disposable income, although this will depend on whether the credit is refundable or non-refundable (with the latter only helping those who earn enough to be subject to income tax). To the extent that cuts to public-service spending occur simultaneously to the implementation of regressive taxation systems, citizens are doubly forced to rely upon the market as service and income provider. This phenomenon has been occurring in various ways in BC since the 1970s, detailed in the section that follows.

THE POLITICS AND ECONOMICS OF BC BUDGETING AND FISCAL POLICY SINCE THE 1970S

Hale (2006, 373) argues that, despite Canadian provincial governments holding greater power and discretion over fiscal matters than subnational governments in most other federal systems, they remain nonetheless constrained in their autonomy by factors such as their economic structures, political cultures, and the impact of changes in fiscal federalism, each of which present their own unique challenges for discretion in spending at the provincial level. To this we might add, or specify, the importance of party ideology and class struggle, international pressure (including economic and financial market volatility), and legacies such as debt and rates of taxation. The composition of the provincial economy is also key and linked to those items.

BC is often thought of as a "staples" economy (see Innis 1954; 1956). As late as the mid-1990s, one could read that:

> BC remains heavily dependent upon the income-generating capability of its resource-based export industries, and especially the forest products industry. In consequence, the cyclical nature of world market prices for resource-based commodities has a considerable impact upon the performance of BC's economy. The capital intensity of BC's resource-based industries also makes its economy vulnerable to world interest rate movements ... as a small open economy, BC is a price-taker for most of its commodity exports, and for virtually all of the goods and services it imports. It is therefore vulnerable to movements in these prices. (Scarfe 1996, 217)

Approximately one-third of BC's annual economic output by the 1990s was based on resource extraction. External trade is dominated by resource extraction, mainly forestry (softwood lumber), natural gas, mining, and quarrying. Fishing is also significant. The "staples approach," which assumes that staple exports (resource-intensive exports) are a leading sector of the economy and set the pace for economic growth (Watkins 1963, 144), holds significant implications for the provincial economy, the political economy, and thus public-sector revenue and budgeting. As the quote by Scarfe (above) implies, when analyzing changes in government revenue and drivers of fiscal policy, we must remain attuned to world prices and vulnerability to international market fluctuations for BC's exports. Not all deficits are structural (when expenditures outstrip revenues regardless of economic conditions), many are cyclical and due to downswings in the economy. Cyclical deficits therefore do not necessarily reflect fiscal mismanagement by government and not all fiscal imbalances are problems to be addressed through austerity.

On the other hand, compared with other resource-rich provinces (see table 1.1), BC's economy is remarkably reliant on services, with goods-producing sectors (which includes forestry, mining and quarrying, oil and gas) contributing only 22.8% of the gross domestic product (GDP) in 2013. Howlett and Brownsey (2001) dub BC a "post-staples" political economy given that the origins of BC economics and politics are indeed rooted in primary product exploitation, with local business elites dominating politics early on. By the 1940s and 1950s, consolidation of resource companies and investment by multinational companies along with significant state expenditures on economic and social infrastructure had begun, leading to a full-fledged service-based economy by the 1980s (ibid., 312–18). This suggests that we should not exaggerate the impact of export market price fluctuations on government budgets. Economic management strategies, revenue, and the political economy of public-sector budgeting in the province has varied over the years, often connected to both upswings/downswings in the economy and the election cycle.

When the New Democratic Party (NDP) came to power (1972–75) under Premier David Barrett, the provincial government created public monopolies to control the marketing of natural gas and oil (the BC Petroleum Company) and public auto insurance (Insurance Corporation of British Columbia, or ICBC), and implemented an accelerated mineral royalty tax as a way of capturing revenue and guiding the economy (Brownsey et al. 2009, 20). The portion of BC's economy reliant upon extraction and exports, mainly forestry and mining, was subject to price volatility in world markets – with booms and busts common in these sectors over this period – leading to fluctuations in provincial economic growth and government revenue. When the Social Credit government (a conservative-populist party) held office from 1975–91, world market prices for these goods were high and the province experienced significant economic growth. Far exceeding the Canadian average, BC's economy grew annually by 5.6% over that period (Malcolmson 1984, 77). Provincial exports in lumber, coal, metal concentrates, and pulp drove the boom, growing by staggering amounts: 137.5%, 96.2%, 92.4%, and 42.8% respectively over that five-year period. Malcolmson (ibid.) argues that this was the basis upon which government expenditures could expand, as could public service provision.

By 1982 BC, along with the rest of the country, was hit hard by recession. Government deficits expanded in concert with low or negative growth, and Premier Bennett's statement that "no government can spend its way to prosperity" seemed to capture the mood of the day, along with the motto of "recovery through restraint" (Schofield 1984, 45). The Social Credit government's austerity measures, as

Table 1.1
Goods-producing sector as a share (%) of provincial GDP, select Canadian provinces (2007–13)

	2007	*2008*	*2009*	*2010*	*2011*	*2012*	*2013*
BC	25.81	26.58	22.37	23.18	23.89	23.11	22.83
Alberta	47.8	50.94	40.86	43.92	45.87	44.58	45.76
Saskatchewan	45.18	53.37	46.76	46.63	49.98	49.24	49.73
Manitoba	29.22	29.64	26.95	26.91	27.08	27.39	27.53
Ontario	25.6	24.01	22.47	23.14	23.30	23.17	22.40
Quebec	29.44	29.11	27.62	28.25	28.10	27.77	27.31

Source: Statistics Canada, CANSIM Table 379-0028 Gross domestic product (GDP) at basic prices, by North American Industry Classification System (NAICS), provinces and territories, annual (percentage share)

implemented through the 1983 provincial budget, introduced a 15% cut to full-time public-sector staff and mandatory budget and staff cuts imposed on schools, colleges, and universities; alongside these cuts, employment at the Ministry of Health was cut by 27% and 1,200 acute care beds were closed (Vogel 2000, 5–6). The subsequent 1984 budget introduced further cuts to employment in the public sector, amounting to a 25% reduction (ibid., 6).

Restraint in the early 1980s in BC came simultaneously with a slump in world export markets, the primary-product sector in particular, and between July 1981 and December 1982 the province lost nearly a third of its employment in goods-producing sectors of the economy. Likewise, the provincial government lost a significant amount of revenue as corporate income tax revenue fell from $580 million in 1981–82 to $180 million in 1982–83 (Malcolmson 1984, 79). A government budget deficit, the first since the mid-1970s, was the result. Overall, the economic effect of the 1982 recession was nearly three times as severe in BC than it was in the rest of Canada (McMartin 2009). Over the rest of the decade, BC saw huge swings in real GDP, dropping by 6.1% in 1982, rising to 6.9% in 1985, seeing stagnation in 1986 at 0.2%, and rising back up to 6.1% a year later (ibid.). By 1991, the year that the NDP government would take power once more, this time holding onto office for a decade, the economy was flat, with growth at 0.2%. BC's economy over the decade of the 1990s was fairly lacklustre but without recession.

The first two budgets introduced by the NDP can be labelled "mildly progressive, in a middle-of-the-road liberal sense" – in other words, relatively minor tax increases for the wealthy, no reductions made to social-service spending, moderate increases in the minimum wage, but no sweeping changes consistent with what might be otherwise expected for a social democratic party (Cohen 1994, 157). Further, government rhetoric in the early 1990s was decidedly neoliberal in its emphasis, with the NDP insistent that it must go after "welfare cheats" and focus on correcting a structural deficit through debt reduction, yet as Cohen (ibid., 156) also points out, there was no serious deficit problem in the province – less than 6% of provincial government revenues were devoted to the interest on the debt at a time when the federal government was paying about 35%. From 1991 to 1998, real per capita public spending dropped by $544, and spending in all areas but health and education were reduced significantly (Vogel 2000, 2). Public-sector employment increased by 19.8% from 1988 to 1998, but over this same period population grew by 28.8% (ibid., 7). By 1998, BC had the second-smallest provincial public sector relative to population size. Real commodity prices were beginning to recover in 2001, the year of a sea change in BC public policy.

During the 2001 provincial election campaign, the NDP claimed the budget was in surplus by $1.5 billion while the Liberals claimed that these numbers had been "fudged" and that the province was actually in a deficit position. Five weeks after the election, the comptroller general and auditor general confirmed surpluses in the consolidated revenue fund and the summary accounts and BC was able to make its then-largest pay down of government debt (McMartin 2005). Upon taking office, under their "New Era" banner (akin to Ontario's 1995 Harris-led "Common Sense Revolution," described by Evans and Fanelli in this volume), the Liberals enacted sweeping tax cuts, buoyed by their landslide victory of seventy-seven of seventy-nine seats. Corporate and personal income taxes were slashed immediately, including an across-the-board 25% cut to personal income tax – the government's largest source of revenue at the time (Cohn 2006). By 2013, tax cuts introduced since 2001 led to a loss of $3.5 billion for government (Ivanova and Klein 2013, 6). This shifted the government's source of revenue, with the province collecting more from sales taxes than from personal income tax (28% of total revenue compared with 27%) (Lee et al. 2011, 2).

Tax cuts have not only hurt government revenue but have also been unequal in their impact on citizens. These cuts have been highly regressive, meaning the wealthy have benefited by paying less in dollar terms and as a share of their income. Whereas lower-income households received an average tax cut–related savings of $200 per year, the top 10% of income-earning households saved an average of $9,200 per year (ibid., 1). Another key regressive tax in the province is the Medical Services Plan (MSP), a Canadian oddity, which imposes annual premiums on households as means of accessing public health care. MSP premiums have increased by 85% (2010–13) and by 2013 the province was earning more revenue off MSP than corporate income taxes (Ivanova and Klein 2013, 6). The net result for BC residents is that the higher the income, the lower the tax rate when all personal taxes are accounted for (income, sales, carbon and property taxes, and MSP premiums).

The "New Era" banner applied far more broadly than taxation and fiscal prudence, it also sought to reinvent government and create private-sector investment opportunities. Upon taking office, the Liberal government quickly began a neoliberal restructuring process involving changes that fundamentally reshaped state–society relations. Whole volumes could be dedicated to a description and analysis of the reforms and restructuring introduced by the Liberals; here we can but summarize some of the most significant initiatives.

First, the influence of the Ministry of Finance has been augmented and its spending control priorities now inform all other areas of the public sector through the 2002 creation of the Capital Asset Management Framework (CAMF) and Partnerships BC. This has institutionalized a bias towards using for-profit public–private partnerships (P3s) to privately design, build, finance, operate, and/or maintain public infrastructure assets such as hospitals, highways, bridges, and transit projects (for more on P3s, see Whiteside 2016; 2015; other authors in this volume also point to P3 emergence and spread – Smith in Saskatchewan, Evans and Fanelli in Ontario, Clancy in Nova Scotia, Graefe and Rioux in Quebec, Hicks in Nunavut – under similar conditions of neoliberal era restructuring and austerity). The CAMF serves as new "rules of the road" for public infrastructure building in BC, including the stipulation that capital project proposals with a provincial cost in excess of $50 million must *first* be considered as a P3 using private for-profit partners and financing. The CAMF applies province-wide. All ministries, public sector agencies, and other public organizations must now comply with these rules when seeking approval and funding for infrastructure projects. Partnerships BC acts as the province's P3 champion, value-for-money evaluator, and knowledge centre. Its services must be used for all large infrastructure projects. Despite being introduced under the auspices of fiscal prudence and value for money, privately financed P3s are more expensive than publicly financed projects because private borrowers pay higher interest rates than public borrowers, P3s have high hidden fees and transaction costs, and project savings are often siphoned off as profit – all of which makes P3 ill suited to austerity, since it is not a cost-savings device (Whiteside 2014).

Second, funding schemes for hospitals and health authorities have been altered by introducing tight spending control and inducing market-oriented restructuring by simultaneously downloading greater responsibilities and risks onto local authorities. Regional health authorities must now comply with performance agreements with the Ministry of Health, which stipulate that budget cuts imposed by the province cannot be dealt with through deficits at the local level. The consequences are hospital restructuring and amalgamations, service cuts (e.g., cancelling elective surgeries), fee hikes (where applicable, e.g., parking lot rates and private hospital rooms), and cuts to labour costs (e.g., freezes on hiring, overtime, and layoffs). In 2010, BC began to move away from line item–based (global lump sum) hospital funding to an "activity-based" model in dozens of hospitals across the province, impacting roughly 20% of hospital funding overall (Cohen et al. 2012, 6). Cast as a "patient-focused" model able to reduce surgical wait times and improve access to emergency services (BC Ministry of Health 2010), under an activity-based model financing for procedures becomes linked to the volume of activity, and payments are made by procedure or by patient. Funds are distributed using metrics such as efficiency, throughput, and lowest price as opposed to other rival considerations such as ensuring patients are receiving the highest quality of care possible or equity of access across the population (Canadian Doctors for Medicare 2008). Patients with the most complex care needs are particularly disadvantaged by this funding model (Cohen et al. 2012).

Third, the province implemented new and unprecedented privatization-enabling and anti-union legislation within the provincial health care system: Bill 29-2002 (*The Health and Social Services Delivery*

Improvement Act), Bill 94-2003 (*The Health Sector Partnerships Agreement Act*), and Bill 37-2004 (*The Health Sector [Facilities Subsector] Collective Agreement Act*). Bill 29 enabled contracting out in BC's health care sector, targeting support staff such as cleaners and food service staff. Bill 94 is the companion legislation to Bill 29, applicable to P3 hospitals. Lower wages, fractured bargaining units, and more precarious employment overall have resulted from both Bill 29-2002 and Bill 94-2003. Bill 37 imposed wage rollbacks affecting 43,000 hospital and long-term health care workers and allowed for greater casualization of health-sector employment.[3]

Anti-austerity and anti-privatization demonstrations (specifically focused on incoming health care cuts and contracting out) by the Hospital Employees' Union (HEU), BC Federation of Labour, and other groups around the province began in 2002. The HEU even erected a blockade to thwart the transportation of contracted-out linen services running from Chilliwack, BC to Calgary, Alberta. In 2003, negotiations were taking place between unions and government to come up with an agreement around wage concessions, vacation time, job losses, and other elements pertinent to the unfolding of Bill 29; but a 2003 tentative agreement was swiftly rejected by 57% of HEU members (Camfield 2006, 20). In an unusual arrangement, the Industrial, Wood and Allied Workers union (IWA) signed "partnership agreements" in July 2003 to take on positions that had been contracted out under the employ of multinational corporations Sodexo, Aramark, and Compass (see Cohen and Cohen 2006). An HEU strike vote, held in March 2004, was endorsed by 90%. The provincial government quickly passed back-to-work legislation (the aforementioned Bill 37) and imposed a new collective agreement. Wildcat solidarity strikes, protests, and new picket lines characterized April 2004, and culminated in a 40,000-strong strike/protest in May 2004 (see Camfield 2006 for details and chronology). However, just as solidarity and union resistance were at their height in spring 2004, an agreement was reached between government and union negotiators. It is worth quoting one staffer at length to capture the street-level sentiment at the time surrounding the elite-driven agreement: "people were really, really angry. People had no idea that was the deal that was being contemplated, people were angry they didn't get to vote on it, people didn't understand why the plug was pulled at this zenith of support ... it was just rage" (quoted in Camfield 2006, 32).

Within a few short years, more than 9,000 HEU members had lost their jobs, and wages were slashed in half (from roughly $20/hour to roughly $10) and benefits lost in newly contracted-out positions (Cohen and Cohen 2006). After attempts by union and health care advocacy organizations to challenge Bill 29 through BC courts had failed, the case was brought before the Supreme Court of Canada. In 2007, in a six-to-one ruling, three sections of the legislation were found to be constitutionally invalid: sections 6.2 (no restrictions on contracting out), 6.4 (no requirement of consultation prior to contracting out), and 9 (relating to layoffs and bumping). The provincial government was given one year to remedy the situation and in May 2008 amendments were introduced through Bill 26-2008 (*The Health Statutes Amendment Act*). The Court also instructed the government to compensate workers for their loss, but it did not terminate the contracts that had been struck with Sodexo, Aramark, and Compass. Privatization was here to stay. The HEU reached a settlement with the government in 2008 and this provided some measure of compensation, retraining, and expanded rights for workers affected by contracting out. Collective bargaining also led to an improvement in pay and benefits, but by 2017, nominal wages for some occupations were still below what they were in 2002.

BC PROVINCIAL BUDGETS: 2006–16

The changes introduced since 2001, and particularly those initiated early on between roughly 2001 and 2004, were of greater significance for public-service recipients and public-sector workers, taxpayers, and the political economy of public infrastructure than was the fiscal austerity that followed the global financial crisis of 2007–08. This does not minimize the impact of either austerity or the recent economic crisis, but it does indicate that BC's "crisis" or watershed shift in its political economy is located earlier in the decade, making malleable the notion of fiscal crisis and fundamentally questioning the necessity of austerity when adopted in 2013.

Table 1.2 presents a scan of surplus/deficit (estimated and actual), rates of taxpayer-supported debt/GDP, and real GDP growth in BC Budgets 2006–14. In October 2008 (following the spring budget), the provincial government announced stimulus measures in the wake of the 2007–08 global financial crisis. The stimulus package featured tax relief for small businesses and cuts to personal income tax

Table 1.2
BC provincial budgets

Year	Revenues – expenditures estimated	Revenues – expenditures actual	Debt/GDP (%)	Real GDP growth (%)
2006	Surplus $600 million	Surplus $2.9 billion	15.8	3.9
2007	Surplus $400 million	Surplus $2 billion	14.8	3.1
2008	Surplus $50 million	Surplus $50 million	14.0	2.4
2009	Deficit $495 million	Deficit $2.8 billion	15.2	-0.9
2010	Deficit $1.7 billion	Deficit $1.3 billion	17.2	2.2
2011	Deficit $925 million	Deficit $2.5 billion	17.5	2
2012	Deficit $968 million	Deficit $1.2 billion	17.6	1.8
2013	Surplus $197 million	Surplus $175 million	18.2	1.6
2014	Surplus $184 million	Surplus $879 million	18.4	2.0
2015	Surplus $284 million	Surplus $377 million	17.4	2.3
2016	Surplus $264 million	Surplus $2.2 billion	17.0	2.4

Source: BC Ministry of Finance 2007; 2008; 2009; 2010; 2011; 2012; 2013; 2014; 2015; 2016.

(3% for the lowest two income brackets) and a three-year, $20 billion infrastructure spending program for investments on projects relating to roads, transit, schools, hospitals, and the like. Through these measures, government hoped to create 88,000 construction jobs over this three-year period, and $3.9 billion over three years was also allocated to health care spending. It is at this moment that the global financial crisis began to translate into a fiscal "crisis" for the state (although a minor one in relative terms). Budget 2009 was in deficit and real GDP had contracted; unlike its neighbour to the north, Yukon, which saw its deficit begin and end that same fiscal year (see Sabin this volume), BC's deficits continued until 2013.

Budget 2009 described the slowdown in the US and global economy as well as financial market instability as the leading causes of BC's economic and fiscal woes. It predicted a rebound in 2010 but the US (and many other leading economies such as the UK) quickly fell back into a recession, contra expectations at the time. BC's 2009 budget maintained the infrastructure stimulus spending announced in fall 2008. It also allocated an additional $920 million to health care, $244 million over three years for education, and $381 million over four years for social services. However, plans for government "streamlining" and cuts to discretionary spending in health, education, and social services were simultaneously enacted. Budget 2010 introduced more additional spending: $447 million on health care, $156 million on education over three years, and $58 million on infrastructure (matched by other levels of government). By Budget 2011, and continuing in 2012, the stated concern shifted to maintaining the province's AAA credit rating; protecting health care, education, and social services; and balancing the budget by FY 2013–14. New spending commitments totalled $604 million for health care and $65 million over three years for social services. Budget 2012 maintained existing commitments. Both budgets emphasized problems relating to export revenue (less demand globally and from Asia in particular), exchange rate volatility, and weaknesses in the US economy.

Making good on the commitment in 2011 to balance the budget by 2013–14, Budget 2013 can be considered BC's first "austerity" budget after the 2008 global financial crisis. Budgets can be balanced in several ways. Aside from achieving surplus through growth, austerity usually comes down to cutting expenditures and/or raising additional revenue through asset sales and taxation. Budget 2013 chose the latter. Revenue was to be raised through the sale of properties and assets (in hopes of earning $625 million over two years), temporary increases in personal income tax for those earning over $150,000, and advancing the effective date of corporate tax increases announced earlier in 2012. Average annual spending was also set to increase by 1.5% for the next three fiscal years, with health program spending targeted in particular ($2.4 billion over three years). However, even within this fiscally privileged area there emerged concerning trends; namely, premiums for MSP were set to increase by 4%. According to analysis by the HEU (2013), this would translate into an additional tax on BC families' incomes amounting to $2.39 billion by 2015–16. Further, though rising in each budget, health spending in BC was falling as a percentage of GDP (Rozworski 2014). Finally, following the spring budget, in October 2013 the province introduced a "managed staffing strategy": an across-the-board hiring freeze for the public sector. Budget 2014 introduced a few additional tax measures such as a BC Early Childhood Tax Benefit (although extremely modest at $55/month and only beginning the following year), and an increase in tobacco taxes. "Expenditure management" for ministry spending continued, leading to cuts of $100 million from 2009 to 2014.

All told, these 2013–2014 austerity measures were far from drastic compared with previous eras, discussed earlier in this chapter. From 2010 to 2014, measured in nominal dollars, overall spending increased. With Budget 2010, total expenses came in at $40.6 billion; by 2014 they were $44.4 billion, and inflation averaged only 1.2% from 2010 to 2014. However – this is a key point to keep in mind – there was not much fat to trim off the BC public sector given previous rounds of fiscal restraint; public sector employment as a proportion of total employment was the smallest of all provinces in 2011, and spending as a percentage of GDP was 2.3% lower in 2011 than 2001, or roughly $5 billion less (Ivanova 2013). Within a few years, estimates were forecasting record-low levels of provincial spending as a percentage of GDP (see Ivanova 2014).

Budget 2015 stuck fast to the neoliberal balanced-budget fixation and tax expenditures continued to feature as the main form of fiscal governance. This budget provided tax credits in areas of marginal significance like children's fitness equipment and interactive digital media despite poor growth; stated concerns with export market demand and exchange rate volatility; and a growing list of social ills relating to a lack of affordable housing in major cities, child poverty, and growing inequality. The expressed focus and purpose behind fiscal policy of this sort was to maintain the province's triple-A credit rating. Clearly, debt payment burdens ought to be a concern for any government, but the central gift bestowed by an excellent rating – low interest rates – was being squandered in the process of meeting ideological criteria, not structural necessity. No, these were not the shock-and-awe, slash-and-burn austerity budgets of Britain or Greece, but they were an entirely lacklustre, "nothing doing" series of tepid neoliberal budgets that dampened growth, did little for employment and social need, and indicated very little creativity or inspiration at the helm. In marked contrast to Alberta's Keynesian-style economic management (see Brownsey in this volume), that BC's economy has remained relatively healthy at all is thanks not to government but instead to tumbling oil prices and a dramatically depreciated dollar – macroeconomic factors that help key BC sectors like timber and natural gas exports, tourism, and the film industry.

Budget 2016 continued the balanced budget trend but also showed some signs of life with a $1.6 billion increase in spending for social support, economic development, and community safety. In detail, the plan remained as dull as before: a $75 million rural dividend,

Table 1.3
Unemployment rate

	2007	2008	2009	2010	2011	2012	2013
BC	4.3	4.6	7.7	7.6	7.5	6.7	6.6
Canada	6	6.1	8.3	8	7.4	7.2	7.1

Source: Statistics Canada, CANSIM Table 282-0002 Labour Force Survey estimates (LFS), males and females 15 years of age and over.

$128 million for a correctional facility, and the like. A sovereign wealth fund of sorts was also established with an initial injection of $100 million, but it was meant to target debt reduction and more tax expenditures in the following years. Economic concerns persisted, budgeted spending increases fell below revenue gains, and greater nominal dollars devoted to social programs did not keep pace with inflation and population growth. Conciliatory changes made to the province's much-loathed Medical Service Plan in this budget are ones that ought to have always been in place, like exempting children from the public health care premium.

Throughout the financial crisis and ensuing recession, BC's labour market performed better than the Canadian average, although the crisis still clearly had an impact: by 2009 the unemployment rate had nearly doubled compared with 2007's rate, jumping by 3.4% as table 1.3 shows. Government intervention through stimulus spending was thus warranted. However, the employment rate dropped nearly every year since 2007, and in 2013 it was at its lowest rate in seven years. The employment rate is often said to be a better indicator of labour market prospects and climate given that the unemployment rate only captures those actively seeking employment, ignoring discouraged workers. Table 1.4 below indicates that an end to stimulus and a switch to austerity in 2013 came at a delicate time for workers and the economy. It furthermore suggests that more needs to be done to support job growth and employment, that efforts to date have not been altogether successful, and that new strategies are required. By 2015, positive growth had returned for the employment rate, albeit by a meagre 0.8%.

In summary, the "crisis" moment in BC fiscal affairs was not 2008 when the financial crisis hit, 2009 when recession ensued, or 2013

Table 1.4
Employment rate

	2007	2008	2009	2010	2011	2012	2013
BC	63.2	63.2	60.5	60.5	60.2	60.6	59.9
Canada	63.4	63.5	61.6	61.6	61.8	61.8	61.8

Source: Statistics Canada, CANSIM Table 282-0002 Labour Force Survey estimates (LFS), males and females 15 years of age and over.

when austerity returned, but in the early years of the 2000s with the implementation of deep tax cuts and regressive taxation. An obvious fix to budgetary pressures would be to permanently restore a more equitable distribution of taxes and reverse previous tax cuts. Creating a more progressive tax system would help more than just social equity, it would mean substantially greater revenue for government (see Ivanova and Klein 2013 for various scenarios). Furthermore, if by 2013 BC had collected the same amount of tax as a share of GDP that it did in 2000, the government would have earned an additional $3.5 billion, eliminating the deficit and enhancing funding for services (ibid., 6). These initiatives might be fought on the basis that they will hurt competitiveness, but thus far the tax cuts over the past decade have not created the prosperity for the BC economy that was promised, opening space for new strategies. Greater investment in public infrastructure assets would be one such strategy. BC chose to do this from 2002 to 2017 by using private financing via P3 agreements – this will lead to higher overall costs and is therefore not sustainable over the long run. Use of public financing rather than a reliance on private capital markets would save money (through lower interest rates) and ensure control and decision making is fully retained by government and the public sector.

Finally, BC revenue generated through royalties from resources like natural gas has been falling in recent years, compared with 2007 and 2008 when market prices were higher. The 2014 budget proposed a new LNG income tax to bring in more revenue, yet the scheme is reliant upon inherently volatile market pricing. Lee (2014, 14) proposes viable alternatives such as setting a minimum public return, applying BC's carbon tax to emissions from LNG facilities and operations, and requiring that a BC Crown corporation hold an equity stake in an LNG operation as a way of ensuring that some share of the profits remain in BC.

CONCLUDING REMARKS

The title of this book refers to an "age of austerity." This age of austerity is also an era of paradox. In BC, austerity budgeting has experienced victory unfettered from success: austerity as an aim has triumphed despite not leading to the ends it has promised. The goals of austerity are seldom exclusively fiscal in nature, and fiscal policy has been used to set priorities and responsibilities, burdens and benefits.

Both the NDP in 1991 and the Liberals in 2001 took power claiming that their predecessor left them with a weak provincial economy, justifying a change in fiscal policy tactics. However, with export revenue–based swings, provincial fiscal policy can help or hinder recovery, but it cannot be pointed to as the sole and decisive factor in dramatic, year-over-year upswings and downswings in both economic and government revenue. Changes in revenue that occur in this fashion are due to cyclical factors, not structural ones. Yet at the same time, upswings and downswings can provide a window for policy shift and serve as a backdrop for justifying claims that restraint or other potentially unpopular maneuvers that redistribute benefits and wealth upward (e.g., regressive taxation) are warranted. Austerity in the early years of the 2000s sought to address budget imbalance (even if fabricated) through tax cuts that led to significant revenue losses for government, tax changes that initiated a highly regressive system of taxation, and policies that favoured greater market-based service provision and more expensive private financing for public infrastructure and support services. The austerity that began in 2013 took aim at tackling what were essentially cyclically induced budget deficits (caused not by profligate government spending but by world economic volatility), using the recession period to justify neoliberal public-sector hiring freezes, tax cuts, and expenditure management. The "solution" to budget imbalances therefore squeezes government finances and could require future rounds of austerity, hardly a successful long-run governance strategy. Victory without success is thus achieved when fiscal policy is used not to create budgetary stability and economic prosperity but as a mechanism of restructuring state–society relations, public-sector employment, and public services along more individualized, flexibilized, and market-oriented lines.

NOTES

1 The Philips curve depicts inflation and unemployment as inversely related: if people are out of work, then the economy should be cooling off, and if price levels are on a tear, people should not have trouble finding a job. Government macroeconomic managers (working in the post-Keynesian tradition) felt they could target the price level or the unemployment rate, but not both at once. With relatively high growth and low unemployment over the post war era, this trade-off did not matter, but when stagflation hit in the early 1970s – simultaneous economic stagnation (which included high unemployment) and inflation – neoclassical economists like Milton Friedman used this opportunity to overturn the dominance of Keynesian and post-Keynesian inspired macroeconomic policy. Profligate government spending, they claimed, was causing stagflation.

2 Put simply, exemptions reduce taxable income, deductions reduce expense items, and credits are usually dollar-for-dollar tax reductions (of the refundable or non-refundable variety).

3 There has been equally egregious legislation applied to public-sector workers in education: Bill 28-2002 (*Public Education and Flexibility Act*) and later Bill 22-2012 (*Education Improvement Act*). In 2011 the BC Supreme Court ruled that the removal of teachers' right to bargain class size and composition through Bill 28 was unconstitutional. In 2014 a similar ruling was made about Bill 22, the replacement legislation for Bill 28, as it included the same provisions. The BC Teachers' Federation began job action (rotating strikes) in late spring 2014, with an agreement reached in fall 2014.

REFERENCES

Alesina, Alberto, and Silvia Ardagna. 1998. *Expansionary Fiscal Contractions in Europe: New Evidence*. European Central Bank working paper number 675.

Alesina, Alberto, and Roberto Perotti. 1995. "Fiscal Expansions and Adjustments in OECD Countries." *Economic Policy* 21: 205–48.

Alesina, Alberto, Roberto Perotti, and Jose Tavares. 1998. "The Political Economy of Fiscal Adjustments." *Brookings Papers on Economic Activity* 1: 197–266.

Battle, Ken. 1999. "Child Benefit Reform: A Case Study in Tax-Transfer Integration." *Canadian Tax Journal* 47 (2): 1219–57.

BC Ministry of Health. 2010. BC *Launches Patient-Focused Funding Provincewide*. Victoria: Government of British Columbia, 12 April. http://www2.news.gov.bc.ca/news_releases_2009-2013/2010HSERV0020-000403.htm.

Block, Sheila, and Allan Maslove. 1994. "Ontario Tax Expenditures." In *Taxes as Instruments of Public Policy*, edited by Allan Maslove, 167–205. Toronto: University of Toronto Press.

Blyth, Mark. 2013a. "Why Austerity Is a Dangerous Idea." *Time*, 18 April. http://ideas.time.com/2013/04/18/why-austerity-is-a-dangerous-idea/.

– 2013b. *Austerity: The History of a Dangerous Idea*. Oxford: Oxford University Press.

– 2013c. "Power & Prejudice: The Politics of Austerity." *New Left Project*, 14 August. http://www.newleftproject.org/index.php/site/article_comments/power_prejudice_the_politics_of_austerity_part_1.

British Columbia. Ministry of Finance. 2007. *Budget and Fiscal Plan 2007/08 – 2009/10*. Victoria: Ministry of Finance, February. http://www.bcbudget.gov.bc.ca/2007/pdf/2007_Budget_Fiscal_Plan.pdf.

– 2008. *Budget and Fiscal Plan 2008/09 – 2010/11*. Victoria: Ministry of Finance, February. http://bcbudget.gov.bc.ca/2008/bfp/2008_budget_fiscal_plan.pdf.

– 2009. *Budget and Fiscal Plan 2009/10 – 2011/12*. Victoria: Ministry of Finance, February. http://bcbudget.gov.bc.ca/2009/bfp/2009_budget_fiscal_plan.pdf.

– 2010. *Budget and Fiscal Plan 2010/11 – 2012/13*. Victoria: Ministry of Finance, March. http://bcbudget.gov.bc.ca/2010/bfp/2010_budget_fiscal_plan.pdf.

– 2011. *Budget and Fiscal Plan 2011/12 – 2013/14*. Victoria: Ministry of Finance, May. http://bcbudget.gov.bc.ca/2011/bfp/2011_budget_fiscal_plan.pdf.

– 2012. *Budget and Fiscal Plan 2012/13 – 2014/15*. Victoria: Ministry of Finance, February. http://www.bcbudget.gov.bc.ca/2012/bfp/2012_budget_fiscal_plan.pdf.

– 2013. *Budget and Fiscal Plan 2013/14 – 2015/16*. Victoria: Ministry of Finance, February. http://bcbudget.gov.bc.ca/2013/bfp/2013_budget_fiscal_plan.pdf.

– 2014. *Budget and Fiscal Plan 2014/15 – 2016/17*. Victoria: Ministry of Finance, February. http://bcbudget.gov.bc.ca/2014/bfp/2014_budget_fiscal_plan.pdf.

– 2015. *Budget and Fiscal Plan 2015/16 – 2017/18*. Victoria: Ministry of Finance, February. http://bcbudget.gov.bc.ca/2015/bfp/2015_budget_and_fiscal_plan.pdf.

– 2016. *Budget and Fiscal Plan 2016/17 – 2018/19*. Victoria: Ministry of Finance, February. http://bcbudget.gov.bc.ca/2016/bfp/2016_budget_and_fiscal_plan.pdf.

Brownsey, Keith, Michael Howlett, and Joshua Newman. 2009. "From Forestry to Film: The Changing Political Economy of British Columbia." In *British Columbia Politics and Government*, edited by Michael Howlett, Dennis Pilon, and Tracy Summerville, 21–39. Toronto: Emond Montgomery Publications.

Camfield, David. 2006. "Neoliberalism and Working-Class Resistance in British Columbia: The Hospital Employees' Union Struggle, 2002–2004." *Labour/Le Travail* 57 (Spring): 9–41.

Canadian Doctors for Medicare. 2008. *Activity-Based Funding in Canadian Hospitals and Other Surgical Facilities*. http://www.canadiandoctorsformedicare.ca/images/stories/ABF_Position_Paper_15OCT08.pdf.

Cohen, Marjorie Griffin. 1994. "British Columbia: Playing Safe Is a Dangerous Game." *Studies in Political Economy* 43 (Spring): 149–59.

Cohen, Marjorie Griffin, and Marcy Cohen. 2006. "Privatization a Strategy for Eliminating Pay Equity in Health Care." In *Social Reproduction: Feminist Political Economy Challenges Neo-Liberalism*, edited by Kate Bezanson and Meg Luxton, 117–44. Montreal and Kingston: McGill-Queen's University Press.

Cohen, Marcy, Margaret McGregor, Iglika Ivanova, and Chris Kinkaid. 2012. *Beyond the Hospital Walls: Activity Based Funding versus Integrated Health Care Reform*. Vancouver: Canadian Centre for Policy Alternatives. January.

Cohn, Daniel. 2006. "Transformative Change and Measuring Success: Public–Private Partnerships in British Columbia, 2001–2005." *Revue Gouvernance* 3 (2).

Cutt, James. 1989. "Budgeting in British Columbia, 1976–1986: Coping and Caring in Tough Times." In *Budgeting in the Provinces*, edited by Allan Maslove, 143–66. Toronto: The Institute of Public Administration of Canada.

Doern, Bruce, Allan Maslove, and Michael Prince. 2013. *Canadian Public Budgeting in the Age of Crises*. Montreal and Kingston: McGill-Queen's University Press.

Giavazzi, Francesco, and Marco Pagano. 1990. "Can Severe Fiscal Contractions Be Expansionary? Tales of Two Small European Countries." In *NBER Macroeconomics Annual*, edited by Olivier Jean Blanchard and Stanley Fischer. Cambridge: MIT Press.

Hale, Geoffrey E. 2006. "Balancing Autonomy and Responsibility: The Politics of Provincial Fiscal and Tax Policies." In *Provinces: Canadian*

Provincial Politics. 2nd ed., edited by Christopher Dunn, 373–412. Peterborough: Broadview Press.

Harder, Lois. 2003. "Tax Expenditures: The Social Policy of Globalization?" In *Global Turbulence: Social Activists' and State Responses to Globalization*, edited by Marjorie Griffin Cohen and Stephen McBride, 59–71. Aldershot: Ashgate Publishing.

HEU (Hospital Employees' Union). 2013. "BC Liberals Balance Election Budget by Cutting Planned Health Spending; MSP Revenues to Outpace Corporate Tax Revenues by 2015." *News Release*, 19 February.

Howard, Christopher. 1997. *The Hidden Welfare State: Tax Expenditures as Social Policy in the United States*. Princeton: Princeton University Press.

Howlett, Michael, and Keith Brownsey. 2001. "British Columbia: Politics in a Post-Staples Political Economy." In *The Provincial State in Canada*, edited by Keith Brownsey and Michael Howlett, 309–34. Peterborough: Broadview Press.

Innis, Harold. 1954. *The Cod Fisheries: The History of an International Economy*. 2nd ed. Toronto: University of Toronto Press.

– 1956. *The Fur Trade in Canada: An Introduction to Canadian Economic History*. 2nd ed. Toronto: University of Toronto Press.

Ivanova, Iglika. 2013. *Reality Check on the Size of BC's Public Sector*. Vancouver: Canadian Centre for Policy Alternatives, April.

– 2014. *What You Need to Know about Budget 2014*. Policy Note. Vancouver: Canadian Centre for Policy Alternatives, February.

Ivanova, Iglika, and Seth Klein. 2013. *Progressive Tax Options for BC*. Vancouver: Canadian Centre for Policy Alternatives, January.

Lee, Marc. 2014. *Path to Prosperity*? Vancouver: Canadian Centre for Policy Alternatives.

Lee, Marc, Iglika Ivanova, and Seth Klein. 2011. *BC's Regressive Tax Shift*. Vancouver: Canadian Centre for Policy Alternatives, June.

Malcolmson, John. 1984. "The Hidden Agenda of 'Restraint.'" In *The New Reality: The Politics of Restraint in British Columbia*, edited by Warren Magnusson et al., 75–87. Vancouver: New Star Books.

McBride, Stephen. 1992. *Not Working*. Toronto: University of Toronto Press.

McMartin, Will. 2005. "Campbell Misled Public on NDP Finances." *The Tyee*, 20 April. http://thetyee.ca/Views/2005/04/20/CampbellMisledPublic/.

– 2009. "BC's Economy: Whose Was Best?" *The Tyee*, 23 April. http://thetyee.ca/Views/2009/04/23/BCEcon/.

Minister of Finance. 2012. *Budget Speech 2012: Jobs, Growth, and Long-Term Prosperity*. Ottawa: Government of Canada, 29 March. http://www.budget.gc.ca/2012/rd-dc/speech-discours-eng.html.

Peck, Jamie. 2014. "Pushing Austerity: State Failure, Municipal Bankruptcy and the Crises of Fiscal Federalism in the USA." *Cambridge Journal of Regions, Economy and Society* 7 (1): 17–44.

Rozworski, Michal. 2014. "Selling Prosperity in a Time of Austerity: Budget Days in BC and Quebec." *Canadian Dimensions*, 23 February. http://canadiandimension.com/articles/5961/.

Scarfe, Brian. 1996. "Public Finance and Fiscal Policy in British Columbia." In *Politics, Policy, and Government in British Columbia*, edited by Kenneth Carty, 217–71. Vancouver: UBC Press.

Schumpeter, J.A. (1918) 1954. "The Crisis of the Tax State." *International Economic Papers* 4: 5–38.

Schofield, John. 1984. "Recovery through Restraint? The Budgets of 1983/84 and 1984/85." In *The New Reality: The Politics of Restraint in British Columbia*, edited by Will Magnusson et al., 41–55. Vancouver: New Star Books.

Vogel, Donna. 2000. *Are Spending Cuts and Privatization the Answer for BC?* Vancouver: Canadian Centre for Policy Alternatives, March.

Watkins, Mel. 1963. "A Staple Theory of Economic Growth." *The Canadian Journal of Economics and Political Science* 19 (2): 141–58.

Whiteside, Heather. 2014. "P3s and the Value for Money Illusion." In *Orchestrating Austerity*, edited by Donna Baines and Stephen McBride, 162–74. Halifax: Fernwood Publishing.

– 2015. *Purchase for Profit: Public–Private Partnerships and Canada's Public Health Care System*. Toronto: University of Toronto Press.

– 2016. *About Canada: Public–Private Partnerships*. Halifax: Fernwood Publishing.

CHAPTER TWO

Alberta and the Great Recession: Neoliberalism, Conservative Government, and Public Finance

KEITH BROWNSEY

In the mid-1990s under the Progressive Conservative (PC) government of Ralph Klein, Alberta established a starkly neoliberal agenda. With a focus on deficit and debt elimination, Klein privatized public services, cut spending in provincial departments in the range of 20% to 30%, reduced public-sector wages and salaries, eliminated a variety of programs, and attempted to deregulate electricity generation and transmission (Taft 1997; Kneebone 2016; Evans and Fanelli in this volume; Whiteside in this volume). As well, the corporate income tax and other taxes were cut for businesses and a flat tax on personal incomes was introduced. The great symbol of the Alberta fiscal regime was the absence of a provincial sales tax. Klein made clear that, in his view, the province did not have a revenue problem; rather, it had a spending problem. This set of policies, which cut spending and taxes, eliminated or privatized services, and deregulated key economic sectors, came to be known as the "Klein Revolution" or the "Alberta Advantage." At the same time, the Klein formula also included delaying spending on infrastructure such as schools, hospitals, water and sewage systems, and transportation projects, which resulted in a massive infrastructure deficit. This neoliberal program occurred as the Alberta population continued to grow due to immigration from elsewhere in Canada and overseas (for an overview of Alberta population growth, see figure 2.1).

A decade and a half later, beginning with the Great Recession that hit with such devastating force in 2008, Alberta again faced a revenue shortfall. The cause of this revenue shortfall was a precipitous decline in oil and natural gas revenues, the general economic downturn created by the world financial crisis and, beginning in 2014, an oversupply of oil and natural gas and a resulting decline in provincial revenues (see also Smith in this volume). Royalties and fees from the oil and natural gas sector fell from a high of 40.65% of provincial revenues in 2005–06 to an estimated 5.76% in 2015–16. The Government of Alberta responded to the decline in revenues by withdrawing billions from a Sustainability Fund[1] created in 2000 by the Klein government and by running deficits, which had reached over $10 billion by 2016. The Sustainability Fund had been created for just such circumstances. Governments would withdraw from the fund to offset declining revenues but would replenish it when oil and gas revenues increased. With volatility in oil and natural gas revenues, the Fund would stabilize public expenditures for program areas such as health care, education, and physical infrastructure. In the mid-2000s and again in the period 2011–14, oil prices sometimes reached USD$100 a barrel and the Fund reached CAD$17 billion by late 2006, as Ralph Klein left office. But the Sustainability Fund declined as successive governments used it to subsidize revenues in the late 2000s and 2010s.

While there was some effort made to reduce expenditures, throughout the 2008–16 period the provincial budget nevertheless increased to take into account both inflation and population growth, as well as a continuing expectation for a consistent level of public services. This was a very different approach to economic policy than the neoliberal agenda of the Klein years. Without stating it so publicly, the Progressive Conservative government from 2008–15 and the New Democratic (NDP) government after it came to office in May 2015 implemented a program of stimulus spending, program restraint, and tax increases, which maintained and even increased the role of the provincial state in the economy during a period of economic volatility. Whether it was a conscious plan or simply a response to political demands, Alberta's fiscal policy under the PC and NDP governments was a combination of a Klein-era low-tax environment and a type of Keynesian economic management.

The financial crisis of 2008–09, the Great Recession, had a global, national, and provincial impact. With the collapse of several key investment banks, including Lehman Brothers and Bear Stearns, and the near-death experience of American International Group (AIG),[2] there was a breakdown in financial markets (Geithner 2014, 206).

Credit markets refused to lend; assets, which had supported the financial system, proved worthless; and the economies of Western Europe and North America were thrown into turmoil. Alberta was not immune from these events. In the province's oil and natural gas sector – which accounts for over 60% of its gross domestic product – both small and large producers had difficulty borrowing and a number of significant projects stalled. As the crisis deepened and the price of natural gas and oil fell, provincial finances became strained. For the first time since the mid-1990s, the Government of Alberta recorded a deficit. Then, as provincial finances seemed to be recovering, another complicating factor emerged in 2014: the world supply of oil and natural gas increased. The result was a lowering of prices for these resources to levels not seen since the 1990s. This continued the already-difficult situation for the Alberta government.

Three factors shaped the PC and NDP governments' response to the fiscal crisis precipitated by the Great Recession and the fall of oil and natural gas prices. These factors prevented the governing Progressive Conservatives from making policy changes to fit a changed fiscal reality. A steady increase in population (see figure 2.1) and the political necessity of providing essential infrastructure and services saw the several PC governments that came after Ralph Klein use a policy mix of low taxes, performance review of provincial programs and policies, and deficit spending to manage the worst economic crisis since the Great Depression of the 1930s. After their election victory in May 2015, the NDP government led by Rachel Notley was faced with a dramatic decline in oil and natural gas revenues. Until the selection of Jim Prentice as PC leader and premier in September 2014, the province drifted through the Great Recession with the same policy set that had been in place since the mid-1990s (Hacker 2004; Lynch 2006). The short-lived Prentice government, on the other hand, broke with the previous policy mix. The Progressive Conservatives proposed various revenue-generating measures such as the reintroduction of a progressive income tax to replace the existing flat tax. They proposed deficit spending, program cuts, and other measures to restrain provincial spending. The New Democratic Party government elected on 5 May 2015 kept much of the Prentice agenda. They moved to place revenues on a sustainable footing with the introduction of a progressive income tax, an increase in the corporate tax rate, and a carbon tax. They sought to provide stable program funding with increases to offset inflation. Still, the new revenue sources cannot compensate entirely for the billions of dollars lost through a decline in oil and natural gas royalties and leases.

Although they had first been elected in 1971 and remained in office for almost forty-four years, the Progressive Conservatives became increasingly entangled with questions of leadership and factional rivalry in the mid-2000s. The party held three leadership contests between December 2006 and September 2014 and had five different leaders: Ralph Klein (1992–2006), Ed Stelmach (2006–11), Alison Redford (2011–14), David Hancock (May to September 2014), and Jim Prentice (2014–15). As well, over the same eight-year period there were eight ministers of finance and seven ministers of energy. This was a very unstable situation in which it was difficult to take decisions despite the increasingly perilous economic circumstances. The various PC premiers, finance ministers, and energy ministers attempted to maintain the neoliberal agenda of balanced budgets, no tax increases, and program reviews; they were reluctant to make the necessary adjustments to program funding or to raise taxes, which would bring spending in line with revenue in a politically uncertain environment. It was not until the fiscal situation reached a near critical point in spring 2015 that the Prentice government proposed to introduce a modestly progressive income tax in its March 2015 budget to replace the flat tax of the Klein years. At the same time, the Progressive Conservative government withdrew monies from the Sustainability Fund to continue program spending. The Prentice Conservatives were unwilling to raise taxes sufficiently to cover the deficit. Instead, they chose a combination of tax increases and withdrawals from the Sustainability Fund. There was little rethinking of economic and fiscal policy to fit the changing circumstances of the Great Recession and the decline in oil and natural gas prices.[3]

A second factor that framed the Government of Alberta's response to the Great Recession was the vague and often contradictory ideology of the PC government. The various governments during the 2006–15 period were unwilling to consider increasing tax revenues. Because a low tax regime had been one of the signature policy initiatives of the Klein years, Klein's successors were committed to keep Alberta taxes at the lowest possible level. Instead, of reforming the tax system to increase revenues, the Redford government, for example, initiated a program review to find efficiencies in program delivery and withdrew money from the Sustainability Fund to maintain program and infrastructure spending. While the realities of a growing population (see figure 2.1) and the consequent demands for physical and social infrastructure forced the Conservative governments to provide a publicly acceptable level of services in education, health care and other areas, they were committed to low taxes, balanced budgets, increased efficiencies in the delivery of public services, and program review.

The third factor that determined the government's response to the Great Recession was the volatility of oil and natural gas revenues. The average annual market price for oil was as low as CAD$56 in 2006 and as high as CAD$81.64 in 2013 but dropped to an average price of USD$48.67 a barrel in 2015 (U.S. Energy Information Agency 2016). The average price for natural gas was CAD$6.68 per thousand cubic feet (Mcf) in 2006, while it less than half that in 2013 at CAD$3.02 in 2013. The decline in oil and natural gas royalties left the provincial with a shrinking revenue base. While personal and corporate income taxes accounted for up to 60% of provincial revenues during the period 2007–15, the province was dependent on oil and natural gas revenues. For example, oil and natural gas royalties formed roughly 40% of the provincial revenues in 2007, but by 2015 this number had fallen to 5.76% (Treasury Board and Finance 2016, 113).

The government's response to the decline in oil and natural gas revenues and the economic slowdown included deficit financing of infrastructure, withdrawals from savings, a low-tax regime, and program reviews and cost reduction measures and, beginning in 2015, measures to increase tax revenues from personal and corporate income taxes. Within the context of neoliberal ideology, political awareness, and continuous personnel change, the Government of Alberta framed its response to the Great Recession of 2008–16 by raising taxes in select areas and withdrawing from the Sustainability Fund. This two-track approach was predicated on the idea that oil and natural gas prices would soon rise sufficiently to offset deficits and rebuild the Sustainability Fund. The province's budgeting strategy seemed contradictory, but it served the political purpose of maintaining spending in the key areas of health care, education, and infrastructure. The result was that despite a significant decline in oil and gas revenues, program spending was maintained, infrastructure was built, and efficiencies were sought. Out of these seeming contradictions emerged an uncoordinated policy of stimulus spending and low taxes, which resembled a Keynesian economic package designed to maintain economic growth and support provincial services.

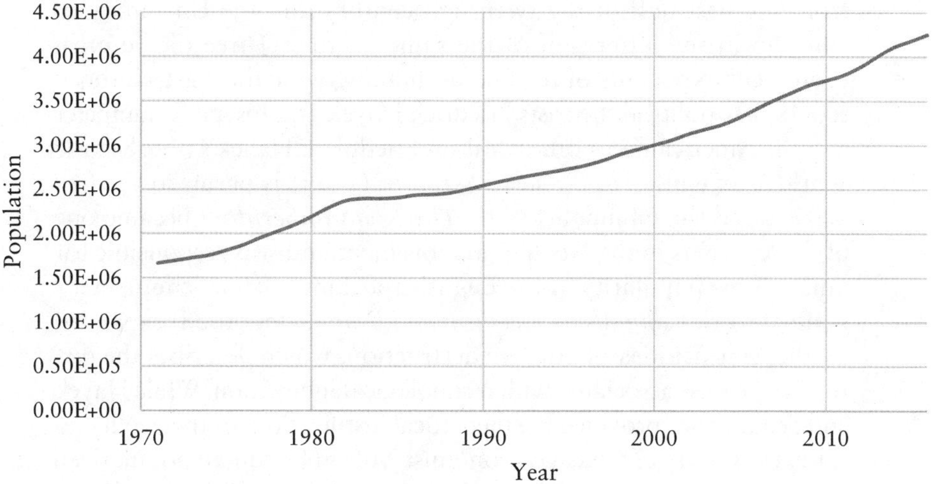

Source: Statistics Canada, CANSIM Table 051-0001

Figure 2.1 Alberta population over time: 1971–2016

NEOLIBERALISM

Neoliberalism is an economic theory that seeks to achieve a free-market economy unfettered by state activity. The system is based on an "institutional framework characterized by strong property rights, free markets, and free trade" (Harvey 2007, 2–3). Under neoliberalism, the role of the state is to establish the conditions in which the free market can exist (see also Sweeney in this volume). It is within this context that the entrepreneurial spirit can thrive. This view of the world holds that new firms will emerge to meet market demands. When a firm no longer responds to the market, it disintegrates and is replaced by one that does. This kind of creative destruction is a key principle of neoliberal thinking and is found in the thinking of Joseph Schumpeter, an Austrian economist who spent much of his career at Harvard. Schumpeter, a fierce critic of Karl Marx and his theories, derived his concept of creative destruction from Marx's idea of accumulation and annihilation (Schumpeter 2008; Greenspan 2009; O'Connor 1979).[4]

While neoliberalism has a variety of antecedents, the current model is closely identified with the Austrian School of economic thought from the first half of the twentieth century and the University of Chicago in the latter half of the same century. Three of the most prominent exponents of neoliberal thinking were the Austrian-born economists/political theorists Friedrich Hayek and Joseph Schumpeter and the American economist Milton Friedman. Hayek's post Second World War work *The Road to Serfdom* (1945) is paean to the free market and the minimalist state. *The Road to Serfdom* became one of the key texts in the Neoliberal movement and was responsible for much of his popularity in the English-speaking world. Schumpeter's seminal work *Capitalism, Socialism and Democracy* (2008) expanded on the Marxist idea of creative destruction, which describes the disruptive process associated with technological innovation. While Hayek and Schumpeter provided the theoretical justification for the neoliberal state, University of Chicago economist Milton Friedman popularized neoliberal, free-market ideas with his manifestos *Free to Choose* (1980) and *Capitalism and Freedom* (1982).

Neoliberalism landed with a thud in Alberta in the late 1980s and early 1990s. In the mid-1980s, oil and natural gas revenues declined, leaving the province's fiscal regime in tatters. The response from the governments in that decade, led by Don Getty and Ralph Klein, was a series of program cuts, privatization of public services, program elimination, and tax cuts. Under Klein, hospitals were shuttered and destroyed, kindergarten was defunded, social assistance was cut and a variety of provincial services such as the sale of alcoholic beverages and registries were privatized. Even the private provincial electricity market was deregulated. Overall department budgets within the Government of Alberta were reduced by an average of 20% (Taft 1997) and a number of major projects were suspended or delayed.

Along with spending cuts, privatization of services, and program elimination, the Klein government reduced taxes. The most important of these reductions was the implementation of a flat tax on personal incomes. In 1999, the Klein government replaced the progressive personal income tax with a 10% flat tax. During the same period, corporate income taxes were cut, and equipment and capital depreciation allowances were increased. A flat tax was introduced on alcoholic beverages, which reduced the cost of high-end products but increased the price of less expensive items. These tax changes were to impose a program of austerity on the province to promote economic growth. The theory was that these measures would free capital for private investment – in the case of Alberta, in the conventional oil and gas sector as well as the rapidly developing oil sands in the northern part of the province. Each department of the provincial government was ordered to create a three-year business plan and establish performance measures by which its programs' successes or failures could be determined. Simply put, the government believed that its neoliberal program would restore business confidence, reduce the cost of public programs, and allow the public to measure the value it received for its tax dollars.

While the provincial government was lowering taxes and cutting services, population growth and expansion of the oil and natural gas sector conspired to increase demand for schools, roads, hospitals, water treatment plants, and other infrastructure and services. Throughout the period from the late 1980s to the mid-2010s, the provincial population increased each year (see figure 2.1). Funding for these programs and services came from oil and gas revenues. Nevertheless, there was sufficient revenue to pay off the provincial debt and establish a provincial savings account, the Sustainability Fund. Unlike the Heritage Savings Trust Fund, which had been established in the mid-1970s as a vehicle for long-term savings, the Sustainability Fund was established "to cover things such as the cost of emergencies, disasters, natural gas rebates, and unexpected declines in budget revenue" (Gartner 2010, 10). With the decline in provincial revenues precipitated by the Great Recession, the Sustainability Fund allowed the Progressive Conservative government to maintain levels of spending without resorting to raising taxes and other fees.

In 2007 and 2008, for example, oil reached USD $100 per barrel and averaged out at CAD$88.53 over the year, based on the Western Canada Select average price of crude oil. Natural gas, in 2007, averaged CAD$6.60 thousand cubic feet (Mcf). While some of the revenues from oil and natural gas were placed in the Sustainability Fund, much of the income from these non-renewable resources was placed in general revenues to fund ongoing programs. By 2007, up to 40% of provincial revenues were from oil and natural gas.

STIMULUS SPENDING, THE GREAT RECESSION, AND ALBERTA

The Great Recession has been characterized in a number of ways. Identified causes include a failure of governments to regulate banks adequately, an increase in income inequality, the use of unethical investment practices, and the political influence of the financial sector. As Mark Blyth (2013, 22) states, the financial crisis was a non-linear, multi-causal process that saw the international financial system come very close to collapse. Its epicenter was a set of problems in the private investment or shadow banking sector. These problems precipitated the collapse of the mortgage-backed securities in the United States and the withering of the overnight-repurchase market (Geithner 2014; Bernanke 2015).[5] Mortgage-backed securities were no longer accepted as credit for overnight borrowing and the entire financial system came to a halt. The result was the failure of several large investment-banking firms and a severe lack of credit in various markets for routine economic transactions (Geithner 2014). Whatever its cause or causes, the Great Recession saw an economic decline reminiscent of the Great Depression of the 1930s (Blyth 2013, 23; McCarty, Poole, and Rosenthal 2013).

In Alberta, however, the economic decline was muted. The province experienced a slower rate of economic growth, but the provincial government increased spending (see table 2.1). In 2007, provincial spending reached $33.1 billion on revenues of $35.3 billion. In 2015, provincial expenditures were estimated at $49.481 billion on total revenues estimated at $48.366 billion.[6] The budget deficit for 2015–16 was estimated at approximately $6.1 billion. Almost all of the budget deficit can be accounted for by the $6.181 billion capital expenditure plan for projects such as schools, hospitals, roads, public transportation, water and sewage facilities, and other improvements to public institutions. From 2013 capital expenditures for items such as roads, schools, and other infrastructure were listed separately. The figures in brackets for 2013, 2014, and 2015 include capital expenditures. These numbers should be considered projected expenditures.

While Capital Plan spending was increased, operational or program expenditures were cut. The reasoning behind this approach to public spending in Alberta was twofold. First, the government wanted to portray itself as a prudent fiscal manager. To achieve this goal, operational expenses were separated from capital spending. This allowed the government to claim that its program spending was in surplus. The Progressive Conservatives, moreover, did little to shrink the civil service other than an occasional hiring freeze (see table 2.2). The numbers in the Public Service Commission of Alberta ranged from approximately 27,000 to 30,000 over the period 2007–15. The government's actions were in stark contrast to the opposition Wildrose

Table 2.1
Provincial revenues and expenditures 2007–15 (millions of dollars)

Year	*Revenues**	*Expenditures***	*Surplus/(Deficit)*
2007	35,332	33,149	2,183
2008	38,571	37,003	1,568
2009	31,661	36,375	(4,714)
2010	33,964	38,712	(4,748)
2011	35,589	38,994	(3,405)
2012	40,263	41,149	(886)
2013	38,612	38,006 (5,209)	606**(1,287)
2014	44,354	40,432 (6,599)	3,922**(2,677)
2015	49,481	48,366 (6,181)	1,115**(6,118)

* Withdrawals from the provincial Stability Fund are not included as revenues.

** Includes operating expenses, debt servicing charges, and capital spending for 2007–12.

Party.[7] Under the leadership of Danielle Smith, a libertarian-styled political activist, the rural-based Wildrose had come very close to defeating the Progressive Conservatives in the April 2012 provincial general election. The Wildrose was fast to criticize any government spending that did not fit its anti-statist, social-conservative ideology, and the party made various statements about shrinking the state sector, especially the public service.

From 2008–15 the PC government committed itself to a program of infrastructure spending. Although the infrastructure spending put the province into a deficit fiscal situation, the government maintained a policy of low taxes. They were not willing to increase revenue through taxation even though royalties from oil and gas had declined dramatically beginning in mid-2014. Instead, the Progressive Conservatives either borrowed the required funds on the money markets in Toronto, New York, and elsewhere or took money out of the Sustainability Fund. In the 2013 budget, for example, the provincial government withdrew $6.157 billion from the $11,192 Sustainability Fund for net capital requirements of a proposed $5.732 billion Capital Plan. While there was a surplus of $2.568 billion on the operational side of the budget – the over 800 programs and services offered by the Government of Alberta – a need was seen for a large expenditure on infrastructure because of the infrastructure deficit left by Klein. As well, the province proposed to borrow approximately $4.5 billion on money markets. Minister of finance and president of Treasury Board Doug Horner stated that the government would obtain a far higher rate of return from its savings through investments than what it would pay in interest from borrowing. "Why would you take your savings account and plow it into something that's making you no money, when your savings is making more than what you're borrowing?" (Wood 2013, A3).

By the end of 2015, oil and natural gas royalties and leasing fees had fallen dramatically as a percentage of provincial revenues. In 2005–06, they constituted 40.65% of provincial spending, while in 2012–13 they were 19.83%. In the October 2015 budget, oil and gas revenues constituted 5.76% of provincial receipts. In 2006, oil and gas royalties and lease sales were $14.447 billion; by 2012–13, they accounted for $7.661 billion. This represented a 53.028% decrease in current dollars in oil and natural gas receipts. Table 2.2 indicates that there is only a marginal relationship between oil and natural gas prices and provincial spending. As revenues from this sector decreased, provincial spending increased. The size of Alberta's public service was stable during this period. It fluctuated by only several thousand employees over the entire 2008–15 period of economic downturn and decline in oil and natural gas prices (see table 2.2). As long as income and corporate tax revenues continued to grow and the Sustainability Fund was available for use, the government did not need to raise taxes and seek other sources of funding.

In contrast to the Klein Revolution of the mid-1990s, there were no across-the-board funding cuts to programs. Health care, for example, had a funding decrease of $21 million from $16.638 billion to $16.617 billion or 0.12% in the 2013 budget. Advanced Education's budget was slashed by $70 million, down from $2.857 billion to $2.787 billion or 2.45%, and Human Services was cut by $13 million from $4.28 billion to $4.267 billion or 0.3%. When inflation was factored into departmental spending, cuts of 2% were likely closer to 4% or greater. Other departments saw funding increases, including Education which saw its budget rise by $9 million, and transportation, which had an increase of $76 million. The funding increases and decreases occurred when oil and gas revenues were estimated to be $7.661 billion, a decline of $3.958 billion or 34.06% from 2012 revenues of $11,619 billion. Overall spending in 2013 increased from $35,688 billion to $37,524 billion in the operational budget, while the Capital Plan or infrastructure spending was estimated at

Table 2.2
Oil and gas revenues in dollars and as percentage of overall revenues and number of civil servants. Values reported in millions of dollars.

Budget year	*Natural gas*	*Oil*	*Bitumen*	*Leases*	*Fees*	*Total*	*Total revenue*	*Percentage of total revenue*	*No. of civil servants*
2005–06	8,388	1,463	950	3,490	156	1,4447	35,542	40.65%	26,811
2006–07	5,988	1,400	2,411	2,463	159	1,2421	38,017	32.67%	27,949
2007–08	5,199	1,655	2,913	1,128	159	1,1054	38,169	28.96%	29,224
2008–09	5,834	1,800	2,973	1,112	160	1,1879	35,811	33.17%	30,643
2009–10	1,525	1,848	3,160	1,165	158	7856	35,658	22.03%	30,128
2010–11	1,416	2,236	3,723	2,635	161	1,0171	35,034	29.03%	28,617
2011–12	1,304	2,321	4,513	3,312	169	1,1619	39,457	29.45%	28,892
2012–13	954	1,918	3,560	1,053	176	7661	38,635	19.83%	29,387
2013–14	960	2,163	5,001	484	186*	8794	48,959	17.96%	27,193
2014–15	989	2,245	5,049	476	172	8931	49,481	18.04%	

Source: Alberta Treasury Board and Finance. 2005–14. *Fiscal Plan Tables 2005–06 to 2014–15*. Edmonton: Government of Alberta. http://finance.alberta.ca/publications/budget/

$5.634 billion.[8] This represented a spending increase of 6.55% in operations spending. Capital or infrastructure spending in 2013 was $5.634 billion, a decline of $98 million or 1.7% from the $5.732 billion allocated in 2012 (Alberta Treasury Board and Finance 2013, 130–40).

The several Progressive Conservative governments from 2008–2014 refused to seek new sources of revenue. Other than small increases in user fees for several provincial services, tax increases or substantial changes to the revenue stream were not considered. The provincial income tax rate remained at 10% for all levels of income, corporate income tax stayed at 10% level of net profits, while taxes on alcoholic beverages and tobacco products remained unchanged. Several academics proposed a sales tax, but this idea faced strong backlash from voters and was rejected by government. A number of polls indicated that a sales tax was unpopular, while voters were more supportive of borrowing to pay for infrastructure improvements (Wood 2013, A1). It was understood by the government that substantial cuts to program and capital spending would slow the provincial economy at a time when the global economy was in decline (Kleiss 2015, A3). In this contradictory situation, the obvious path for the PC government was to withdraw money from the Sustainability Fund and borrow on capital markets to finance infrastructure and program spending.

The New Democrats took a slightly different approach to the province's finances. In the June 2015, legislative sitting the party had only three bills including Bill 2, *An Act to Restore Public Fairness to Public Revenue*. The 10% Klein flat tax was replaced by a progressive personal income tax with five rates of up to 15% on incomes over $300,000. Bill 2 also increased the corporate income tax rate from 10 to 12%. This measure had two goals. The first was the social democratic goal of implementing a progressive tax system. Social democratic parties such as the Labour parties in the United Kingdom and Australia, as well as the New Democrats when in government in other provinces in Canada, have pursued the goal of an equitable tax system in which those at the top end of the income scale assume a proportionately larger share of the tax burden. The second objective of Bill 2 was to stabilize revenue. Oil and natural gas prices had fallen dramatically beginning in mid-2014 and were not expected to increase in the near- to mid-term. The provincial government, simply put, needed the revenue from these tax increases if it was going to support program and infrastructure spending without an unacceptable level of deficit financing.

POLITICAL INSTABILITY (OR WAS IT CHAOS?)

Although the Progressive Conservative Party continued in power through the Great Recession of 2008–16, the political situation was unstable. Between December 2006 and September 2014, the PC government in Alberta had five premiers, seven ministers of finance, and seven ministers of energy, and the Progressive Conservative party had three leadership races. In office since 1971, the Progressive Conservatives entered the 2000s under the leadership of Ralph Klein. Klein had successfully resurrected the party from what appeared to be certain defeat at the hands of the provincial Liberals in the June 1993 election. After his victory, Klein introduced a radical reordering of the provincial state. This neoliberal agenda, however, could not match the expectations of provincial voters for programs and services. By the early 2000s, Klein's neoliberal program had seen significant modifications with program spending in all areas increasing to meet the demands of a growing population. While Klein won the 2001 and

2004 provincial elections his – at times – erratic behaviour and his deviation from the neoliberal ideology created dissatisfaction within the party. In 2006, he struggled through a leadership review with 55% of the delegate vote. At this point, his choices were limited and after some deliberation, he resigned. Klein's supporters, nevertheless, were bitter, feeling that the popular premier had been ousted in what amounted to a coup. In the ensuing leadership contest, the little-known Minister of Intergovernmental Affairs Ed Stelmach won the leadership and became premier in early December 2006.

Stelmach won a massive victory in the 2008 provincial election with 52.72% of the popular vote and seventy-two of eighty-three seats. Within eighteen months, however, the Stelmach government ran into trouble. In early 2007, the provincial government initiated a Royalty Review on conventional oil, natural gas, and bitumen production. The Alberta Royalty Review Panel recommended the increase of royalties in all categories of the oil and gas sector. The reaction from the industry was ferocious. The political result of this act was a stunning by-election loss for the Progressive Conservatives in a Calgary riding on 12 September 2009 to the Wildrose Alliance Party. Within two months, the Wildrose Alliance Party, itself at least partially the product of the anger of the energy industry over the Royalty Review, had elected a media-savvy former television host, Danielle Smith, as leader. To the political right of the Progressive Conservatives, the Wildrose Alliance criticized the government for taking monies out of the Sustainability Fund to finance capital and operational expenses. Stelmach's first minister of finance and president of the Treasury Board Lyle Oberg was replaced after the 3 March provincial election by Iris Evans. Evans stayed at Treasury Board and Finance for twenty-two months. In January 2010, Ted Morton, a former university professor, was named to the position. Morton delivered the 2010 budget but resigned in January 2011 over differences with the premier on spending. At the same time that Morton resigned from cabinet, Stelmach announced that he was stepping down as premier. Morton's replacement at finance, Lloyd Snelgrove, lasted until the new leader and premier, Alison Redford, was selected in early October 2011. After winning a very close leadership contest, she chose a long-time party activist, Ron Liepert, for Treasury Board and Finance. Liepert was in the position for seven months before he was replaced in May 2012 by Doug Horner, a member of the legislature from the Edmonton region. In September 2014, the Progressive

Conservatives held another leadership contest to select a replacement for Alison Redford, who had resigned in March of that year. David Hancock, a long-serving member of the Legislative Assembly from Edmonton was named interim leader after Redford's resignation. He described his position as "the best summer job he had ever had" (Henton 2014, A1).

The drama that was the Progressive Conservative party continued with the 2014 leadership race. With the exception of Alison Redford and two ministers who quit to run in the leadership race, the cabinet, under the interim premier Dave Hancock, remained in place. Doug Horner was left at Treasury Board and Finance until a new leader, Jim Prentice, was selected leader by the party on 6 September 2014. Prentice replaced Horner with Robyn Campbell, the seventh Progressive Conservative finance minister in seven years (Mason 2014).

Horner, as the longest serving finance minister in the period of the Great Recession, continued the pattern of spending which had begun under the Klein government in the 2000s. Horner withdrew monies from the Sustainability Fund, refused to raise taxes, and initiated a comprehensive review of the over 800 Government of Alberta programs. As official opposition, Wildrose refused to accept the idea that any increase in tax revenues was required. Instead, they insisted on substantial cuts to government spending. In the 2013 budget, Horner responded to the opposition demands by implementing a series of small cuts to department budgets such as Innovation and Advanced Education, while increasing funds for Health and Education. Horner also separated out what he called the operational budget – the financing of programs – from the capital budget, which was to fund physical infrastructure. The monies for the capital budget were drawn from the Sustainability Fund. The actual capital spending in 2014–15 was $6.181 billion (Alberta. Treasury Board and Finance 2016, 113). While the government had been making withdrawals on the Sustainability Fund since 2008, it had not separated capital funds from the operational side of the budget until 2012 under Doug Horner.

Along with maintaining the low rate of taxation and readjusting provincial spending, Horner introduced a comprehensive program review. In a province that had seen dramatic spending cuts in the mid-1990s, the five years of deficit spending was perceived by many pundits as politically damaging to the government. A program of performance-based budgeting was viewed in the media as a way to reduce and eventually eliminate the provincial deficit in the same way that the Klein government had used performance-based budgeting as a justification for its austerity program of the mid-1990s. Moreover, it would create a narrative of the government as fiscally responsible managers of public funds. While performance-based budgeting policy – or, as it was called by the Government of Alberta, Results-based Budgeting – may have been inspired by political motives, it soon became a central feature of provincial fiscal management.

The *Results-based Budgeting Act* was introduced in the provincial legislature in February 2012. The Bill outlined the rationale and processes of fiscal and program review that would occur under the *Results-based Budgeting Act*. There would be three "cycles" of program review with approximately one-third of all provincial activity reviewed at one time. The various provincial departments, boards, agencies and commissions would be assessed for program outcomes. Although it was not advertised as a cost-cutting exercise, the Results-based Budgeting process was used to reallocate funds and, in some cases, reduce spending. It was an effort to establish the relevance, effectiveness, and efficiency of programs and services of the provincial state. This program review was a key element of the Government of Alberta's response to falling oil and natural gas prices as well as the unstable situation in the various financial markets during the Great Recession.

The Prentice government announced the end of the Results-based Budgeting program in its December 2014 Throne Speech. It was not until the March 2015 budget that the minister of finance, Robyn Campbell, announced changes to the tax system. Campbell introduced a modest progressive income tax on incomes of over $50,000. The tax, he stated, would "end Alberta's dependence on volatile energy royalties" (Wood 2015, A1). This was not the policy of the previous Klein government, which had stated emphatically that spending, not revenues, needed to be curtailed. Campbell made it clear that to maintain provincial services, new sources of revenue had to be found. While it was argued that a sales tax would have been the most efficient way of raising new monies, the government made clear that this was not an option. The political consequences of such a policy were too difficult for any government to consider it (Wood 2015, A1).

With the election of the New Democrats on 5 May 2015, the new government appointed the ninth minister of finance in less than ten years, Joe Ceci. Ceci, a member of the legislature from a downtown Calgary riding, faced a trifecta of fiscal problems: declining revenues due to low oil and natural gas prices, promises to reverse Progressive

Conservative funding cuts, and other campaign promises that ranged from a review of royalties paid by the oil and gas sector to building new schools. The new minister brought a degree of stability to the position and quickly brought in a progressive income tax and an increase to the corporate income tax. As with the former Conservative governments, Ceci was constrained by a very difficult fiscal situation. Yet, the New Democrats refused to move on a sales tax, which had been recommended for years by university researchers, policy institutes, and the civil service as a fast and efficient method to stabilize revenues. Instead, in an effort to deal with very high provincial carbon emission as well as to increase revenues, the New Democrats proposed a carbon tax. This broad-based tax began at $10 per ton of emissions and will rise to $50 per ton by 2022. The increase in tax revenues have been marked for program funding. As well, it is hoped that the carbon tax will assuage criticism of Alberta's environmental record, which many observers argue has been an impediment to the construction of pipelines to transmit oil and natural gas to markets. This sales-tax-by-another-name is opposed by the Progressive Conservative and Wildrose opposition parties, both of whom claim it will erase any tax advantages that Alberta may have enjoyed and, thereby, deter investment. Still, with mounting deficits and a campaign promise to reduce Alberta's greenhouse gas emissions, the carbon tax indicates that the provincial government has decided not simply to continue to rely on volatile royalties and other fees from the oil and natural gas sector. The Prentice government and the New Democrats raised taxes and maintained program and infrastructure spending. The difference between the two governments' approaches was one of degree. The New Democrats raised corporate taxes and levied a carbon tax. The Progressive Conservatives refused to do either, instead relying on non-renewable natural resource revenues to pay for programs and infrastructure.

CONCLUSION

Alberta's response to the financial crisis and crash of oil and natural gas prices of 2008–16 was shaped by several factors. First, the PC government was ideologically committed to an agenda of low taxes, a type of neoliberalism that relied on unstable revenue from oil and natural gas royalties, licences, and fees to maintain program and infrastructure spending. While the political and economic circumstances had changed since the Klein revolution of the 1990s, the government refused to raise taxes, sought savings through a performance review of all programs, and pursued an uneven mix of austerity and stimulus spending. For example, the provincial government could have raised taxes by several means including the introduction of a sales tax. It was only after the collapse of oil and natural gas prices that the Prentice government decided to introduce a progressive income tax and raise other fees and taxes. However, they were defeated before their budget could pass. It was the NDP who introduced a progressive income tax system, raised the corporate tax, and raised other taxes and fees.

The Progressive Conservatives and the New Democrats were, however, constrained by popular expectations of low taxes and a high level of provincial government spending, which had been labelled as the "Alberta Advantage." To meet popular expectations of low taxes and high levels of spending, the various PC governments withdrew monies from the Sustainability Fund and borrowed on international money markets to meet voter expectations of program delivery, keep up with population growth (see figure 2.1) and fill ever-growing gaps in the infrastructure deficit that Klein had left behind. There was, as well, a comprehensive performance review of all government programs. While mandated to determine the relevancy, effectiveness, and efficiency of government programs, the Results-based Budgeting process was seen by many of the participants in it as a cost-savings exercise to minimize state involvement in civil society.

The second factor that shaped the response to the Great Recession was the political turmoil within the Progressive Conservative party. From December 2006 to September 2014, the province had four premiers and seven ministers of finance. The result was a lack of a strategy beyond maintaining a low level of taxation, spending reductions of selected programs, and withdrawing funds from the Sustainability Fund. There was an unwillingness or inability to explore policy alternatives. The New Democrats have adopted a more directed policy of raising taxes and maintaining levels of spending. These polices reflect a new direction in Alberta's fiscal policy, away from a reliance on oil and natural gas revenues.

The third variable that shaped the Alberta government's response to the Great Recession was the fluctuation in the price of oil and natural gas. Royalties and lease payments from the two non-renewable resources have comprised up to 40% of the provincial budget. When prices for these products declined in mid-2014, a Sustainability Fund consisting of savings from these non-renewable resource revenues saved the day – at least for a while. The monies derived from the oil and natural gas industry allowed the several Conservative governments to avoid difficult decisions to either cut provincial spending or raise taxes.

These factors – neoliberal ideology, political instability in the governing party, and the dependence on oil and natural gas revenues – prevented the governing Progressive Conservatives from exploring policy alternatives during the Great Recession. While the fiscal crisis shifted the policy context significantly, the PCs were unable and, to some extent, unwilling to alter the status quo. Their dependence on oil and natural gas revenues and general unwillingness to seek out other sources of revenue through an increase in taxes prevented the government from addressing a fundamental problem of Alberta's political and economic life – dependence on revenues from price-volatile, non-renewable natural resources. While spending continued with money from provincial savings and from borrowing in money markets, the provincial government could not make the fundamental changes necessary to address the changing economic and political context of Alberta society. The contradictory approach of borrowing, withdrawal from savings, performance reviews of programs, selective spending cuts and low taxes blocked any substantive change in provincial policy.

The New Democrats have altered this situation. They have responded to the decline in oil and gas revenues by abandoning the neoliberal agenda. Instead, they have implemented a progressive personal income tax and raised corporate taxes and other fees. And, for the near-term, they have maintained program and infrastructure spending. During the Great Recession of 2008–16, both the Progressive Conservatives and New Democrats relied on a localized version of Keynesian spending on infrastructure and programs to maintain services and, it is hoped, maintain a level of economic activity that generates employment and growth. The Conservatives, constrained by their past policies of low taxes, spending reductions, and program consolidation and elimination, could not embrace the new economic and political circumstances of low oil and gas prices and an increasing demand for infrastructure and services. Although the New Democrats are constrained by the political context from implementing a sales tax and other revenue measures, they have broken with the recent past in an effort to stabilize the revenue and spending patterns of the Government of Alberta.

NOTES

1 The Sustainability Fund was renamed the Contingency Account in the 2013 Budget.
2 American International Group (AIG) is the insurer for millions of American households and approximately 180,000 businesses in the United States, which employ two-thirds of the workforce. It also provides "much of the financial system with protection against disaster" (Geithner 2014, 188).
3 The Progressive Conservative budget of 26 March 2015 proposed to replace the flat tax of 10% on all incomes with a progressive income tax. This budget, however, was never passed and did not come into effect.
4 In the midst of the financial and economic turmoil in 2009, Alan Greenspan told a Calgary audience he would prefer to have the economy endure the financial collapse of 2007–08 so as to preserve the creative destruction of the markets.
5 Mortgage-backed securities (MBS) refers to bundles of mortgages sold by lenders to third parties. This allows mortgage lenders access to enormous capital pools. As well, the securities can be structured in ways that increase purchaser diversification by, for example, combining mortgages from different risk levels. MBS can also be divided into segments or branches to meet the risk preferences of investors (Bernanke 2015, 85). The overnight-repurchase market, or repos, is a form of overnight lending which shifts cash and securities between lenders and borrowers. The Bank of New York Mellon, one of the largest repurchase (repo) institutions, acted as an intermediary between borrowers such as mortgage companies and lenders, providing credit and pricing collateral (Geithner 2014, 124).
6 The expenditure numbers are a combination of all expenses including $822 million for 2013 flood relief; debt servicing, $326 million; debt servicing – capital, $452 million; amortization, $2.262 billion; inventory consumption, $821 million; and Capital Plan, $6.181 billion. The total of these expenditures was included in the provincial fiscal plan tables.
7 The Wildrose Alliance Party (WRAP) changed its name to the Wildrose Party at its June 2011 general meeting in Calgary.
8 It should be noted that the budget lines for Disaster and Emergency Assistance, General Debt Servicing Costs, Amortization, Inventory Consumption, and Inventory Acquisition are not included in these figures.

It had been standard practice in Alberta not to include these expenses in the Operations and Capital budgets.

REFERENCES

Alberta. Treasury Board and Finance. 2005. *Budget 2005: Investing in the Next Alberta – Fiscal Plan.* Edmonton: Government of Alberta. http://finance.alberta.ca/publications/budget/budget2005/index.html.

– 2006. *Budget 2006: Strengthening Today, Securing Tomorrow – Fiscal Plan.* Edmonton: Government of Alberta. http://finance.alberta.ca/publications/budget/budget2006/index.html.

– 2007. *Budget 2007: Managing Our Growth – Fiscal Plan.* Edmonton: Government of Alberta. http://finance.alberta.ca/publications/budget/budget2007/index.html.

– 2008. *Budget 2008: The Right Plan for Today and Tomorrow – Fiscal Plan.* Edmonton: President of the Treasury Board and Minister of Finance. http://finance.alberta.ca/publications/budget/budget2008/index.html.

– 2009. *Budget 2009: Building On Our Strength – Fiscal Plan.* Edmonton: Government of Alberta. http://finance.alberta.ca/publications/budget/budget2009/index.html.

– 2010. *Budget 2010: Striking the Right Balance – Fiscal Plan.* Edmonton: Government of Alberta. http://finance.alberta.ca/publications/budget/budget2010/index.html.

– 2011. *Budget 2011: Building a better Alberta – Fiscal Plan.* Edmonton: Government of Alberta. http://finance.alberta.ca/publications/budget/budget2011/index.html.

– 2012. *Budget 2012: Investing in People – Fiscal Plan.* Edmonton: Government of Alberta. http://finance.alberta.ca/publications/budget/budget2012/index.html.

– 2013. *Budget 2013: Responsible Change – Fiscal Plan.* Edmonton: Government of Alberta. http://finance.alberta.ca/publications/budget/budget2013/index.html.

– 2014. *Budget 2014: The Building Alberta Plan – Fiscal Plan.* Edmonton: Government of Alberta. http://finance.alberta.ca/publications/budget/budget2014/index.html.

– 2015. *Budget 2015: Supporting Jobs, Supporting Families. The Alberta Way – Fiscal Plan.* Edmonton: Government of Alberta. http://finance.alberta.ca/publications/budget/budget2015/index.html.

– 2016. *Budget 2016: The Alberta Jobs Plan – Fiscal Plan.* Edmonton: Government of Alberta. http://finance.alberta.ca/publications/budget/budget2016/index.html.

Bernanke, Ben S. 2015. *The Courage to Act: A Memoir of a Crisis and Its Aftermath*. New York: W.W. Norton and Company.
Blyth, Mark. 2013. *Austerity. The History of a Dangerous Idea*. New York: Oxford University Press.
Friedman, Milton. *Capitalism and Freedom*. 1982. Chicago: University of Chicago Press.
Friedman, Milton, and Rose Friedman. 1980. *Free to Choose: A Personal Statement*. New York: Harcourt Brace.
Gartner, Brett. 2007. "Alberta's Money Jars: Current Provincial Savings and Endowment Funds." In *Alberta's Energy Legacy. Ideas for the Future*, edited by Robert Roach, 9–26. Calgary: Canada West Foundation.
Geithner, Timothy F. 2014. *Stress Test: Reflections on Financial Crises*. New York: Crown Publishers.
Greenspan, Alan. 2009. Speech in Calgary. 3 November.
Hacker, Jacob. 2004. "Privatizing Risk without Privatizing the Welfare State: The Hidden Politics of Social Policy of Retrenchment in the United States." *American Political Science Review* 98 (2): 243–60.
Harvey, David. 2007. *A Brief History of Neoliberalism*. Oxford: Oxford University Press.
Henton, Darcy. 2014. "Premier Dave Hancock Retiring from Politics." *Calgary Herald*. 12 September.
Hayek, Fredrich A. 1945. *The Road to Serfdom*. London: George Routledge and Sons.
Kleiss, Karen. 2015. "Deficit Could Help Avoid a Recession: Prentice." *Calgary Herald*, 17 January.
Lynch, Julia. 2006. *Age in the Welfare State: The Origins of Social Spending on Pensioners*. Cambridge: Cambridge University Press.
Mason, Gary. 2014. "Jim Prentice Shrinks Alberta Cabinet, Appoints Two Outsiders." *Globe and Mail*, 14 September.
McCarty, Nolan, Keith T. Poole, and Howard Rosenthal. 2013. *Political Bubbles: Financial Crises and the Failure of American Democracy*. Princeton: Princeton University Press.
O'Connor, James. 1979. *The Fiscal Crisis of the State*. New York: St Martin's Press, 1973.
Schumpeter, Joseph. 2008. *Capitalism, Socialism and Democracy*. 3rd ed. New York: Harper Perennial.
Statistics Canada. 2016. *Table 051-0001 – Estimates of Population, by Age Group and Sex for July 1, Canada, Provinces and Territories Annual*. CANSIM (database). http://www5.statcan.gc.ca/cansim/a26?lang=eng&retrLang=eng&id=0510001&pattern=&tabMode=dataTable&srchLan=-1&p1=-1&p2=9.

Taft, Kevin. 1997. *Shredding the Public Interest: Ralph Klein and 25 Years of One-Party Government*. Edmonton: University of Alberta Press.

U.S. Energy Information Agency. 2016. "Short Term Energy Outlook." November. https://www.eia.gov/forecasts/steo/archives/nov16.pdf.

Wood, James. 2013. "Alberta Finances Grate on Voters: Poll Reveals Support for Infrastructure Borrowing." *Calgary Herald*, 24 April.

Wood, James. 2015. "Budget: Personal Income Taxes to Rise Sharply, Province Moves toward Progressive System." *Calgary Herald*, 25 March.

CHAPTER THREE

Active Incrementalism and the Politics of Austerity in the "New Saskatchewan"

CHARLES W. SMITH

In 2007, the people of Saskatchewan elected the obscurely named Saskatchewan Party to provincial government. Although the party's name conceals its right-wing ideological position, the Saskatchewan Party's rise to power did not represent a radical departure from the sixteen years of New Democratic Party (NDP) rule that preceded it. In fact, when one examines the last twenty-five years of NDP/Saskatchewan Party rule, there is a striking similarity in both tone and substance between policies regulating economic growth, job creation, and social spending. For both parties, the frame of public policy creation has represented what one analyst has termed "a rush to the centre," in which both parties prioritize active market-oriented policies to drive economic growth (Leeson 2008, 4). As a result, both parties have repositioned their policy priorities to loosely align with business interests to expand the extraction of Saskatchewan's rich abundance of natural resources. Since 1991, those policies have overwhelmingly favoured lowering business and personal taxes, decreasing royalty rents, weakening laws protecting workers and labour unions, and utilizing the politics of austerity to restructure the internal workings of the state.

Notwithstanding the broad consensus between the two main parties regarding a host of economic issues, differences remain. Indeed, throughout the 1990s and 2000s, the NDP remained in power primarily because it positioned itself as a defender of the province's large and influential Crown corporations. This position proved popular among large sections of the electorate, as the Crowns contribute to political stability for governments while also symbolizing a collective sense of economic ingenuity for citizens primarily living in a natural resource and agriculturally based society (Pitsula and Rasmussen 1990, 71–2). In view of this reality, the viability and health of the Crowns have become the third rail of Saskatchewan politics. Any government that seeks to privatize the powerful Crowns risks quickly falling out of favour with the electorate. Recognizing this, one of the secrets of the NDP's success in the 1990s and 2000s was to instill the narrative that the Saskatchewan Party had a secret agenda to privatize the Crowns while also significantly weakening the province's welfare state (McGrane 2007; 2008).

In many ways, the admiration of the Crowns and the widespread popularity of the health and education components of the modern welfare state have limited the extent to which both of Saskatchewan's political parties can fully embrace neoliberal reforms. That being the case, the central question in this chapter is how the openly conservative Saskatchewan Party continues to transform the provincial state along neoliberal lines while remaining popular with the electorate. In answering this question, the chapter will argue that the Saskatchewan Party has embraced a form of political pragmatism that I term "active incrementalism." While certainly a paradox, the concept of active incrementalism refers to a conscious political strategy to weaken vital components of the social welfare state to shake loose public support for these institutions over time. When examining ten years of Saskatchewan Party rule, it becomes clear that the party guardedly but consistently implements austerity measures to transform the state further toward private market power while slowly undermining – but not outright privatizing – the largest Crowns and other public services in the province.

To map out this argument, this chapter is divided into five sections. In the first section, I briefly outline the concepts of neoliberalism and austerity, which are then used in the second section to analyze Saskatchewan politics from 1944–2007. In that section, the chapter argues that the Saskatchewan Party is not the author of neoliberalism in the province; rather, it inherited a radically transformed state from both its Conservative and New Democratic predecessors. In the third section, the chapter examines the Saskatchewan Party's record in government, concentrating on the party's market-oriented policy priorities for economic growth and many of its budgetary considerations to further the process of neoliberal accumulation. In the last two sections, the chapter provides an overview of the Saskatchewan

Party's incremental embrace of privatization and its usage of public–private partnerships (P3s) to build public infrastructure in the province. Finally, the chapter concludes by scrutinizing the Saskatchewan Party's continued attack on the province's organized labour movement, which is the one area where the government has ignored its actively incremental policy paradigms and embraced an openly austere approach to labour relations. Taken together, these sections demonstrate that the Saskatchewan Party has utilized actively incremental forms of austerity to deepen neoliberalism in the province.

NEOLIBERALISM AND AUSTERITY

The ascendency of neoliberalism has transformed political and economic relations throughout Western capitalist societies. The foundation of neoliberal thinking is the relatively simple belief that individual market forces can only excel when free from government regulations or collective pressure from workers (see Evans and Fanelli's introduction to this volume, as well as Brownsey in this volume). Politically, neoliberals have promoted policies such as trade liberalization, lower taxation, deregulation, and the privatization of public assets on the belief that these actions foster free and more efficient societies (Albo 2010; Peck 2010; Harvey 2005). These freedoms are presupposed to flow from the preservation and deepening of private property rights. For neoliberals, the extension of property rights seeks to redefine the relationship "that people have towards each other in regard to the use and disposal of socially necessary objects" (Teeple 2004, 82). In other words, the extension of private property rights leads to individual claims of ownership over socially necessary goods. For this to occur, the state must be restructured to create an institutional framework that promotes market freedoms. Along these lines, neoliberals place important emphasis on the coercive elements of state power, including legal, military, police, and defence. These powers then become instrumental in protecting individual property claims against alternative collective interests.

In different ways, the forces of neoliberalism seek to deepen the power of individual economic actors as owners of property. An important way that governments have reinforced the power of private property is through a retrenchment of the social capacities of the state. In order to accomplish this, neoliberal governments have utilized the politics of austerity to weaken and undermine public redistribution of public goods and services (Albo and Fanelli 2014, 5–7; Peck 2013). Austerity thus "serves as a broader paradigm of neoliberalism" because citizens become more closely tied to the market, both as consumers of necessary services and as workers in privately run organizations (McBride 2014, 15). For workers, the forces of neoliberalism have unleashed increased worker competition while transforming the way work is conducted. Throughout North America, workplaces in both the public and private sectors have adopted so-called "lean-production" methods and have squeezed worker compensation, which has resulted in "widening gaps between the share of value taken by capital and that taken by workers" (Crow and Albo 2005, 13). These "austere" policy measures can include long-term tax restructuring, deregulation, restructuring public services along market lines, and utilizing various forms of privatization that can include selling public assets to private capitalists or implementing P3s to build necessary public infrastructure.

When government resorts to these austere measures, it ultimately reduces the redistributive capacities of the public sector. Such reforms have long-term implications for workers because austerity policies restructure equity-based public services and transform them into private commodities. In so doing, those who benefit from or work in public services are tied even more closely to the market to meet basic human needs. The limitations of privatization become obvious when examined against the broader goals of public services to fulfill universal social values based on fairness and equitable redistribution of public goods. As Jeff Noonan has articulated,

> The ongoing privatization of public institutions is not only an attack on public sector workers, but on the universally life-valuable principle that those institutions through which social self-conscious agency is developed ought to be open and accessible to all, because [it is] necessary to a fully human life. (Noonan 2013, 20–1)

Given this reality, important components of neoliberalism in Canada and its provinces have been government attempts to weaken the collective ability of workers to resist the power of employers from dictating the conditions (and remuneration) of work in both the public and private sectors (Evans and Smith 2015). Among the numerous changes to workers' freedoms in the neoliberal era have been limits on the right to organize, bargain, and strike (Panitch and Swartz 2003). These top-down restrictions on the rights of labour have severely weakened the movement, especially limiting its influence in the private sector. Internally, neoliberal reforms have led to a crisis of worker solidarity, limiting the economic and political influence of unions in all Western states (Gindin 2013; Swartz and Warskett 2012). Restrictions on workers' freedoms have also extended to basic employment standards, making it more difficult for workers in non-unionized, non-traditional workplaces to be paid a living wage or to be protected from employer abuse (Fudge and Vosko 2003). While uneven, the social forces associated with neoliberal austerity have been central to governing Saskatchewan over the past thirty years.

SASKATCHEWAN'S NEOLIBERAL TURN

When Tommy Douglas and the social democratic Co-operative Commonwealth Federation (CCF) won the 1944 Saskatchewan provincial election, it transformed politics in the province for nearly four decades. Under Tommy Douglas, Woodrow Lloyd and, later, when the CCF was succeeded by the NDP, NDP leader Allan Blakeney, the provincial state became the primary tool for the advancement of economic growth (Rasmussen 2001). Over several decades, the CCF/NDP prioritized Keynesian-style economic diversification through large-scale infrastructure developments in the extraction of natural resources. The state was able to enter into these industries through publicly owned Crown corporations, which included a significant public stake in the extraction of potash, oil, gas, and uranium (Pratt and Richards, 1979; Dyck 1996; Warnock 2004, 345; Praud and McQuarrie 2001, 147–8). Governments also generally increased economic rents on the private extraction of natural resources, using that income to fund Saskatchewan's relatively inclusive welfare state (Warnock 2005). Alongside these large-scale industrial projects, the CCF/NDP prioritized building necessary public infrastructure and delivering important public services, which included rural electrification in the 1940s and 1950s, public auto insurance in 1945, new hospitals in the 1950s and 1960s, and universal medical care in 1961. The CCF/NDP was also active in promoting the rights of workers, passing a wide range of workplace laws including the country's first *Trade Union Act* (TUA) in 1945, which outlined the right of workers in all sectors to organize, bargain, and strike. The CCF/NDP likewise created the country's first meaningful Workers' Compensation Board and slowly expanded employment standards protections for non-unionized workers over the course of almost thirty years in government (Warren and Carlisle 2005; Smith 2011).

Throughout the postwar period, politics in the province oscillated between a populist, social democratic left with roots in rural areas and the urban working class of the province against more urban, elite-driven, pro-business coalitions. By the early 1980s, however, the once-populist roots of the NDP seemed to wane against the now openly pro-business and market reformers in the newest right-wing coalition in the province, the Progressive Conservative Party. Under the leadership of Grant Devine, the Conservatives ushered in an era of pro-business and austere reforms through massively subsidizing industry with public funds, privatizing public assets, cutting back the welfare state, curtailing the ability of labour unions to organize, and drastically scaling back employment standards for unorganized workers (McCuaig, Sass, and Stobbe 1991; Pitsula and Rasmussen 1990, 235–47). Devine made these changes arguing that a combination of free-market capitalism and conservative social values would more effectively provide jobs and benefits to individuals and families (Pitsula and Rasmussen 1990, 14–21). While many of these reforms were implemented in a fiscally irresponsible manner, Devine's neoliberal revolution fundamentally transformed the political economy of the province. In his two terms in government, Devine ran a series of deficits, recklessly lowered taxes, dramatically lowered the royalty rates on oil and gas (and other minerals) and sold off many of the province's prized Crown corporations, including large parts of SaskOil and Saskatchewan Potash Corporation while the Saskatchewan Mining Development Corporation (uranium), the Saskatchewan Fur Marketing Corporation, SaskMedia, and the Prince Albert Pulp Company were sold outright.

Perhaps surprisingly, when the NDP swept back to power in a wave of anti-Conservative and thus anti-austerity public sentiment in 1991, the social democrats did not seek to radically reverse Devine's reforms. Rather, under the leadership of Roy Romanow and, later, Lorne Calvert, the NDP deepened neoliberalism in the province (Conway and Conway 2015). For instance, notwithstanding the large deficits left by the Conservatives, the party did not reverse the Devine tax cuts or raise royalty rates on natural resource extraction. Nor did the NDP seek to build other revenue-generating resources, such as reacquiring sold-off public assets. In fact, the Romanow government engaged in a series of privatizations of its own, selling off the province's remaining public shares in Saskatchewan Oil (SaskOil), Saskatchewan Potash Corporation, and Cameco, and privatizing a heavy oil upgrader in Lloydminster (Praud and McQuarrie 2001, 158). The NDP's privatization of public assets took place alongside a significant program of austerity, which included raising a flat sales tax, refusing to raise resource royalties, and implementing some minor tax increases on income (Brown, Roberts, and Warnock 1999, 57–9; Conway and Conway 2015, 239–41). Many of these tax changes were introduced alongside deep reductions to social programs, which included cuts to health and education alongside the closing of rural hospitals. Together with its austerity program, the party also was slow to amend Devine's changes to the TUA, only bringing in minor reforms in 1994 (Smith 2011). In the late 1990s, the NDP's unwillingness to expand the rights of labour resulted in significant battles with its public-sector workers, culminating in the province wide strike of nurses in 1999 (Panitch and Swartz 2003).

Although the NDP took a more moderate and less austere course under the leadership of Lorne Calvert after 2003, the party's new political and economic philosophy never altered from the politics of austerity. Indeed, in its last two budgets, the Calvert NDP reduced corporate and individual taxes that were prefaced on expanding private-sector development in the province's natural resource sectors (McGrane 2011). In the lead up to the 2007 election, for instance, the Calvert government phased out the general corporate capital tax, cut corporate taxes to 14% (from 17%), with a further planned cut down to 12% if the party was re-elected. The budget also cut the provincial sales tax by two percentage points and reduced royalty rates on oil, gas, potash, coal, and uranium (Ministry of Finance 2007). These modifications made Saskatchewan's corporate tax rates comparable to those in Liberal British Columbia and Progressive Conservative Alberta (Saskatchewan Ministry of Finance 2006; Whiteside in this volume; Brownsey in this volume).

Notwithstanding the embrace of neoliberalism by the Saskatchewan NDP, Devine's legacy destroyed the Progressive Conservative Party in the province. Forced to regroup under a new political banner, the pro-business and right-wing forces created a new non-controversial and seemingly non-ideological party brand: the Saskatchewan Party. Founded in 1997, the Saskatchewan Party was a coalition of disgruntled Liberal and Conservative MLAs, Reform Party members, business elites, and social and fiscal conservatives concentrated largely in rural areas of the province (Blake 2008, 169). Electing former Reform Party MP Elwin Hermanson as the leader, the Saskatchewan Party positioned itself as a right-wing, populist alternative to the NDP. Throughout the 1990s and early 2000s, the Party argued that the NDP had lost touch with the voters of Saskatchewan, stifled private-sector development, and driven whole generations of young workers and entrepreneurs out of the province. While those positions certainly resonated with its core supporters on the political right, they did nothing to alleviate fears that the Saskatchewan Party's real agenda was to privatize large segments of the province's remaining Crown corporations, especially the big five utilities: Saskatchewan Power (SaskPower), Saskatchewan Telecom (SaskTel), Saskatchewan Energy, Saskatchewan Government Insurance (SGI), and Saskatchewan Liquor and Gaming (SLGA).[1] The NDP's defence of the Crowns against what it claimed was the secret privatization agenda of the Saskatchewan Party worked effectively to keep the NDP in power during the 1999 and 2003 elections.

To combat the NDP's claims that the Saskatchewan Party had a hidden privatization agenda, the party sought to reassure large segments of the province's middle class that it was a moderate political movement. Many of the Saskatchewan Party's internal changes included moderating the party's platform on privatization and economic reform, jettisoning social conservative promises (such as implementing "chain gains" and youth boot camps in provincial correction services), and electing former Progressive Conservative staffer and seemingly moderate Brad Wall as leader (Blake 2008, 174–81). In making these changes, the party was deliberately aligning its traditional rural conservative base with urban business supporters and elements of the province's (especially male) working and middle classes. By 2007, a culmination of internal party changes and sixteen years of NDP rule contributed to voters electing its first Saskatchewan Party government and elevating Brad Wall to the premier's chair.

THE SASKATCHEWAN PARTY IN POWER: INCREMENTALISM AND THE NEW RIGHT

In most of the country, the 2007 and 2008 market collapse contributed to significant fiscal challenges for governments. In Saskatchewan,

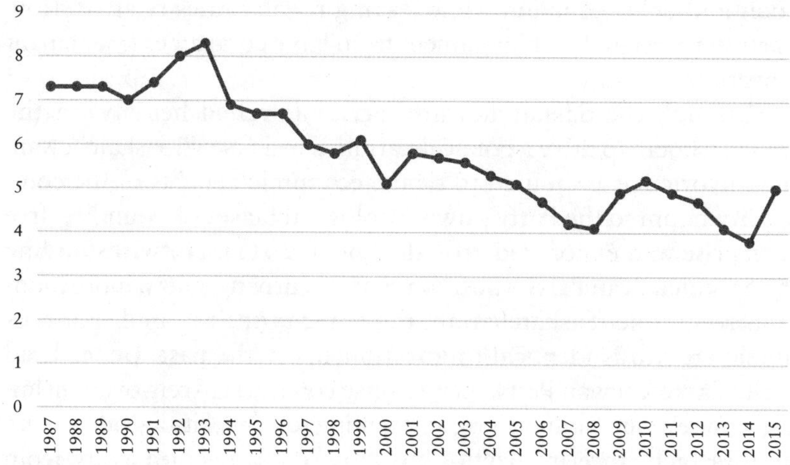

Source: Statistics Canada, CANSIM Table 282-0055 Saskatchewan unemployment rate 2002–15; Table 282-0123 1987–2001.

Figure 3.1 Saskatchewan unemployment (percentage), 1987–2015

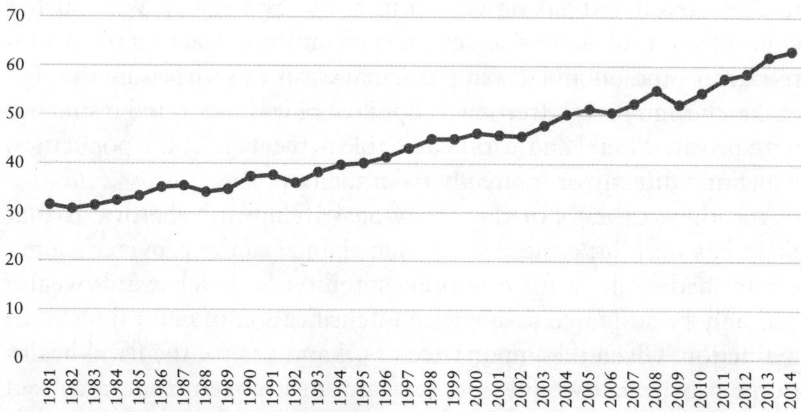

Source: Statistics Canada, CANSIM Table 384-0038, CANSIM Saskatchewan, chained (2007) dollars, GDP (market prices), 1981–2014

Figure 3.2 Saskatchewan GDP growth (billions), 1981–2014

however, world demand from emerging markets (especially China and India) for natural resources and food commodities contributed to steady levels of growth and consistent job creation in the province (figure 3.1 and figure 3.2). The low unemployment levels allowed the government fiscal room to implement its stated agenda of lower taxes and debt reduction while leaving royalty rates relatively low to attract foreign direct investment from large companies (Lieutenant Governor 2008).

Although the Saskatchewan Party has relied heavily on the resource boom to drive a political narrative of a "New" Saskatchewan, the rhetoric has been used to tie the economic benefits of the commodity boom to the Party's own ideological biases surrounding free enterprise and export-led growth (Enoch 2011). Notwithstanding the Saskatchewan Party's position that it is driving a new, more modern, free-market Saskatchewan, the government's formula for economic growth is identical to governments in the past. Under Brad Wall's Saskatchewan Party, the province continues to rely overwhelmingly on revenue from oil, gas, and mining to propel its agenda (figure 3.3). In fact, since its election in 2007, the transition away from goods-producing sectors (which include oil, gas, mining, and manufacturing) toward service-based economies that is prevalent in other advanced capitalist regions in the country (notably Ontario, Quebec, and British Columbia) has declined in Saskatchewan, with the exception of the oil and gas downturn in 2015 (figure 3.4). With such a concentration of economic dependence on the extraction of natural resources (and oil and gas in particular), it is not surprising that the Saskatchewan Party's free-market philosophies have found resonance with private capital and within a sizable percentage of the population benefiting directly or indirectly from the boom.

Yet, the weakness of the "New Saskatchewan" rhetoric is that there has been little macroeconomic change to the province's long-established formula for economic stability: Saskatchewan's wealth can only be sustained through an intensification of natural resource extraction. Given the importance of oil and gas for the fiscal health of the province, it would seem logical for the government to extract more of that surplus for long-term stability through heritage savings trust funds and high-quality public goods and services. Provincial governments in Western Canada open Crown (public) lands for exploration through an initial auction bid (termed a "bonus" or opening bid) and then tax the resource once it is extracted, usually through a graduated scheme that increases taxes as more of the commodity is taken from the ground (Busby, Dachis, and Dahlby 2011). Yet, since coming to power in 2007, the Saskatchewan Party has not altered the royalty structure for natural resources, notwithstanding that Saskatchewan's public royalty structure on its non-renewal commodities remain overly complicated and are some of the lowest in North America (Warnock 2005). Even as world markets for oil and gas began to cool significantly in 2015 and 2016, the government's stated commitment to "keep Saskatchewan strong" is entirely reliant on finding new markets for the raw commodities of oil, gas, and potash (figure 3.3). This overreliance on the oil and gas industry explains Saskatchewan's sharp economic downturn in 2015. Nevertheless, the Saskatchewan Party has made no indication that it intends to move away from oil and gas extraction as the province's engine for economic growth. This explains why questions of economic diversification, moving towards greener economic alternatives, or simply moving away from carbon-intense industries are simply not compatible with Brad Wall's self-described "new" Saskatchewan.

Recognizing that Saskatchewan's economic health is intimately tied to natural resource exports, Brad Wall's fiscal priorities in his first term in office were similar to the Calvert NDP's priorities of low taxes and low spending. Between 2008 and 2011, the Saskatchewan Party went out of its way to highlight razor-thin budget surpluses while limiting spending in most areas outside of public health. In its first series of budgets, the Saskatchewan Party emphasized that a "strong and steady" hand would guide the province through the economic crisis gripping the Western world (Ministry of Finance 2009). Budget priorities in its first term in government included reworking the education funding formula, which limited local school board autonomy in budgeting and paying for local programing, paid down provincial debt, initiated a new tax cut for families, and increased some funding to hospitals. Recognizing the volatility of Saskatchewan's dependence on natural resources, however, the Saskatchewan Party's finance minister was forced to shelve almost $1 billion of the campaign commitment to expand infrastructure development when potash prices fell in the spring of 2009. Based on the weakness of potash prices, the government also made a series of cuts and spending deferrals to offset taking the province into deficit (White 2009).

Similar forms of incrementalism were adopted in the Saskatchewan Party's approach to its Crown corporations, as it announced a "SaskFirst policy" that required the Crowns to disinvest from any businesses not physically in the province. In 2009 alone, this policy required SaskTel to sell off portions of its business holdings in Alberta and Manitoba (Neil 2009; see also Camfield in this volume). Throughout 2010 and 2011, SaskTel, SaskPower, and SaskEnergy

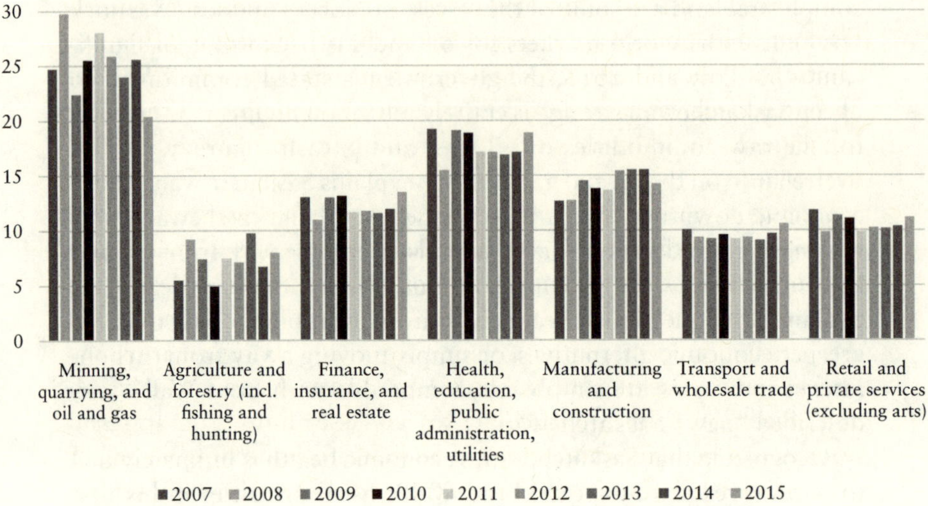

Source: Statistics Canada, CANSIM, Table 379-0028 gross domestic product (GDP) at basic prices, by North American Industry Classification System (NAICS), provinces and territories, annually (percentage share)

Figure 3.3 Saskatchewan gross domestic product (percentage), 2007–15

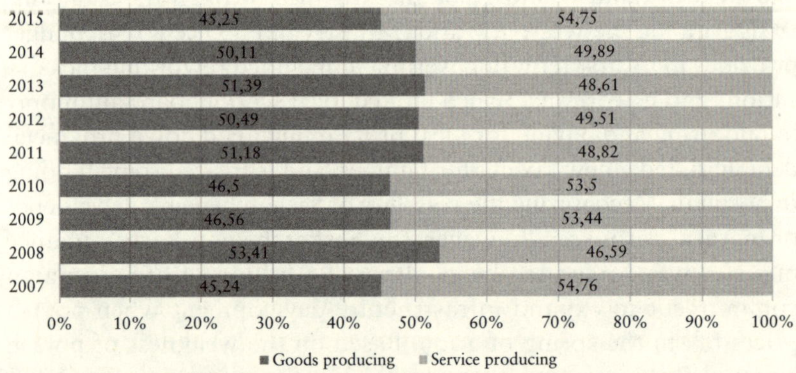

Source: CANSIM Table 379-0028 gross domestic product (GDP) at basic prices, by North American Industry
Classification System (NAICS), provinces and territories, annually (percentage share)

Figure 3.4 Goods-producing and service-producing values, 2007–15

were forced to sell off additional investments throughout the country, resulting in millions of public assets lost to the private sector (Canadian Centre for Policy Alternatives Saskatchewan 2015, 16–18). While not an outright privatization, SaskFirst certainly undermined the fiscal capacities of the Crowns, weakening their ability to grow and expand in the future.

In its 2010–11 budget, the Government of Saskatchewan emphasized its priority to "reduce the overall government footprint" while also striving "for a more efficient delivery of public services" (Ministry of Finance 2010, 25–6). Recognizing that the government did not introduce a single revenue enhancement during the boom, it took the unusual step of asking the public sector (and workers in the health and education field in particular) to "consider how programs and services can be made more efficient and effective and how we might get by with less" (ibid., 25). To meet this goal, the government set out to reduce the size of the public service by 15%, while imposing similar restructuring on the province's Crown corporations. In the same budget, the Saskatchewan Party also embraced the language of the neoliberal New Public Management from the 1990s (Osborne and Gaebler 1992) and enhanced its experimentation in the healthcare system with the private sector management philosophy known as "Lean." As a system of management, Lean was developed by managers in the Toyota auto company in the late 1980s in order to devise a "systemic approach to identify and eliminate waste through continuous improvement; flowing the product at the pull of the customer ..." (Bhasin 2015, 2). In adopting these private-sector management techniques to the delivery of health care, the government advocated for:

> A customer-focused approach to evaluating the entire process, from the beginning to its end. The goal may be to make the process more effective (thereby improving services) and/or make it more efficient (eliminating waste). (Ministry of Finance 2010, 9)

Over the next five years, Lean became the government's primary policy program to restructure the delivery of health care to reduce costs (see also Conrad in this volume).

Part of the government's priority in introducing Lean in the health care field was to find an undescribed amount of "savings" in the delivery of health. To achieve these savings, the Saskatchewan Party contracted out the implementation of Lean to private-sector consultants,

John Black and Associates. Between 2010 and 2015 when the contract was terminated, the government spent $33 million on Black consultants (CBC Saskatchewan News 2015a). Aside from the costs of contracting out the implementation of Lean, the government was also determined to implement LEAN in a top-down manner, with little consultation with workers in the health field. According to the Saskatchewan Union of Nurses (SUN) and Services Employees International Union West (SEIU West), LEAN represented a top-down process that had little to do with patient care. In fact, SUN (2014) argued that the

> primary focus is on creating efficiencies, waste reduction, and budgetary savings only, it fails to take into account patient acuity and complexity and is unfortunately proving to have little impact on direct care at the bedside and patient outcomes. We are constantly hearing this from our members and it is concerning.

When the Saskatchewan Party cancelled its Lean contract in 2015, the government claimed that the process had resulted in $125 million in savings, but offered few details on whether those savings came from administrative changes, frontline cuts, or outright layoffs (Mandryk 2015). Recognizing this, frontline health care workers concluded that Lean did nothing to improve the quality of healthcare delivery for patients, while offering little in enhanced healthcare across the province.

After the Saskatchewan Party was re-elected in 2011, its budget priorities continued to reflect elements of incremental austerity in numerous areas. With ongoing Lean initiatives in healthcare, the government continued to increase funding to this social program at roughly 3% per year. Nevertheless, in its second term the government began to experiment with privatization in the health care field, announcing in 2015 that it would begin to allow patients to pay for magnetic resonance imaging (MRI) in private, for-profit clinics (CBC Saskatchewan News 2015b). In other areas, the government continued to prioritize lower taxes to enhance competiveness. In the 2012 Speech from the Throne (Saskatchewan Lieutenant Governor 2012, 6), the government announced that it would lower Saskatchewan's business tax rate from 12% to 10%. In the same speech, the government announced that it would continue to remove regulatory barriers to businesses, while also reducing the size of the public service by 15%.

Recognizing these priorities, the government's fiscal objectives in its 2013–14 and 2014–15 budgets remained the same: lower business taxes and moderate spending increases in social programs. Where the government felt emboldened to implement a new form of austerity was in its intention to reinvest in public infrastructure. In this plan, the government committed to a new relationship with the private sector through privatization and the embrace of P3s.

INCREMENTAL PRIVATIZATION AND THE P3 TURN

Since 2007, the Saskatchewan Party has slowly turned toward privatizing secondary and tertiary services in health, education, and other areas of service delivery. In its first term, many of these privatizations emerged in the Crown sector, as the SaskFirst policy imposed strict limitations on which investments the Crowns could hold outside of the province. Although the province engaged in some small privatizations, including selling off $750 million in shares in a public fertilizer plant (Saskferco) and the small Saskatchewan educational television station (Saskatchewan Communications Network), it left the large Crowns relatively untouched.

When the Saskatchewan Party was re-elected in 2011 with a dramatically increased mandate, it continued to move incrementally toward its privatization agenda. Between 2011 and 2015, the Saskatchewan government announced that it would privatize the construction of new liquor stores in the province, thus weakening the reach of the SLGA. The government also sold off the Information and Services Commission (ISC), which was responsible for the registration of land sales in the province along with numerous vital statistics. In addition, it outsourced laundry services in the Saskatoon Health Region and contracted out food servicing in the province's correctional services, the latter resulting in the loss of over sixty public-sector jobs (CUPE Saskatchewan 2015). To be sure, these privatizations have certainly weakened the strength of the public sector, while also eliminating good public jobs. Yet, as they have occurred largely on the margins of the large Crowns and other vital public programs, these privatizations have not resulted in antagonism towards the government or a rise in support for the provincial NDP.

A far less incremental turn toward the market-oriented growth occurred in the Saskatchewan Party's embrace of P3s. In its 2012 Speech from the Throne, the government announced the creation of a new Crown corporation entitled SaskBuilds. As a commitment to P3s, SaskBuilds was a major investment by the province with $150 million committed to the Growth and Financial Security Fund in the new Crown. The mandate of SaskBuilds remains to plan and manage large-scale ($100 million or more) infrastructure in the province. Consistent with the Saskatchewan Party's ideology, SaskBuilds is mandated to fund new infrastructure projects through traditional or alternative financing (SaskBuilds 2012). In its first report in 2012, SaskBuilds confirmed that all new infrastructure planned for the province would be "alternative" in nature and would include P3 "opportunities" to fund nine "new joint-use elementary schools" in Regina and Saskatoon, a new hospital in North Battleford, Swift Current's new long-term care facility, and the massive new highway surrounding the city of Regina (the Regina Bypass). In dealing with new infrastructure projects, SaskBuilds (2015) has outlined several overarching policies to implement P3s. Each project must be a government priority, should be significantly large, produce value for taxpayers, and be competitive and transparent. Having committed to these programs, the Saskatchewan Party emphasized in 2014 that P3s would "leverage the forces of innovation and competition through public-private partnerships" to "save hundreds of millions of dollars on P3 capital projects" (Saskatchewan Lieutenant Governor 2014).

While the adoption of P3s for all future public infrastructure projects is certainly consistent with the government's free-market ideology, the fixation on these relationships is not without controversy. In its 2015 report, the Saskatchewan Auditor General raised serious concerns about the government's claims regarding P3 savings (Saskatchewan Auditor General 2015, 183–204). In the Auditor's mind, SaskBuilds P3 process was "full of estimates, full of assumptions, and a small change in an assumption can have a huge dollar impact" (Garney 2015). The Saskatchewan Auditor's findings on P3 projects are consistent with similar Auditor General reports across the country, which have consistently found that the true costs of P3s are usually higher than when government delivers these projects through public financing. For example, the Ontario Auditor General examined seventy-four P3s in Ontario between 2005 and 2014 working on areas similar to SaskBuilds: municipal infrastructure (roads, bridges), schools, and hospitals. In the 2014 Ontario report, the Auditor concludes that, over the last nine years, P3s have cost Ontario citizens $8 billion more over the traditional public-procurement model due to higher borrowing costs, risk premiums, and ancillary fees (Ontario Office of the Auditor General 2014, 193–215). Interestingly, the Auditor in Saskatchewan has raised similar early concerns, yet the Saskatchewan Party continues to see P3s as a viable model for building necessary public infrastructure.

ACTIVE INCREMENTALISM ABANDONED: THE CONTINUING ASSAULT ON ORGANIZED LABOUR

If part of the Saskatchewan Party's success has been its embrace of incremental neoliberal reforms, it has strategically ignored that framework in its labour relations policies. The government abandoned incrementalism in this policy area for political reasons, as a retrenchment of workers' rights appealed to its pro-business and anti-union base, while also weakening an important and powerful social movement that opposed the Saskatchewan Party's agenda. Moreover, in weakening the province's labour movement, the government also tied individual workers even more closely to the redistributive powers of the market.

The assault on the province's labour movement began as early as the 2007 election campaign. During the campaign, the Saskatchewan Party promised to "establish a fair and balanced labour environment," by ending what it characterized as "pro-labour" biased legislation passed during the NDP years (Saskatchewan Party 2007, 19–20). While describing the labour legislation from the NDP years as overtly "pro-labour" is certainly problematic (Smith 2011), it resonated with the pro-business and anti-labour sentiments of many on the political right. As part of its attack on unions during the 2007 campaign, the Saskatchewan Party also targeted public-sector workers and promised that it would "protect the public" by limiting workers' ability to strike in "essential services"; the party also promised that it would amend the TUA to "require secret ballots on any vote to certify a union in a workplace and a 50% plus one result for successful certification" (Saskatchewan Party 2007, 19–20; Johnstone 2007, A8). The Saskatchewan Party also stated that it would extend the abilities of employers to speak out during certification drives in order to combat aggressive union organizing.

In the Saskatchewan Party's first Speech from the Throne, the government stated that the statutory rights of workers were not absolute and had to be balanced with business priorities so that labour laws could be "competitive with other Canadian jurisdictions, if the Saskatchewan economy is to realize its potential" (Saskatchewan Lieutenant Governor 2007, 5). In making this claim, the Saskatchewan Party believed that the abilities of workers to bargain or strike were not stand-alone freedoms. Rather, the government clearly believed that workers' ability to collectively challenge public- or private-sector employers risked interfering with the low-tax and regulatory environment that the Saskatchewan Party believed was contributing to Saskatchewan's natural resource boom. After briefly consulting with its partners in business, the new government introduced two pieces of hastily crafted labour legislation: Bill 5, *The Public Service Essential Services Act* (PSESA), and Bill 6, *Trade Union Amendment Act* (Wood 2008, A7; Graham 2008b).

The PSESA had one primary objective: to weaken public-sector workers' ability to effectively bargain by restricting their ability to strike. Prior to 2007, Saskatchewan governments avoided outright bans on public-sector strikes, knowing that back-to-work legislation was always possible when disputes became a political liability. In fact, during the NDP's time in office, the Romanow government consistently argued that it was unable to introduce anti-scab legislation without a corresponding limitation on public-sector workers' ability to strike (Smith 2014). The Saskatchewan Party, however, was determined to limit public-sector disputes before they began. To accomplish these objectives, the government adopted the broadest definition of "essential services" in the country (Graham 2008a; *Saskatchewan v. Saskatchewan Federation of Labour* 2012, SKQB 62, para 205). In the PSESA, any work stoppage that caused (i) danger to life, health, or safety; (ii) the destruction or serious deterioration of machinery, equipment, or premises; (iii) serious environmental damage; or (iv) disruption of any of the courts of Saskatchewan is deemed essential, and thus illegal (Saskatchewan Lieutenant Governor 2007, 2). Additionally, any worker employed by the Government of Saskatchewan, provincial Crown corporations, regional health authorities, post-secondary institutions, municipalities, and provincial police services are extremely limited in their right to legally strike (or be locked out) (Saskatchewan Lieutenant Governor 2007, 2–3).

The bill also empowered the government to unilaterally extend "prescribed services" if deemed necessary to protect the public. The PSESA broadened the definition of public-sector strikes to include collective actions that "limit output." In other words, any collective decision to refuse to work overtime or to engage in on-the-job action could be constituted as an illegal strike. In a trend that has become increasingly common across the country, the PSESA also imposed immense fines for any union that contravened the Act. A union participating in an illegal strike is subject to an initial fine of $50,000 and, thereafter, $10,000 for each day the strike continues. If an individual or group of individuals violates the essential service agreement, they are subjected to a fine of $10,000 and, thereafter, $400 for each day the strike continues.

The Saskatchewan Party claimed that the PSESA was necessary to protect public safety in the event of a public-sector strike. While certainly a viable goal, the government presented little evidence that public-sector strikes constitute such danger. According to many of the public-sector unions in the province, most public-sector negotiations end with a mutually agreed settlement. During the 1990s and 2000s, for instance, 96% of all public-sector agreements were settled without a strike (CUPE Saskatchewan 2008, 27). In the few instances where strikes actually jeopardized public safety, workers often voluntarily agreed to provide necessary levels of service (Cameron 2008, 3). In the early 1990s, for example, members of the Saskatchewan General Employees Union (SGEU) resisted the government's austerity measures and wage restrictions through a series of rotating strikes, thus preserving necessary services (Panitch and Swartz 2003, 200). When the Saskatchewan Union of Nurses (SUN) defied the NDP's back-to-work legislation in 1999, the union also continued to provide essential services in the health care field (Wyatt 1999, A1–2).

In addition to introducing the new essential services bill, the Saskatchewan Party also made several changes to the province's decade old *Trade Union Act*. Bill 6, *Trade Union Amendment Act*, amplified the restrictions on public-sector workers' ability to strike. Among its many changes, the bill strengthened the rights of individual employers while making it more difficult for workers to organize into new unions. Under the Saskatchewan Party's TUA amendments, employers are given new legal freedoms to communicate "facts and its opinions to its employees" about the implications of possible unionization (Saskatchewan 26th Legislature 2007b, 2). This change loosens the legal restrictions on an employer's ability to intimidate or threaten union supporters (Saskatchewan Federation of Labour 2008, 10–11). Bill 6 also alters the province's long-standing certification procedure by making certification votes mandatory and raising the threshold to obtain certification to 50% plus one of those in the new bargaining unit (rather than a simple majority of those voting). This change to the voting procedure, referred to as the double quorum, places a significant barrier to unions winning a certification election, as any non-voter is counted against the union (Warren 2008). The government defended its workplace legislation as promoting "democratic workplaces" (Ministry of Advanced Education, Employment and Labour 2008, 10). While business also leaned on the democratization argument, groups like the Canadian Federation of Independent Business were blunter in characterizing the government's labour law changes as "tip[ping] the scales" and thus the balance of power in the workplace away from organized labour (Graham 2007).

The province's labour movement opposed the government's austere labour legislation in two ways. First, it continued to financially and organizationally support the Saskatchewan NDP. While the NDP opposition certainly disapproved of the legislation, its weakened political position and poor labour relations history gave it little clout. The second tool was more unorthodox for workers' organizations. Rather than rallying on the steps of the legislature or opposing the bills through workplace action, the province's labour leaders chose to challenge the bills in court. At the centre of these legal arguments were the unions' claims that Bills 5 and 6 violated the Charter of Rights and Freedom's guarantee of freedom of association. Upon launching its legal challenge, the Saskatchewan Federation of Labour (SFL) and eighteen separate unions claimed that "the government has not been able to, to this point, justify this rolling back of workers' rights" and suggested that both of the Saskatchewan Party's labour bills violated the constitution (Hall 2008). Over the next seven years, the unions continued their constitutional challenges, winning in the Court of Queen's Bench while losing before the Saskatchewan Court of Appeal (*Saskatchewan Federation of Labour v. Saskatchewan* 2012, SKQB 62; *Saskatchewan v. Saskatchewan Federation of Labour* 2013, SKCA 43). When the Supreme Court of Canada (SCC) ruled in January 2015, it made the decision that workers had the constitutional right to strike as part of a process of meaningful collective bargaining (*Saskatchewan Federation of Labour v. Saskatchewan* [2015] 1 S.C.R. 245). In arriving at this conclusion, the SCC struck down numerous sections of the PSESA but upheld the government's amendments to the *Trade Union Act*. Although not a complete legal victory for the province's workers, the SCC decision certainly reflected a public embarrassment for the government, as Premier Wall publicly mused about implementing the Charter's notwithstanding clause to override the SCC's decision (Trembath 2015). The government backed away from that threat relatively quickly, introducing Bill 183, *The Saskatchewan Employment Amendment Act (Essential Services)* in fall 2015. Under the provisions of Bill 183, the definition of essential services was removed, replaced with a provision for workers and management to determine what is essential in their sectors. While that change certainly favoured the workers, it did not end the Saskatchewan Party's insistence that labour law was not a tool to protect workers but rather a legislative way to improve business competitiveness in the province.

Bills 5 and 6 were the Saskatchewan Party's significant labour policy reforms during its first term. After its re-election in 2011, the government continued to antagonize the unions through legislative reform. In early 2012, the government released a paper to begin an online consultative process designed to "update" and "modernize" the province's labour laws. In that paper, the government asked leading questions about limiting labour unions' ability to participate politically, removing or allowing workers to opt out of the mandatory dues formula (the so-called Rand formula) while also allowing employers greater freedom to decertify unions. The paper also contemplated weakening employment standards by raising the length of time required before non-unionized workers could access vacation pay and other workplace benefits (Saskatchewan Ministry of Labour Relations and Workplace Safety 2012). Although business and labour took their traditional opposing views on the scope and substance of labour law reform, there were some surprising agreements (see Smith 2008). For instance, many of the large businesses in the province could see no benefit in undermining the mandatory union dues structure, fearing instability in their industries (Potash Corporation 2012; Construction Labour Relations Association 2012).

The short, four-month consultative process resulted in a massive legislative omnibus bill, Bill 85, which combined twelve pieces of legislation – including *the Trade Union Act*, employment standards legislation, and occupational health and safety legislation – into a single act. While many of the contentious issues surrounding the mandatory dues checkoff (the Rand formula) and union financing were dropped by the government, the Saskatchewan Party did scale back some of the freedoms that unions had to collect fines from members crossing a picket line, imposed a statutory obligation for unions to provide audited financial statements to its members, and delayed strike action by imposing mandatory conciliation and a further fourteen-day cooling-off period, while also expanding the statutory definition of "manager" in the Act to include current members in a bargaining unit. Existing members of a bargaining unit who have "duties related to labour relations, business strategic planning, policy advice or budget planning" could thus be pushed out-of-scope (Lieutenant Governor 2012; Stevens 2013). Outside of reforms affecting labour unions, Bill 85 also made several amendments to employment standards legislation. Among the numerous changes to the limited rights of unorganized workers were modifications to overtime requirements, limits to time off for workers in small businesses, and a host of other small deviations that made it easier for employers to alter conditions of work and overtime pay with little to no input from workers. The government also indexed future minimum-wage increases to inflation, providing stability in future wage increases to both employers and workers, but kept that wage comparatively low and thus unable to seriously address poverty in the province.

Although labour unions raised serious concerns about the government's earlier musings regarding the elimination the mandatory dues checkoff (the Rand formula), the more moderate provisions in Bill 85 allowed it to pass with little opposition. Notwithstanding these changes, the new *Saskatchewan Employment Act* represents the amalgamation of almost seventy-five years of labour regulation into a single bill. Not only was the new legislation pursued quickly; it also did little to advance the causes of workers in either the public or private sector. The most that can be said about labour law reforms under the Saskatchewan Party is that it is now hard to create, maintain, and advance the cause of unions in the province. That reality suggests that workers are less equipped to fight future austerity in Saskatchewan.

CONCLUSION: ABANDONING ACTIVE INCREMENTALISM?

In some ways, the Saskatchewan Party's two-term government does not represent a radical break from the NDP governments that preceded it. Both the Saskatchewan Party and the NDP were both committed to the neoliberal principles of decreasing resource royalty rents and keeping personal and business taxation low. Nevertheless, in its eight years in power the Saskatchewan Party has continued to pursue neoliberal reforms through an actively incremental approach to austerity. These policies have included small-scale privatizations in a host of secondary amenities in core public services, weakening – but not outright privatizing – the core Crown corporations and restructuring the internal workings of the state through new public management initiatives such as Lean.

Although many of these restructuring initiatives have proven controversial, none has dented the popularity of the party or its leader, Brad Wall. In fact, Wall's popularity continued to propel the Saskatchewan Party forward, allowing the party to easily navigate the 2016 provincial election, winning a third straight majority government. Notwithstanding this impressive electoral victory, the government's overreliance on the oil and gas industry suggests that more austere times are ahead for the people of Saskatchewan. Already, the premier has floated the idea of "transformative change" in the public sector, which includes amalgamating health and school boards and the possibility of privatizing SaskTel, a move that many would not have envisioned prior to the economic downturn. Whether or not these moves will come to fruition or if the "transformative change" rhetoric signals an end to the active incrementalism of the Saskatchewan Party remains unclear.

The province's economic woes will also do little to change the Saskatchewan Party's approach to labour relations. In this field, the government has consistently and repeatedly weakened the ability of the province's labour unions to organize, bargain, and strike. While the unions were able to challenge some of those labour reforms through the courts, all of the amendments to the *Trade Union Act* (now the *Employment Act*) remain. Over the long-term, these changes to workers' rights will weaken the capacity of workers to bargain higher wages and benefits, tying them even closer to the precarity to the labour market. As Saskatchewan's economy enters what many are perceiving as a long-term downturn in the price of oil and gas commodities, the government's stated commitment to market-driven reforms will stretch the welfare state even further, resulting in even greater pressure for the government to use austerity to bring its inflating deficits under control, downsize the public service, and privatize (or partially privatize) important public assets such as SGI, SaskPower, and SaskTel.

NOTE

1 It is worth noting that these are not the only Crown corporations in Saskatchewan. There are numerous others in the province, including Saskatchewan Transportation Company, SaskGaming, Saskatchewan Research Council, and a host of others. A full list can be accessed here: https://www.saskatchewan.ca/government/government-structure/crown-corporations.

REFERENCES

Albo, Gregory. 2010. "'The New Economy' and Capitalism Today." In *Interrogating the New Economy: Restructuring Work in the 21st Century*, edited by Noreen Pupo and Mark P. Thomas, 3–20. Toronto: University of Toronto Press.

Albo, Greg, and Carlo Fanelli. 2014. *Austerity against Democracy: An Authoritarian Phase of Neoliberalism?* Toronto: Centre for Social Justice.

Bhasin, Sanjay. 2015. *Lean Management beyond Manufacturing: A Holistic Approach*. New York: Springer.

Blake, Raymond B. 2008. "The Saskatchewan Party and the Politics of Branding." In *Saskatchewan Politics: Crowding the Centre*, edited by Howard Leeson, 165–88. Regina: Canadian Plains Research Centre.

Brown, Lorne A., Joseph K. Roberts, and John W. Warnock. 1999. *Saskatchewan Politics from Left to Right, '44 to '99*. Regina: Hinterland Publications.

Busby, Colin, Benjamin Dachis, and Bev Dahlby. 2011. *Rethinking Royalty Rates: Why There Is a Better Way to Tax Oil and Gas Development*. C.D. Howe Institute Commentary 333. Toronto: C.D. Howe Institute. September.

Cameron, Dan. 2008. "Essential Services Legislation: Will It Facilitate or Impair Industrial Relations?" *Canadian Centre for Policy Alternatives: Saskatchewan Notes* 7 (February): 1–4.

Canadian Centre for Policy Alternatives, Saskatchewan Office. 2015. *The Wrong Track: A Decade of Privatization in Saskatchewan, 2004–2015*. Regina: Canadian Centre for Policy Alternatives. October. https://www.policyalternatives.ca/publications/reports/wrong-track.

CBC Saskatchewan News. 2015a. "Government of Saskatchewan's Lean Contract Comes to an End." *CBC News*, 31 March. http://www.cbc.ca/

news/canada/saskatchewan/government-of-saskatchewan-s-lean-contract-comes-to-an-end-1.3017218.

– 2015b. "Saskatchewan to Allow More Private MRI Scans for Paying Customers." *CBC News*, 6 May. http://www.cbc.ca/news/canada/saskatchewan/saskatchewan-to-allow-more-private-mri-scans-for-paying-customers-1.3063849.

Construction Labour Relations Association of Saskatchewan. 2012. *Response to Government Paper on Renewal of Labour Legislation in Saskatchewan.*

Conway, Aiden, and John Conway. 2015. "Saskatchewan: From Cradle of Social Democracy to Neoliberalism's Sandbox." In *Transforming Provincial Politics: The Political Economy of Canada's Provinces and Territories in the Neoliberal Era*, edited by Bryan M. Evans and Charles W. Smith, 226–54. Toronto: University of Toronto Press.

Crow, Dan, and Greg Albo. 2005. "Neo-Liberalism, NAFTA, and the State of the North American Labour Movements." *Just Labour* 6&7: 12–22.

CUPE Saskatchewan (Canadian Union of Provincial Employees). 2008. *Tilt: How the SaskParty Plans to Shift the Scales in Favour of Employers.* CUPE Saskatchewan.

– 2015. *Privatization & P3s.* CUPE Saskatchewan. http://sk.cupe.ca/privatization-p3s/.

Dyck, Rand. 1996. *Provincial Politics in Canada: Toward the Turn of the Century.* Scarborough: Prentice Hall.

Enoch, Simon. 2011. "The 'New Saskatchewan' Neoliberal Renewal or Redux?" *Socialist Studies* 7 (1/2): 191–215.

Evans, Bryan M., and Charles W. Smith. 2015. "Introduction: Transforming Provincial Politics: The Political Economy of Canada's Provinces and Territories in a Neoliberal Era." In *Transforming Provincial Politics: The Political Economy of Canada's Provinces and Territories in the Neoliberal Era*, edited by Bryan M. Evans and Charles W. Smith, 3–18. Toronto: University of Toronto Press.

Fudge, Judy, and Leah F. Vosko. 2003. "Gender Paradoxes and the Rise of Contingent Work: Towards a Transformative Political Economy of the Labour Market." In *Changing Canada: Political Economy as Transformation*, edited by Wallace Clement and Leah F. Vosko, 183–209. Montreal and Kingston: McGill-Queen's University Press.

Garney, Emma. 2015. "Auditor Urges Changes on P3s, School Division." *StarPhoenix*, 4 June.

Hall, Angela. 2008. "Constitutional Challenge Filed," *Regina Leader Post*, 30 July.

Harvey, David. 2005. *A Brief History of Neoliberalism*. Oxford: Oxford University Press.

Gindin, Sam. 2013. "Rethinking Unions, Registering Socialism." In *The Question of Strategy: Socialist Register 2013*, edited by Leo Panitch, Greg Albo, and Vivek Chibber, 26–51. London: Merlin Publishers.

Graham, Jennifer. 2007. "Labour Groups Call New Sask. Legislation 'an Attack' on Workers' Rights." *Canadian Press*, 19 December.

– 2008a. "Internal Notes Suggest Sask. New Essential Services Bill 'Broadest' in Canada." *Canadian Press*, 9 April.

– 2008b. "Union Alleges Sask. Gov't Sought Support on Labour Bill Prior to Its Tabling." *Canadian Press*, 14 March.

– 2008c. "Unions Upset, but Saskatchewan Minister Defends Firing of Labour Board Officials." *Canadian Press*, 7 March.

Johnstone, Bruce. 2007. "Chamber Wants Change; Business Lobby Pushes Labour Laws as Election Issue." *StarPhoenix*, 23 October.

Leeson, Howard. 2008. "The 2007 Saskatchewan Election: Watershed or Way Station?" In *Saskatchewan Politics: Crowding the Centre*, edited by Howard Leeson, 119–40. Regina: Canadian Plains Research Centre.

Mandryk, Murray. 2015. "Explanations for Lean Costs Ridiculous." *Regina Leader-Post*, 4 March.

McBride, Stephen. 2014. "'In Austerity We Trust.'" In *Orchestrating Austerity: Impacts and Resistance*, edited by Donna Bains and Stephen McBride, 10–20. Halifax: Fernwood Publishing.

McCuaig, Ian, Bob Sass, and Mark Stobbe. 1991. "Labour Pains: The Birth of a New Industrial Relations Order in Saskatchewan, 1982–1990." In *Devine Rule in Saskatchewan: A Decade of Hope and Hardship*, edited by Leslie Biggs and Mark Stobbe, 149–75. Saskatoon: Fifth House Publishers.

McGrane, David. 2007. "The 2007 Provincial Election in Saskatchewan." *Canadian Political Science Review* 2 (1): 64–71.

– 2008. "Which Third Way? A Comparison of the Romanow and Calvert NDP Governments." In *Saskatchewan Politics: Crowding the Centre*, edited by Howard Leeson, 143–64. Regina: Canadian Plains Research Centre.

– 2011. "Balancing Conflicting Purposes: Saskatchewan Taxation Policy from 1991–2011." In *New Directions in Saskatchewan Public Policy*, edited by David McGrane, 91–120. Regina: Canadian Plains Research Centre.

Neil, Scott. 2009. "SaskTel to Sell DirectWest Holdings." *Regina Leader Post*, 6 November.

Noonan, Jeff. 2013. "The Historical and Contemporary Life-Value of the Canadian Labour Movement." *Labour/Le Travail* 71: 9–27.

Ontario. Office of the Auditor General. 2014. *Annual Report 2014*. Toronto: Queen's Printer for Ontario. http://www.auditor.on.ca/en/content/annualreports/arbyyear/ar2014.html.

Osborne, David, and Ted Gaebler. 1992. *Reinventing Government: How the Entrepreneurial Spirit is Transforming the Public Sector*. New York: Plume.

Panitch, Leo, and Donald Swartz. 2003. *The Assault on Trade Union Freedoms: From Consent to Coercion*. 3rd ed. Toronto: Garamond.

Peck, Jamie. 2010. *Constructions of Neoliberal Reason*. Oxford: Oxford University Press.

– 2013. "Pushing Austerity: State Failure, Municipal Bankruptcy and the Crises of Fiscal Federalism in the USA." *Cambridge Journal of Regions, Economy and Society* 7 (1): 17–44.

Pitsula, James M., and Kenneth A. Rasmussen. 1990. *Privatizing a Province: The New Right in Saskatchewan*. Vancouver: New Star Books.

Potash Corporation. 2012. *Response to "A Consultation Paper on the Renewal of Labour Legislation in Saskatchewan."*

Pratt, Larry, and John Richards. 1979. *Prairie Capitalism: Power and Influence in the New West*. Toronto: McClelland and Stewart.

Praud, Jocelyne, and Sarah McQuarrie. 2001. "The Saskatchewan CCF-NDP from the Regina Manifesto to the Romanow Years." In *Saskatchewan Politics: Into the Twenty-First Century*, edited by Howard A. Leeson, 143–68. Regina: Canadian Plains Research Centre.

Rasmussen, Kenneth A. 2001. "Saskatchewan: From Entrepreneurial State to Embedded State." In *The Provincial State in Canada: Politics in the Provinces and Territories*, edited by Keith Brownsey and Michael Howlett, 241–76. Toronto: Broadview Press.

Saskatchewan 26th Legislature. 2007a. *An Act respecting Essential Public Services* (Bill 5). 1st session. http://www.publications.gov.sk.ca/freelaw/documents/english/FirstRead/2007-08/Bill-5.pdf.

– 2007b. *An Act to Amend the Trade Union Act* (Bill 6). 1st session. http://www.qp.gov.sk.ca/documents/english/FirstRead/2007-08/Bill-6.pdf.

Saskatchewan 27th Legislature. 2012. *An Act respecting Employment Standards, Occupational Health and Safety, Labour Relations and Related Matters and making consequential amendments to certain Acts (Saskatchewan Employment Act)* (Bill 85). 2nd session (amended 2013). http://www.publications.gov.sk.ca/freelaw/documents/english/FirstRead/2012/Bill-85.pdf.

Saskatchewan. Auditor General. 2015. 2015 Report Volume I. Government of Saskatchewan, 3 June. https://auditor.sk.ca/publications/public-reports/item?id=138

Saskatchewan. Court of Appeal. 2013. *Saskatchewan v. Saskatchewan Federation of Labour*, 2013 SKCA 43.

Saskatchewan. Court of Queen's Bench. 2012. *Saskatchewan v. Saskatchewan Federation of Labour*, 2012 SKQB 62.

Saskatchewan Federation of Labour. 2008. *Brief to Minister Norris: Bill 5, The Public Service Essential Services Act and Bill 6, An Act to amend the Trade Union Act*. Regina: Saskatchewan Federation of Labour.

Saskatchewan. Lieutenant Governor. 2007. *Speech from the Throne 2007: Securing the Future*. Regina: Government of Saskatchewan, 10 December.

– 2008. *Speech from the Throne: A Stronger Saskatchewan, A Better Life*. Regina: Government of Saskatchewan, 22 October.

– 2012. *Speech from the Throne 2012: Planning for Growth*. Regina: Government of Saskatchewan, 25 October.

– 2014. *Speech from the Throne: Keeping Saskatchewan Strong*. Regina: Government of Saskatchewan, 22 October.

Saskatchewan. Ministry of Advanced Education, Employment and Labour. 2008. *Annual Report, 2007–2008*. Regina: Government of Saskatchewan. http://www.finance.gov.sk.ca/annreport/AEELAnnualReport200708.pdf.

Saskatchewan. Ministry of Finance. 2006. *A Plan for Growth and Opportunity: Business Tax Reform in Saskatchewan*. Regina: Government of Saskatchewan. http://finance.gov.sk.ca/budget/budget06/SKBusinessTaxReform.pdf.

– 2007. *Saskatchewan Provincial Budget 2007–2008*. Regina: Government of Saskatchewan. http://www.finance.gov.sk.ca/budget/budget07/0708budgetsummarybook.pdf.

– 2009. *Saskatchewan Provincial Budget 2009–2010: Strong and Steady*. Regina: Government of Saskatchewan. http://www.finance.gov.sk.ca/budget2009-10/Budget200910SummaryBook.pdf.

– 2010. *Saskatchewan Provincial Budget 2010–2011: Balanced. Forward-Looking. Responsible*. Regina: Government of Saskatchewan. http://www.finance.gov.sk.ca/budget2010-11/2010-11BudgetSummary.pdf.

Saskatchewan. Ministry of Labour Relations and Workplace Safety. 2012. *A Consultation Paper on the Renewal of Labour Legislation in Saskatchewan*. Regina: Government of Saskatchewan. http://www.seiuwest.ca/files/2012/05/consultation-paper-renewal-labour-legislation.pdf.

Saskatchewan Party. 2007. *Securing the Future: New Ideas for Saskatchewan*. Saskatchewan Party. https://www.poltext.org/sites/poltext.org/files/plateformes/sk2007skp_plt_12072011_95625.pdf.
Saskatchewan Union of Nurses. 2014. "The Real Story about Lean." http://sun-nurses.sk.ca/index/presidents-message/march-2014-the-real-story-about-lean.
SaskBuilds. 2012. *About SaskBuilds*. http://www.saskbuilds.ca/about-us/.
– 2013. *Annual Report for 2012–13*. Regina: Government of Saskatchewan. http://www.saskbuilds.ca/about-us/AnnualReport.html.
– 2015. *Annual Report for 2014–15*. Regina: Government of Saskatchewan. http://www.saskbuilds.ca/about-us/AnnualReport.html.
Smith, Charles W. 2008. "The Politics of the Ontario Labour Relations Act: Business, Labour, and Government in the Consolidation of Post-War Industrial Relations, 1949–1961." *Labour/Le Travail* 62 (Fall): 109–51.
– 2011. "The 'New Normal' in Saskatchewan: Neoliberalism and the Challenge to Workers' Rights." In *New Directions in Saskatchewan Public Policy*, edited by David McGrane, 121–52. Regina: Canadian Plains Research Centre.
– 2014. "We Didn't Want to Totally Break the Law: Industrial Legality, the Pepsi Strike, and Workers' Collective Rights in Canada." *Labour/Le Travail* 74 (Fall 2014): 89–121.
Stevens, Andrew. 2013. "Saskatchewan: A Beachhead of Labour Law Reform?" *Socialist Project E-Bulletin* 812, 29 April.
Supreme Court of Canada. 2015. *Saskatchewan Federation of Labour v. Saskatchewan*, [2015] 1 S.C.R. 245.
Swartz, Donald, and Rosemary Warskett. 2012. "Contextualizing Labour and Working-Class Politics: Canadian Labour and the Crisis of Solidarity." In *Rethinking the Politics of Labour in Canada*, edited by Stephanie Ross and Larry Savage, 18–32. Halifax: Fernwood Publishing.
Teeple, Gary. 2004. *Globalization and the Decline of Social Reform: Into the Twenty-First Century*. Toronto: Garamond Press.
Trembath, Sean. 2015. "NDP Slams Wall's Notwithstanding Comment on Labour Law." *StarPhoenix*, 9 February.
Warnock, John W. 2004. *Saskatchewan: The Roots of Discontent and Protest*. Montreal: Blackrose Books.
– 2005. *Natural Resources and Government Revenue: Recent Trends in Saskatchewan*. Regina: Canadian Centre for Policy Alternatives.
Warren, Jim. 2008. *Joining the Race to the Bottom: An Assessment of Bill 6, Amendments to the Trade Union Act, 2008*. Regina: Canadian Centre for Policy Alternatives.

Warren, Jim W., and Kathleen Carlisle. 2005. *On the Side of the People: A History of Labour in Saskatchewan*. Regina: Coteau Books.

White, Patrick. 2009. "Surplus Forecasts Slashed as Potash Prices Plunge." *Globe and Mail*, 15 August.

Wood, James. 2008. "Calvert Questions Role of Lawyer in Crafting Sask. Party Labour Laws; Private-Sector Lawyer Only Advising Gov't." *StarPhoenix*, 18 March.

Wyatt, Mark. 1999. "8,400 Nurses Hit Picket Lines Province Wide." *StarPhoenix*, 8 April.

CHAPTER FOUR

Manitoba: Fiscal Policy and the Public Sector under "Today's NDP"

DAVID CAMFIELD

To analyze the Manitoba experience in the years 2007–15, it is essential to first look critically at the nature of fiscal policy in capitalist societies.[1] Most discussions of government taxation and spending treat these issues as fundamentally technical, not political. Former Nova Scotia NDP finance minister Graham Steele gives us a good example of this attitude: "Provincial finance is complicated ... But on some level, provincial finance is also very simple. Revenue has to equal or exceed expenditure. Taxes pay for services. Services are paid for with taxes. If you want your taxes to go down, we have to figure out what services we'll no longer offer. If you want your services to improve, we have to figure out who will pay. You can run deficits, but not forever. Don't let anyone tell you it's more complicated than that" (Steele 2013). Underlying most discussions of fiscal policy is the assumption that this is the policy of a neutral institution, the state, that functions in the general interest of society.

These commonplace notions – fiscal policy as technical and the state as neutral – are classic cases of ideas whose apparent obviousness registers the extent to which the specific character of the social phenomena in question has been obscured (see also Evans and Fanelli's introduction to this volume). Let us begin with the state. There is no question that states in capitalist societies are institutionally separate from private enterprises. However, "the separation of the state from civil society in no way implies the 'neutrality' or 'autonomy' of the state. The essential feature of the liberal form of the state is the formal and abstract character of state power most adequately embodied in the rule of law and money ... The state secures the reproduction of civil society by enforcing the rule of money and the law, which are at the same time its own presuppositions" (Clarke 1988, 127). In so doing, the state reproduces society as capitalist society.

Because it does this as a set of institutions that exist separately from so-called private interests, the state appears as "the embodiment of the general interest of society and as the neutral arbiter of all particularistic claims" (ibid., 128). This appearance is not mere illusion; the state really is institutionally separate. This is the most important reason why state power is so often seen as essentially neutral. Yet, the appearance of neutrality is deceiving: states in capitalist societies are capitalist states, no matter which party or group is in government. This is not because they are captured by businesspeople, though capitalists try in all manner of ways – including lobbying, influencing political parties and cultivating connections with politicians and senior civil servants, and promising to invest or to relocate – to get states to act in their interests. Rather, it is because the state's "existence as a material force and the forms of its social intervention are subordinated to the need to secure the expanded reproduction of capitalist social relations of production" (Clarke 1983, 123). In other words, the ability of capitalist states to function and carry out their activities of politically administering society depends on capitalist economic expansion. This orients states toward, and disciplines states into, trying to ensure that capital is profitable.

Since capitalism is a global system, states are subject to pressures from within and beyond their borders. For example, the exchange rates for currencies and the interest rates for the bonds that governments issue to raise money are shaped by international forces. A serious crisis of capital will tend to cause a serious crisis of state power as, for example, tax revenue falls drastically and state expenditure related to growing unemployment rises. However, although states are not neutral "the state is not simply a tool of capital" (ibid.). Because capitalist production generates conflict between capital and the working class, the state is "an arena of class struggle" and its "forms and limits are themselves an object of that struggle" (ibid.). In addition to not being neutral in terms of class, state power is also distinctly gendered and racialized (Gordon 2007). All this must be borne in mind when examining the actions of the Manitoba provincial government, which should be understood as a subordinate component of the Canadian state.

Fiscal policy is the policy of states that have a class, gender, and racial character. However, in Canada today fiscal policy – like economic policy in general – is often treated as, at root, a technical exercise that transcends ideology. This reflects the degree to which neoliberal ideology, which treats the elimination of deficits as a prized and supposedly non-ideological objective, has taken hold in all major political parties, the mainstream media, and, to a lesser extent, popular consciousness. Internationally, one way of trying to shift responsibility for economic policy away from governments has been to bind them to rules in multilateral or bilateral investment and trade deals, such as the North American Free Trade Agreement (NAFTA), or more elaborate arrangements like those of the European Union. Another has been to give policy-making authority to state institutions other than the government itself, such as central banks, or to pass legislation that restricts what governments can do, such as Manitoba's balanced-budget legislation. These can be seen as efforts to "depoliticize" economic management. It is not that policy actually becomes non-political. Rather, "depoliticisation as a governing strategy is the process of placing at one remove the political character of decision-making" (Burnham 1999, 47). Shifting responsibility in this way makes economic policy even less subject to democratic influence – with democracy understood here as popular power (Cairns and Sears 2012) – than when decisions are made by elected governments.

In the case of fiscal policy in particular, governments must deal with how their decisions about spending and taxation (and other matters of economic policy) will be treated by the financial markets to which they resort when they wish to raise money by issuing securities (see Brownsey in this volume). Here, the power of the agencies that set the credit ratings of governments is crucial, since these ratings influence the rates of return that governments must offer to sell bonds. This is an eminently political matter that is often treated as technical or non-ideological. Hugo Radice (2011, 94) observes that "It is striking that at no point in the past forty years of debate on public finances did the monetarist economists – or their neoliberal successors – explain why any particular limit to public deficits and debt was *economically necessary*. Instead we have been offered, then as now, an entirely circular argument. We are told by supposed economic experts that deficit cuts are necessary because international bond markets require them. So why do the investors in international bond markets require cuts? Because the economic experts say they are necessary!"

This is not an innocent confusion. The ratings assigned by credit rating agencies to government bonds reflect agency managers' commitment to neoliberal ideology. "While the agencies 'disavow any ideological content' in their ratings, this is implausible – particularly in light of the evaluation of economic policy that lies at the heart of sovereign rating. Indeed, adherence to the agencies' conception of 'orthodox' economic policy – and the avoidance of 'policy errors' associated with deviating from it – appears to be central to the agencies' rating actions" (Bruner 2008, 137). Today the agencies operate in an ideological environment in which, despite the concerns voiced by some supporters of neoliberalism (e.g. Ostry, Loungani, and Furceri 2016), austerity has "become the *objective* of policy, rather than a policy whose objective is macroeconomic stabilisation" (Konzelmann 2014, 35).

This is illustrated by the downgrading of France's credit rating by Standard and Poor's (S&P) in 2013, despite the French government's "exemplary" (Krugman 2013) fiscal restraint. Paul Krugman argues that the ratings move was driven by S&P's opposition to the French government's decision to raise taxes instead of "dismantling the welfare state" (Krugman 2013). Thus, Steele's earlier-cited claim about provincial government spending – "You can run deficits, but not forever" – obscures how and why fiscal policy is deeply ideological. This point is reinforced by Richard Seymour's reminder that because of the dynamics of bond markets, "in general, large deficits are unsustainable," but "this doesn't mean that cutting spending solves the problem. The Keynesian critics are right about this. It just means that in a sense *all the options are bad*" (Seymour 2014, 124–5; emphasis in original).

Before moving to look at Manitoba, a few words on concepts and context are necessary. The term neoliberalism is used in a number of different senses in popular and academic writing. In what follows, neoliberalism is understood as, following Al Campbell (2005), at its most basic level a particular organization of capitalism. It is the product of what Jamie Peck, Nik Theodore, and Neil Brenner call "neoliberalization": a "historically specific, unevenly developed, hybrid, patterned tendency of market-disciplinary regulatory restructuring" (Peck, Theodore, and Brenner 2012, 269). State power plays an absolutely central active role in this process, and states are restructured, not dismantled (Wacquant 2012). Neoliberalism developed as a response to the crisis of capitalism in the mid-1970s that put an end to the long postwar economic boom. One of its features has been "incremental and cumulative changes ... to public sector management and operation" that "have had a negative impact – especially on public services, public service employment, and public sector collective bargaining" (Peters 2012, 126; see also Smith in this volume). The neoliberal reorganization of capitalism generated a period of global economic expansion that lasted from the early 1980s until the recession of 2008–09 that opened the present era of global slump (McNally 2011). As non-Marxist analysts like Philip Mirowski and Marxist analysts like David McNally both argue, while this began as a financial crisis it was not simply a crisis of finance. The ensuing growth of state deficits and debt has been a consequence of this crisis. Thus, what Canadian provincial governments have been grappling with since 2008 is "at base a crisis of capitalism, and only derivatively a fiscal crisis of the state" (Mirowski 2013, 18).

THE TRANSITION TO NEOLIBERALISM IN MANITOBA

Sterling Lyon, Progressive Conservative (PC) premier from 1977 to 1981, was an early supporter of neoliberalism. However, his government did not actually unleash neoliberalization in Manitoba, although it did implement some cuts in spending and taxes while raising a number of user fees (Stewart and Wesley 2010). Neoliberal federal government policies affected people in Manitoba beginning in the early 1980s, but the turn to neoliberalism at the provincial level was made by the PC government of Gary Filmon (1988–99). Moving slowly during the minority government of 1988–90, the PCs set to work after winning a majority in 1990. Their achievements of the 1990s included the privatization of Manitoba Telecom Services and changes to labour law that made it harder for workers to unionize. Perhaps most important was their balanced-budget legislation. This required that government spending be equal to or less than revenue, except in the event of a natural disaster, war, or a fall in revenue of over 5% as a result of unexpected circumstances. It also stipulated that the rates of the four major provincial taxes could be raised only if authorized by majority support in a public referendum. Its aim was to lock in neoliberal priorities, tie the hands of government, and force cuts to jobs and services whenever revenue fell below the existing level of expenditure (Saunders 2010; Loxley 1995–96). The government's measures met with considerable protest, including a significant number of strikes in 1995–96.

The NDP was able to win a majority of seats in the legislature in 1999. It went on to win re-election as a majority government in 2003, 2007, and 2011, only losing office in 2016. During its years in office, it demonstrated "a general alignment with twenty-first century neoliberalism" (Evans 2012, 80). More precisely, its ideology and practice can be characterized as social-liberal, with social democratic themes subordinated to an overall acceptance of neoliberalism. It did relatively little to actively deepen neoliberalization in the province. However, its generosity to mining investors (Baragar and Loxley 2011, 11) was noteworthy, as was its expansion of policing and imprisonment, including its support for the federal Conservative government's "tough on crime" *Safe Streets and Communities Act* (Dobchuk-Land 2017; Burrows 2011).[2] It should be seen as a government of mild neoliberal consolidation, in contrast to the preceding PC government of neoliberal reorientation, to use Neil Davidson's terms (Davidson 2016). Its economic policy was "largely consistent with the interests of Manitoba capital, keeping those interests from mobilizing politically against the NDP" (Evans 2012, 79–80). In 2003, one NDP strategist described the party leadership's policy strategy as one of "inoculation": "giving their traditional enemies at least a bit of what they demand, much as we inoculate ourselves against a disease by injecting into our bodies a bit of the disease" (Black and Silver 2008, 166). As a result, the NDP "end[ed] up *defining* their governing strategy by the demands of their traditional enemies" (ibid., 168) in the capitalist class. Cuts to personal and corporate taxes were a hallmark of this approach (ibid., 167).

POLITICAL ECONOMY AND FISCAL POLICY IN MANITOBA, 2007–15

Capital accumulation in Canada has been hit much less severely than in other advanced capitalist countries in the current crisis. Arguably, this is because a "profitability crisis of colossal proportions" from 1990 to 1992 was followed by "high profitability and strong business investment" that "acted to stabilize the macroeconomic environment for capital and allowed the country to weather the financial storm" (McCormack 2013, 8, 2). Within Canada, capital in Manitoba has been significantly less affected by the crisis than in most other regions.

A number of conventional economic indicators register how Manitoba has been touched relatively mildly. Gross domestic product (GDP) in Manitoba grew faster than Canada's from 2006 through 2008. Nominal GDP in 2009 was 2.5% below the 2008 level, but 2010's figure was up 4.5% over 2009's. Nominal GDP growth was 4.3% for 2011 and 5.6% the following year. More significantly, in

2012 when measured in dollars as valued in 2008, real GDP was 5% higher than the pre-recession level of 2008 and 8.7% larger than the low level of 2009 (calculated from Statistics Canada 2014a). Over the years 2007 through 2012, Manitoba average annual GDP growth was 2.1%, compared to 1.1% for Canada (Manitoba Ministry of Finance 2013a, A3). Private capital investment declined in 2009 but has since grown significantly; public capital investment did not fall in 2009, dipped in 2011, and then rebounded. From 2007 to 2012, capital investment in the province grew by 38%, twice the pan-Canadian level (ibid., A10). In terms of unemployment, the impact of the crisis "was less severe and more protracted" (Baragar 2011, 20) than it was in Canada as a whole. The official unemployment rate rose from 4.3% at the end of 2008 to 5.8% in October 2009 (ibid.) before declining to 5.3% in 2012, a full 2% below the pan-Canadian level. Labour force participation stayed higher than in Canada as a whole, registering 68.2% in Manitoba in December 2013 compared to 66.4% for Canada (Statistics Canada 2014c).

This recent regional economic record is best explained as a consequence of the quite diverse nature of the Manitoba economy, in which no single industry plays a key role akin to fossil fuel extraction in Alberta (Brownsey in this volume) or manufacturing's former role in Ontario (Evans and Fanelli in this volume). The public sector is proportionately larger than in most regions (final consumption spending by all levels of government as a percentage of Manitoba GDP was 27.6% in 2012, in comparison to 21.7% at the pan-Canadian level, 22.2% in Ontario, and 15.1% in Alberta [calculated from Statistics Canada 2014a]). In addition, the performance of capital in Manitoba has been shaped by the shift within manufacturing toward exporting to markets other than the US, construction by Manitoba Hydro, and the provincial government's policy course (Baragar 2011).

During the NDP's years in office, its fiscal policy did not stray from the party's overall social-liberal orientation. Business lobby groups never ceased to push for more of what they wanted, while the almost-complete lack of mobilization by Manitoba unions, community, and student organizations to place demands on the NDP meant the government felt very little pressure to deliver more for the working class or specific groups of oppressed people. The result was "relative stability of the economic and political landscape" (Levasseur 2014, 185).

The government ran surpluses in the 2007–08 and 2008–09 fiscal years. Following the requirements of the province's *Balanced Budget,*

Fiscal Management and Taxpayer Accountability Act (the current name of the balanced budget law, which was amended in 2008 to require that budgets be balanced over a four-year period rather than annually), in both years $110 million of the surplus was allocated to debt repayment. The province's fiscal stabilization or "rainy day" fund was assigned $128 million in the first year and $46 million in the second.

In November 2008, the government announced an economic stimulus plan that involved spending $4.7 billion over four years on infrastructure. The 2009 budget accelerated spending in the short term as a countercyclical measure, with a majority of the year's stimulus spending directed at building or upgrading roads and highways, post-secondary educational institutions and schools, and health care facilities (Manitoba Ministry of Finance 2009a). The negative impact of the crisis on government finances was first registered in the 2009–10 year: in nominal terms revenue fell by 1% from the previous year while spending rose by 5.5%.

In 2010, the government announced a Five-Year Economic Plan. This was presented as a "more responsible and balanced approach" (Wowchuk 2010, 1) to a recession than the PCs' cuts to public services and privatizations in the 1990s. It emphasized economic stimulus measures and eschewed across-the-board cuts to government spending in favour of a more selective combination of measures. Faced with the straightjacket of the balanced-budget law, which would have forced cuts and undermined the economic stimulus program, the government amended the legislation in order to allow the tabling of deficit budgets during an "economic recovery period" lasting from April 2010 to as late as the end of March 2014. The government pledged an end to deficit spending by 2014. The 2010 budget devoted a majority of new spending to health care, with half of government departments seeing reductions in spending (see also Conrad in this volume). Funding for public schools and post-secondary institutions continued to grow; university and college tuition fees, which had been frozen, were increased. A planned cut in corporate taxes was postponed until "the economy strengthens" (Wowchuk 2010, 7). The budget also announced the intention of negotiating "for a pause in wage increases" (ibid., 6) in the public sector. In practice, this led to employer demands, in bargaining with government workers and workers in the broader public sector, for collective agreements that included two years with no wage increases (discussed further below).

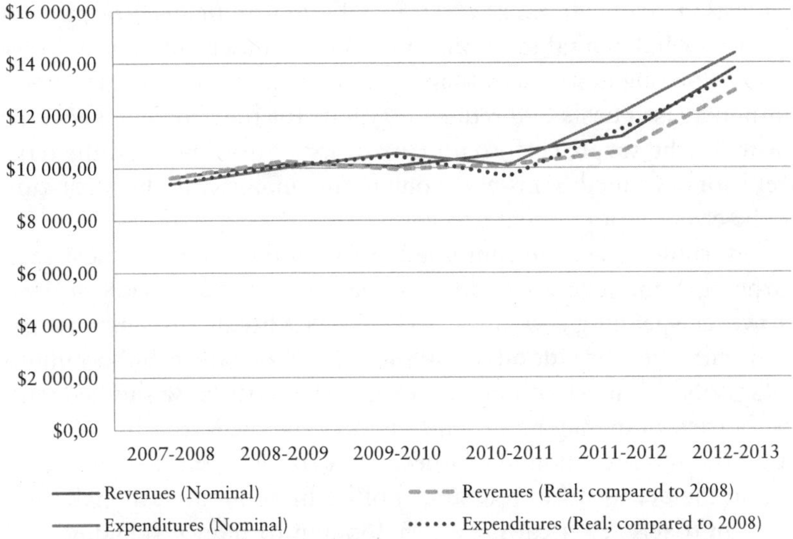

Source: Manitoba Ministry of Finance 2008; 2009; 2010; 2011; 2012; 2013.

Figure 4.1 Manitoba core government revenues and expenditures, 2008–13 (in millions)

The 2010–11 fiscal year saw a growth of government revenue, although when measured in 2008 dollars revenue was still 1.2% below the 2008–09 level. Nominal spending was up $321 million over the previous year. The gap between revenue and expenditure came in at $340 million, less than the $501 million of the year before (Manitoba Ministry of Finance 2011b).[3] The 2011 budget was introduced in an election year. The NDP looked unlikely to win a fourth term in office, as the PCs had been consistently leading in the polls since the autumn of 2010. The budget continued the infrastructure spending program but made the improvement of listing public housing as a higher priority. Road building continued to be the leading area of investment, followed by housing, health facilities, and all levels of education (Manitoba Ministry of Finance 2011a, 18). In terms of transfers to the broader public sector, universities were prioritized with 5% increases to their grants promised for three years. University tuition increases were pegged to the inflation rate. On the tax front, the government could proclaim that this year would be the first in which small businesses would pay no provincial income tax. The general corporation capital tax was also eliminated, and financial institutions with capital of up to $4 billion were made exempt from the provincial capital tax (ibid., 17). Unfortunately, there was widespread flooding in southern Manitoba in the spring of 2011. The flood both increased costs and reduced revenue for the provincial government. To the surprise of even many of its own supporters, the NDP were not defeated but instead won another majority in the legislature in the election of October 2011.

Government revenue continued to rise in the 2011–12 fiscal year, surpassing the level of 2008–09 when measured in 2008 dollars. However, spending shot up by 11%, in part because of costs associated with the 2011 floods, resulting in a shortfall of $910 million (Manitoba Ministry of Finance 2012). The NDP, now saddled with the burden of managing provincial public finances for another term at a time when economic prospects looked much bleaker than they had in the decade after it assumed office in 1999, took a "half-and-half approach" to fiscal pressures, looking to reduce spending and raise revenue in equal measure to manage the deficit (personal interview with a source close to the government, 15 November 2013). It announced a number of mergers, chosen both to cut costs in the broader public sector and for their high profile; Manitoba's eleven regional health authorities would be reduced to five, and the Manitoba Liquor Control Commission merged with the Manitoba Lotteries Corporation. Government departments were directed to combine and reorganize programs to trim costs without worsening frontline services. The provincial gas and tobacco taxes were raised. The base of the provincial sales tax (PST) was broadened by applying the tax to insurance services, cosmetic services, and expensive haircuts, a move designed to minimize negative impacts on people living in poverty. In addition, a "concerted effort" began to restrain labour costs in the civil service through vacancy management, but without layoffs (personal interview with a source close to the government, 15 November 2013). At the end of 2012, the government announced a privatization decision: the province's Property Registry, which had been turned from a government service into a special operating agency by the previous PC government, was sold to Teranet Manitoba for $75 million (Regier and Fernandez 2013).

Nominal spending was $248 million lower in 2012–13 but revenue also dipped slightly, resulting in a shortfall of $690 million (Manitoba Ministry of Finance 2013c). The 2013 budget promised "more responsible, innovative ways to reduce the cost of government and to increase efficiency" (Manitoba Ministry of Finance 2013b, 10) and moved the deadline for eliminating the deficit from 2014–15 to 2016–17. The "responsible, innovative" ways amounted mainly to a reduction of the ranks of the provincial civil service by 600 positions over three years and a number of office amalgamations within departments. The government also raised the PST from 7% to 8% as of July 2013, with the expressed intentions of dedicating the additional revenue to infrastructure spending and reversing the increase in a decade after matching funds from the federal government's Building Canada Fund had come to an end (Beaudette 2013). It was estimated that the rate increase would bring in close to $278 million more annually. Individuals would pay 54% of that total, with three-tenths of that share coming from households with annual incomes below $60,000. Businesses would pay 41% of the additional revenue; of that, four-tenths would be paid by construction firms, many of which could expect to profit from more spending on new infrastructure projects.[4]

Since the sales tax increase contravened the balanced-budget law, the government introduced a bill to suspend the need for a referendum along with its bill to increase the PST rate. The PCs responded with extensive filibustering in the legislature (Canadian Press 2013). Along with the Canadian Taxpayers Federation, they attempted with some success to use the tax increase to weaken popular support for the NDP. In the 2011 election, the NDP had received 46% of votes cast, the PCs 43.9%, and the Liberals 7.5% (CBC News 2011). By March 2014 one poll reported PC support at 46% among decided voters, the NDP at 28%, and the Liberals at 23% (Canadian Press 2014). This suggests that NDP support was eroded by having to politically administer Manitoba in a period of economic slowdown in which hostile media outlets amplified popular resentment of a tax increase that affects most people directly.

One post-budget move made at the end of 2013 and worthy of mention was the government's decision to impose a retroactive 4% cut, amounting to $3.1 million, on social service agencies during the 2013–14 fiscal year. While media coverage suggested a link between the cut and the government's desire "to have a stash of money available to act on recommendations" (Welch 2014) arising from the commission of inquiry into the 2005 death of an indigenous girl, Phoenix Sinclair, one informed observer reported that the money clawed back represented the value of worker positions left vacant by agency managers (personal communication with U-1, 18 February 2014).[5]

The 2014–15 budget introduced in March 2014 reflected continuity in the direction of fiscal policy. However, its commitment to implementing "lean management across government to maximize value and eliminate duplication and repetitive processes" (Manitoba Ministry of Finance 2014a, 11) and the accompanying decision to create an advisory "lean council" chaired by a manager at aircraft maintenance firm Standard Aero (Owen 2014) was an initiative without precedent in the province. Although lean methods of work organization have been introduced in some companies and public-sector institutions in Manitoba, the provincial government's workforce itself had not yet been subjected to them to any significant degree. This initiative was probably motivated by the desire to reduce labour costs without cutting services. The application of lean work reorganization could be expected to intensify work and lead to the redeployment of workers, layoffs, or a combination of both.[6]

One concern undoubtedly high on the minds of those who designed the budget was the decline in per capita federal transfer payments to Manitoba caused by changes in federal government policy and a reduction in the province's population estimate by Statistics Canada. In 2014–15, total transfers were essentially the same in nominal terms as in 2009–10. On a per capita basis, this represented a decline of 5.7%. When adjusted to account for inflation, the real decline was 13.9% (Manitoba Ministry of Finance 2014b, D2–3). By 2014–15, federal transfers accounted for 25.8% of provincial revenue, down from 31% in 2010–11 (Manitoba Ministry of Finance 2015, 45). All efforts by the provincial government to persuade the federal government to revise its policy on transfers and to challenge the Statistics Canada population figure were unsuccessful, as Harper's Conservatives were quite hostile to the Manitoba NDP (personal communication with a source close to the government, 18 March 2014).

The 2015 budget was brought in by a government that, over the previous six months, had been wracked by a leadership crisis caused by the NDP's dismal performance in opinion polls. Faced with five cabinet ministers publicly asking him to consider resigning, Premier Selinger hung on and won a very narrow victory in the leadership vote at the NDP convention in March. The provincial budget that followed was very much a pre-election document that featured further investments in infrastructure. It made significant cuts to some departments, most notably Finance, Labour and Immigration, the Civil Service Commission, Mineral Resources, and Infrastructure and

Transportation. In contrast, Housing and Community Development saw its budget grow by 12.5% (Levasseur 2015). It is hard not to interpret the decision by Moody's Investors Service to downgrade Manitoba's credit rating from AA-1 to AA-2, announced in July 2015 (Lambert 2015), as a reprimand for the government's failure to embrace the orthodox neoliberal austerity agenda. Contrary to the impression given by media coverage of this decision, the cost of servicing Manitoba's growing public debt actually remained low and manageable, thanks to low interest rates: 5.7% of provincial revenue in 2014–15, down from 6.2% in 2012–13 (Manitoba Ministry of Finance 2015, 39). The media also failed to report that in 1998–99, the last full fiscal year under the previous PC government, about 8.5% of revenue had been spent on servicing the public debt (calculated from Manitoba Ministry of Finance 1999).

Fiscal policy is a crucial part of how, after the onset of the global slump, the NDP government sought to use the limited provincial tools of state power available to it to reproduce capitalist society within its jurisdiction in a manner that met its objectives. The way the NDP acted in office reflected its version of social-liberalism as well as the pressures to which all provincial governments are subjected. The government showed respect for the fundamental parameters of neoliberalism – witness its efforts to hold down public-sector wages and reassure bond markets by, for example, proclaiming its plan for eliminating the deficit by a specific year. Within those limits, it attempted to boost economic activity by sustaining the overall level of spending by government and broader public-sector institutions, minimizing cuts to government services and jobs, directing public funds to infrastructure construction, and trying to attract new investment to the province in targeted ways. The decision to suspend the "depoliticizing" rules of the balanced-budget law suggests that concerns about demonstrating fidelity to the budget-slashing version of anti-deficit ideology were trumped by a pragmatic commitment to avoid cuts that would probably have hurt the NDP at the polls and by an appreciation that austerity would slow economic growth (a concern recently voiced by analysts at the International Monetary Fund [Ostry, Loungani, and Furceri 2016]).

During its last term in office, the NDP sought to reduce the deficit by both increasing revenue and slowing the growth of government spending rather than simply one or the other; the increase to the PST in 2013 was part of this strategy, as was the pledge to apply lean work organization methods to the provincial government. While inspired in some ways by New Labour in the UK – the Manitoba party proclaims itself "Today's NDP" in implicit contrast with the Keynesian social democratic NDP of the past – the government did not try to emulate New Labour's very significant neoliberalization of the public sector by pushing privatization, contracting out or engaging in public–private partnerships (see also Graefe and Ouimet in this volume). The overall result of the mild impact of the global slump in Manitoba and the government's approach was that provincial government revenue in the 2012–13 fiscal year was, when measured in 2008 dollars, 7.5% above the 2007–08 level. However, the level of real expenditure on health (administered by the Ministries of Health and Healthy Living) was 18.6% higher. The real amount spent on education was up 5.1% (calculated from Manitoba Ministry of Finance 2008; 2013).

THE EFFECTS OF FISCAL POLICY

The significance of the NDP government's policy course is best understood by examining its effects on public-sector workers, public services, and the users of these services, bearing in mind the political economy and policy pressures examined above. The most obvious way that fiscal policy plays out for public-sector workers is its impact on collective bargaining. The public sector is even more highly unionized in Manitoba than in Canada as a whole: Manitoba's union density was 77.9% in 2012, compared to 74.5% in Canada (Statistics Canada 2014b). The government's 2010 decision to insist on a "wage pause" led to the officials of most public-sector unions in the province agreeing on settlements, usually of four years in length, that contained two years with no wage increases and two years with increases of 2.9%, followed by ratification of these deals by workers ("Manitoba Public Sector" n.d.). The settlement for nurses was sweetened by a 2% lump-sum payment in the contract's first year (*Winnipeg Free Press* 2010). The most notable hiccup along the way was the January 2011 rejection by provincial government workers of the tentative agreement negotiated by the leadership of the Manitoba Government and General Employees' Union (MGEU). The deal contained a no-layoff clause along with the two-year wage freeze that proved to be the target of worker ire (Welch 2011). The 54% "no" vote on the tentative agreement came as a shock, given that there is no recent history in MGEU of rank-and-file militancy or activist self-organization independent of the union's officialdom. MGEU officials quickly sat down and negotiated a slightly different contract, campaigned in favour of it, and secured a two-thirds majority for ratification (Manitoba Government and General Employees' Union 2011).

Workers whose employers do not rely solely or primarily on provincial government funding fared better than those who do. Teachers were the largest exception to the "wage pause." The Manitoba Teachers' Society, which lacks the right to strike, reached settlements with school divisions containing 3% increases in 2010–11 and 2% in each of the following three years (Manitoba Teachers' Society 2013). City of Winnipeg workers, represented by Canadian Union of Public Employees Local 500, managed to get 1% for 2012 and 2.5% for the following two years (CUPE Local 500 2011).

Nevertheless, support workers in health care and education, along with many workers in social services, found their employers "definitely trying to keep wages down." Many such workers received wage increases "less than inflation" (personal interview with U-4, 26 February 2014). Although reliable data is not available, anecdotal evidence suggests that the presence of workers of colour in these parts of the public sector is especially significant. As a result, wage restraint is probably being experienced in a racially inequitable way.

Fiscal policy's effects on public-sector workers are certainly not limited to what is negotiated at the bargaining table. Workloads, staffing levels and other aspects of labour processes are also affected. Provincial government employees report that they are "doing more than they used to ... doing more with less" in the words of one union official (personal interview with U-1, 13 November 2013). The Manitoba civil service – whose employees in 2013 were, thanks in part to employment equity policy, 54% women, 13.6% indigenous, and 8.3% people of colour, making it an important source of better jobs for oppressed people (Manitoba Civil Service Commission 2013, 7) – has not been hit by layoffs. Rather, small workforce reductions have taken place through attrition, with some vacant positions left unfilled (personal interview with U-1, 13 November 2013). As a result, the total number of provincial government employees in 2013 was 1.1% below the 2012 level (data provided by U-1). Attrition has been most noticeable among administrative support staff. Seasonal workers at the Department of Conservation and Water Stewardship have also been particularly affected, with their number of weeks of employment reduced and spending on basic supplies and equipment trimmed (personal interview with U-1, 13 November 2013). While only slightly over 3% of the provincial workforce are classified as casual employees, their numbers have been rising (data provided by U-1).

Outside the civil service, the situation is often worse. Even though health care spending – which, it must be recalled, is highly reliant on federal transfer payments to the province – has increased significantly, nurses report growing pressures on the job. The number of patients per nurse is up and, in addition, there are "less support services and less resources" (personal interview with U-2 and U-3, 9 December 2013). Nurses indicate that supplies are sometimes not available. This adds to workload, since "staff are running around trying to find things that they need to deliver the care" (ibid.). It has become more common for nurses to skip meal breaks and other breaks, even working twelve-hour shifts without any break. Both hospital-based and public health nurses report that when they are sick or on vacation they are less likely to be replaced, which adds to the workload of the staff on the job, or they are replaced temporarily with a health care aide rather than a nurse. Vacant positions are regularly not posted for a period of time. In some cases, when full-time positions become vacant they are replaced with less than full-time positions, particularly when the job does not involve direct care to patients. Registered nurse (RN) vacancies are sometimes reposted as licensed practical nurse (LPN) jobs, a trend best explained as "about deskilling" since LPNs are "a cheaper workforce" but one that, in some cases, does the same work as RNs (ibid.). Management is also changing. Nursing managers are more likely now than in the past to not possess a nursing background or even experience as a health care provider, but instead come from another line of work such as food services or accounting. Nevertheless, "that could be the person you're calling at three o'clock in the morning regarding patient care decisions" (ibid.). Nurses report seeing a shift toward decisions about staffing being made at the level of the regional health authority (RHA) rather than the individual health care facility, with facility managers facing pressures from the RHA "to decrease expenses." In addition, "lean management has been implemented" in some facilities (personal interview with U-2 and U-3, 9 December 2013). What this suggests is that increased provincial spending on a health care system in which not only hospital costs but also physician fees and drug costs have been rising rapidly (Canadian Institute for Health Information 2013) has been accompanied by incremental neoliberalization, to the detriment of the quality of nurses' jobs.

Nurses are certainly not the only public-sector workers experiencing such neoliberal pressures. Work intensification is happening in many workplaces. For example, RHA managers have reduced the time allowed per task for some of the tasks carried out by home care workers. In personal care homes, where residents' health is poorer because home care allows some people to stay longer in their own homes, "the job is more strenuous" and some managers do not bring in relief staff when regular workers are sick or absent for other reasons (personal interview with U-1, 13 November 2013). Employers are "demanding more flexibility with people's schedules and their job descriptions" (personal interview with U-4, 26 February 2014), and larger employers are increasingly adopting forms of electronic monitoring. It is more common to find workers who are officially part-time nonetheless working full-time hours. There is evidence of a trend by employers to reduce the number of "high-end jobs," such as trades and information technology (IT), "by attrition, by restructuring, by whatever means they can" (ibid.). The contracting out of such work is spreading. Where such work is still being done by public-sector workers, employers are "squeezing them all the time" (ibid.). In particular, IT workers "in many sectors report being overworked" (ibid.). Reports of workers close to retirement being subjected to pressures from management that make them "miserable so they'll leave sooner" (ibid.) are multiplying. Not surprisingly, workers' physical and mental health suffers in these conditions. Although the desire to reduce labour costs is an important factor driving managers, one union observer adds that employers also want workers with lower expectations. The expectations of new hires in public-sector positions and those of employees in firms that handle work that was previously done by public-sector workers are generally lower than those of long-serving, unionized public-sector workers (ibid.).

As we have seen, provincial and provincially funded public services in Manitoba did not experience significant spending cuts under the NDP. Where staffing and/or resources were reduced, it seems that in many cases public-sector workers were able to preserve the same quality and level of services by putting in greater efforts. For example, health care workers "have to work a lot harder ... to keep the care good" (personal interview with U-2 and U-3, 9 December 2013). Nevertheless, services have not gone unaffected by fiscal policy decisions. Where casualization of the health care workforce has happened, "you just can't provide the high level of service if people have these jobs where they don't know what's coming next" (personal interview with U-4, 26 February 2014). Child services are an important example of an area where growing demands are straining services. The number of children in care in Manitoba – over 80% of whom are indigenous (Puxley 2014) – grew by nearly half between 2006 and 2012. Funding has not kept up, and the result has sometimes been "unmanageable workloads [for social workers], which increase the likelihood of a child or family not getting the care they need" (Manitoba Government and General Employees' Union 2013, 8).

Employment and Income Assistance (EIA), Manitoba's welfare program, has also been affected by fiscal policy priorities. Between 1992 and the early years of the twenty-first century, EIA rates in real terms declined significantly for persons deemed employable, persons with disabilities, and couples with children. With indigenous people massively overrepresented among the poor in Manitoba (MacKinnon 2013; see also Hicks in this volume), this erosion was no more race-neutral than the overburdening of child services. Between 2007 and 2013, real EIA rates for single employable people grew by just over 10% but were still about 3% below their value in 1999 when the NDP took office. In contrast, over the same period the benefits for persons with disabilities on EIA declined in real terms by 2%, rates for single parents fell by close to 7%, and rates for couples with children shrank by 6% (calculated from Tweddle, Battle, and Torjman 2013, 80. Percentages rounded). The 2014 budget brought a measure of relief for people collecting EIA, in the form of a new program called Rent Assist that resulted in small increases in money for housing costs for the 15,500 EIA recipients who rent from private landlords. Rent Assist is also available to the lowest-paid wage-earners (Fernandez and McCracken 2014). This was accompanied by the ongoing construction of affordable housing. The 1,500 units built compared favourably to the records of the federal government and most other provinces (Brandon 2014).

WAS THERE AN ALTERNATIVE?

Manitoba's experience since the onset of the global economic crisis demonstrates that a relatively mild recession and a course of provincial economic policy that eschewed calls for large spending cuts and a rapid return to balanced budgets still resulted in negative effects on public-sector workers and, to a lesser extent, public services. That the damage done under the NDP was much less than what was inflicted in many other jurisdictions should not obscure the reality that some harm was done (or that services and working conditions in the public sector were far from adequate prior to 2008). It is also important to remember Mirowski's point, cited earlier in this chapter, that the ultimate cause of the damage was a crisis of capitalism, mediated by an aggressively neoliberal federal government and a social-liberal provincial government.

Considerations of alternative policies in defence of the public sector need to bear these structural pressures in mind. It is also undeniable that provincial governments have much less room to maneuver than the federal government, since only the latter has monetary policy tools at its disposal. Different decisions at the federal level would have had a significant impact on the ability of the provincial government to preserve public-sector jobs and services since, as mentioned above, in real terms per capita federal–provincial transfers in Manitoba have fallen considerably. A recalibration of how the overall costs of social programs are shared between the federal and provincial governments could make an enormous difference. That said, within the existing constraints the provincial government still had some ability to steer a different course.

During its years in office the NDP made its fiscal position more difficult through a series of small tax cuts and credits, some of which were mentioned earlier. These included a staged reduction for all senior citizens, regardless of income, of the education portion of the property tax, which was eliminated altogether in 2016. Another was a 30% tax credit for investments in companies engaged in mineral exploration. Reversing or eliminating these policies would have boosted revenue. The government could also have found new ways to improve the quality of services while spending the same amount or even somewhat less money by adopting popular planning across the public sector. The heart of this element of what has been called the democratic administration approach to public administration is "the utilization of the first-hand, uncodified knowledge of state workers and clients as the best route to improving the efficiency of the public sector and of enhancing its responsiveness to client needs" (Shields and Evans 1998, 119). Driven as it is by the needs of those who deliver and use public services, popular planning is qualitatively different from the managerial agenda of lean work reorganization that the NDP government endorsed in its last term.

These alternatives are far from revolutionary. However, it was always extremely unlikely that the Manitoba NDP would move to raise more revenue by making capital pay or that they would begin promoting popular planning. Such measures could have been attempted but were inconceivable to the leadership of "Today's NDP." They would only have been adopted as the result of a great deal of external pressure. This could only have come from highly mobilized unions and community organizations. However, after the NDP came to office in 1999 the labour officialdom and leaders of community groups almost without exception tailed the NDP rather than challenging it. No heed was taken of the argument made by two left-wing NDP members that it was vital "to mobilize the rank and file to put the pressure on the ... government to respond to the needs of workers with progressive legislation and programs" (Black and Silver 2004). Errol Black and Jim Silver also suggested "mobilizing workers for extra-parliamentary action against this government would prepare the labour movement to take on the next Conservative government" (ibid.). The absence of this kind of mobilization contributed to the remarkably dormant condition of most unions in Manitoba. This will probably have dire consequences for efforts to defend public-sector jobs and services from the PC government that was elected in 2016.

NOTES

1 Thanks to Craig Adolphe for indispensable research assistance; to Fletcher Baragar, Ian Hudson, and a reader who wishes to remain anonymous for their comments on a draft; and to Monique Woroniak for providing me with a number of relevant articles. Thanks also to all those who agreed to be interviewed as part of my research.

2 This expansion of the carceral state is not a process separate from neoliberalization. As Loic Wacquant argues, "The growth and glorification of the penal wing of the state are an integral component of the neoliberal Leviathan," and a "stunning rehabilitation and stupendous expansion of the penal apparatus of the state ... have accompanied the wave of market dominance" (Wacquant 2012, 74). Readers interested in the relationship between neoliberalism and the carceral state can consult the 2010 issue of *Theoretical Criminology* (14.1) devoted to discussing Wacquant's work.

3 Here and in what follows, I discuss the core issues of revenues and expenditures rather than officially reported deficit figures.

4 Calculated from "Impact of Sales Tax Rate Increases on Households & Businesses" (unpublished Manitoba government document, n.d.).
5 Sources who are union officials are designated U-[Number].
6 On lean work organization, see Parker and Slaughter 1994.

REFERENCES

Baragar, Fletcher. 2011. *Report on the Manitoba Economy 2011.* Winnipeg: Canadian Centre for Policy Alternatives Manitoba.

Baragar, Fletcher, and John Loxley. 2011. "The Staple Economy in Manitoba: Neo-Liberalism and the Challenge of Development." Unpublished.

Beaudette, Teghan. 2013. "Manitoba to Hike PST to 8%." *CBC News*, 16 April. http://www.cbc.ca/news/canada/manitoba/manitoba-to-hike-pst-to-8-1.1310688.

Black, Errol and Jim Silver. 2004. *Is Labour's Future in the Streets?* Fast Facts. Winnipeg: Canadian Centre for Policy Alternatives, 10 October. https://www.policyalternatives.ca/publications/reports/fastfacts-labours-future-streets.

– 2008. *Building a Better World: An Introduction to Trade Unionism in Canada.* 2nd ed. Halifax: Fernwood Publishing.

Brandon, Josh. 2014. *Provincial Record on Housing a Welcome Achievement.* Fast Facts. Ottawa: Canadian Centre for Policy Alternatives, 14 April. https://www.policyalternatives.ca/publications/commentary/fast-facts-provincial-record-housing-welcome-achievement.

Bruner, Christopher M. 2008. "States, Markets and Gatekeepers: Public-Private Regulatory Regimes in an Era of Economic Globalization." *Michigan Journal of International Law* 30: 125–76.

Burnham, Peter. 1999. "The Politics of Economic Management in the 1990s." *New Political Economy* 4 (1): 37–54.

Burrows, Sel. 2011. "Andrew Swan Might Fit as New Tory Leader." *Winnipeg Free Press*, 26 November. http://www.winnipegfreepress.com/opinion/analysis/andrew-swan-might-fit-as-new-tory-leader-134524933.html.

Cairns, James, and Alan Sears. 2012. *The Democratic Imagination: Envisioning Popular Power in the Twenty-First Century.* Toronto: University of Toronto Press.

Campbell, Al. 2005. "The Birth of Neoliberalism in the United States: A Reorganization of Capitalism." In *Neoliberalism: A Critical Reader*, edited by Alfredo Saad-Filho and Deborah Johnston, 187–98. London: Pluto.

Canadian Institute for Health Information. 2013. *National Health Expenditure Trends, 1975 to 2013*. Ottawa: CIHI.

Canadian Press. 2013. "Bureaucrats Told Manitoba to Follow Law on PST Tax Hike." 9 October. http://www.cbc.ca/news/canada/manitoba/bureaucrats-told-manitoba-to-follow-law-on-pst-tax-hike-1.1931406.

– 2014. "New Poll Suggests Manitoba's NDP Struggling to Regain Support." 7 April. http://globalnews.ca/news/1254891/new-poll-suggests-manitobas-ndp-struggling-to-regain-support/.

CBC *News*. 2011. "Manitoba NDP Wins Majority Government." 4 October. http://www.cbc.ca/news/canada/manitoba/manitoba-ndp-wins-majority-government-1.1100791.

CUPE (Canadian Union of Public Employees) Local 500. 2011. *Collective Agreement Wage Rates*.

Clarke, Simon. 1983. "State, Class Struggle, and the Reproduction of Capital." *Kapitalistate* 10/11: 113–34.

– 1988. *Keynesianism, Monetarism and the Crisis of the State*. Aldershot: Edward Elgar.

Davidson, Neil. 2016. "Crisis Neoliberalism and Regimes of Permanent Exception." *Critical Sociology* 43 (4–5): 613–34. doi:10.1177/0896920516655386.

Dobchuk-Land, Bronwyn. 2017. "'Tough on Crime, Tough on the Causes of Crime': Liberal Carceral Logics and the Reproduction of Settler Colonial Violence in Winnipeg, MB, Canada." PhD diss., City University of New York.

Evans, Bryan. 2012. "From Protest Movement to Neoliberal Management: Canada's New Democratic Party in Era of Permanent Austerity." In *Social Democracy after the Cold War*, edited by Bryan Evans and Ingo Schmidt, 45–97. Edmonton: Athabasca University Press.

Fernandez, Lynne, and Molly McCracken. 2014. *Manitoba Budget a Leap Forward for Poverty Reduction*. Winnipeg: Canadian Centre for Policy Alternatives, 6 March. https://www.policyalternatives.ca/publications/commentary/manitoba-budget-leap-forward-poverty-reduction.

Gordon, Todd. 2007. "Towards an Anti-Racist Marxist State Theory: A Canadian Case Study." *Capital and Class* 91: 1–29.

Konzelmann, Suzanne J. 2014. "The Political Economics of Austerity." *Cambridge Journal of Economics* 38 (4): 701–41. doi:10.1093/cje/bet076.

Krugman, Paul. 2013. "Ideological Ratings." *New York Times*, 8 November. https://krugman.blogs.nytimes.com/2013/11/08/ideological-ratings/.

Lambert, Steve. 2015. "Manitoba's Credit Rating Downgraded Due to Growing Debt." *CBC News*, 10 July. http://www.cbc.ca/news/canada/manitoba/manitoba-s-credit-rating-downgraded-due-to-growing-debt-1.3147120.

Levasseur, Karine. 2014. "The Growing Instability in Manitoba: The Selinger Majority, Budgetary Reductions, and Increasing Taxes." *Manitoba Law Journal: Underneath the Golden Boy* 36 (2): 181–99.

– 2015. "On We Go to Manitoba's Next Provincial Election: Whither the NDP?" *Manitoba Law Journal: Underneath the Golden Boy* 38 (2): 102–22.

Loxley, John. 1995–96. "Balanced Budget Legislation or Bad Budget Legislation?" *Canadian Dimension* 19–20 (December–January): 54.

MacKinnon, Shauna. 2013. *First Nations Poverty and the Canadian Economy: Aligning Policy with What Works*. Ottawa: Canadian Centre for Policy Alternatives, 10 July. https://www.policyalternatives.ca/publications/commentary/first-nations-poverty-and-canadian-economy.

Manitoba. 2017a. "Employment and Income Assistance for Single Parents." https://www.gov.mb.ca/fs/eia/.

– 2017b. "Employment and Income Assistance for Persons with Disabilities." https://www.gov.mb.ca/fs/eia/.

– 2017c. "Employment and Income Assistance for the General Assistance Category." https://www.gov.mb.ca/fs/eia/.

Manitoba Government and General Employees' Union. 2011. "Civil Service Accepts Offer." 11 March. https://www.mgeu.ca/news-and-multimedia/news/read,article/398/civil-service-accepts-offer#sthash.4lJn9XiD.dpbs.

– 2013. *Services First: Commonsense Proposals for the 2013 Manitoba Budget*. 13 February. http://www.mgeu.ca/uploads/ck/files/mgeu_complete_services_first_final.pdf?t=1363465030.

Manitoba. Manitoba Civil Service Commission. 2013. *Annual Report 2012–2013*. Winnipeg: Civil Service Commission. http://www.manitoba.ca/csc/publications/annrpt/pdf/2012-13_annualrpt_en-fr.pdf.

Manitoba. Ministry of Finance. 1999. "Province of Manitoba Notes to the Preliminary Unaudited Financial Statements for the Year Ended March 31, 1999." Winnipeg: Ministry of Finance. http://www.gov.mb.ca/finance/publications/pubs/quarterlyreports/4qr9899.pdf.

– 2008. *The Province of Manitoba Annual Report For the Year Ended March 31, 2008*. Winnipeg: Ministry of Finance. http://www.gov.mb.ca/finance/publications/pubs/annualreports/annreport_1_08.pdf.

– 2009a. *Manitoba Budget 2009*. Winnipeg: Ministry of Finance. https://www.gov.mb.ca/finance/budgets/provincialbudgets.html.

– 2009b. *The Province of Manitoba Annual Report for the Year Ended March 31, 2009*. Winnipeg: Ministry of Finance. http://www.gov.mb.ca/finance/publications/pubs/annualreports/public_accounts_v1_09.pdf.

– 2010. *The Province of Manitoba Annual Report for the Year Ended March 31, 2010*. Winnipeg: Ministry of Finance. http://www.gov.mb.ca/finance/publications/pubs/annualreports/pubacct_1_10.pdf.

– 2011a. *Manitoba Budget 2011*. Winnipeg: Ministry of Finance. https://www.gov.mb.ca/finance/budgets/provincialbudgets.html.

– 2011b. *Province of Manitoba Annual Report for the Year Ended March 31, 2011*. Winnipeg: Ministry of Finance. http://www.gov.mb.ca/finance/publications/pubs/annualreports/pubacct_1_11.pdf.

– 2012. *The Province of Manitoba Annual Report for the Year Ended March 31, 2012*. Winnipeg: Ministry of Finance. http://www.gov.mb.ca/finance/publications/pubs/annualreports/pubacct_1_12.pdf.

– 2013a. *Budget Paper A: Economic Review and Outlook*. Winnipeg: Ministry of Finance. https://www.gov.mb.ca/finance/budget13/pubs/economy.pdf.

– 2013b. *Manitoba Budget 2013*. Winnipeg: Ministry of Finance. https://www.gov.mb.ca/finance/budgets/provincialbudgets.html.

– 2013c. *The Province of Manitoba Annual Report for the Year Ended March 31, 2013*. Winnipeg: Ministry of Finance. http://www.gov.mb.ca/finance/publications/pubs/annualreports/pubacct_1_13.pdf.

– 2014a. *Manitoba Budget 2014*. Winnipeg: Ministry of Finance. https://www.gov.mb.ca/finance/budgets/provincialbudgets.html.

– 2014b. *Budget Paper D: Update on Fiscal Arrangements*. Winnipeg: Ministry of Finance. https://www.gov.mb.ca/finance/budget14/papers/fiscal_arrangements.pdf.

– 2015. *The Province of Manitoba Annual Report for the Year Ended March 31, 2015*. Winnipeg: Ministry of Finance. https://www.gov.mb.ca/finance/publications/pubs/annualreports/pubacct_1_15.pdf.

– n.d. *Impact of Sales Tax Rate Increases on Households & Businesses*. Unpublished government document.

"Manitoba Public Sector Collective Bargaining Settlements – 2010 and 2011." n.d. http://umanitoba.ca/admin/human_resources/services/media/MB_Public_Sector_revised%285%29.pdf.

Manitoba Teachers' Society. 2013. *Annual Report 2012–2013*. Winnipeg: MTS. http://www.mbteach.org/pdfs/ar/AR_12-13.pdf.

McCracken, Molly. 2013. *Federal Off-Loading Hurts Us All.* Ottawa: Canadian Centre for Policy Alternatives, 23 July. https://www.policyalternatives.ca/publications/commentary/fast-facts-federal-loading-hurts-us-all.

McCormack, Geoffrey. 2013. "The Great Exception? Canada and the Global Slump." Paper presented at Rethinking Marxism Conference, University of Massachusetts Amherst, 21 September.

McNally, David. 2011. *Global Slump: The Economics and Politics of Crisis and Resistance.* Oakland: PM Press.

Mirowski, Philip. 2013. *Never Let a Serious Crisis Go to Waste: How Neoliberalism Survived the Financial Meltdown.* London: Verso Books.

Ostry, Jonathan D., Prakash Loungani, and Davide Furceri. 2016. "Neoliberalism: Oversold?" *Finance and Development* 53 (2). http://www.imf.org/external/pubs/ft/fandd/2016/06/ostry.htm.

Owen, Bruce. 2014. "The Dean of Lean." *Winnipeg Free Press*, 7 March. http://www.winnipegfreepress.com/local/the-dean-of-lean-248954871.html.

Parker, Mike, and Jane Slaughter. 1994. *Working Smart: A Union Guide to Participation Programs and Reengineering.* Detroit: Labor Notes.

Peck, Jamie, Nik Theodore, and Neil Brenner. 2012. "Neoliberalism Resurgent? Market Rule after the Great Recession." *South Atlantic Quarterly* 111 (2): 265–88.

Peters, John. 2012. "The Remaking of Leviathan: The State and Public Sector Reform in Advanced Capitalist Countries." *Socialist Studies/Études Socialistes* 8 (2): 109–33. https://www.socialiststudies.com/index.php/sss/article/viewFile/23548/17432.

Puxley, Chinta. 2014. "Manitoba Has No Right to Know about Apprehended Kids on Reserves, Says Chief." *CBC News*, 20 April. http://www.cbc.ca/news/canada/manitoba/manitoba-has-no-right-to-know-about-apprehended-kids-on-reserves-say-chiefs-1.2616245.

Radice, Hugo. 2011. "Cutting Government Deficits: Economic Science or Class War?" *Alternate Routes* 22: 87–102.

Regier, Andy, and Lynne Fernandez. 2013. *First a Ripple, Then a Wave.* Ottawa: Canadian Centre for Policy Alternatives, 28 February. https://www.policyalternatives.ca/publications/commentary/fast-facts-first-ripple-then-wave.

Saunders, Kelly L. 2010. "Manitoba's Progressive Conservative Party: A 'Great Renewal' or Continued Disarray?" In *Manitoba Politics and*

Government: Issues, Institutions, Traditions, edited by Paul G. Thomas and Curtis Brown, 96–127. Winnipeg: University of Manitoba Press.

Seymour, Richard. 2014. *Against Austerity: How We Can Fix the Crisis They Made*. London: Pluto Press.

Shields, John, and Bryan Evans. 1998. *Shrinking the State: Globalization and Public Administration "Reform."* Halifax: Fernwood Publishing.

Statistics Canada. 2014a. *Table 384-0038 Gross Domestic Product, Expenditure-Based, Provincial and Territorial, Annual (Dollars x 1,000,000)*. CANSIM (database). http://www5.statcan.gc.ca/cansim/pick-choisir?id=3840038&p2=33&retrLang=eng&lang=eng.

– 2014b. *Table 282-0078 Labour Force Survey Estimates (LFS), Employees by Union Coverage, North America Industry Classification System (NAICS), Sex and Age Group, Annual (Persons)*. CANSIM (database). http://www5.statcan.gc.ca/cansim/a05?lang=eng&id=2820078&pattern=2820078&searchTypeyValue=1&p2=35.

– 2014c. *Table 282-0087 Labour Force Survey Estimates (LFS), by Sex and Age Group, Seasonally Adjusted and Unadjusted, Monthly (Persons Unless Otherwise Noted)*. CANSIM (database). http://www5.statcan.gc.ca/cansim/a26?lang=eng&retrLang=eng&id=2820087&paSer=&pattern=&stByVal=1&p1=1&p2=37&tabMode=dataTable&csid=.

– 2014d. *Table 183-0002 Public Sector Employment, Wages and Salaries, Seasonally Unadjusted and Adjusted, Monthly*. CANSIM (database). http://www5.statcan.gc.ca/cansim/a26?lang=eng&retrLang=eng&id=1830002&pattern=public+sector+employment&tabMode=data Table&srchLan=-1&p1=1&p2=-1.

Steele, Graham. 2013. "Eavesdropping on the Minister of Finance." *CBC News*, 19 December. http://www.cbc.ca/news/canada/nova-scotia/graham-steele-eavesdropping-on-the-minister-of-finance-1.2470119.

Stewart, David and Jared Wesley. 2010. "Sterling Lyon, 1977–1981." In *Manitoba Premiers of the 19th and 20th Centuries*, edited by Barry Ferguson and Robert Wardhaugh, 308–30. Regina: Canadian Plains Research Centre.

Tweddle, Anne, Ken Battle, and Sherri Torjman. 2013. *Welfare in Canada 2012*. Ottawa: Caledon Institute of Social Policy.

Wacquant, Loic. 2012. "Three Steps to a Historical Anthropology of Actually Existing Neoliberalism." *Social Anthropology/Anthropologie Sociale* 20 (1): 66–79.

Welch, Mary-Agnes. 2011. "MGEU Workers Nix Austerity Deal." *Winnipeg Free Press*, 23 January. https://www.winnipegfreepress.com/local/mgeu-workers-nix-austerity-deal-114443124.html.

– 2014. "Agencies Hit with Cash Cuts." *Winnipeg Free Press*, 30 January. http://www.winnipegfreepress.com/local/agencies-hit-with-cash-cuts-242708251.html.

Winnipeg Free Press. 2010. "Manitoba Nurses Reach Tentative Deal." 29 May. https://www.winnipegfreepress.com/local/manitoba-nurses-reach-tentative-deal-95173069.html.

Wowchuk, Rosanne. 2010. *The 2010 Manitoba Budget Address*. Winnipeg: Ministry of Finance. https://www.gov.mb.ca/finance/budgets/pubs/budget2010/speech10.pdf.

CHAPTER FIVE

Ontario in an Age of Austerity: Common Sense Reloaded

BRYAN EVANS AND CARLO FANELLI

Given the importance of the provincial state and the array of public institutions that compose it in providing the mechanisms for the political management of social and economic development, it is astonishing that there is so little analysis concerned with Canada's provinces. The paucity of province-focused analysis is still more curious given that the Canadian constitution, by omission rather than design, assigns to the provinces responsibility for crucially important social and public services such as primary, secondary, and post-secondary education; health; and social services. These social policy fields have accounted for between 66% and 71% of Ontario's provincial expenditures from the late 1960s through to 2006 and then jumped to roughly 80% of total expenditures as the Dalton McGuinty Liberals entered their second term of government (Public Accounts of Ontario 1996–08). Given the prominence of social program expenditures within the Ontario budget (as well as that of other provinces) and the high rate of unionization of the workers who deliver these services, it makes sense that some of the most aggressive forms of neoliberal experimentation in Canada have been observed at the level of the provincial state. Ontario's turn to neoliberalism tends to be identified with the election of the Progressive Conservatives under the leadership of Mike Harris. While the election of the "Common Sense Revolutionaries" was indeed a significant moment politically, it was, in historical perspective, a particularly triumphal episode in a process that stretched back to the late 1960s when, just as Ontario set out in earnest on a province-building project, certain voices raised alarms about the scope and cost of that project.

THE LONG ROAD TO COLLECTIVE BARGAINING IN THE PUBLIC SECTOR

In 1944, Ontario premier George Drew announced the formation of the Joint Advisory Council (JAC) to be made up of government and the representatives of provincial public-sector associations to voluntarily discuss employer–employee relations. Four years later, drawing on federal Order-in-Council P.C. 1003, which first established the provisions for union certification, legal obligations for both parties, and prohibitions on unfair labour practices, the Ontario government passed the Ontario Labour Relations Act (OLRA). OLRA extended the right to strike and bargain collectively to workers in the private sector as well as state agencies at an arm's length from core public-service workers, including those at the municipal scale. Ontario's civil servants, however, continued to be denied the right to organize and bargain collectively, just as public servants in the other provinces save for Saskatchewan. Through the 1950s, the JAC was virtually extinguished as a means of useful consultation.[1]

By the 1960s many public-sector workers' pay and benefits began to lag behind their unionized private-sector counterparts, making retention a significant concern (White 2002). This was partly due to unprecedented economic growth and militant demands by industrial unions, which raised the expectations of an incipient working class (Palmer 1992). As a result of the significant growth brought about by the extension of the welfare state – including militancy in the federal public sector, municipalities, and public-sector workers in other provinces, particularly Saskatchewan and Quebec who had recognized the collective bargaining rights of public-sector workers in 1944 and 1965 – many Ontario public-sector workers began demanding the right to unionize and bargain collectively (Hodgetts 1995).

In light of increasing labour strife in the public sector as well as tensions in the mining, auto, and steel industries, in 1967 the Conservative government of John Robarts established a special advisory committee on Collective Bargaining in the Ontario Government Service headed by Judge Walter Little. The government requested that Judge Little examine the appropriate scope of bargaining units, forms of negotiation, and methods for resolving disputes. In brief, Judge Little's report recommended giving the Civil Service Association of Ontario (CSAO) – predecessor to the Ontario Public Service Employees Union – representation rights for the entire civil service; excluding management and professionals from the scope of bargaining; and resting ultimate authority with management over the determination of merit, job classification, and pay (Little 1969). Although Judge Little believed that the right to strike and lockouts were appropriate in the private sector, he argued that these actions were inappropriate for public-sector workers by citing the ultimate sovereignty of government and the fact that the public was owed uninterrupted public services.

Soon after Little released his report, the government appointed the Committee on Government Productivity (COGP 1969–74). The ten reports published by the COGP between 1969 and 1974 put forward a catalogue of restructuring initiatives, including identifying opportunities for privatizing and outsourcing services as alternatives to direct public provisioning. The endorsement of the Little Report and COGP by the Tories signalled that the guiding minds – both political and public service – were considering how to restructure the provincial apparatus and service-delivery mechanisms to better align with fiscal capacity. Since entering government in 1943, Ontario's Red Tories – pragmatic to a fault – had lead the incremental building of the Ontario version of the welfare state. The mid to late 1960s saw major new initiatives led by the federal government that required the provinces to take up significant roles in policy and delivery – post-secondary education, social services, and of course, publicly financed health care. But the golden age of province building came with a price. Announcing the establishment of the COGP in early 1969, Ontario's Treasurer told the Legislature that this review committee was necessary, given that "During the 1960s this Legislature has approved an increasingly broad range of public services, greatly expanding its contribution in such areas as health, education and welfare" (Archives of Ontario, Records of Charles McNaughton 1969).

The COGP's ultimate concern was to reduce public spending, as this was outstripping the capacity and willingness of government to raise sufficient revenues (Ontario Ministry of Treasury, Economics and Intergovernmental Affairs 1972a, 31–2). Key members of Ontario's state and businesses saw it necessary to constrain public-sector expansion and to do so by reasserting the power and authority of the political leadership over policy formulation and decision making. The membership of the COGP included senior executives from the brewing, mining, oil, and steel sectors as well as the most strategically located senior public servants including the deputy treasurer and the cabinet secretary. The composition of the COGP may not have been precisely indicative of capitalist class control and colonization of the Ontario state apparatus, but it certainly was indicative of "decisive influence" in shaping a much more constrained expansion of public services (Barrow 2008, 91). In part the COGP sought to assert political control over policy and to establish a distinction between policy development and program delivery so that privatization and contracting could be more readily entertained (Ontario Ministry of Treasury, Economics and Intergovernmental Affairs n.d., 6). The principles expressed here of policy centralization and delivery decentralization presage David Osborne and Ted Gaebler's paean to neoliberal public administration – *Reinventing Government* – published some twenty years later. This reconsideration took place within a context of economic turmoil. From 1975 to 1980 economic growth slowed to 1.7% and then shrunk in 1980 by 0.2% as inflation swelled to 10.2%. The effect on personal income was significant as inflation nullified any gains in employment income (Ontario Ministry of Treasury and Economics 1981a; 1981b, 4). The change in economic environment was the first indication of a rupture with postwar growth. It was indeed the "beginning of a new approach to fiscal policy for the Province" (Ontario Ministry of Treasury and Economics 1981a, 5).

In 1970 the OLRA was amended, paving the way for binding arbitration. Two years later, the shift toward a more formalized and confrontational approach to collective bargaining for core public-service workers was codified with the establishment of the Crown Employees Collective Bargaining Act (CECBA 1972). Introduced against the backdrop of striking hydro workers and Toronto civic workers, for the first time public-service workers were granted the right to collective bargaining. However, the legislation included significant restrictions and thus was far from a real breakthrough.[2] In response to the Davis government's unwillingness to bargain with teachers' unions, as well as unilaterally imposing wage ceilings, layoffs, school-board mergers, increases in workloads and class sizes, and the cancellation of school programs, in December 1973, 80,000 of Ontario's 105,000 primary and secondary teachers went on strike. Striking teachers employed work-to-rule tactics and letter-writing campaigns, held large demonstrations at Queen's Park, and submitted mass resignations. As Richter (2006, 7) noted, teachers "demanded free collective bargaining, the right to negotiate any term or condition of employment, and the right to strike."

While Davis's government had tried to compel workers into accepting binding arbitration without the right to strike, mass public sympathy backed by teachers and support from the broader labour movement subsequently pressed Davis to extend collective bargaining with the right to strike to teachers. In 1974, the Davis government amended the CECBA to include casual and temporary employees and expanded the scope of bargaining to include issues related to promotion, transfers, layoffs, job evaluations, reappointment, pay, and successor rights. However, issues related to classification, merit, performance evaluation, and pensions remained the exclusive domain of management (Carson 2011). As a result of ongoing protests, work-ins, walkouts, and solidarity strikes by education, health care, utilities, administration, and transport workers, the right to strike was extended to other public-sector workers throughout the decade. The right to strike continued to elude the Ontario civil service proper, as there were no major changes to the CECBA legislation until the 1990s.

In 1975, Premier Bill Davis appointed the Special Program Review Committee (SPRC) "to enquire into ways and means of restraining the costs of Government, through examining issues such as the usefulness of programs, alternative lower costs means of accomplishing objectives, and the problem of increased public demand for services in an inflationary period" (Special Program Review Committee 1975, ix). The work of the SPRC set the primary objective of Ontario's budget policy for the remainder of the 1970s as one of controlling inflation, a serious problem at the time, and reducing the costs of government that were being driven by inflation. The rate of growth in public expenditures decelerated significantly from a high of 24.7% in 1974–75 to 6.4% in 1978–79. This fiscal policy agenda was concerned with slowing the rate of public expenditure growth, not reducing public expenditures in and of themselves and not a wholesale attack on public services. This is a crucial political and ideological difference between this period of restraint and the neoliberal austerity that would emerge in full force in 1995. Nevertheless, the Ontario Tories did reduce the rate of public-sector spending growth, increased industrial incentives, froze the salaries of senior public-service staff, and discharged over 1,000 civil-service staff. As well, highway maintenance and snow plowing services were contracted out, psychiatric hospitals were closed down, the number of available hospital beds was reduced, and health labs were sold to the private sector. Between 1975 and 1980, 7,000 public-sector jobs were eliminated along with real reductions to health care and educational spending (Roberts 1994; Ontario Ministry of Treasury and Economics 1981). In sum, while important reductions with real impacts, these hardly amounted to a Thatcherite assault on public services. Indeed, the Davis government years were also marked by progressive interventions and legislative reforms to occupational health and safety, post-secondary education, environmental regulation (specifically, regulations governing acid rain), rent controls, and changes to employment standards.

But fiscal restraint proved unpopular as the Conservatives lost their legislative majority in the 1975 election and failed again in 1977 to win more than half the seats. Indeed, the period of minority government from 1975 to 1981 saw many of the above-mentioned reforms tabled and passed. Yet, it was increasingly clear, if not fully recognized, that the postwar political-economic foundations that enabled the success of Ontario's pragmatic Conservatives was coming unhinged (Brownsey and Howlett 1992). Through this period, the Canadian Union of Public Employees (CUPE), Ontario Public Service Employees Union (OPSEU), and other unions continued to organize workers at universities, colleges, and administrative services, as well as in utilities, medical, and correctional facilities. Over the next decade major strikes by both private- and public-sector unions would galvanize the province, enshrining the mandatory adoption of the Rand formula in the labour code in 1980. The composition of public-sector unionism also shifted with women now comprising some 50% of membership, although they continued to be largely under-represented in private-sector unions (Warskett 1997). Once-marginalized issues, such as maternity leave, child care, health and safety concerns, sexual harassment, and sex discrimination related to pay and promotion, were increasingly understood as part of the broader catalogue of bargaining issues. Women also challenged traditional leaderships to become more accountable and democratic, organized women's committees, and pushed unions to be more representative across race and gender (Briskin 2010).

In 1980–81, roughly 10,000 health care workers at fifty Ontario hospitals organized by CUPE struck against mandated arbitration and laws prohibiting strikes by hospital employees. The strike was ended one week later and resulted in thirty-four workers being fired and 3,400 suspensions. Three union leaders, including CUPE president Grace Hartman, were jailed for contempt of court for supporting striking workers. Later that year, 11,000 striking hospital workers at Riverdale Hospital organized with CUPE were legislated back to work; the union was charged with criminal contempt and fined $250,000.

The Conservatives fought the 1981 election on a platform that sought to deploy the powers and capacities of the provincial state as an instrument for economic development and to reassemble the "One Ontario" politics that had served the "red" Tories so well since 1943.[3] With the Conservatives returned to power with a majority government, the province was engulfed by the "Reagan recession" of 1981 (MacDermid and Albo 2001). Unprecedented interest rates reaching 21% in 1981 and explosive energy costs fueled by the second oil shock pushed Ontario into an even deeper recession. Between 1979 and 1982, Ontario recorded double-digit inflation that peaked at 12.1% and drove unemployment up to 9.8% in 1982. The 1982 *Inflation Restraint Act* suspended the right to strike and extended all collective agreements by one year. The *Act* also prohibited wage increases in excess of 5% for roughly 500,000 broader public-sector workers. In 1983, the *Public Sector Prices and Compensation Review Act* mandated that arbitrators consider employers' ability to pay in the arbitration process and made all collective agreements subject to review by the Restraint Board. This was a blatant intervention by the state that not only undermined free collective bargaining but also sought to shift the burden of recession from the private to the public sector as convenient scapegoats of economic recession. The seeds of the Common Sense Revolution were beginning to be sown, as the attack against the welfare state intensified and the postwar class compromise came unhinged.

PROGRESSIVE COMPETITIVENESS AND THE LAST GASP OF SOCIAL DEMOCRACY

Frank Miller replaced Davis as leader in 1985. His leadership convention victory was seen as a rejection of the "Red Tory" politics that had served the Conservatives well over the postwar period (Speirs 1986). Of course, the Ontario Progressive Conservatives, as with any party, was a broad tent encompassing various ideological tendencies. The memoirs of Darcy McKeough, Ontario's treasurer through much of the 1970s, reveal that serious political differences were present in the party during that decade. McKeough sought to balance the budget through public expenditure restraint while key figures around Premier Davis preferred to raise corporate taxes (McKeough 2016, 159). In this respect, Miller too was closely identified with restraint. He served as treasurer as well; however, his restraint legacy was not a formula for electoral success. On 2 May 1985, the Progressive Conservatives saw their share of the popular vote plummet from 44% to 37%. Twenty-eight seats were lost, leaving them with only fifty-two seats, still the largest party in the Legislature. The Liberals won 37.9% of the popular vote to the Conservatives 37.0%. They gained fourteen seats for a total of forty-eight. The New Democratic Party (NDP) finished with twenty-five seats, thus holding the balance of power with significant leverage.

In the wake of the election, Miller reassembled a government under his premiership; however, this would be short-lived. On 28 May 1985, the two opposition leaders, Liberal David Peterson and New Democrat Bob Rae, co-signed a common program referred to as the "Accord." It was derived from shared campaign themes and marked a departure from the era of restraint. Instead, the Liberals and NDP were both committed to forging an enabling state with a capacity to guide Ontario's social and economic development. Several proposals captured this: a priority to create employment and training programs aimed at young workers who had been left behind by the long recession, new employment security legislation, significant new investment in co-operative and non-profit housing, employment and pay equity, and new environmental regulations (Peterson and Rae 1985).

The Liberals came to government just as the full effect of the 1983 to 1989 mini-boom took hold and Ontario growth and unemployment rates achieved levels not seen since the 1960s. The Liberals did little to change the Ontario state's structure, but they did seek to provide it with greater policy and coordinative and program delivery capacities that were evident in fairly significant growth in both the broader public sector and the core Ontario Public Service (White 2002). Between 1985 and 1989, the Ontario public-sector workforce grew by 131,300 workers (15.2%), while the Ontario Public Service expanded by more than 8,000. This increase in the public-sector workforce corresponded to a 50% increase in provincial public expenditures over the same period (Ontario Ministry of Finance

1989). The Peterson government sought "to restructure Ontario's industrial base to meet high-tech competition on world markets, plan for an aging society, check rising health care costs without reducing the quality of care and improve the education system to produce the highly skilled workers" (Gagnon and Rath 1992). The Liberals established a new corporatist structure to provide policy advice and build consensus – the Premier's Council – comprised of representatives from business, labour, government, and the universities.[4] Peterson's new chief public servant said that Ontario's recent good economic fortune had "spared the province the budget-slashing and continued restraint seen in other jurisdictions," but he warned that the welfare state "can no longer be afforded, unless a new entrepreneurial economy can greatly increase a jurisdiction's productivity" (Carman 1988, n.p.). In response, the production and delivery of public services required reconsideration where direct service delivery by the state could be replaced with greater use of contracting out in the non-profit and for-profit sectors. Doing so required a new style of public-service leadership, one armed with a "corporate" and global perspective and an understanding of business.

With the Accord exhausted in terms of its legislative agenda, Peterson called an election for 10 September 1987. The Liberals captured 47.3% of the popular vote and took ninety-five of the Legislature's 130 seats. The New Democrats became the official opposition while the Conservatives lost thirty-four seats and were reduced to just sixteen. The stock market crash of October 1987 presaged a changing economic environment; layoffs in Ontario's industrial sector began to mount through 1988–89. Peterson opted for an early election before the political situation became unmanageable. But this was seen as a rash of political opportunism, and the 6 September 1990 election unexpectedly made Bob Rae the premier and the New Democrats the majority government just as a recession was firmly taking hold. The New Democrats continued the work of the Premier's Council by seeking to deepen multi-class consensus toward adjustment (Jenson and Mahon 1995). The objective was to adapt Ontario to a more competitive economic context by promoting "a highly qualified labour force, strategic investments by firms in higher-value-added activities, and investment by government in the necessary social and physical infrastructure" (Rachlis and Wolfe 1997, 349). The NDP also amended both the *Employment Standards Act* (ESA) and the OLRA, improving workers' ability to recover unpaid wages, enhancing pay equity provisions, expanding the rights of domestic and agricultural workers to organize, placing restrictions on the use of replacement workers, increasing the remedial powers of the Ontario Labour Relations Board (OLRB), and extending the rights of unions to "combine" bargaining units within the same company. They also reformed the grievance arbitration process, expanded successor rights, extended the right to first contract arbitration, expedited the hearings process, and lowered the threshold for triggering certification.

But before these efforts could fully take hold, the Rae government dramatically shifted its focus toward controlling the deficit and all but abandoned the experiment with progressive competitiveness. In 1992, provincial expenditures shrunk $3 billion (the largest proportional decrease in expenditures since 1953), and by 1993 finance ministry officials projected a deficit of $17 billion (Rae 1996, 204). Ontario social democracy would respond through an aggressive and unprecedented reduction in public expenditures. The objective was to control the deficit by both reducing expenditures by $6 billion and increasing revenues by $2 billion. This included a three-year wage freeze for 900,000 workers and a 5% reduction in wages through twelve unpaid days off, known as the social contract, and an Expenditure Control Plan that would potentially result in a loss of 9,000 to 11,000 jobs (Walkom 1994, 137).

The Public Services Coalition, comprised of public-sector unions, rejected the government's invitation to participate in the cost-cutting exercise "because the only matter on which the government was prepared to negotiate was on how cuts could be made, and even on that issue some felt there was little flexibility" (McBride 1995, 50). On 14 June 1993, the government introduced the *Social Contract Act*. The legislation empowered the cabinet and the minister of finance to impose outcomes where negotiations failed (Sack Goldblatt Mitchell 1993). By the deadline to complete negotiations in August 1993, 30% of public-sector workers had not agreed to a sectoral agreement (Hebdon and Warrian 1999, 199). Consequently, the finance minister moved to impose agreements overriding existing collectively bargained contracts. The NDP also amended the *Crown Employees Collective Bargaining Act*, extending the right to strike to the core public service. The great irony was, however, that soon after the NDP passed the Orwellian-titled *An Act Respecting the Collective Bargaining Rights of Employees of the Crown*, they statutorily prohibited workers from exercising those very rights.

The Social Contract may not have marked a concession to the ideology that "there is no alternative" to globalization and free markets, but it did fracture the electoral base of the NDP and particularly its trade-union allies who were thrown into civil war. The failed effort at negotiating an agreement between many of the public-sector unions and the government spoke as much to a flawed process as it did to the capacities of the various parties to engage in a large-scale experiment in social concertation. Regardless, the result was a slowing in the rate of growth for Ontario's public expenditures. For the first time since 1942, there was an absolute shrinkage in government expenditures: in 1990–91, program spending grew by 14.7%, but by 1993–94 spending had contracted by 3.4% (Ontario Ministry of Finance 2010, 69). It was a historic turning point in the history of Canadian social democracy that reached beyond Ontario (see, for instance, Sweeney and Hicks in this volume).

NEOLIBERAL ONSLAUGHT: THE COMMON SENSE REVOLUTION MOVES CENTRE STAGE

On 8 June 1995, the Conservatives, led by Mike Harris, formed a majority government. An era of aggressive neoliberal assault by the Conservatives, whose campaign manifesto was provocatively titled "Common Sense Revolution," was about to begin. The PCs' platform contained six key themes that sought to remake the Ontario state: (1) cut the provincial income tax rate by 30%; (2) cut "non-priority" government spending by 20%; (3) rescind and reduce various regulations, laws, and taxes deemed to impede economic growth; (4) reduce the size of the Ontario Public Service; (5) introduce performance standards; and (6) balance the budget (Ontario Progressive Conservative Party 1994). The sweeping reforms were concerned with more than technical legislative tinkering; they committed to a deep transformation in the very logic of the Ontario state. Critical to this commitment was the dismantling of important regulatory and redistributive functions of the welfare state. Prosperity could only return by reorienting the role of the Ontario state to better facilitate capital accumulation. This included repealing the *Employment Equity Act*, which had provided Aboriginal people, people with disabilities, members of racial minorities, and women – all social categories that had experienced higher rates of unemployment than the population in general – with some special consideration in public-sector employment.

The PCs also introduced Bill 7, *An Act to Restore Balance and Stability to Labour Relations and to Promote Economic Prosperity*, which repealed the amendments to the OLRA introduced by the NDP. This included substantially rewriting Ontario's labour and employment laws to make the province "open for business" by replacing automatic certification following card signing with an election model using secret ballots, eliminating the prohibition on replacement workers during strikes, reducing the threshold to trigger decertification, putting limitations on when unions could call a strike vote, removing successor rights for public-sector unions, imposing a twelve-month ban on a lost certification vote and repealing the rights of agricultural and domestic workers to unionize. Similarly, the employee wage protection fund under the *Employment Standards Act* that ensured workers would receive their unpaid wages when an employer went bankrupt was also rolled back.

By the end of 1995, the PCs had also introduced the omnibus Bill 49 *Savings and Restructuring Act*, which proposed amendments to more than forty pieces of legislation. This included reductions to social expenditures, the introduction of workfare, and an expected loss of 13,000 public sector jobs; the Act stipulated new powers that unilaterally allowed Queen's Park to restructure municipalities and hospitals, as well as new constraints on the scope of arbitrators' adjudication powers, limitations on the remedial powers of the OLRB, and freezing of the minimum wage at $6.85 (Sinclair, Rochon, and Leatt 2005, 19–20). Bill 49 also reduced the time limit for workers to register formal complaints with the OLRB from two years to six months, and capped awards at $10,000 regardless of the damages incurred (Thomas 2009). There were also numerous rule changes that resulted in tens of thousands of recipients becoming ineligible for social assistance.

On 26 February 1996, over 50,000 OPSEU members went on strike to protest the changes made by the Mike Harris Conservatives. For the first time, core public-service workers in Ontario were able to strike as a result of the 1993 amendments to the CECBA. Despite wages being frozen at 1991 levels, the union did not ask for a wage increase. Instead, OPSEU was most concerned about issues related to job security, successor rights, and retraining guarantees. The strike reached a turning point on 18 March, at the start of the spring parliamentary session, when union activists and protestors violently clashed with the Ontario Provincial Police (Reshef and Rastin, 2003). The government used the legal system to undermine OPSEU job actions by filling out more than thirty applications at the OLRB and eighty-two court actions seeking to reduce the visibility of strikers and limit picketing. Within a year, the Conservatives laid off upwards of 11,000 staff; however, arbitration awards in favour of the union would slow further attempts at privatization (Reshef and Rastin 2003, 64).

In light of the experiences of the OPSEU strike – the government had accomplished its goals and not suffered serious political blowback – the PCs continued along the path of privatization and contracting out. In 1997, the provincially run temporary employment agency GO Temp was privatized. At the same time, dozens of meat inspectors were laid off and later rehired as self-employed workers prohibited from unionizing, while the government increased its reliance on part-time and temporary contracts. The PCs also passed the *Public Sector Accountability Act* to "ensure that the private sector has an open opportunity to compete to provide services," which included setting new private-sector performance benchmarks for the public sector (Ontario Ministry of Finance 1997). Before the end of Harris's first term, more than 126,000 teachers across Ontario took part in extra-legal job actions in protest to the *Education Quality Improvement Act*. The *Act* unilaterally centralized control over education curricula, repealed employment equity initiatives, abolished Grade thirteen, standardized testing and report cards, and amalgamated school boards while reducing the number of trustees (MacLellan 2009).[5]

By 1999, the Conservatives had introduced ninety-nine different tax cuts, with income taxes reduced by 30% compared with pre-1990s levels. The Tory government also moved quickly to privatize water analysis and health care laboratories, including the elimination of twenty-nine hospitals, over 10,000 hospital beds, and more than 6,000 nurse jobs. Power was also significantly concentrated in the hands of the premier and his closest advisors in the Premier's Office. Ontario public expenditures as a proportion of the total economy shrank dramatically. In 1995–96, Ontario government expenditures comprised 19.2% of the gross provincial product (GPP), but by 2000–01 they had dropped to 14.8% of GPP and remained in that range until 2005 (Ontario Ministry of Finance 1997; 2003). On a per capita basis, provincial expenditures were essentially frozen between 1990 and 2005.

The budgets of key ministries were also cut by significant amounts. Some of the most egregious included economic development (cut by nearly 79%), municipal affairs and housing (reduced by 73%), labour (cut by 58%), environment (cut by 37%), natural resources (reduced by nearly 31%), community and social services (shrunk by nearly 20%), and education and training (reduced by 14%). As such, employment in the core Ontario Public Service fell from 81,300 in 1995–96 to 54,952 in 1999–2000. From 1,042,000 employees in 1992, the broader Ontario public-sector workforce had been reduced to 938,500 by 1997 (a decline of nearly 10%). For the Ontario Public Service this meant a return, in terms of numbers, to dimensions not seen since 1967–68, despite the massive demographic growth of the province over the same period. The proportion of public-sector workers as compared to the overall Ontario workforce fell from 21% in 1992 to 15.9% in 1998 (Statistics Canada 2001). This was an astonishing decline of more than a quarter of the public-sector workforce. In 2002, Harris stepped down as premier and was replaced by Finance Minister Ernie Eves. Eves's premiership was a short eighteen months and was characterized by significant policy indecision, especially with regard to privatizing Ontario Hydro and the Liquor Control Board of Ontario (LCBO).

The PCs deployed the power of the state to create new laws, regulations and institutions "designed to reproduce a neoliberal future" (Hackworth 2008). The Harris-era 30% cut in the tax rate and the elimination of several dozen taxes on various business-related activities left in place a more regressive tax regime, and by the 2003 election the Common Sense Revolution had reached an impasse. In the run up to the election, the largest private- and public-sector unions explicitly campaigned against the PCs while implicitly supporting the Liberals through non-partisan campaigns such as, and most notably, the Working Families Coalition. Offering both financial and third-party campaigning support, the shift toward Liberal support symbolized the political realignment of labour in Ontario. This shift was also symptomatic of an ideological divide expressing trade unions' adaptations to the conditions of neoliberalism in turning to defensive strategies and tactics. In October 2003, the Dalton McGuinty–led Liberals won a landslide electoral victory, gaining seventy-two of 130 legislative seats, while the Conservatives were reduced to only twenty-four seats and seven remained for the NDP.

COMMON SENSE REDUX: THE MCGUINTY-WYNNE LIBERALS

The Ontario electoral landscape had shifted decisively toward the right since 1995. However, rather than reversing the core of the Common Sense Revolution, the Liberals moved to deepen and extend the conflagration of neoliberal policies. The first two terms (2003, 2007) of the McGuinty government were concerned with embedding existing reforms and avoiding a direct assault on public services and confrontation with public-sector unions. However, by the Liberals' third term (2011) the writing was on the wall; confrontation loomed. The Liberals had campaigned as "centrists" promising to reinvest in public services, particularly health care and education. But rolling back the fiscal legacy of the Conservatives was not an option. They promised to hold the line on taxes for consumers, reduce corporate taxes, and balance the budget (Ontario Liberal Party 2003).[6] In prioritizing the reduction of the $5.6 billion deficit inherited from the PCs, the Liberals intimated their affinity to neoliberalism.

In a telling sign of things to come, three months before the Liberals introduced their first budget in 2004, Premier McGuinty raised the possibility that public-sector workers might be subjected to a wage freeze or required to take unpaid days off if wage demands were not moderated. In delivering their first budget, modest savings were made through the privatization of services formerly covered by the Ontario Health Insurance Plan, like chiropractic therapy, physical rehabilitation, and optometry exams. The McGuinty government also spearheaded the expansion of private health care clinics. The Liberals also announced the introduction of a graduated health care premium, which would exclude individuals with a taxable income of less than $21,000 and then rise from $60 to $900 per year depending on income level (see also Conrad in this volume). Thus, rather than overturn the regime of tax cuts and marketization put in place through the Common Sense Revolution, the Liberals streamlined it.

As the tailwinds of the 2008 recession swept across Ontario, the Liberal government responded by calling for a decade of austerity. The major policy plank of this program was the Open Ontario Plan (OOP), which called for tax relief, a wage freeze for public-sector workers, the privatization of public assets, and regressive reforms to employment standards legislation (Fanelli and Thomas 2010). The OOP signalled a new era of austerity in the course of reorganizing neoliberalism in an effort to reassert its legitimacy as a political philosophy, economic program, and social policy framework. The general corporate income tax (CIT) rate was reduced from 14 to 10% by 2013. The CIT rate also decreased from 12 to 10% for manufacturing and processing firms, and there was a reduction of the preferential small-business CIT rate from 5.5 to 4.5%, along with the elimination of the small-business deduction surtax. The tax rate on the first $37,106 of personal taxable income was also reduced by more than 16%, from 6.05% to 5.05%, while those earning up to $80,000 per year saw a tax cut of 10%. This made Ontario's tax regime among the lowest among the countries belonging to the Organisation of Economic Co-operation and Development (OECD).[7] The OOP also called for the marginal effective tax rate to be cut in half by 2018, equivalent to some $4.6 billion in tax cuts on income and capital (Ontario Ministry of Finance 2010).

The omnibus *Open for Business Act* marked the revival of state coercion in the form of a legislative assault that introduced over a hundred amendments to legislation across ten ministries, and its stated objective was to create a more competitive business climate (Gellatly et al., 2013). The climate of restraint was further amplified through less-than-genuine consultative negotiations with the Ontario government over 2010, which sought to develop an austerity "framework agreement" that would see private- and public-sector unions moderate their bargaining demands (Evans 2011). This dynamic stifled free collective bargaining by using the recession as an excuse to extract concessions while extending new forms of corporate welfare and furthering the neoliberal remaking of the state.

The Liberals also enacted the *Public Sector Compensation to Protect Public Services Act* and *Broader Public Sector Accountability Act*. The Acts imposed a two-year wage freeze for 350,000 non-unionized public-sector workers, while also indirectly affecting 710,000 unionized public-sector workers through a proposed "voluntary" two-year wage freeze, and concentrated new powers in the Management Board of Cabinet. The Liberals clearly stated that they would not fund net compensation increases to operational costs associated with collective agreements. Throughout the consultations, they maintained that all options were on the table, including legislated wage freezes and furloughs, as well as a 5% reduction to local transfers if municipalities failed to hold the line on expenditures (Fanelli 2016). Following the two-year freeze, wage increases were to be kept below inflation and not exceed the province's 1.9% cap on expenditure growth. The Liberals also solicited CIBC World Markets and Goldman Sachs to come up with a plan to monetize the province's $60 billion worth of public assets. The idea behind "SuperCorp" was to combine Ontario's Crown assets, including nuclear power plants, power generation facilities, 29,000 kilometres of electrical transmission and distribution lines, and over 600 liquor stores and gaming operations. The politically sensitive task of liquidating Ontario's assets was put on hold, however, to deal with the more immediate issue of reducing the deficit through public-sector service and employment cuts.

As part of the OOP, Bill 68 replicates Alberta's and British Columbia's "self-help" model for complaints and enforcement under the *Employment Standards Act* (see Brownsey and Whiteside in this volume for background and context). Under the changes, employees are required to address employment grievances directly with their employer in advance of government intervention. In other words, employees are expected to make all "reasonable efforts" to resolve the dispute individually on a case-by-case basis. The implications of this amendment to the ESA are twofold. First, it promotes voluntarism by creating the potential for employers to resist the process if they feel it will not work in their favour. Second, it privileges a mediated settlement over an actual award, which may expedite the claims process but could reduce the value of the settlement achieved by a worker. Regardless of the outcome of individual settlements, this orientation represents a transformation in the role of Employment Standards officers from those who make judgments based on fact-finding to mediators in a process that assumes two equal parties when, in fact, the parties are far from equal (Fanelli and Thomas 2011).

It is equally telling to review what the McGuinty government chose not to do. Avoiding the question of raising taxes meant explicitly agreeing to allow Ontario's public economy to shrink. The Liberals had made reinvesting in public services a central policy plank of their campaign, yet a year-over-year review of the province's five principal social policy ministries (health, education, post-secondary, social services and children's services) reveals modest enhancements: aggregate program spending increases (2003–07) varied from 6.5 to 8% through their first term (2003–07) and tended toward less than 7%

in their second (2007–11) (Ontario Ministry of Finance 1996–2011). By the 2011 budget, the Liberals had come full circle back to the Common Sense Revolution. They pledged to restrain expenditure growth to 2% annually which, given inflation and population growth, continues the aggressive restraint measures that had been a hallmark of the Harris regime. The budget also vowed not to raise taxes and to freeze non-priority program spending by reining in union wages. Finance Minister Duncan indicated a hardening climate of austerity when he suggested that upwards of 1,500 positions in the Ontario public sector could be eliminated (Ontario Ministry of Finance 2011). Tax cuts amounted to the second largest platform item in their 2011 budget, estimated to cost the treasury $327 million by fiscal year 2015–16 (Mackenzie 2011).

The McGuinty government also established the Commission on the Reform of Ontario's Public Services, headed by former TD Bank chief economist Don Drummond.[8] The Commission argued that without new forms of revenue generation (their mandate explicitly prevented them from exploring these options), program spending would need to be cut "more deeply on a real per capita basis, and over a much longer period of time, than the Harris government did in the 1990s" (Commission on the Reform of Ontario's Public Services 2012, 10). Released the same year – to much less fanfare – the Social Assistance Review Commission's report recommended over a hundred reforms to the way public services, particularly social assistance, could be enhanced through realigned and integrated service arrangements, from child care and long-term care to income and employment reforms, as well as supportive public housing (Lankin and Sheikh 2012). The public policy decisions made since 2011 have reinforced pressures for "competitive austerity" (Albo and Fanelli 2014), and seems to confirm Hackworth's (2008) hypothesis that "soft edge" neoliberal governments may actually be able to go further than its most aggressive proponents (see also Graefe and Ouimet as well as Clancy in this volume).

The 2012 Liberal budget implemented a range of austerity measures: Children's Aid societies were restructured and wages frozen in order to find $9 million in efficiencies; Social Assistance and Disability payments were to be reduced by $200 million over three years, resulting in benefits that were less in real dollars in 2015 than they were in 1986; correctional services and legal aid were to be cut by 1.6% every year until 2017–18; municipal and local infrastructure funding was to be cut by $48 million from 2011 levels; hospitals lost $1 billion and OHIP another $1.5 billion in cuts and wage freezes, despite having the highest out-of-pocket health expenses and fewest hospital beds per person than any other province; primary and secondary schooling were to be cut by $660 million over three years, while post-secondary education transfers stagnated and fees rose as much as 3% annually (Ontario Ministry of Finance 2012). From 2010 to 2012, Ontario fell from seventh to last place among Canada's ten provinces in total social program spending (Ontario Common Front 2012).

As Mackenzie (2012) has noted, the crowning irony of McGuinty's ninth budget was that it completed the job of cutting government down to the size it was during Harris's tenure. The budget increased fiscal capacity by increasing revenues to the treasury by $1.6 billion but also cut $10.7 billion (equal to 1.5% of GDP) from expenditures. With inflation, by 2012–13 social assistance had lost 5.5% of funding and disability lost some $200 million when compared with when Harris left government (Mackenzie 2012). The budget also legislated a pay freeze for 1.2 million broader public-sector workers, nullifying some 4000 agreements. All said, the 2012 budget took $17.7 billion out of the economy over the next three years (Walkom 2012). Citing the sale and lease-back of eight government buildings, the end of Ontario Northland Transportation Railroad Commission, and the need for more private-sector involvement in the Ontario Lottery and Gaming Corporation, Finance Minister Dwight Duncan said, "I expect to see a lot of people [protesting] on the front lawns here [at Queen's Park]" (Benzie 2012). The 2013–14 budget further reduced expenditure growth to 1.5% (below the rate of inflation and expectations to meet new population growth) and back-end loaded austerity measures, with each year of restraint being more aggressive than the last. From 2014–16, program spending growth was to be held to 1.1% and 0.4%, and by 2016–17, as the final year of the government's fiscal plan shows and based on trends observed by fiscal forecasters in 2013–14, Ontario would need to freeze program spending and then cut spending by an additional 1% in 2017–18 to meet its stated goal of budget surpluses (Ontario Ministry of Finance 2013). As others have shown, these reductions to public spending were not an economic necessity but a political choice, as Ontario's budgetary deficit has been on track to surplus without the additional austerity targets (Mackenzie 2014).

On 3 January 2013 the Liberals imposed concessionary contracts on the province's teachers, which followed 2012 legislation restraining spending in the education system. This included wage controls, layoffs, and the freezing of pension contributions for five years. Teachers responded with a number of one-day strikes, work-to-rule campaigns, the withdrawal of extracurricular activities, and mass protests. Despite the labour discontent, the job actions did not see a repeat of the Harris-era confrontations. Some teachers have since raised questions about the capacities of educational workers and organized labour more broadly to fight back against concessionary demands (Hewitt-White 2015). Amid mounting unpopularity, Dalton McGuinty stepped down as party leader in early 2013. This was followed by the resignation of McGuinty's long-time finance minister, Dwight Duncan, in what was portrayed as a period of renewal. In McGuinty's place, Kathleen Wynne emerged as new party leader and premier of Ontario. Wynne positioned herself as the "social justice" and "activist" premier against the old guard. In power, however, much of the McGuinty legacy has continued uninterrupted.

The Liberals continued to put forward the privatization and contracting out of public services, assets, and employment as a testament to New Public Management. Having launched the largest expansion of public–private partnerships (P3s) in Ontario history (Coulter 2009), in 2014 the province was engaged in over eighty P3s (known as Alternative Financial Procurement). However, of twenty-eight P3s undertaken between 2007–10, Siemiatycki and Farooqi (2012) found them to be 16% more expensive than traditional public procurement. Likewise, a major report undertaken by the Auditor General (2014) found that of the seventy-four completed P3 projects between 2003 and 2014, Ontario could have saved up to $8 billion through traditional public procurement.[9] In June 2013, Wynne launched a blue-ribbon panel headed by president and former CEO of TD Bank, Ed Clark. The panel was created to advise the government how to get more than $3 billion through the "recycling" of public assets. Reporting in late 2014, the panel suggested the sell-off of Ontario's estimated $3.3 billion lottery, which brought in $883 million in revenue in 2012–13 alone (Benzie 2014). Following the panel's recommendations, lottery and LCBO lands were put on sale, as well as Hydro One Brampton and Hydro One Networks' distribution arm, worth some $2-3 billion in one-off monies, although the government expects to retain a 40% majority stake. In doing so, the Wynne government completes the sell-off of Hydro One started by Harris and revives the idea behind "SuperCorp" first raised in 2010.

Upon the recommendation of Wynne, on 2 May 2014, Lieutenant Governor David Onley called an election after the NDP announced it would vote against the minority Liberal government's proposed budget. Throughout the election, the Liberals made a concerted effort to emphasize that they had implemented 80% of the Drummond Commission's recommended austerity measures. Throughout the election, Wynne promised to eliminate the deficit in three years without cuts to public services or staffing levels (Babbage 2014). The election saw the NDP move sharply right, while the Conservatives raised the spectre of so-called "right-to-work" laws and cutbacks to the public service. The Liberals, who had characterized their 2014 budget (which the NDP voted against) as "the most progressive budget in decades," were not only re-elected but surprisingly regained a majority in the Legislature by winning fifty-eight seats. In 2010–11, total public program spending represented 17.9% of GDP in Ontario. Wynne's 2014 budget plan aimed to cut this to 14.6% by 2017–18 – equivalent to roughly $20 billion in public sector spending cuts, or some 3.3% of GDP (Mackenzie 2014). At the same time, the share of Ontario's public health care paid by employers though the Employer Health Care Tax dropped, having decreased from 17.2% in 1991 to 12.4% in 2014. John Stapleton of Open Policy Ontario notes that welfare incomes adjusted for inflation have dropped by 34% and disability support payments have fallen by 14% since the Liberals took over in 2003 (Goar 2014). With population growth and inflation, the 2017 Liberal budget decreased total program spending by the largest amount per person since 1995.[10] Wynne's 2014 budget reduced per capita spending by $179 in 2017 compared with 2013 levels (Alstedter 2014). With roughly half of each ministry's budget going to wages, that will put more pressure for departments to choose between fewer staff, lower wages, or fewer services.

The 2015 budget emphasized public expenditure reductions, of which a key component was a continued "net zero" policy in public-sector labour negotiations, meaning that no budget would be allotted to departments for increased wages. A financial accountability officer was also hired "to provide independent analysis to the legislature about the state of the Province's finances, including the Ontario Budget" (Ontario Ministry of Finance 2015, 222). The "net zero" policy was tested in a labour dispute between the provincial government and the Ontario teachers' union in September 2015. The tactics of teachers included a reframing of "net zero" as austerity budgeting. For example, the Elementary Teachers' Federation of Ontario (ETFO) released a poster brief titled "Top 10 Reasons Why Ontario's Austerity Budget Is Misguided." The document argued that Ontario's program spending was the lowest per capita in the country, and that Ontario's financial situation was not a crisis given that its debt-to-GDP ratio was still quite low. In reality, Ontario's debt-to-GDP ratio was the highest of all provinces with the exception of Quebec. Ultimately, the Ontario government caved on the "net zero" policy, mostly due to the timing. Kathleen Wynne had placed her support behind Justin Trudeau's Liberal party during the federal election and a prolonged labour dispute would affect their chances in a large number of Ontario seats.

In June of 2015, the Wynne government also set out a plan to sell parts of Hydro One – Ontario's largest power utility – and use the funds to expand transit and roads (Morrow 2015). On 5 November 2015, 15% of the company would be sold on the stock market and further portions at regular intervals until the Government of Ontario held only 40% of the stock. No single entity could obtain greater than 10% of the company, meaning Ontario would continue to control the majority of operations in the company. The Premier's Advisory Council on Government Assets argued that while selling the Crown corporation would lead to lost revenue, such costs needed to be measured against the opportunity costs of not spending on road, bridge, and transit infrastructure (Premier's Advisory Council 2015). This recommendation was surprising because the focus of stakeholder engagement activities by the Council was originally on a merger of Brampton Hydro and three smaller local distribution units (LDUs) to increase economies of scale in the local distribution of electrical energy. In a report examining the fiscal impacts of the Hydro One sell-off, Ontario's former financial accountability officer Andre Leclerq noted: "In years following the sale of 60% of Hydro One, the Province's budget balance would be worse than it would have been without the sale. The Province's net debt would initially be reduced, but will eventually be higher than it would have been without the sale" (Financial Accountability Office 2015, 1). The report went on to note how Hydro One brings in close to $750 million annually, making its sale roughly equivalent to five years of continued public ownership.

The results of these measures were mixed. Ontario had an increase in revenues of about $10 billion dollars over 2014–15, but expenses in health care, social services, and justice were above spending projections. The more discretionary general government expenses account, targeted as a source for budgetary constraint, was reduced but at a lower rate than what was projected. Nonetheless, the tightening of expenses was sufficient for Wynne to announce a removal of the "net zero" policy for labour negotiations in September of 2016. But Premier Wynne, who ran ostensibly to the left of the NDP and claimed the progressive ground, was looking to increasingly overt neoliberal solutions to her government's fiscal challenges.

CONCLUSION: CONSOLIDATING AUSTERITY

Although the Common Sense Revolution is over, the neoliberalization of the Ontario state and its public policies is not. This chapter has outlined the long and often painful transformation of the Ontario public sector over the postwar period. However, despite the Peterson-Rae interregnum, the transformation of the Ontario Progressive Conservative party in the late 1980s into an explicit vehicle for neoliberal politics and policies and the election of that party to government in 1995 marked the definitive end of Ontario's particularly slow turn toward neoliberalism compared to several other provinces and especially Alberta, British Columbia, Manitoba, and Saskatchewan. The ensuing eight years would be transformative, as the pragmatic centrist politics that had marked Ontario since the 1940s were replaced by an unprecedented polarization.

The style and strategy of the "Common Sense" Conservatives, aggressive and uncompromising, was new to Ontario. Ontario's public sector shrunk in terms of workforce and economic size to a level not seen since the 1960s. The McGuinty Liberals offered an alternative in tone and style and an interest in rebuilding health and education. While not anti-neoliberal, the strategy was different. The sharp edges of the "Revolution" were dulled and investment in key social programs were noteworthy, but this was all part of the normalization of the neoliberal project along "Third Way" lines. The ideological legacy of the Common Sense Revolution essentially prohibited any mature discussion of the need to increase taxes to adequately fund public services. The Wynne government's neoliberal practices and policies have proven themselves to be flexible and perhaps even opportunistic in navigating public opinion. In this regard, the 7 June 2018 general election, and what follows in terms of fiscal and other policy directions, will demonstrate if the Wynne government exercises more continuity with the Third Way–ism of McGuinty or charts a different, perhaps slightly more redistributional course.

NOTES

1 The OLRA established Ontario's first independent labour relations board, which was given the power to certify and decertify unions as well as remedial powers of reinstatement. Moreover, the OLRA established new procedures for certification, mandated bargaining in good faith, prohibited strikes and lockouts during the terms of a collective agreement, defined unfair labour practices, and established new conciliation protocols, although mandatory automatic dues check-off was still three decades away (Hodgetts 1995).

2 The CECBA provisions designated the Management Board of Cabinet as the employer of the public service and outlined twenty-one exclusive managerial rights such as training, classification, job evaluations, staffing levels, technical changes, and pensions. Drawing on the recommendations of Little's report, the Act also excluded professionals and management, as well as casual, contract, and temporary employees (less than six months' experience), from the provisions of the CECBA (Carson 2011).

3 The term "One Ontario" used here draws on the nineteenth-century "One nation" doctrine within British Toryism. At its heart, the doctrine suggests that class and other sectional interests are to be overridden by appeal to social unity and a rejection of polarization. In the Ontario context, the doctrine accurately characterizes the style of governing that marked the Progressive Conservative dynasty of 1943 to 1985. In essence, it was a political practice that sought to dullen class and other sectional conflicts and to integrate elements of the working class, peripheral regions, and other subordinate socio-economic sections into a non-ideological, declassed, and consumerist social consensus. With the notable exception of the Common Sense Revolution, the dominant political narrative across the twentieth century has been that of "One Ontario" (revived by the McGuinty-Wynne Liberals).

4 The objective of the Premier's Council was to design a broadly acceptable progressive competitiveness strategy that rejected a "race to the bottom" dynamic caused by international competition and the continual cutting of

wages and work standards. The strategy of progressive competitiveness accepts the inevitability of globalization but seeks to enact policies that increase a region's competitiveness within the international marketplace, particularly in those sectors most exposed to global competition. To the highest ranks of the Ontario executive, a different kind of state was required.

5 Minister of education at the time John Snobelen spoke of "creating a crisis" in the education sector as a means of achieving political goals: weakening teacher unions and reducing education expenditures. Moreover, under the provisions of the Act teaching and staff positions were reduced by nearly 7,000 positions, upwards of 8,000 principals and vice-principals were removed from bargaining units, and the government retained absolute power to determine class sizes, teacher preparation time, student-teacher ratios, and the length of the working day and school year (MacLellan 2009).

6 At the same time, the Liberals suggested a return to some of the progressive competitiveness economic policies that characterized the Peterson and Rae governments. It was in some respects an homage reassembling of Red Toryism and "One Ontario" ideology, which glossed over class, ethnic, linguistic, and other divides cutting through Ontario society, and it appealed to a vision of an inclusive and ever-prosperous province. However, despite some modest investments in support of skills and knowledge, including generous financial incentives for firms in key economic sectors (e.g. automotive, pharmaceutical and biotechnology, financial services, agriculture and food processing, information and communications technologies, and entertainment and culture), there was no going back to the era of progressive competitiveness; industrial strategy largely focussed on supply-side incentives, absent an industrial strategy and long-term economic planning.

7 The corporate minimum tax was reduced from 4 to 2.7% in 2010, with more small- and medium-sized businesses made exempt. Likewise, the capital tax was completely eliminated. This was a small surcharge of 0.3% on the first $400 million of taxable capital, 0.54% for non–deposit taking financial institutions with taxable capital over $400 million, and 0.67% on deposit taking financial institutions with over $400,000 million in taxable capital. Together, this translates into $500 million per year in lost in revenues (Ontario Ministry of Finance 2010).

8 In a poignant subsection titled "Reforming Public Service Delivery," the 2011 budget pointed to increasingly aggressive austerity measures: "Just because a government department is delivering a program or service today does not mean it should deliver that program or service in the future. The

government will focus on outcomes and results as opposed to how programs and services are delivered … the [Drummond] Commission will examine long-term, fundamental changes to the way government works. The Commission's work will include exploring which areas of service delivery are core to the Ontario government's mandate, which areas could be delivered more efficiently by another entity and how to get better value for taxpayers' money in the delivery of public services" (Ontario Ministry of Finance 2011). The report put forward over 600 recommendations suggesting the elimination or reduction of a range of services, with the private sector filling any remaining voids. The report was harshly criticized for its "lack of evidence or data to support its recommendations" (OCUFA 2012, 1–2), flawed methodology, accounting oversights, exaggerated spending increases, and fidelity to neoliberal policy making (Noonen 2012).

9 The report also went on to criticize the Liberals' continuing practice of "high risk" loans, particularly the $308 million loan to the research incubator Medical and Related Sciences as part of a failed real estate deal. The report also criticized the Liberal government for not acting on leftover recommendations from the Walkerton Water tragedy, tracking vaccinations, duplicitous physician billing, weak childcare oversight, lack of services for people with developmental disabilities, and ineffective energy "smart meters."

10 The deputy minister of finance during the Harris years, Bryne Purchase, noted, "She's [Wynne's] not talking about war with the public-sector unions, but that's what those numbers imply to me. I think the reality is a lot of strikes in the public sector." Don Drummond added that he "wouldn't be surprised" to see 100,000 fewer public-sector workers in 2017 if the Liberals achieve the spending targets that they have put in the budget (Siekierski 2014).

REFERENCES

Albo, Greg, and Carlo Fanelli. 2014. "Austerity Against Democracy: An Authoritarian Phase of Neoliberalism?" *Teoria Politica: An International Journal of Theory and Politics*, 65–88.

Alstedter, Ari. 2014. "Wynne's Budget Fortells Biggest Ontario Cuts since Harris." *Bloomberg*, 3 June. http://www.bloomberg.com/news/articles/2014-06-03/wynne-s-budget-fortells-biggest-ontario-cuts-since-harris.

Archives of Ontario. 1969. Records of Charles McNaughton. Operational Plans II-40. RG 18-527, Box Y69.

Auditor General of Ontario. 2014. *Annual Report of the Office of the Auditor General of Ontario*. Toronto: Queen's Printer.

Babbage, Maria. 2014. "Ontario Liberals Promise to Eliminate $12.5-Billion Deficit in Three Years without Cuts." *National Post*, 3 July. http://news.nationalpost.com/news/canada/canadian-politics/liberal-throne-speech-promises-combination-of-big-spending-and-restraint-will-balance-ontario-budget.

Barrow, Clyde. 2008. "Ralph Miliband and the Instrumentalist Theory of the State: The (Mis)Construction of an Analytic Concept." In *Class, Power and the State in Capitalist Society: Essays on Ralph Miliband*, edited by Paul Wetherly, Clyde Barrow, and Peter Burnham, 84–108. Houndmills, Basingstoke, Hampshire: Palgrave.

Benzie, Robert. 2014. "Ontario Betting on Bell, Rogers to Bid on Lotto Takeover." *Toronto Star*, 8 September. http://www.thestar.com/news/queenspark/2014/09/08/ontario_aims_to_get_bell_rogers_to_big_on_lotto_takeover.html.

Briskin, Linda. 2010. "Militancy and Resistance in the New Economy." In *Interrogating the New Economy: Restructuring Work in the 21st Century*, edited by Norene Pupo and Mark P. Thomas, 217–34. Toronto: University of Toronto Press.

Brownsey, Keith, and Michael Howlett. 1992. "Class Structure and Political Alliances in an Industrialized Society." In *The Provincial State: Politics in Canada's Provinces and Territories*, edited by Keith Brownsey and Michael Howlett, 147–74. Toronto: Copp Clark Pitman Ltd.

Carman, Bob. 1988. *The Ontario Public Service in the Year 2000: The Challenge of Renewal*. Unpublished paper prepared for Executive Resources by Robert Carman. Toronto, Ontario.

Carson, Jonathan. 2009 *Two Steps Forward, One Step Back: Legislating Labour Relations in the Ontario Public Service*. Paper presented at the 2009 Meetings of the Canadian Political Science Association. http://www.cpsa-acsp.ca/papers-2009/Carson.pdf.

CEBCA (*Crown Employees Collective Bargaining Act*). 1972. Toronto: Queen's Printer.

Commission on the Reform of Ontario's Public Services. 2012. *Public Services for Ontarians: A Path to Sustainability and Excellence*. Toronto: Queen's Printer for Ontario.

Coulter, Kendra. 2009. "Patriarchy at the Pink Palace. Gender and Work Inside the Ontario Legislature." *Atlantis: Critical Studies in Gender, Culture and Social Justice* 34 (1): 16–26.

Evans, Bryan. 2011. "The Politics of Public Sector Wages: Ontario's Social Dialogue for Austerity." *Socialist Studies/Etudes Socialistes* 7 (1/2): 171–90.

Fanelli, Carlo. 2016. Megacity *Malaise: Neoliberalism, Public Services and Labour in Toronto*. Halifax: Fernwood Publishing.

Fanelli, Carlo, and Mark P. Thomas. 2011. "Austerity, Competitiveness and Neoliberalism Redux: Ontario Responds to the Great Recession." *Socialist Studies/Etudes Socialistes* 7 (1/2): 140–71.

Financial Accountability Office of Ontario. 2015. *An Assessment of the Financial Impact of the Partial Sale of Hydro One*. Toronto: Queen's Printer. http://www.fao-on.org/web/default/files/publications/FAO%20Hydro%20One%20EN.pdf.

Gagnon, Georgette, and Dan Rath. 1992. *Not without Cause: David Peterson's Fall from Grace*. Toronto: Harper Collins.

Gellatly, Mary, John Grundy, Kiran Mirchandani, J. Adam Perry, Mark P. Thomas, and Leah F. Vosko. 2011. "'Modernising' Employment Standards? Administrative Efficiency and the Production of the Illegitimate Claimant in Ontario, Canada." *The Economic and Labour Relations Review* 22 (2): 81–106.

Goar, Carol. 2012. "Outsourcing: The New Way to Balance Government Budgets in Canada." *Toronto Star*, 21 February. http://www.thestar.com/opinion/editorialopinion/2012/02/21/outsourcing_the_new_way_to_balance_government_budgets_in_canada.html.

– 2014. "Ontario Gives with One Hand, Takes with the Other." *Toronto Star*, 13 July. http://www.thestar.com/opinion/commentary/2014/07/31/ontario_gives_with_one_hand_takes_with_the_other_goar.html.

Hackworth, Jason. 2008. "The Durability of Roll-Out Neoliberalism under Centre-Left Governance: The Case of Ontario's Social Housing Sector." *Studies in Political Economy* 81: 7–26.

Hebdon, Bob, and Peter Warrian. 1999. "Coercive Bargaining: Public Sector Restructuring under the Ontario Social Contract, 1993–1996." *Industrial and Labor Relations Review* 52 (2): 196–212.

Hewitt-White, Caitlin. 2015. "The OSSTF Anti-Bill 115 Campaign: An Assessment from a Social Movement Unionism Perspective." *Alternate Routes: A Journal of Critical Social Research* 26: 170–99.

Hodgetts, John E. 1995. *From Arm's Length to Hands-On: The Formative Years of Ontario's Public Service, 1867–1940*. Toronto: University of Toronto Press.

Jacobs, John. 2012. *CETA's Constraining Effects on Ontario*. Toronto: Canadian Centre for Policy Alternatives Ontario.

Jenson, Jane, and Paule Rianne Mahon. 1995. "From 'Premier Bob' to 'Rae Days': The Impasse of the Ontario New Democrats." In *Late Twentieth Century Social Democracy*, edited by Jean-Pierre Beaud and Jen-Guy Prevost, 149–72. Saint-Foy: Presses de l'Université du Quebec.

Lankin, F., and M.A. Sheikh. 2012. *Brighter Prospects: Transforming Social Assistance in Ontario*. http://www.mcss.gov.on.ca/documents/en/mcss/social/publications/social_assistance_review_final_report.pdf.

Little, Walter. 1969. *Collective Bargaining in the Ontario Government Service: A Report of the Special Advisor, His Honour Judge Walter Little*. Ontario: Queens Park Printers.

MacDermid, Robert, and Greg Albo. 2001. "Divided Province, Growing Protests: Ontario Moves Right." In *The Provincial State in Canada: Politics in the Provinces and Territories*, edited by Keith Brownsey and Michael Howlett, 163–202. Peterborough: Broadview Press.

Mackenzie, Hugh. 2011. *Platform Costing and the Politics of Fiscal Policy in Ontario*. Ottawa: Canadian Centre for Policy Alternatives Ontario.

– 2012. *Ontario's Fiscal Reality: Cup Half Empty or Half Full?* Ottawa: Canadian Centre for Policy Alternatives Ontario.

– 2014a. "The Staying Power of Ontario's Deficit Games." *Behind the Numbers*. http://behindthenumbers.ca/2014/01/29/the-staying-power-of-ontarios-deficit-games/.

– 2014b. "Tackling Ontario's Public Services Deficit." *Behind the Numbers*. http://behindthenumbers.ca/2014/02/03/tackling-ontario-public-services-deficit/.

MacLellan, Duncan. 2009. "Neoliberalism and Ontario Teachers' Unions: A 'Not-So' Common Sense Revolution." *Socialist Studies/Etudes Socialistes* 5 (1): 51–74.

McBride, Stephen. 1995. "Coercion and Consent: The Recurring Corporatist Temptation in Canadian Labour Relations." In *Labour Gains, Labour Pains: 50 Years of PC 1003*, edited by Cy Gonick, Paul Phillips, and Jesse Vorst, 79–96. Winnipeg: Fernwood Publishing.

McKeough, Darcy. 2016. *The Duke of Kent: A Memoir*. Toronto: ECW Press.

McKeough, Darcy, and Grant Henderson. 1975. *Report of the Special Program Review*. Toronto: Queen's Printer.

Monsebraaten, Laurie. 2015. "Ontario's Affordable Housing Wait List Hits Record High." *Toronto Star*, 4 May. https://www.thestar.com/news/gta/2015/05/04/ontarios-affordable-housing-wait-list-hits-record-high.html.

Morrow, Adrian. 2015. "Hydro One: Ontario's Privatization Plan Explained." *Globe and Mail*, 3 June. http://www.theglobeandmail.com/news/politics/hydro-one-ontarios-privatization-plan-explained/article24743446/.

– 2016. "Union to Sue Ontario Government over Hydro One Sell-Off." *Globe and Mail*, 14 September. http://www.theglobeandmail.com/news/national/union-to-sue-ontario-government-over-hydro-one-sell-off/article31869405/.

Noonen, Jeff. 2012. *Academic Freedom Endangered in Ontario*. Toronto: Canadian Centre for Policy Alternatives Ontario, 1 April. https://www.policyalternatives.ca/publications/monitor/academic-freedom-endangered-ontario.

Ontario Confederation of University Faculty Associations. 2012. *OCUFA Analysis of the Drummond Report: Long on Cuts, Short on Insight*. http://ocufa.on.ca/assets/OCUFA-Drummond-Report-Analysis-Feb.-22-2012Final.pdf.

Ontario Common Front. 2012. *Falling Behind: Ontario's Backslide into Widening Inequality, Growing Poverty and Cuts to Social Programs*. http://www.weareontario.ca/wp-content/uploads/OCF-RPT-Falling Behind-20120829.pdf.

Ontario Liberal Party. 2003. *Achieving Our Potential: The Ontario Liberal Plan for Economic Growth, Book #3*. Toronto: Ontario Liberal Party.

Ontario Ministry of Finance. 1989. *Table C6: Ten-Year Review of Selected Financial and Economic Statistics ($ millions), Ontario Budget 1989*, 49. Toronto: Queen's Printer. http://books2.scholarsportal.info/viewdoc.html?id=586155.

– 1996–2011. *Public Accounts of Ontario*. Toronto: Queen's Printer.

– 2010. *Ontario Economic Outlook and Fiscal Review 2010*. Toronto: Queen's Printer. http://www.fin.gov.on.ca/en/budget/fallstatement/2010/paper_all.pdf.

– 2011. *Ontario Budget 2011: Turning the Corner to a Better Tomorrow*. Toronto: Queen's Printer. http://www.fin.gov.on.ca/en/budget/ontariobudgets/2011/papers_all.pdf.

– 2012. *Ontario Budget 2012: Strong Action for Ontario*. Toronto: Queen's Printer. http://www.fin.gov.on.ca/en/budget/ontariobudgets/2012/papers_all.pdf.

– 2015. *Ontario Budget 2015: Building Ontario Up*. Toronto: Queen's Printer. http://www.fin.gov.on.ca/en/budget/ontariobudgets/2015/papers_all.pdf.

Ontario Ministry of Treasury and Economics. 1981. *1982 Budget Speech*. Toronto: Queen's Printer.

– 1981a. *1981 Ontario Budget*. Toronto: Queen's Printer.

– 1981b. *Budget paper 'A': Fiscal developments in Ontario in the 1970s*. 1981 Ontario Budget. Toronto: Queen's Printer.

– 1981c. *Budget paper 'C': Ontario's fiscal management strategy*. Ontario Budget. Toronto: Queen's Printer.
– n.d. Committee on Government Productivity. *Organizing for Program Delivery*. File: Ross Structures of Government. RG 18-527, Box Y82.
Ontario Ministry of Treasury, Economics and Intergovernmental Affairs. 1972. Committee on Government Productivity. *Agencies, Boards and Commissions: A Discussion Paper* (25 February). File: Boards and Commissions. RG 18-527, Box Y82.
– 1972a. Committee on Government Productivity. *Report to the Executive Council of the Government of Ontario*. Toronto: Queen's Printer.
Ontario Progressive Conservative Party. 1994. *The Common Sense Revolution*. Toronto: Ontario Progressive Conservative Party.
Osborne, David, and Ted Gaebler. 1992. *Reinventing Government: How the Entrepreneurial Spirit Is Transforming the Public Sector*. Reading: Addison-Wesley Publishing Co.
Palmer, Bryan. 1992. *Working-Class Experience: Rethinking the History of Canadian Labour, 1800–1991*. Toronto: McClelland and Stewart.
Panitch, Leo, and Donald Swartz. 2003. *From Consent to Coercion: The Assault on Trade Union Freedoms*. Aurora: Garamond Press.
Peterson, David, and Bob Rae. 1985. *An Agenda for Reform: Proposals for a Minority Parliament*. Toronto: The New Democrats.
Poverty and Employment Precarity in Southern Ontario. 2013. *It's More than Poverty Employment Precarity and Household Well-Being*. Hamilton: McMaster University-United Way.
Premier's Advisory Council on Government Assets. 2015. *Improving Performance and Unlocking Value in the Electricity Sector.* Toronto: Queen's Printer. https://www.ontario.ca/page/improving-performance-and-unlocking-value-electricity-sector.
Rachlis, Chuck, and David Wolfe. 1997. "An Insider's View of the NDP Government of Ontario: The Politics of Permanent Opposition Meets the Economics of Permanent Recession." In *The Government and Politics of Ontario*, 5th ed., edited by Graham White, 331–64. Toronto: University of Toronto Press.
Rae, Bob. 1996. *From Protest to Power: Personal Reflections on a Life in Politics*. Toronto: Viking Press.
Reshef, Yonatan, and Sandra Rastin. 2003. *Unions in the Time of Revolution: Government Restructuring in Alberta and Ontario*. Toronto: University of Toronto Press.
Richter, Barbara. 2006. *It's Elementary: A Brief History of Ontario's Public Elementary Teachers and Their Federations*. Toronto: ETFO.

Roberts, Wayne. 1994. *Don't Call Me Servant: Government Work and Union in Ontario, 1911–1984*. Toronto: Ontario Public Service.

Sack Goldblatt Mitchell LLP. 1993. *An Analysis of Bill 48: The Social Contract Act*. Toronto: Sack Goldblatt Mitchell LLP.

Shillington, Richard. 2014. *Which Pays Better: Public or Private Sector Jobs? Settling the Debate*. Ottawa: Canadian Centre for Policy Alternatives Ontario. https://www.policyalternatives.ca/sites/default/files/uploads/publications/Ontario%20Office/2014/09/Which%20Pays%20Better%20Public%20or%20PrivateFINAL.pdf.

Siemiatycki, Matti, and Naeem Farooqi. 2012. "Value for Money and Risk in Public–Private Partnerships." *Journal of the American Planning Association* 78 (3): 286–99.

Siekierski, B.J. 2014. "100,000 Fewer Public Sector Jobs Possible under Wynne: Don Drummond." *iPolitics*, 26 June. http://www.ipolitics.ca/2014/06/26/100000-few-public-sector-jobs-possible-under-wynne-don-drummond/.

Sinclair, Duncan, Mark Rochon, and Peggy Leatt. 2005. *Riding the Third Rail: The Story of Ontario's Health Services Restructuring Committee, 1996–2000*. Montreal: IPAC.

Special Program Review Committee (SPRC), Ministry of Treasury, Economics, and Intergovernmental Affairs. 1975. *Report of the Special Review Committee (November)*. Toronto: Queen's Printer.

Speirs, Rosemary. 1986. *Out of the Blue: The Fall of the Tory Dynasty in Ontario*. Toronto: Macmillan.

Statistics Canada. 2001. "Table CD1T07 Employment by Class of Worker, Public and Private Sector, Sex, Industry, Canada, Province, Annual Average (Table)." *Labour Force Historical Review 2001*, Revised edition, CD 1. Statistics Canada Catalogue no. 71F0004XCB. CD-ROM.

Stinson, Scott. 2014. "Ex-Liberal Finance Minister Warned His Party That Deep Spending Cuts Are Needed to Balance Ontario Budget." *National Post*, 9 May. http://news.nationalpost.com/news/canada/canadian-politics/even-an-ex-liberal-finance-minister-warned-wynne-that-deep-spending-cuts-are-needed-to-balance-ontarios-budget.

Thomas, Mark. 2009. *Regulating Flexibility: The Political Economy of Employment Standards*. Montreal and Kingston: McGill-Queen's University Press.

Tiessen, Kaylie. 2014. *Seismic Shift Ontario's Changing Labour Market*. Toronto: Canadian Centre for Policy Alternatives Ontario.

Walkom, Thomas. 1994. *Rae Days: The Rise and Follies of the NDP*. Toronto: Key Porter Books.

– 1997. “The Harris Government Restoration or Revolution?” In *The Government and Politics of Ontario* 5th ed., edited by Graham White, 402–17. Toronto: University of Toronto Press.
– 2012. “Wrong-Headed Ontario Budget Tough on Public Sector, Vague on Rest.” *Toronto Star*, 27 March. http://www.thestar.com/news/canada/2012/03/27/walkom_wrongheaded_ontario_budget_tough_on_public_sector_vague_on_the_rest.html.
Warskett, Rosemary. 1997. “Learning to Be ‘Uncivil’: Class Formation andFeminization in the Public Service Alliance of Canada, 1966–1996.” PhD diss., Carleton University.
White, Graham. 2002. *Change in the Ontario State 1952–2002*. Paper prepared for the Role of Government Panel, available at http://www.ontla.on.ca/library/repository/mon/8000/244111.pdf.

CHAPTER SIX

From the Bailiffs at Our Doors to the Greek Peril: Twenty Years of Fiscal "Urgency" and Quebec Politics

PETER GRAEFE AND X.H. RIOUX OUIMET

When discussing austerity and public services in the Canadian provinces, there may be a tendency to cast Quebec in a favourable light given the Maple Spring of 2012. This event, starting with a broad-based student strike and expanding into a larger set of concerns for public services and the right to protest, reflected particularities of the organization of social interests in Quebec and pointed to certain possibilities in terms of alternatives. At the same time, a focus on this experience may divert attention from other features of post-crisis budgeting and statecraft in Quebec. While the scale of the fiscal challenge from the 2008 crisis is quite minor compared to that of its neighbours in Ontario and New Brunswick (Gillies in this volume), the ebb and flow of Quebec's partisan politics seems to have made austerity a powerful card for conservative forces that have long sought to restructure the state.

The fact that the 2012 student strike was resolved by the election of a weak and short-lived Parti Québécois (PQ) minority government seems to have emboldened Quebec's Liberals to embark on a much more profound set of cuts to services and to the employment conditions of civil servants. Having said that, Quebecers came into the crisis with a far more robust and redistributive welfare state than Canada's other provinces, a characteristic that is unlikely to be undone in the course of a single mandate. This, in turn, provides some additional opportunities to craft alternative socioeconomic paths. Put another way, Quebec's governments over the past two decades have pursued budgetary austerity, and this has shown up in budgets and public-sector employment. However, given that Quebec started with a larger and more redistributive state and better organized unions and social movements, there remain possibilities and resources for constructing alternatives.

This chapter starts by looking at the big picture of Quebec budgeting as well as the more specific features of post-2008 restructuring, capturing a trajectory with similarities to other provinces, and indeed other nation-states. Despite this similarity in trajectories, Quebec's had a different starting point, which the chapter develops by discussing the relative performance of the Quebec welfare state and the situation of its labour movement. This has allowed for political opposition to austerity and restructuring to take different forms than can be seen in other provinces. Nonetheless, the labour movement has had a difficult time translating its power into either a broad-based alliance against austerity or an effective insider bargaining strategy to protect public services.

The chapter concludes with some reflection on alternatives. It is difficult to see a clear and all-encompassing path away from austerity, particularly since positive-sum, cross-class strategies (e.g. development strategies that bring sustained profits and rising standards of living) seem relatively unlikely (Pineault 2014). However, in this chapter we seek to point to some smaller-scale possibilities, such as minor departures achieved by the PQ minority government between 2012 and 2014, as reminders that there is always some potential to start crafting these elements into something more encompassing.

THE BIG PICTURE: RE-ENGINEERING PUBLIC FINANCES

A month after the Liberals' electoral victory in April 2014, Quebec's finance minister Carlos J. Leitão told economic journalist Gérald Fillion (2014) that if nothing was done to curb public spending, the province would be in the same financial situation as Greece or Portugal within five years. Yet, taken as a percentage of gross domestic product (GDP), Quebec's net debt amounted to 50.8% in 2013–14,[1] compared with 115% and 176% for Portugal and Greece. Since 2009–10, this proportion had only moved up from 49.7%. Between 2007 and 2014, despite slow economic growth, accumulated deficits also remained stable, at 32.8% of provincial GDP.[2] Moreover, consistent with Quebec's *Act to Reduce the Debt and Establish the Generations Fund*, the government aims to bring that last figure down to 17% by 2025–26. Thus, not only will financial restraint be the norm for the next decade, but even if nothing had been done to change existing budgetary trends, Minister Leitão's would have remained a manifest overstatement (Fortier and Tremblay-Pépin 2014).

Hyperbole about the unsustainability of Quebec's public finances dates back at least to the mid-1990s. It would thus be a mistake to discuss Quebec's public-sector restructuring since 2007 without reference to the late 1990s' budgeting trends, and the previous Liberal administration's efforts in "modernizing the state," from 2003 onward. The late 1990s profoundly influenced perceptions of Quebec's finances, notably through an accounting reform that, in 1997, changed how public debts are computed. In 1996–97, Quebec's net debt amounted to 36% of its GDP; in 1997–98, it was established at 47% of the GDP. Accumulated deficits followed the same trend: between 1996 and 1998, they increased by 8% as a proportion of the GDP, up to 44%. Such drastic increases took place because Quebec chose to revise its bookkeeping practices (Ministère des Finances 1998a), thereby adding billions in pension fund liabilities to the net debt as well as amalgamating capital expenditures and accumulated budget deficits (Ministère des Finances 1998b).

This reform was implemented at a time when the PQ government was dedicated to restoring budget balance while fiscal imbalance between provinces and the federal government reached problematic proportions (Rioux Ouimet 2014). From 1994 to 1999, operating expenses grew at an average annual rate of 0.3%, with two successive cutbacks between 1994 and 1996 (Imbeau and Leclerc 2002, 71). As a consequence of the 30% drop in federal transfers between 1995 and 1998, budget restraint was institutionalized with the 1996 *Act Respecting the Elimination of the Deficit and a Balanced Budget*; budget deficits were generally prohibited and governments forced to restore balance within five years after incurring one. These choices aimed at binding subsequent administrations but also, not unlike in Ontario's case, the public sector as a whole (see Evans and Fanelli in this volume). Although the PQ adopted a number of structuring, social-democratic policies (McGrane 2014; Noël 2002; Vaillancourt and Thériault 2008) and increased operating expenses at an average rate of 5.3% between 2000 and 2003 (Databank of Official Statistics on Québec, see note 1), precedents were thus established upon which the post-2003 Liberal government could work.

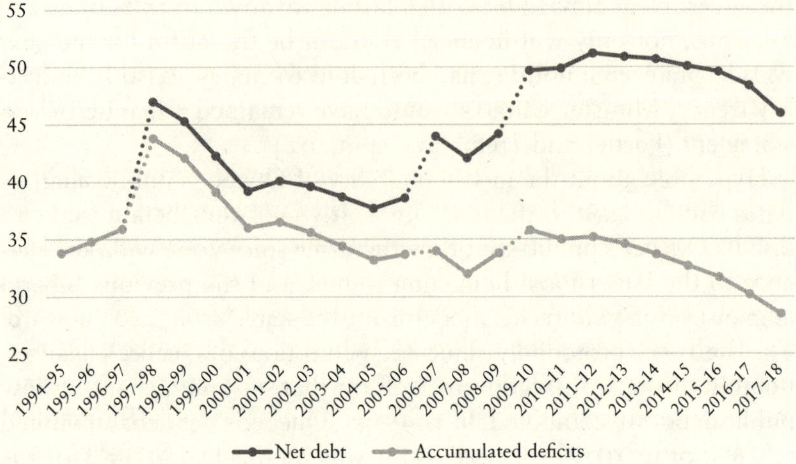

Sources: Databank of Official Statistics on Québec; Quebec. Ministère des Finances 2016. Breaks represent accounting reforms.

Figure 6.1 Debt and deficits (% of Quebec's GDP)

Changes were already perceptible in 2003–04: overall, operating expenses were increased by 3.8%, 1.5% less than the 2000–03 average and 1.8% less than the previous administration's plans for 2003–04 (Treasury Board 2003). This rate also concealed important alterations in the distribution of spending; budget allocations for economic development, for instance, dropped by almost 14%, while those for the Treasury Board were increased by more than 33%. Such figures say a lot about the centralization and tightening of expenditure management. The influence of the Department of Finance and Treasury Board indeed rose noticeably under the Liberals, in part as a result of the Treasury's "Modernization Plan" (Conseil du Trésor 2004).

According to this plan, Quebec was caught in a "budget trap," with higher public spending, public spending growth, debt, and income taxes than Canadian averages. Ignoring the political roots and income side of the problem – with federal transfers reaching a historic low point in 2003–04, Liberals argued that new budgetary priorities had to be set and the state refocused on "essential missions." Spending growth was reduced to 2.9% in 2004–05; mandates of state corporations were revised to subordinate development responsibilities to market performance (Rioux Ouimet 2012); a policy framework favouring public–private partnerships (P3s) for major highway and hospital projects, as well as a Public–Private Partnership Agency, were established; and the size of the public-service workforce was further reduced by replacing only 50% of retirees and favouring casual jobs.

Well before 2007, Liberals were thus engaged in a "re-engineering" of the public sector. Two reforms were then implemented in 2006–07 that had significant impacts on public finances: first was the establishment of the "Generations Fund," retaining substantial revenues from, notably, Hydro-Québec's royalties, and second was the inclusion of the health and education networks' liabilities to the public debt, adding more than $18 billion to the net debt (see figure 6.1; Ministère des Finances 2007b, 21). Before this accounting reform, the net debt and accumulated deficits had been declining, as a percentage of GDP, between 1997 and 2006 (Databank of Official Statistics on Québec, see note 1). Now, their sudden rise put even more pressure on health and education departments to control expenditures. Unsurprisingly, the implementation of user fees and an expansion of the role of private clinics and insurance were recommended as early as 2008 (Task Force on the Funding of the Health System 2008).

On top of that, Finance Minister Jérôme-Forget (simultaneously chair of the Treasury Board) introduced tax cuts in 2007–08. By raising the tax tables' income thresholds, mostly benefiting high-income households (Ministère des Finances 2007c, F10), and by phasing out the tax on capital by 2011, this budget ultimately deprived the state of over $3 billion in annual revenues (Couturier, Hurteau, and Pépin 2010). Notwithstanding the budget surplus, revenues from income and corporate taxes remained stagnant, with slightly rising federal transfers bridging the gap (Ministère des Finances 2008a, 119). By 2008, it was clear that political choices, at least as much as financial imperatives, were driving the Liberals' budget strategies. The appointment of a Task Force on Fees for Public Services in late 2007 was clearly another indication of this. In its report (2008), the Task Force on Fees advised the "urgent" implementation and indexing of user fees for water consumption, highways, electricity rates, university tuition, and child care. With the financial crisis in full swing, GDP growth revised downwards for 2008, and decreasing inputs from the personal income tax (PIT) and corporate taxes (Ministère des Finances 2008b; 2009b), this report was timely for the Liberals.

Post-Crisis Restraint

The 2008–09 budget, with a 4.2% growth in operating expenses, hardly qualified as a stimulus even when considering the new credits on payroll taxes and investments (Ministère des Finances 2008b). As figure 6.2 suggests, post-crisis tax expenditures were mainly aimed at stimulating consumption. After a rise in 2008–09, corporate tax expenditures actually declined between 2009 and 2012, while credits on PIT and consumption taxes rose substantially. Combined with these billions in additional tax credits, the recession of 2009, with a 1.4% decline in real GDP and close to 40,000 lost jobs, seriously undermined Quebec's revenues. Between 2008 and 2010, consolidated autonomous revenues declined by almost 2% (Ministère des Finances 2010a). Compared with previous recessions, these effects were relatively mild, but the upturn also proved much less vigorous. Most interesting are the moves that led to this timid recovery, a somewhat paradoxical mix of budget austerity, user fees, and consumption stimulation (Pineault 2013a).

Alongside the 2009–10 budget, a "Policy for the Funding of Public Services" was implemented, which incorporated some recommendations of the aforementioned Task Force on user fees (Ministère des Finances 2009a). Applying to all public bodies, it required the cost of all fee-based and potential fee-based services to be determined. Based in part on this cost, new fees would be introduced and, as with existing ones (except for child care), adjusted annually from 2011 onward. Quebec's *Financial Administration Act* was modified in 2010 to this end. Only "pure public goods," such as justice and security, would ultimately be funded through income taxes, while "mixed" (health, education, transport) and "private" (insurance, electricity) goods were to be partly or wholly fee-based (Ministère des Finances 2009a, 10). From 2004 to 2008, consolidated user-fee revenues had already grown by more than 20% (Ministère des Finances 2009d, 53); between 2007 and 2011, the proportion of services' costs covered by user fees rose to over 52% for public bodies (Ministère des Finances 2012, 16).

User fees were also accompanied by consumption taxes. Consistent with the recommendation of the Advisory Committee on the Economy and Public Finances to lower income taxes while raising user fees and consumption taxes (Ministère des Finances 2009c), two successive increases of the Quebec sales tax (QST) were announced in 2009 and

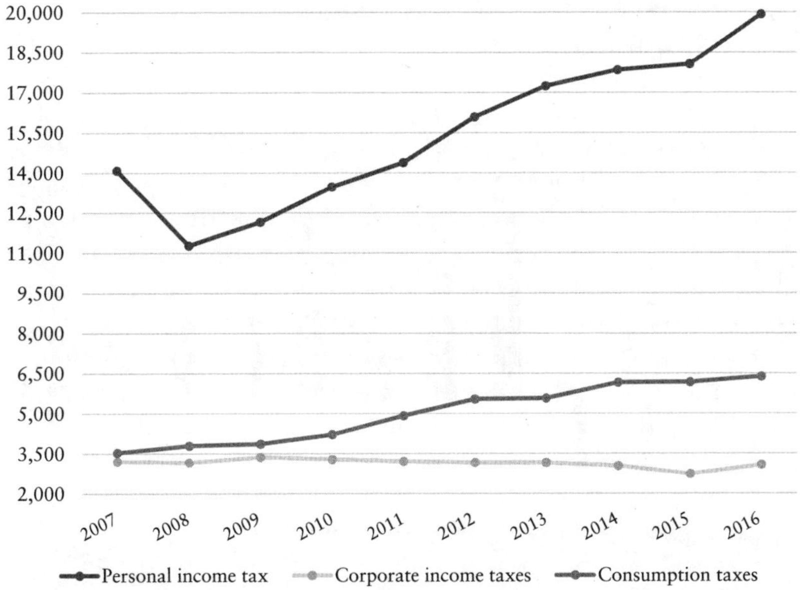

Sources: Québec. Ministère des Finances 2010c; 2015b; 2017.

Figure 6.2 Quebec's tax expenditures (millions of dollars)

2010 (Ministère des Finances 2010b), establishing it at 9.5% for 2012. In fact, consumption tax revenues had already been growing faster than PIT revenues: from 2007 to 2012, even if consumption tax credits were the fastest growing tax expenditure, consumption taxes were catching up to PIT as the state's main source of revenues (see figure 6.3). Although this trend receded after 2012, it has been promoted again by the Commission d'examen sur la fiscalité québécoise, created by the Liberals in 2014 and chaired by Luc Godbout, ex-member of the above-mentioned Advisory Committee.

With operating expenses increasing more rapidly than consolidated revenues for 2009–10, a $3 billion deficit was incurred and the return to balance planned for 2013–14 (Ministère des Finances 2009d). The persistence of the deficit beyond this date was due in good part to constant overestimations of GDP growth; in the 2009–10 budget, an average of 2.5% was forecast for 2011, 2012, and 2013, when the actual rate was a mere 1.4% (Ministère des Finances 2013, 27). A vicious cycle thus formed – as GDP growth stagnated

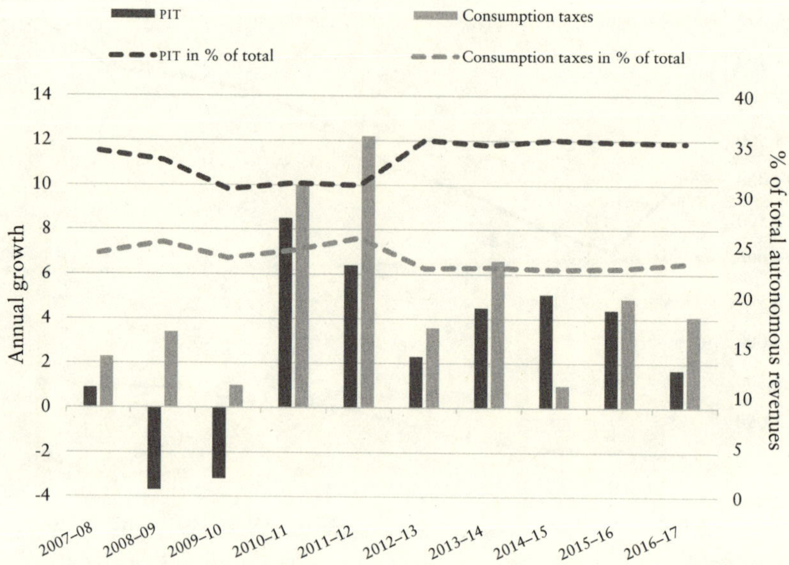

Sources: Treasury Board, "Public Accounts" (2007–08 to 2016–17)

Figure 6.3 Quebec's revenues from PIT and consumption taxes

below expectations, so did revenues; with deficits persisting, public spending growth was decelerated, thereby affecting economic growth. In 2010–11, the growth of operating expenses was reduced to 2.9% (Ministère des Finances 2010b), and the trend downwards carried on for the next five years (see figure 6.4). To compensate for stagnating revenues and to modify revenue sources, a payroll freeze was also imposed on the public sector until 2013–14, and many new fees were implemented.

First, an "annual health contribution" (similar to the McGuinty government's "health care premium" in Ontario) was introduced in 2012 as a regressive, across-the-board tax. Added to the QST hikes, this contributed to boost revenues from PIT and consumption taxes in 2010–11, while revenues from corporate taxes, with the tax on capital disappearing, stagnated (Treasury Board 2011, 139). Then, to curb the university network's deficit, a 75% increase in tuition fees over five years (2012–17) was imposed (Ministère des Finances 2011). In a context of stagnating salaries, this hike had a mixed reception to say the least.

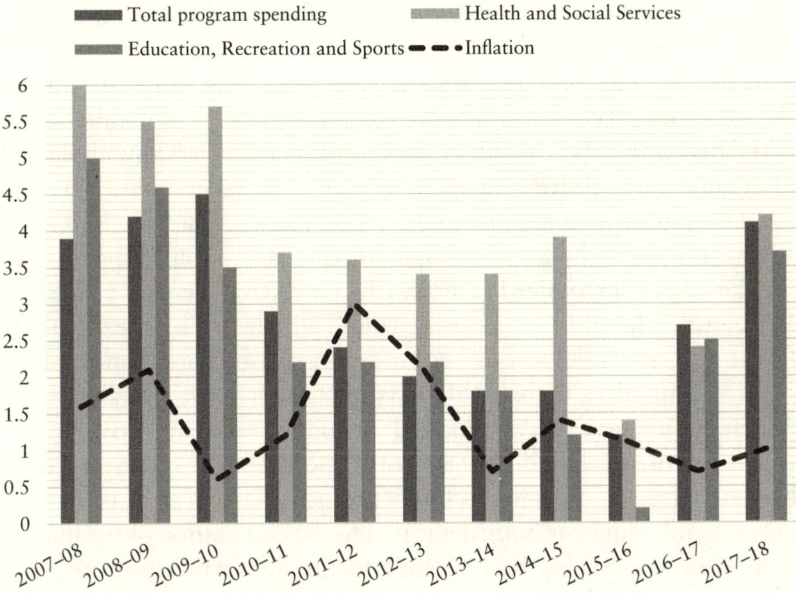

Sources: Treasury Board, "Expenditure Budgets" (2007–08 to 2017–18).

Figure 6.4 Quebec's operating expenses and inflation (% annual growth)

Overall, between 2007 and 2012, consolidated public spending (including debt servicing) as a proportion of Quebec's GDP rose from less than 21% to over 23% (*Observatoire* 2013). This arguably had less to do with increased spending than with slow GDP growth, but it does qualify arguments about austerity in the post-crisis years. Yet, as figure 6.4 shows, the fact remains that successive administrations did indeed follow budget restraint strategies, as a response to the financial crisis but also to growing vertical fiscal imbalance with the federal government (Rioux Ouimet 2014; Bourque and Bibeau 2014). The first three post-2009 budgets all included substantial drops in spending growth: from 4.5% in 2009–10, the annual growth of operating expenses moved to only 1.2% by 2015–16. In 2011–12 and 2012–13, growth rates were actually lower than inflation and can, therefore, be effectively interpreted as cutbacks. This had very concrete impacts on central departments, such as Health and Social Services or Education, Recreation and Sports, with clear downward pressures on their expenditure budgets.

The Brief PQ Interregnum and the Return of the Liberals

Without altering these trends, some divergence was noticeable during the PQ's minority government interregnum between September 2012 and April 2014. The health contribution was completely abolished or significantly reduced for 65% of people and increased by $1000 for individuals with net incomes over $150,000. The hike in tuition fees was replaced by a 3% annual indexing, and a fourth income tax bracket was reintroduced at a rate of 25.75% for incomes exceeding $100,000. The old "fifteen-year rule," which forced the Régie de l'assurance maladie du Québec to defray the full price on publicly covered drugs despite the availability of cheaper generic versions after patent expiry, was also abandoned. Beyond this, the PQ government was too short-lived to draw firm conclusions about how far it would have departed from previous budget trends. What is clear is that the new Liberal administration, dedicated to the elimination of the budget deficit in 2015–16, has been moving further down the austerity path.

Based on projections from the *Rapport d'experts sur l'état des finances publiques*, ordered by the Liberals after the 2014 elections, spending growth rates were reduced to 1.8% and 1.2% for the next two years respectively and the 2014–15 budget established that any surplus from 2016 onward would be spent equally on debt and tax reductions. In addition, a hiring freeze for the public sector was imposed and was to last up to March 2016. In addition, corporate tax rates for small and medium manufacturing businesses were reduced, a "safety catch" was established by the Treasury Board requiring that any new public expense must be counterbalanced by an equivalent saving, and Bill 3 forced the retroactive restructuration of municipal pension plans on the basis of fifty-fifty financing by employees and employers. This last measure included the non-indexation of current retirees' pensions in the case of underfunded plans, and contributions to the plans could not exceed 18% of total payroll going forward. The 2016–17 budget maintained this austere course; while it forecast a $2 billion surplus, this was based on increasing the health budget by 2.4%, which is below cost inflation for the sector, and the education budget by 2.5%, which amounts to very little new money once inflation and enrollment growth are factored in (see figure 6.4).

Finally, a Commission de révision permanente des programmes, loosely modeled on Ontario's Drummond Commission (see Evans and Fanelli in this volume), was mandated to evaluate the relevance of existing public services and recommend alternative funding methods. At first, it seemed like this Commission's first report, published in November 2014, was received coldly because of its radicalism. With hindsight, it now appears that some of its recommendations were implemented. Most significantly, provincial transfers to municipalities were reduced by $300 million for 2015, following a "transitory fiscal pact" aimed at facilitating the attainment of budget balance in 2015–16. Consistent with principles set out by the Commission, fees for public child care services were also increased and scaled to income, at between $8 and $20 a day per child before provincial and federal tax deductions.

In one case, the Liberal administration went even further than the Commission by putting an end to a fifty-five-year-old agreement with France, according to which French students paid the same fees as the province's citizens for higher education. It is also noteworthy that social assistance, which was largely left alone by Jean Charest's Liberals, was again subject to cuts. This began with an attempt by the PQ to find $20 million in cuts by reducing benefits for certain categories, which the Liberals resumed by cutting $200 million from the Ministry of Labour, Employment and Social Solidarity's budget. Some of this came from cuts to other programs, such as the network of youth employment centres (the Carrefours Jeunesse-Emploi), but the rest came from clawing back benefits. In November 2015 the government introduced Bill 70, which was filled with punitive measures such as cutting benefits in half for recipients who refuse to take a job or training program. The bill was held up, for a time, given the strong response from the Commission des droits de la personne, welfare rights groups, and opposition parties, but was finally adopted in November 2016. Although many austerity measures have engendered concern and disquiet within the public sector and labour movement since 2003, it remains unclear how effective the scattered opposition to austerity can prove to be in the long run.

QUEBEC'S PUBLIC SECTOR AND LABOUR MOVEMENT

This story of recurrent pulses of austerity over the past two decades is not without parallels in other provinces, notably in neighbouring Ontario (see Evans and Fanelli in this volume). Nevertheless, given Quebec's unique starting point, the similar trajectories do not mean convergence. Recent studies of social spending across the provinces reveal large differences in both outlays and redistributive effects that are comparable to divergences between "worlds of welfare" in the main welfare state typologies (Haddow 2013; 2015). In the Canadian case, Quebec has been an outlier since the 1970s in terms of the size of its provincial state apparatus, with higher levels of indebtedness, taxes, and redistribution than the other large provinces. Since the 1990s, social policy choices, particularly around encouraging the labour force participation of mothers with young children and supplementing the income of families with kids, have further set Quebec apart (van den Berg and Raïq 2014). This is seen by the fact that the tax and transfer system in Quebec does more to reduce inequality (as measured by the Gini coefficient) than other provincial welfare states, and has managed to prevent increased labour market inequality translating into increased overall income inequality (Noël 2013). The fact that households at the median family income are still net beneficiaries of the tax and transfer system is politically significant in terms of providing a broader base of voters with an interest in shielding the redistributive state from austerity and restructuring.

For Haddow (2013), and for Noël (2013) to a lesser extent, the explanation for this divergence rests on the higher rates of union density in Quebec. Whereas density has declined for Canada as a whole over the past two decades, it has scarcely moved in Quebec, remaining at about 40% (versus 30% in the rest of Canada and 28% in Ontario). Beneath the near constant level of density, there have been some shifts in the makeup of the labour movement. In particular, the decline in unionized manufacturing employment, particularly since 2000, as well as continued weakness in organizing the private-service sector, has been compensated with large membership gains in the booming construction sector (although this only makes up roughly 7% of total membership, compared to the 45% of members drawn from the public sector). In terms of the constant tension within unions between protecting members' immediate interests and developing a broader socio-political vision (see Collombat 2014), this shift in membership has likely served to draw the already more conservative Fédération des travailleurs et travailleuses du Québec (FTQ) away from more contentious political activity.

The degree of inter-federation rivalry also sets Quebec apart, with three separate federations involved in representing public employees and on occasion engaging in raiding or poaching behaviour. All told, the Confédération des syndicats nationaux (CSN) is the main representative of public-sector employees, particularly those in the provincial public service and hospitals. This includes 130,000 members in its health and social services federation, 60,000 in its public-service employees federation, and another 30,000 in its education federation (largely CEGEP/college teachers and university sessionals). The FTQ – the largest federation in the province – is less present in the public sector, although it is much more visible at the municipal level, particularly through the Canadian Union of Public Employees; it also has some new presence at universities through Public Service Alliance of Canada organizing. While the Centrale des syndicats du Québec (126,000 members, with 60,000 members of its core teachers' federation) has recently tried to diversify its membership, it remains first and foremost the representative of the province's teachers. There are also a variety of independent unions, such as the Fédération interprofessionelle de la santé (63,000 members), which largely represents nurses, and the Syndicat de la fonction publique et parapublique du Québec (35,000 members). If this was not already complex enough, the negotiation of public-sector contracts passes through a heavy bureaucratic process wherein the union centrals must try to develop a common front in negotiating with the government employer.

Public-sector employees have obviously not been left unaffected by the big picture struggle over budgetary policy discussed above and its translation into staffing levels and working conditions. Each wave of austerity leaves its own mark. In the mid-1990s, the main approach was a thinning of the public sector. Between 1993 and 1998, Quebec shed nearly 43,000 public-sector jobs (from 704,900 to 662,000). In 2008–09, this dipped by 2,500 from 804,400 before climbing back to 868,700 in 2013. In the early years of Charest's Liberal administration, the focus was less on staffing levels than on restructuring the collective bargaining situation. This took the form of changes to legislation on contracting out so as to strip successorship rights for unionized workers; in other words, the changes removed the ability of workers to retain the terms of employment when their work is subcontracted (Haddow and Klassen 2006). More significantly for public-sector unions, the government unilaterally decreed a new framework of union representation within the health sector, ending the existing set of union accreditations and agreements. The result was an intense period of campaigning and raiding between the different public-sector unions as they attempted to represent employees under the new system (Collombat 2014).

On the bargaining front, after months of negotiations, the Charest administration unilaterally imposed a five-year collective agreement in December 2005, without much effective push back. This was in notable contrast with the student movement, which had struck in the spring of 2005 and managed to push back an attempt to cut about $100 million from student grants. For the renegotiation in 2009–10, the unions managed to form the largest and most encompassing Common Front in Quebec history. This Front was able to mount massive gatherings and demonstrations in support of their demands. Nevertheless, the leadership agreed to an early deal, which was less lucrative than anticipated and disappointed many activists. It seemed at the time that the leadership was willing to take a less beneficial deal simply to be able to return to negotiated contracts, rather than legislatively imposed ones (Collombat 2014; Charest 2009; Mandel 2010). In 2015, the unions faced an emboldened Liberal government that proposed a five-year contract with wage freezes in the first two years and 1% increases in the final three. The government's initial proposal also sought to increase class sizes and the length of teachers' work weeks in public schools, to increase patient-to-nurse ratios in hospitals, and to remove bonuses for working night shifts. Despite the government's austere budgetary language, recent Supreme Court decisions on freedom of association meant that the government was willing to show some limited flexibility in bargaining, resulting in agreements that would raise wages about 9% over five years, which would be ever-so-slightly above the rate of inflation. The unions conceded a one-year increase in the retirement age (to sixty-one) and straightened out some inequities in the government's salary grid, which would bring a one-time salary bump of up to 2.4% for affected employees.

The net result has left the provincial civil service in a relatively underpaid situation, and its levels of pay have continued to slide in the post-crisis period. In 2014, the wages of Quebec government employees were, on average, 11.5% lower than those of other Quebecers working in the same types of jobs and 8.4% lower than Quebecers working in the same types of jobs in the private sector. When one looks at total compensation, Quebec government employees are more or less at parity with the private sector, but they are behind other public-sector employees in Quebec (e.g. municipal employees and broader public-sector employees) (Institut de la Statistique du Québec 2015).

This suggests that when talking of austerity, different groups of public workers start from different places: municipal workers and workers in the broader public sector have done relatively better than provincial public servants or many parts of the private sector. The public sector advantage over the private sector, particularly compared to non-unionized and service workers, flows more strongly from benefits than from wages. It is therefore not surprising that the Philippe Couillard Liberals' Bill 3 targeted municipal workers and their pension plans, and that Common Front negotiations are also trying to find savings in pension adjustments. It is also worth noting that the conditions of work have changed somewhat over the period. Public-sector employees show a higher rate of atypical (e.g. part-time, contract, part-year) work (25.9%) as compared to the private sector (19.1), although this is an increase of only 0.7 percentage points from 1997–99 to 2011–13 compared to a 1.5 percentage point increase in the private sector over the same time period.

The bigger change has been within atypical public–sector work, with the largest category moving from being permanent part-time (from 41.8% of atypical jobs in 1997–99 to 34.2% in 2011–13) to being temporary full-time (44.5% in 2011–13, up from 35.9% in 1997–99) (Cloutier-Villeneuve 2014, 8). Although Quebec has not seen much direct privatization of public-sector work in the form of contracting out, tight finances coupled with new delivery models have meant that job growth in certain care sectors has been skewed to the private sector. This is, for instance, the case in health care and social assistance, the second largest job category in Quebec behind retail (and ahead of manufacturing). While public-sector employment has increased by about 50,000 from 200,000 jobs in 1991 to 250,000 in 2010, private-sector jobs have increased from 100,000 to 180,000 over the same period, now making up 43% of sector employment. It is noteworthy that private employment really started growing in 1998, about a year after public-sector employment dropped by 20,000, and no doubt this is related in part to job cuts flowing from the 1996 austerity drive (Cloutier 2011, 7).

OPPOSITION

Strategies to resist public-sector austerity obviously predate the 2008 crisis. In the mid-1990s, the preferred strategy was to use mechanisms of multi-stakeholder social dialogue in an attempt to trade-off balanced budgets (and the public-sector job cuts needed to get there) for state and public-sector commitments to expand employment and innovate in social policy. The highest profile examples of such multi-stakeholder dialogue and concerted action were two summits held in 1996, bringing together the union federations, key employer groups, and a number of other leading social actors to find a consensual path to balanced budgets. This strategy was roundly criticized in the years following the 1996 summits, resulting for instance in the CSN stepping back from the Partners in Sovereignty organization in protest of the PQ's job cuts (Piotte 1998; 2013). However, our interviews with the senior staff of one labour central indicated that they felt their own members supported measures to balance the budget, so they had their hands tied (personal interview, February 2005). With the election of Jean Charest's government in 2003, the space for multi-stakeholder concerted action evaporated. As such, the response to changes to the labour code around successorship rights in cases of subcontracting took the form of a National Day of Disruption in December 2003. While there was a push to extend the disruption into a broader social strike, the strength of attachment to the existing legal regime, particularly at the FTQ, meant that labour ultimately pulled back (Collombat 2014).

As the 2008 crisis started to turn toward the adoption of austerity, actors seeking to combat the latter had both strengths and weaknesses. In terms of strength, the Liberal administration's ongoing interest in the user-pay principle had spurred counter-organization. The first to form, in the fall of 2009, was the Coalition opposée à la tarification et à la privatisation des services publics, which brought together unions, popular groups, civil society organizations, and, importantly, the radical student union Association pour une solidarité syndicale étudiante (ASSÉ). Local unions and sectoral union federations were part of this group, but the FTQ, CSN, and Centrale des Syndicats du Québec (CSQ) were not. They instead formed a Social Alliance in partnership with the two more mainstream student federations, the Fédération étudiante universitaire du Québec (FEUQ) and the Fédération étudiante collégiale du Québec (FECQ), in 2010. In terms of weakness, the unions' preferred political relay, the PQ, had mostly been critical of the government's recourse to deficit spending during the crisis and called for a rapid return to budget balance.

The preparatory work around fees enabled a more wide-ranging response to the government's announced tuition increase in its 2011–12 budget. Through strategies of organizing students, but also through much reflection on positioning and messaging, the more radical ASSÉ group was able to exert a lot of influence on the student response, pushing it toward striking. While the response was at first largely focused on student concerns about tuition, the earlier coalition work meant that it was already tied into a broader reflection around the value of public services, and that there were relays within the union movement and other social movements who could represent the strike in those terms (see Nadeau-Dubois 2013; Collombat 2014). As the strike lengthened and the government's heavy-handed response became less tenable, it developed into a more general strike against austerity and for the value of public services. When the government suspended classes as well as tightly regulated protest, the strike also expanded into a more general defense of democratic association (Piotte 2013).

In this context, favourable to bringing the labour movement's big-picture strategies forward, the actual response of labour centrals was mixed. At a grassroots level, labour organizations and activists provided forms of financial and moral support to the strike. At the peak level, support was more in the form of declarations, which nevertheless was already better than the hostilities seen during the 2005 student strike. For the labour centrals, in fact, the possibility of the student strike spurring a more general social strike was worrisome. Particularly for the FTQ, where the leadership saw the students as unlikely to be able to sustain their mobilization, the desire was to push the students to find a settlement with the government and to avoid the possibility of a wider social confrontation (Collombat 2014).

With the election of a PQ government in September 2012, the unions generally returned to trying to use insider strategies to influence government decisions. There was a good degree of unhappiness with the government's backtracking on a number of files. Student organizations had been hoping for a tuition freeze and were disappointed with the decision to index fees to inflation. The union-backed Coalition Solidarité Santé and others criticized the decision to modulate the health tax rather than scrap it as promised. But overall, the presence of a PQ government confused strategies, as progressive actors split over whether to engage the PQ as a "friendly" government through insider strategies or whether to protest from outside and position the anti-austerity movement closer to a smaller and younger left party, Québec Solidaire (QS).

The re-election of the Liberals in 2014 has revived the earlier split around user fees. On one hand, the Coalition opposée à la tarification et à la privatisation des services publics (or Coalition Main rouge) continues to draw on a large number (sixty-nine) of member groups to oppose public-sector cuts and to instead propose more progressive taxation and a crackdown on tax evasion. The membership draws together organizations working on a wide range of social justice pursuits (women's rights, housing, anti-poverty, student movements, etc.). Unions are well represented in the membership but at the level of labour council or sectoral federation rather than at the level of the labour centrals themselves. The coalition's message has hit a chord with the broader population, where there are concerns about cuts to core public services. This is seen, for instance, in the "Je protège mon école publique" demonstrations that started in the fall of 2015, where parents formed human chains around public schools to protest the government's cuts. This is an example of a new set of actors, namely school-based committees of parents, organizing autonomously in the anti-austerity/pro-public services space developed by the more radical actors.

Parallel to the Coalition Main rouge but with stronger labour control and a less radical set of tactics is the Refusons l'austérité group. Whereas the former group is organizing in the hope of building from the experience of the Maple Spring to launch a form of social strike, the latter appears to be geared toward using large public demonstrations to increase the political cost of the government continuing with austerity policies. Nevertheless, the Refusons l'austérité group is broader than the earlier Social Alliance, and includes the ASSÉ and a number of other groups of more radical persuasion.

The tensions between the leadership of the labour movement and a broader movement against austerity were renewed during the public-sector negotiations of 2015. For the actors around the Coalition Main rouge, these negotiations provided an opportunity to build a union–community common front against austerity, with union demands being tied to ensuring the survival and improved quality of public services. When the union leadership scaled back mobilization and then agreed to a moderate wage agreement ahead of a planned day of action in early December 2015, there was a palpable feeling of betrayal among rank-and-file activists (see Pelletier and Theurillat-Cloutier 2016). The union leadership likely felt that a rejection of the offer would have emboldened the government to legislate the unions back to work and did not feel that they could win an illegal strike against the government. For the rank and file, this was seen as putting the short-term financial interests of public-sector union members ahead of building a wide public coalition against austerity, and this reduced the union's credibility as a defender of public services and ally of public service users. As well, the example of how the students had organized to keep their negotiators in close and constant contact with their members had created expectations that the Common Front negotiators would respond to their members, but this expectation was disappointed as the union negotiators preferred to maintain the tradition of relatively closed negotiations. They wished to be able to turn on and turn off the tap of base-level mobilization to serve their strategy, rather than having to be in dialogue with the base about defining the strategy (Lacoursière 2016).

Parallel to this, there were a range of demonstrations against Bill 3, although these had a difficult time moving beyond trying to protect the pensions of specific groups of workers. Indeed, the framing of the issue, "On n'a rien volé (nous)," was less around austerity than around the blamelessness of the workers whose pensions were cut compared to the cabal of engineering companies, contractors, and morally pliable politicians who paraded before the Commission of Inquiry on the Awarding and Management of Public Contracts in the Construction Industry between 2012 and 2014. Resistance for the sake of resistance can only go so far, however. A purely defensive strategy may block certain austerity moves, but if it does not open doors toward other possibilities, it only forestalls the inevitable.

ALTERNATIVES

To speak of alternatives, one needs to think of both ideas and of a program for change but also of the political agencies and strategies that might translate them into practice. Drawing on the Quebec experience, but reflecting more broadly, Pineault (2014) underlines the difficulty of developing alternatives in the current context. While austerity plays havoc with the macro economy, it does not prevent ongoing accumulation through financialization (i.e. practices of financial value extraction), on one hand (see Pineault 2014, 97), and labour suppression in the productive economy on the other. As such, attempts to cast austerity as negative for everyone runs up against the fact that it is productive for a number of influential interests. Put otherwise, there is a disconnect between the effective framing of the current situation as an attack by the 1% on the extended middle class and the political agencies that could translate this framing into policy changes.

The framing of austerity as wrong-headed and self-defeating macroeconomic policy that should be replaced by a "win-win" expansionary policy cannot catch on if the business community does not feel that it needs that "win." Indeed, while expansionary policy would provide some benefits, it would also dampen some of the labour repression of austerity. As such, those opposed to austerity are left in a box if the solution is "growth" for its own sake, since the main door left to growth then becomes further extractivism, be it mineral development in the North or shale gas and oil throughout Quebec. Given the current parameters of resource extraction, this poses high environmental costs in return for bargain-basement royalties (Pineault 2013b; 2014).

Framing austerity in terms of social conflict with clear winners and losers (as opposed to a shared burden) nevertheless retains its use (see also Clancy in this volume). The same can be said about educational work on budgets and deficits – such as that of think-tanks like the Institut de recherche et d'informations socio-économiques (IRIS) and the Institut de recherche en économie contemporaine (IRÉC), for instance – that serves to de-dramatize the situation, thereby reducing the power of crisis narratives that justify broad and indiscriminate cuts. However, this work ultimately needs to be translated into a more aggressive program of public investment in collective utility goods, such as public services or community-based innovation, and of popular support for the range of taxes that such investment would require. It is not clear where the political agencies to advance such a project might be found in the short term. The political energies of the 2012 student strike were not enough to push the subsequent PQ government past a return to the *status quo ante*, and it remains to be seen whether the new PQ leader will significantly chart new directions on the welfare state and taxation. On the other hand, Québec Solidaire's relatively marginal position means that if it can keep these ideas alive, it remains unlikely to be in a position to implement them itself.

The danger of looking for a big-picture alternative to austerity in the here and now is that its implausibility may blind us to smaller alternatives that might provide new trajectories over time. A few examples can be invoked, less to champion any one as particularly valuable than to remind that there are materials out of which to fashion anti-austerity politics. One place to look is back to the short-lived PQ government of 2012–14. While our discussion above highlights the continuity of this government's budgetary policies with the preceding Liberals, there were nevertheless a few attempts to broaden debate. These included proposing measures to give greater recognition to the role of the social economy, to enable municipalities to implement inclusionary zoning as a means of increasing social housing, and to put in place a new public "autonomy insurance" plan to enable people to get access to professional care and services to aid while aging in place (see Graefe and Rioux 2017). While only the first was passed before the government fell, they are signs there are spaces for alternatives and innovation even within governments that largely follow the austerity script.

More controversially, another place to look is at some of the attempts of the current administration to modulate fees to income. This has been seen most clearly in the field of child care policy, where the universal $7 a day program is set to be replaced by one where parents pay based on income. This move has been widely attacked, and with good reason since it seems based more on encouraging the growth of private providers and saving money than on its announced goals of expanding service to poorer neighbourhoods that are currently underserved. Nevertheless, targeted transfers, such as with child benefits and old-age benefits, have proven effective in pushing more money into low-income households without eroding the broad political support associated with universal programs. One wonders if a future government could adopt a "take-the-money-and-run" strategy of fencing in the new revenues coming from the modulation of fees and using them to expand and improve services without then needing to demand as much new taxation.

In emphasizing the agency of parties and unions, as this chapter has, other agencies fall out of view. Clearly, we cannot discount the capacity of the student movement, or indeed of larger coalitions, to develop and move both alternatives but also larger social imaginaries of what is possible. Nadeau-Dubois (2013) is right to underline the need for the student movement, and particularly the more radical ASSÉ group, to rethink the question of the state; while a strategy of non-involvement was useful in avoiding co-optation or internal splits, it also led to a dead end once Premier Charest called elections. While that leads us back to parties and to movement–state interactions, we should not forget that the movement managed to monopolize political debate for months, affected the agendas of political actors, and changed people's relationships to institutional and protest politics (Dufour and Savoie 2014). These effects are not innocent in terms of drawing the boundaries of alternatives.

One final source of alternative agency would be nationalism and, more particularly, a renewed sovereignty movement. Indeed, opening up the question of Quebec's constitutional situation, especially with regards to the persisting flaws of Canadian fiscal federalism, would be one way of pushing its citizens and their representatives to think about the disconnect between their imagined future and the status quo. The PQ's new leader, along with established sovereigntist parties such as QS, might question the province's economic position within Canada with more insistence down the road. The 2014 Scottish referendum, for instance, was instructive for Quebec's nationalists. Whether or not one is skeptical about the ability of the Scottish National Party (SNP) to deliver a clear break to austerity either in Scotland's current situation or in a future independent state, one cannot deny that the referendum itself opened spaces to politicize Westminster's austerity measures, and subsequently gave the SNP additional ginger on this front. There is little doubt Quebec's nationalist movement will have learned from the massive mobilization of social forces around both an opposition to British conservatism and the attainment of renewed fiscal autonomy as a tool to develop alternatives.

CONCLUSION

This chapter can be read in a couple of ways. On one hand, it is consistent with common forms of Quebec exceptionalism; Quebec is a more egalitarian political community, as the result of decisions to tax, redistribute, and provide social services at a scale not seen in other provinces. While austerity policies deliberately move Quebec in a direction similar to other provinces, it does so from a very different starting point. In addition, austerity seems to meet a firmer resistance than elsewhere, as seen with the Maple Spring of 2012, which suggests that Quebec may also be better placed to start developing alternatives that might prove instructive to public employees, their unions, and social movements elsewhere in Canada.

On the other hand, while much of that is true, it also hides some significant commonalities. Like elsewhere, in a period of stagnant wages and living conditions, public-sector workers are increasingly subject to backlash. This public–private divide also plays out in the union movement and handcuffs attempts to mobilize a strong and sustained challenge to austerity programs and imaginaries. While Quebec's social movements do throw up impressive challenges to austerity, the limited ability to find and form relays in institutional politics to block or stymie neoliberal initiatives begins to resemble the situation elsewhere.

If both of these claims are true, then perhaps the appropriate answer is an analysis that does less to essentialize the Quebec exception and instead does more to understand the sources of Quebec's difference, and the manner in which these are reproduced or exhausted in the more recent conjuncture. As we wrote this, it seemed that the austerity agenda was delayed in Quebec by the lack of legitimacy left in the Charest Liberal government and then by the election of a PQ government that, arguably, treated austerity as a necessary evil rather than a virtue. It is with the historic defeat of that government that a re-energized Liberal party played the austerity card for farther-reaching state restructuring. That defeat might as well have taught opposition parties and movements some lessons, which could trigger a reorganization of historically linked political alternatives in nationalism and social democracy. The inability of the two main sovereigntist parties (PQ and QS) to form some kind of electoral alliance in 2018 indicated that such a reorganization remains to be achieved.

NOTES

1 Unless otherwise noted, the figures for Quebec's debt, budgetary balance, and spending growth in this chapter are drawn from tables generated by the Databank of Official Statistics on Québec. In this paragraph, we draw from: http://www.bdso.gouv.qc.ca/pls/ken/Ken213_Afich_Tabl.page_tabl?p_iden_tran=REPERL3X8O33619672397161091XV3&p_lang=1&P_M_O=MFQ&P_ID_RAPRT=2679 and http://www.bdso.gouv.qc.ca/pls/ken/Ken213_Afich_Tabl.page_tabl?p_iden_tran=REPERL3X8O33619672397161091XV3&p_lang=1&P_M_O=MFQ&P_ID_RAPRT=2680. Later in the paper, we also use "Opérations budgétaires, Fonds général": http://www.bdso.gouv.qc.ca/pls/ken/Ken213_Afich_Tabl.page_tabl?p_iden_tran=REPERXB4XOL56456089713289S%293&p_lang=1&P_M_O=MFQ&P_ID_SECTR=423&P_ID_RAPRT=2666

and "Fonds des générations," Databank of Official Statistics on Québec: http://www.bdso.gouv.qc.ca/pls/ken/Ken213_Afich_Tabl.page_tabl?p_iden_tran=REPERRPVZ3E15528045808 11NjEyb&p_lang=2&P_M_O=MFQ&P_ID_RAPRT=2671.

2 On Quebec's debt concepts, see http://www.finances.gouv.qc.ca/en/Quebecs_debt329.asp.

REFERENCES

Bourque, Gilles L., and France Bibeau. 2014. "Déséquilibre fiscal: l'éternel recommencement." Montreal: Institut de recherche en économie contemporaine, 26 November. http://www.irec.net/upload/File/noteinterventionno34octobre2014vd.pdf.

Charest, René. 2009. "Le mouvement syndical Québécois à la croisée des chemins." *Nouveaux Cahiers du Socialisme* 2: 175–83.

Cloutier, Luc. 2011. "L'emploi dans les soins de santé et l'assistance sociale au Québec: tendances depuis les 20 dernières années." *Flash-Info* 12 (2): 5–11.

Cloutier-Villeneuve, Luc. 2014. "Évolution de l'emploi atypique au Québec depuis 1997." *Flash-info* 15 (3): 1–13. http://www.stat.gouv.qc.ca/statistiques/travail-remuneration/bulletins/flash-info-201410.pdf.

Collombat, Thomas. 2014. "Labour and Austerity in Québec: Lessons from the Maple Spring." *Labor Studies Journal* 39 (2): 140–59.

Conseil du Trésor. 2004. *Modernizing the State: Promoting Quality Services to the Population.* http://collections.banq.qc.ca/ark:/52327/bs52106.

Couturier, Eve-Lynne, Philippe Hurteau, and Simon Tremblay-Pépin. 2010. *Budget 2010: Comment financer les services publics.* Montreal: Institut de Rercherche et d'Informations Socio-économiques. March 18. http://iris-recherche.s3.amazonaws.com/uploads/publication/file/Note-Budget2010.pdf.

Dufour, Marie-Josée. 2011. "La croissance salariale au Québec chez les salariés syndiqués en 2009 et 2010." *Flash-info* 12 (2): 1–4.

Dufour, Pascale, and Louis-Philippe Savoie. 2014. "Quand les mouvements sociaux changent le politique: le cas du mouvement étudiant de 2012 au Québec." *Canadian Journal of Political Science* 47 (3): 475–502.

Fillion, Gérald. 2014. "Les chiffres, les mots, les faits." *Blogue Économie*, 12 May. http://blogues.radio-canada.ca/geraldfillion/2014/05/12/leitao-coiteux-syndicat-austerite/.

Fortier, Francis, and Simon Tremblay-Pépin. 2014. "État de la dette du Québec 2014." *Institut de recherche et d'Informations socio-économiques*. 26 November. http://iris-recherche.s3.amazonaws.com/uploads/publication/file/Dette-Web-05.pdf.

Graefe, Peter, and X.H. Rioux. 2017. "Austerity of Imagination: Quebec's Struggles in Translating Resistance into Alternatives." In *Austerity: The Lived Experience*, edited by Stephen McBride and Bryan Evans, 272–92. Toronto: University of Toronto Press.

Haddow, Rodney. 2013. "Labour Market Income Transfers and Redistribution: National Themes and Provincial Variations." In *Inequality and the Fading of Redistributive Politics*, edited by Keith Banting and John Myles, 381–409. Vancouver: UBC Press.

– 2015. *Comparing Quebec and Ontario: Political Economy and Public Policy at the Turn of the Millennium*. Toronto: University of Toronto Press.

Haddow, Rodney, and Thomas Klassen. 2006. *Partisanship, Globalization, and Canadian Labour Market Policy*. Toronto: University of Toronto Press.

Imbeau, Louis M., and Mélissa Leclerc. 2002. "L'élimination du déficit budgétaire au Québec: contexte et réalisation d'un engagement electoral." In *Le Parti Québécois. Bilan des engagements électoraux 1994–2000*, edited by François Pétry, 67–81. Quebec: Presses de l'Université Laval.

Institut de la Statistique du Québec. 2015. *Rémunération des salariés. État et évolution comparés, 2015*. Quebec: Institut de la Statistique du Québec. http://www.stat.gouv.qc.ca/statistiques/travail-remuneration/remuneration-salaries-2015.pdf.

Lacoursière, Benoît. 2016. "Le Front Commun 2015 et la démocratie syndicale." *Nouveaux Cahiers du Socialisme* 16: 203–8.

Mandel, David. 2010. "Fighting Austerity? The Public Sector and the Common Front in Quebec." *The Bullet* 396. http://socialistproject.ca/bullet/396.php.

McGrane, David. 2014. *Remaining Loyal: Social Democracy in Quebec and Saskatchewan*. Montreal and Kingston: McGill-Queen's University Press.

Nadeau-Dubois, Gabriel. 2013. "Enseignements printaniers." *Nouveaux cahiers du socialisme* 9: 188–97.

Noël, Alain. 2002. "Une loi contre la pauvreté: la nouvelle approche québécoise de lutte contre la pauvreté et l'exclusion sociale." *Lien social et Politiques* 48: 103–14.

– 2013. "Quebec's New Politics of Redistribution." In *Inequality and the Fading of Redistributive Politics*, edited by Keith Banting and John Myles, 256–82. Vancouver: UBC Press.

Observatoire de l'administration publique – ENAP. 2013. "L'État québécois en perspective: les dépenses totals." Montreal: École Nationale d'Administration Publique. http://cerberus.enap.ca/Observatoire/docs/Etat_quebecois/a-depenses-totales.pdf.

Pelletier, Louis-Raphaël, and Fanny Theurillat-Cloutier. 2016. "Autopsie d'un rendez-vous manqué." *Nouveaux Cahiers du Socialisme* 16: 196–202.

Pineault, Éric. 2013a. "Cette fois, est-ce différent ? La reprise financiarisée au Canada et au Québec." *Institut de recherche et d'informations socio-économiques*. http://iris-recherche.s3.amazonaws.com/uploads/publication/file/Reprise-WEB-11.pdf.

– 2013b. "Quebec's Red Spring: An Essay on Ideology and Social Conflict at the End of Neoliberalism." *Studies in Political Economy* 90: 29–56.

– 2014. "Neoliberalism and Austerity as Class Struggle." In *Orchestrating Austerity: Impacts and Resistance*, edited by Donna Baines and Stephen McBride, 91–104. Halifax: Fernwood Publishing.

Piotte, Jean-Marc. 1998. *Du combat au partenariat*. Montreal: Nota Bene.

– 2013. *Démocratie des urnes et démocratie de la rue*. Montreal: Québec/Amérique.

Quebec. Ministère des Finances. 1998a. *Rapport du Comité d'étude sur la comptabilité du gouvernement*. Quebec: Gouvernment du Québec. http://www.budget.finances.gouv.qc.ca/budget/1998-1999/fr/PDF/raptech.pdf.

– 1998b. *Réforme de la comptabilité gouvernementale*. Quebec: Gouvernment du Québec. http://www.budget.finances.gouv.qc.ca/budget/1998-1999/fr/PDF/comptafr.pdf.

– 2007a. *The Budget at a Glance*. Quebec: Gouvernment du Québec. http://www.budget.finances.gouv.qc.ca/budget/2007-2008a/en/documents/pdf/BudgetGlance.pdf.

– 2007b. *The Québec Government's Debt*. Quebec: Gouvernment du Québec. http://www.finances.gouv.qc.ca/documents/Autres/en/AUTEN_Debt_gouvQC.pdf.

– 2007c. *2007–2008 Budget Plan*. Quebec: Gouvernment du Québec. http://www.budget.finances.gouv.qc.ca/budget/2007-2008a/en/documents/pdf/BudgetPlan.pdf.

– 2008a. *Public Accounts 2007–2008. Vol. I*. Quebec: Gouvernment du Québec. http://www.finances.gouv.qc.ca/documents/Comptespublics/en/CPTEN_vol1-2007-2008.pdf.

– 2008b. *2008–2009 Budget Plan*. Quebec: Gouvernment du Québec. http://www.budget.finances.gouv.qc.ca/budget/2008-2009/en/documents/pdf/BudgetPlan.pdf.

– 2009a. *Politique de financement des services publics*. Quebec: Gouvernment du Québec. http://www.finances.gouv.qc.ca/documents/Ministere/Fr/MINFR_PolitiqueFSP.pdf.
– 2009b. *Public Accounts 2008–2009, Vol. I*. Quebec: Gouvernment du Québec. http://www.finances.gouv.qc.ca/documents/comptespublics/en/cpten_vol1-2008-2009.pdf.
– 2009c. *Quebec and Its Challenges. Documents 1 to 3*. Quebec: Gouvernment du Québec. http://www.groupes.finances.gouv.qc.ca/Consultprebudg/2010-2011/media/pdf/quebec-and-its-challenges-document-1.pdf.
– 2009d. *2009–2010 Budget Plan*. Quebec: Gouvernment du Québec. http://www.budget.finances.gouv.qc.ca/budget/2009-2010/en/documents/pdf/PublicServices.pdf.
– 2010a. *Economic and Financial Profile of Quebec*. Quebec: Gouvernment du Québec. http://www.finances.gouv.qc.ca/documents/autres/en/auten_profil2010.pdf.
– 2010b. *2010–2011 Budget Plan*. Quebec: Gouvernment du Québec. http://www.budget.finances.gouv.qc.ca/Budget/2010-2011/en/documents/BudgetPlan.pdf.
– 2010c. *Tax Expenditures*. Quebec: Gouvernment du Québec. http://www.finances.gouv.qc.ca/documents/Autres/en/AUTEN_TaxExpenditures2010.pdf.
– 2011. *A Fair and Balanced University Funding Plan*. Quebec: Gouvernment du Québec. http://www.budget.finances.gouv.qc.ca/Budget/2011-2012/en/documents/Educationen.pdf.
– 2012. *Rapport sur le financement des services publics 2010–2011*. Quebec: Gouvernment du Québec. http://www.finances.gouv.qc.ca/documents/Ministere/Fr/MINFR_rapportFSP2010-2011.pdf.
– 2013. *Economic and Financial Profile of Quebec*. Quebec: Gouvernment du Québec. http://www.finances.gouv.qc.ca/documents/Autres/en/AUTEN_profile2013.pdf.
– 2014. *Dépenses fiscales – Édition 2013*. Quebec: Gouvernment du Québec. http://www.finances.gouv.qc.ca/documents/Autres/fr/AUTFR_DepensesFiscales2013.pdf.
– 2015. *Les concepts de dette*. Quebec: Gouvernment du Québec. http://www.finances.gouv.qc.ca/fr/La_dette_du_Quebec328.asp.
– 2015b. *Dépenses fiscales*. Quebec: Gouvernment du Québec. http://www.finances.gouv.qc.ca/documents/autres/fr/AUTFR_DepensesFiscales2015.pdf.
– 2016. *The Québec Economic Plan*. Quebec: Gouvernment du Québec. http://www.budget.finances.gouv.qc.ca/budget/2016-2017/en/documents/EconomicPlan.pdf.

– 2017. *Dépenses fiscales*. Quebec: Gouvernement du Quebec. http://www.finances.gouv.qc.ca/documents/Autres/fr/AUTFR_DepensesFiscales2016.pdf
– Quebec. Treasury Board. 2003. *2003–2004 Expenditure Budget. Volume II: Estimates of the Departmentsand Agencies*. Quebec: Gouvernement du Québec. http://www.tresor.gouv.qc.ca/fileadmin/PDF/budget_depenses/03-04/11-mars/03-04nv_vol2_en.pdf.
– 2007 to 2017. *Expenditure Budget*. Quebec: Gouvernement du Québec. http://www.finances.gouv.qc.ca/.
– 2008 to 2017. *Public Accounts*. Quebec: Gouvernement du Québec. http://www.finances.gouv.qc.ca/.
– 2011. *Public Accounts 2010–2011, Vol. I*. Quebec: Gouvernement du Québec. http://www.finances.gouv.qc.ca/documents/comptespublics/en/cpten_vol1-2010-2011.pdf.
Rioux Ouimet, Hubert. 2012. "Entre réingénierie et continuité: réforme libérale des sociétés d'État et nationalisme économique (2003–2012)." *Papers in Political Economy* 44. http://interventionseconomiques.revues.org/1602.
– 2014. "Quebec and Canadian Fiscal Federalism: From Tremblay to Séguin and Beyond." *Canadian Journal of Political Science* 47 (1): 47–69.
Task Force on Fees for Public Services. 2008. *The Right Fees to Live Better Together.* Quebec: Gouvernement du Québec. http://www.groupes.finances.gouv.qc.ca/GTTSP/RapportENG_GTTSP.pdf.
Task Force on the Funding of the Health System. 2008. *Getting our Money's Worth*. Quebec: Gouvernement du Québec. http://www.groupes.finances.gouv.qc.ca/financementsante/en/rapport/pdf/RapportENG_FinancementSante.pdf.
Vaillancourt, Yves, and Luc Thériault. 2008. "Social Economy, Social Policy and Federalism in Canada." *Canadian Social Economy Research Partnerships*, Occasional Paper Series, no. 4.
Van den Berg, Axel, and Hicham Raïq. 2014. "Les familles, inégalement protégées par la redistribution." In *Miser sur l'égalité*, edited by Alain Noël and Miriam Fahmy, 79–90. Montreal: Fides.

CHAPTER SEVEN

Between "The Rock" and a Hard Place: Fiscal Policy in New Brunswick since 2007

JAMIE GILLIES

Many New Brunswickers lionize the past provincial leadership eras of Louis J. Robichaud (1960–70), Richard Hatfield (1970–87), and Frank McKenna (1987–97). The period from 1960 to the end of the 1990s coincided with a modernization of New Brunswick's infrastructure and economy, as well as the development of official bilingualism as a cornerstone of provincial society. Prioritized focus and attention was given to New Brunswick's public institutions, like health services and education, and standards were developed to keep the province in line with the rest of Canada (see also Conrad in this volume). Since Frank McKenna, and especially in the last decade, however, New Brunswickers are far less certain of the ability of government to continue to build the province the way these three long-standing premiers had done.

New Brunswick has returned to a period of government fiscal instability and, with that, an uncertainty about whether the welfare state institutions that have been built and the innovations to its economy that underscored this modernization and development in the twentieth century are really things of the past. The major impetus on the province in the early 1990s to pursue a more explicitly neoliberal policy direction was largely a result of the Jean Chrétien/Paul Martin federal budgeting initiatives that offloaded fiscal responsibility for government programs to the provinces and forced provincial governments to cut expenditures. Without the pressures resulting from federal constraint, New Brunswick has drifted back into a chronic structural deficit period. Talk concerning fiscal policy has also shifted from an optimistic, forward-looking perception to one of general uneasiness over protecting past legacies within the provincial budget. Without the development of natural resources such as those that buoyed the economies of Alberta (Brownsey in this volume), Saskatchewan (Smith in this volume), and Newfoundland (Sweeney in this volume), and without the manufacturing, tourism, or retirement sectors to provide a base of economic drivers as in Ontario (Evans and Fanelli in this volume) and British Columbia (Whiteside in this volume), New Brunswick finds itself in a cycle of largely unsuccessful government attempts to stimulate the economy, with limited fiscal solutions.

In this chapter, government responses to the fiscal challenges New Brunswick faces will be explored, with emphasis on what has occurred since the global economic crisis in 2007 and 2008. It is argued that there are very few economic and fiscal opportunities available to New Brunswick governments today that do not involve dramatic restructuring of the provincial economy, either through investment in non-renewable resources or through essentially picking and choosing communities by realigning resources from declining rural populations to urban centres. It is also argued that the last four premiers have struggled with innovative ideas to help the province, and this perceived lack of leadership both in addressing worrisome fiscal concerns and thinking strategically about ways to diversify and alter New Brunswick's economy is creating a political climate where the only "solutions" are austerity measures. If New Brunswick is to survive and grow its economy, it must both address fiscal pressures and grow revenues through sustainable economic development.

The chapter begins with a historical analysis of the pre-2007 political and economic environment in the province, before addressing recent challenges. The more neoliberal economic policies of Frank McKenna serve as a useful benchmark for when New Brunswick was actively in line with the fiscal regime of the 1990s, in which that government lowered the deficit and promoted job growth in an era of economic expansion. It then provides a synopsis of the historical trends in the economic and demographic trajectory of the province and the challenges faced by McKenna's successors, including the Liberal government of Brian Gallant that was elected in 2014. The chapter looks closely at the governments of Shawn Graham (2006–10) and David Alward (2010–14) and the economic and fiscal strategies each government employed; then, it attempts to address why their major economic policies largely failed. It concludes with the very difficult financial situation New Brunswick finds itself in as of the

2018–19 fiscal year and considers what the provincial government is likely going to have to do to stave off perpetual, structural deficits and stagnant economic and labour force growth for the foreseeable future.

THE FADING McKENNA MIRACLE LEGACY

Frank McKenna's legacy looms large over New Brunswick politics. The last politically successful premier of the province and one of the very few provincial politicians during the last forty years to finish his term relatively unscathed and with widespread popular support, McKenna is still widely praised because of his tenacity and work ethic in trying to expand, diversify, and market the New Brunswick economy. The economic programs enacted after the McKenna shutout of 1987, in which his provincial Liberals won every seat in the province, put New Brunswick on a stronger fiscal and economic footing. But his policies also aligned with the neoliberal economic policies and fiscal restraint that would become the focus of Canadian federal and provincial economic legislation under Chrétien. His budgets represented the shift from the Keynesian-style policies of his predecessors to the far more fiscally oriented neoliberal order of the 1980s and 1990s. While McKenna is praised by many in the province, during his tenure real wages stagnated and the union workforces, especially well-paid, blue-collar jobs, declined dramatically (Workman 2003, 40–9).

McKenna's "miracle" was in attracting business and corporate money to the province. The legacy he left was one of a renewed focus on attracting higher-paying technology jobs as well as a series of grant programs for startup businesses and, secondly, the more transparent legacy of attracting thousands of call centre jobs located in New Brunswick's three largest cities (Lee 2001, 167–98). By 1999, New Brunswick was bucking the trend of have-less provinces, paying down its provincial debt and reducing the annual deficit in spite of the 1995 Canada Health and Social Transfer, which cut millions in federal transfer payments. McKenna left on top after ten years as premier, and for the first half-decade of the 2000s, many of McKenna's "miracle" economic legacies remained in place, especially corporate tax incentive lures once designed to attract companies with call centre needs (Savoie 2001, 177–8).

McKenna's miracle, however, was short lived without McKenna at the helm. Deprived of the international corporate tilling McKenna and his advisors initiated in drumming up business and incentivizing

New Brunswick as a business destination, the policies went into slow decline, unable to match the intensity of his leadership. His successor Camille Thériault failed to win the 1999 election, and the Progressive Conservatives, out of power for over a decade, returned to government under Premier Bernard Lord. The tougher economic times following the 1990s boom years continued through Lord, his successor Shawn Graham, David Alward, and now Brian Gallant.

Part of the problem was that McKenna's economic policies fit specifically the time and place of when McKenna came to power. They were, in many respects, neoliberal laboratory experiments in an era of fiscal restraint that shifted labour forces in different directions, away from established and traditional unionized industries to growth sectors where there was scant labour movement organization. American state and Canadian provincial jurisdictions competing against each other for business opportunities was part of the governing game during McKenna's time. The big examples, like middle-southern American states attracting auto plant jobs or New Brunswick finding a niche with North American call centres, had started to play themselves out by the time McKenna left office. His successors have not had the acumen or the same energy in attracting economic development opportunities. While neoliberal in spirit, and certainly fitting with the Brian Mulroney and Jean Chrétien era's embrace of global neoliberal fiscal policies, McKenna seemed to want to balance austerity-style policies and fiscal conservatism with genuine concern for working New Brunswickers. Nevertheless, those policies were indicative of an era with a sharp decline in well-paying union jobs in the province.

The ideas that followed McKenna's government seem to generate a pattern of all-eggs-in-one-basket policies for moving the province away from increased debt payments and trying to expand the economy. The last two major attempts at comprehensive policy change – the attempted sale of the provincial power utility and the attempted development of a provincial shale gas industry – have failed and have given New Brunswickers renewed reason to question whether their provincial government even understands their best interests. Both governments, those of Graham and Alward, were unsurprisingly defeated after only one term.

The limitations of the McKenna miracle, then, demonstrate both the upside and severe downside of trying to diversify the New Brunswick economy through relatively low-paying call centre employment. The

McKenna years have been characterized as a testing ground for economic policy development, as the government tried a great many initiatives to diversify and alter the economy (Milne 1996, 9). Some of these policies did not work in the long term, but McKenna created an environment in New Brunswick that made it a model, even temporarily, for what have-less provinces could achieve (Savoie 2001, 177–9).

THE DEMOGRAPHIC AND ECONOMIC PROBLEMS OF NEW BRUNSWICK OVER THE LAST TWO DECADES

While provincial executive leadership since McKenna has been questionable and finance ministers tasked with lowering the deficit have found it difficult to make sizeable cuts to lower the debt burden, the premiers and cabinet ministers are not entirely to blame for the lack of another economic miracle. New Brunswick faces a larger challenge that has been growing since the McKenna era. Demographic shifts have dramatically lowered the rural population and have increased, at higher rates than most of the country, the average age of the province. This is alarming as government allocates more funding for health care and programs for the elderly, while the tax base shrinks as younger New Brunswickers leave the province in their prime earning years. Despite offering incentives to keep young New Brunswickers here and attract young people to the province, the government is struggling even to maintain its population. Without new employment and economic opportunities that keep talented and educated people in the province and without employers that can recruit from larger pools of talent and relocate people there, New Brunswick is in serious economic distress. This is not a new phenomenon; demographic statistics going back to the 1980s have indicated a growing problem with an out-migration "brain drain" of university graduates and skilled workers. Even in the McKenna years, there were high numbers of New Brunswick university graduates leaving the province (Milne 1996, 17–19). This brain drain, as well as the phenomenon of population outflow of people in their late teens and twenties to other parts of the country, has accelerated in the last decade (Haan 2014). The fact is New Brunswick has a demographic crunch of low youth retention and increasing pressures placed on the system, especially in the health sector, by an aging population.

The other economic problem of the post-2007 era is one experienced by all of the have-less provinces, and it can be characterized as "Alberta and Newfoundland Envy." One of the narratives that the David Alward government tried to utilize during its 2010 election campaign was the concern that young New Brunswickers were heading to energy-rich provinces like Alberta, so the government needed to focus on solutions to bring them home. Ironically, the severe contraction of the Alberta oil sands economy in 2015 did bring much of this transient workforce back to New Brunswick, albeit unemployed and without opportunities.

Therefore, the Alward government decided to make shale gas development the economic focus of this strategy. However, with no clear election mandate to do this, the government was caught off guard by localized public backlash and protests against the strategy. Despite shale gas development being an endeavor started by the previous Liberal government, Alward made it the cornerstone of his economic strategy. After protests near Rexton, New Brunswick, in 2013 culminated in violence, the issue became less of a government solution to years of economic decline and more of a communications problem representing the inability of the government to win tacit agreement from all public stakeholders before potentially risking New Brunswick's environmental future on a strategy that might not lead to newfound wealth. Despite pleas from McKenna and other political and business elites that New Brunswick needed to embrace a natural resource extraction ethos and avoid a "death spiral" of declining government revenues and population, voters turfed the Alward Progressive Conservatives in the 2014 election (McKenna 2014). They selected one of the youngest premiers in Canadian history, Liberal leader Brian Gallant, who almost immediately put in place a shale gas extraction moratorium.

For the province's economic health to improve, the ideas of the three most recent governments are not models to follow. Without significant diversification in New Brunswick to meet the new dynamics of the second decade of the twenty-first century, the entire economy could be headed "over the cliff" (Saillant 2014, 1–8). While the Gallant government seems well aware of these challenges – and while the premier tries to be seen employing a leadership style more reminiscent of Robichaud and McKenna, publicly stating that he is willing to make hard decisions to control the provincial budget (CBC News 2014b) – it does not mean that New Brunswick can save itself. Fiscal discipline requires political will but expanding the economy is another story, something that Gallant's immediate predecessors have been unable to accomplish.

THE AUSTERITY-ERA CONTEXT

New Brunswick, like Canada, did not fare as badly as it could have as a consequence of the global financial crisis in 2007 and 2008. However, in the province's case, that is more a result of its continued status as an economic laggard in Eastern Canada, relying significantly on federal transfer payments. Unlike high-flying provincial economies, New Brunswick was more immune to the immediate challenges most jurisdictions faced as a result of the Great Recession. The adage in New Brunswick was that the economic predicament was no great hurdle, given that the province had been in recession since Confederation. However, the truth is more complicated; the fiscal picture has indeed shifted since 2007 because of Ottawa's tightening of provincial transfers, the rule changes in programs like employment insurance that have adversely affected New Brunswick, and the provincial government's struggle with finding innovative ideas to grow the economy and simultaneously control the deficit.

It should be noted that New Brunswick has had the highest rate of government turnover in Canada since 2007, as two successive governments have lasted only one term. One of the results of this instability is that the provincial government faced renewed calls for fiscal discipline from both inside the province by key private sector voices and outside the province by Ottawa and credit rating agencies in the United States. Gallant, like premiers David Alward and Shawn Graham before him, faces the same set of challenges. Still worse, the Gallant government has started with over $12.2 billion in accumulated government debt for a province of less than 750,000 people. That forced the government to do a comprehensive strategic review process after their election and culminated in a 2% increase in the harmonized sales tax. New Brunswick continues to have one of the highest per capita debt-to-GDP ratios in the country and has now implemented among the highest levels of provincial income taxation in Canada.

The Shawn Graham Years

In 2006, Jeannot Volpé, Bernard Lord's finance minister, introduced the final budget of the Lord-led Progressive Conservative government. This budget marked the end of a fiscal discipline that had been part of both the McKenna and Lord years. In their previous budgets, the Lord government had focused on lowering the annual net debt-to-GDP ratio each year of its mandate and concluded with a \$22 million surplus and another balanced provincial budget (Department of Finance 2006). Much of this government discipline was the result of McKenna's economic effect. Lord had adopted similar practices, recognizing in the 2000s that this would be the key to continued success in government.

Lord's economic stewardship often gets ignored in light of the perceived successes of McKenna. Lord was able to build and continue job creation strategies during his seven years, culminating in New Brunswick's unemployment rate falling to below 10% for the first time in decades. The net debt-to-GDP ratio, on which New Brunswick governments have focused given the ratio's importance in neoliberal narratives about fiscal health, was around 27% in 2006 and had been in decline since the middle of the McKenna years (Goodwin and Ruggeri 2004, 30–1). By 2015, that had grown to 38% (Office of the Auditor General 2015b). Lord's major problem from a leadership standpoint was that, although he inherited an improved New Brunswick economy and was able to continue prosperity and grow, he had an overly cautious nature and his risk-adverse economic ideas occurred at a time of expansion of the Canadian economy (Poitras 2004, 341–8). New Brunswick missed an opportunity to take a fiscal house that was in order, as well as a more prosperous economy, and do the hard work to diversify and make it competitive in the future.

Shawn Graham and the provincial Liberal Party campaigned on a promise of economic and energy self-sufficiency, which they called "Charter for Change," during their successful 2006 election victory over Lord's Progressive Conservatives. A problem for both the Lord and Graham governments was that while there continued to be a focus on fiscal responsibility, the overall economic outlook and projections for the future offered very little long-term sustainability. New Brunswick is one of the least diversified economies in Canada. It maintains business investment because two of Canada's wealthiest business families are located in the province. The collected companies under both the Irving and McCain umbrellas are the largest private-sector employers in New Brunswick. Growth, however, has been in sectors that do not fit twenty-first-century challenges, especially around information technology. McKenna had worked on diversification and Lord and Graham both sought to continue this. Tax breaks and incentivizing relocation did not change the narrative of a province with a steady but slightly declining population and few "new economy" prospects.

The Graham government's fiscal performance is perhaps the best example of this inability to shift economic fortunes in new directions. Their first move was to develop a more transparent budgeting and fiscal environment and communicate more closely with the public about the real fiscal pressures the province faced. Subsequent budgets and a lack of key decision making plagued the government. On initiatives to improve service in line departments, like Education and Health, and contain costs, policies were announced and approved only to be dropped later. These major policy shifts, a 2007 recommendation to convert three university campuses to polytechnic institutes to better control post-secondary education spending, a 2008 change in the start date for French immersion education, and a 2009 attempt and memorandum of understanding to sell NB Power's assets to Hydro-Québec were all scuttled after public response proved negative.

Tax rates were maintained, and tinkering around the edges of the budget did little to stem the issues that had been problematic in the late 1970s and early 1980s. As a result, New Brunswick returned to increasing annual deficits and debt-to-GDP ratios (Department of Finance 2007). Further, the Graham government spent a lot more than did the previous government in developing programs. These included more investment and more budget share for environmental cleanup, small business investment, and regional funding for infrastructure, all designed in an attempt to build self-sufficiency into the system and turn New Brunswick into a province that would not need to rely on equalization.

Unfortunately, Graham's fiscal policies did not have the economic growth accompanying them to justify the additional spending. Finance ministers Victor Boudreau and, later, Greg Byrne explained each new policy investment in each budget speech from 2007 to 2010, as well as a fiscal update following the 2008 economic crisis, but the New Brunswick economy was slowing even more than anticipated and estimated government revenues were consistently above actual revenues. Rosy projections and best-case scenario budget rhetoric did not align with what was actually occurring with the provincial economy.

Despite warnings by independent auditors that the economy was slowing and that fiscal imbalance was building, Graham tried to invest in new programs and business opportunities with government dollars.

By late 2008, the budget was already out of balance and the surplus had disappeared. Campaign promises – including the elimination of the Lord-initiated gas tax, giving university students a $2,000 first-year credit to offset tuition, multi-million dollar investments in renewable energy, a harbour cleanup in Saint John, a river cleanup in Moncton, and additional funding for nursing home and long-term care facilities – while popular with the public, further lowered government revenues in Graham's first fiscal year (Department of Finance 2008). The early 2008 budget speech forecasted another surplus, but the economic crisis was looming and the government's overly optimistic forecast, despite warnings that the problems in the United States and elsewhere were headed to Canada, suggested a somewhat naïve take on the fiscal situation. Further, the Lord-initiated legislation, the *Fiscal Responsibility and Balanced Budget Act* that passed in 2006, required balanced budgets through the 2010–11 fiscal year. The rapidity of the economic maelstrom that engulfed the world economy caught New Brunswick, and most provinces, off guard.

In late 2008, Victor Boudreau's fiscal update speech on the economic crisis warned that government revenues had already declined to send the budget out of balance despite legislation requiring a balanced budget (CBC News 2008a). The Auditor General, Mike Ferguson, then provided an update after making clear that the balanced budget target, which Boudreau still maintained would occur in 2010, was at risk (CBC News 2008b). Business and income tax revenue declined that fiscal year, as it did elsewhere, but New Brunswick seemed closer to a precipice than other Canadian jurisdictions in that this year was a demarcation between the after-effects of the McKenna miracle and the province's continued economic decline.

Graham's government, trying to stave off the worst effects of the global crisis, cut taxes and tried a modest stimulation of the provincial economy in 2009. The 2009–10 fiscal budget cut corporate taxes to their lowest levels in years, and for a time were actually the lowest in Canada. That shift from a 12% to an 8% corporate tax rate in 2012 was designed to stimulate private-sector investment in the province (McHardie 2009). Part of *The Plan for Lower Taxes in New Brunswick*, personal income tax brackets were decreased, cutting taxes to almost every New Brunswicker in an effort to stimulate investment and growth. Nearly $150 million in government revenue was cut as a result in the first fiscal year alone, and Boudreau presented a budget that forecasted a $741 million deficit (Department of Finance

2009a). Further, provincial debt increased to above $8 billion and the decade-long reductions in debt-to-GDP ratio began climbing rapidly.

To make matters worse for Graham, the signature policies developed in each year of his mandate lacked widespread public support. In his first year, a strategy to convert the University of New Brunswick's Saint John campus, as well as satellite campuses of the Université de Moncton in Shippagan and Edmunston, into polytechnic schools met with immediate dissatisfaction and the plan was shelved. In his second full year, the attempt to change the beginning grade year for immersion education led to public inquiries and accusations of doctored independent reports aligning with government priorities (Savoie 2010, 58). The recommendations were modified but the episode angered the public.

The 2010–11 fiscal year's budget further increased the deficit; a billion-dollar infrastructure spending program was developed as part of a longer-term strategy from the election campaign to improve provincial works and as a shorter-term stimulus after the economic crisis (Department of Finance 2009b). New finance minister Greg Byrne sought to ease fears about the growing deficit by rolling out, with the premier, a memorandum of understanding between NB Power and Hydro-Québec that would sell the public utility to another province. For Graham, this was his last chance before the 2010 election to put forward a signature policy for addressing the pressing economic concerns of the province. Having campaigned in 2006 on a plan to create self-sufficiency in New Brunswick, the sale of NB Power was going to be the crowning achievement. The terms of the deal did not include the actual sale of the power utility, which would still be managed in New Brunswick, but instead included selling the assets and transmission lines necessary for Quebec to expand further into the Eastern seaboard's energy market. In return, the deal essentially retired the Crown corporation's sizeable debt, which was a large proportion of the total provincial debt. On top of that, the billions of dollars Quebec was willing to pay could have been used to essentially halve the total provincial debt (*Toronto Star* 2009).

Graham had hoped to communicate to the public that the election year plan to sell NB Power was a good deal for the province and that the terms would offer the province a fresh fiscal start. But he never got the chance. Public backlash was swift and with the power of social media, the forces opposed to the sale of NB Power quickly mobilized with little money (Desserud 2011, 103–4). Despite popular media support for the deal, and business support especially in regards to the possibility of lower power pricing and a structure that would result in New Brunswick being included in Hydro-Québec's much larger energy generation and transmission system, localized opposition materialized far faster than the government's message. The government faced the additional problem that, if they did not sell the crown corporation, provincial finances were in the worst shape they had been in over a decade and on the worst fiscal trajectory since the Hatfield years.

The impetus for the NB Power sale came in part from longstanding concerns about the power utility's mismanagement. Despite changes and a new corporate board that stressed efficiency and transparency, public opinion of the utility had traditionally been low. Further, the refurbishment of Point Lepreau Nuclear Generating Station was already leading to multi-billion dollar cost overruns and a timeline that stretched years beyond intended completion targets. Even with these public concerns about the utility's problems, the government was unprepared for the opposition to the proposal. Further, other Maritime provinces expressed regional concerns about Quebec controlling access to transmission lines in Atlantic Canada, most notably Newfoundland Premier Danny Williams who stressed to New Brunswickers the struggles his province had been facing for decades as a result of power deals between Quebec and Newfoundland concerning the Churchill Falls power generation facilities (McCarthy 2010).

A scaled back version of the deal, $3.2 billion involving only particular assets, was also criticized severely by the public and Graham was forced to abandon that memorandum of understanding amidst such public hostility (Marotte 2010). The Liberal Party had maintained anywhere from a 20- to 35-point lead over the Progressive Conservatives in public opinion polling for almost four years. That support evaporated with the NB Power announcement. The deal would have been a chance to essentially clear the red off the government books and start again, but today few in the province speak of any possibility of selling the power utility. The localized opposition, especially in the major cities, caught the government off guard and in an untenable position when they were forced to backtrack on the deal. Further, the deal itself showcased the short-term thinking of the government. In trading the future of its power generation to pay off the provincial debt, it demonstrated the lack of innovative ideas even by a government that promised innovation. The public recognized the long-term implications of selling off a revenue generator and helped scuttle the deal (Desserud 2015, 122–5).

The NB Power deal is also a watershed of sorts in that, like other jurisdictions faced with austerity choices as a result of declining economies and neoliberal fiscal realities, the "solutions" presented by government are often short-term strategies out of a playbook that began in the 1980s. The NB Power arrangement fits with this larger trend toward austerity, from local municipalities selling off key assets or privatizing services, to governments getting out of entire aspects of service provisions. That New Brunswickers had the good sense to reject a bad deal suggests that there are still some opportunities for innovative policies in the future.

The provincial Progressive Conservatives easily won the 2010 election on a platform that included retaining NB Power. However, the election campaign itself lacked any kind of vision for the future and Premier David Alward was left with the task of filling in an economic development and fiscal strategy. Meanwhile, Shawn Graham, the first premier of New Brunswick not to have his government re-elected, had left the province in worse financial and economic shape than he had when he started. Graham's lack of a signature policy in four years came at a bad time, given the economic problems after the 2007–08 crash. Further, the government made some bad bets on keeping jobs in the province, especially in providing close to $70 million in loans to the Atcon Group, a company based in Miramichi, that ultimately closed shop, declared bankruptcy, and laid off its work force after securing the government loans (CBC News 2010). Mired in scandal following allegations of impropriety in the Atcon loan deals, and defeated at the polls, Graham's legacy was not what he had intended.

The David Alward Years

The 2010 election was a referendum on the Graham government in light of the series of failed policy issues, with particular focus on NB Power. Previous elections had revolved around single issues that often had little to do with the economic future of the province. The NB Power deal went to the heart of New Brunswick's fiscal and economic predicament. It represented a change in thinking around the art of the possible with respect to the ability of the provincial government to influence and shape the economic climate. The New Brunswick economy experienced regular growth from the McKenna years until the 2007–08 financial crisis (Saillant 2014, 86–7). The economic contraction that has occurred since is not just a result of global decline but also the lack of innovation in diversifying and altering the economy to meet the new needs of the workforce.

David Alward and the Progressive Conservatives understood this going into their first year, especially given the hostility to the economic ideas of the previous government. The first budgetary moves suggested new leadership that understood the acute challenges present since the end of the McKenna years and arguably squandered during the Graham years. Given the fiscal problems in the province and the economic challenges the incoming government faced, there should have been a renewed focus on opportunities to significantly rework and change the New Brunswick economy. The trajectory of the Lord and Graham governments had been off course, and at least some of this was the result of severe mismanagement, not only among the politicians but also due to the lack of a powerful, independent and accountable public service enacting sound economic policies (Savoie 2010, 54). Fresh ideas were needed that relied on concrete metrics and better utilization of the public servants who were trying to challenge government decisions that flew in the face of their best non-partisan advice.

Unfortunately, the Alward government could not match the rhetoric of developing a more robust and transparent governance apparatus. Despite selecting Blaine Higgs as finance minister, a former Irving Oil executive and self-described non-politician, Alward could not find a strategy to focus his government that the public was willing to support. From a fiscal prudence standpoint, Higgs worked hard to control public spending and find short-term solutions to the mounting concerns over government debt. Even with Higgs informing the public that spending promises during the campaign complicated the fiscal challenge, he was never able to get the government to adhere to a more rigorous fiscal responsibility ethos in the face of the global financial crisis.

Higgs's first budget, presented in March 2011, outlined just how dire the fiscal shape of the province really was. The Tories, after extensive budget review and external accounting, discovered the deficit had increased to over $820 million for the fiscal year. Efficiencies were found and cuts were made to reduce the projected deficit to $739.9 million. Higgs sounded the alarm about needing solutions other than spending reductions. As he argued in the budget speech, government expenses increased over 12% from the time Graham's government took office until they were defeated, while government revenue remained stagnant. That created structural deficits for the first time since the mid-McKenna years, and no amount of cost cutting was going to return the provincial budget to balance. Higgs also noted that the provincial net debt had increased over 20% in just four years, to $8.4 billion (Department of Finance 2011).

The government cut over $220 million in spending to try to lower the deficit for their first fiscal year and found a further $100 million in enhanced revenues from increased taxes, especially from doing away with the previous government's gas rebate. This lowered the 2011–12 projected deficit to $448 million. Higgs warned that even with restraint in spending, net debt was estimated to increase to over $10 billion by the end of the 2011–12 fiscal year (Department of Finance 2011). While the tone of the budget speech was pessimistic, Alward sought a bold strategy for economic growth. Tired of New Brunswick workers leaving the province to energy-rich provinces for better opportunities, positive resource extraction data about the potential for shale gas extraction in the province led the government to almost unilaterally adopt hydrofracking industry development as its sole economic development strategy. In the spring and summer of 2011, despite almost no mention of shale gas as a viable option and little discussion of fracking in the Progressive Conservative platform, the Alward government announced a massive investment in the shale gas industry and hurriedly encouraged energy companies to start testing for viable shale gas in the province. While the shale leases had been already allocated by the previous Liberal government, Alward and Natural Resources Minister Bruce Northrup branded shale gas the potential saving grace for the New Brunswick economy. In early 2011, Northrup did fact-finding trips to American states that had expanded their shale gas industries and, by the spring, messaging for the government had shifted to shale gas as the new solution for the province (*CBC News* 2011).

Business support, especially from corporate observers outside of New Brunswick, was certainly a factor in this strategy. The Saint John base of the PCs was clearly fired up about the possibility of expanding its resource hub beyond oil refining and paper mills. But given that the Tories won an election based on the issue of transparency in the NB Power deal, they underestimated the public response and badly rolled out the shale gas plan. Almost immediately, public reaction to the proposal was skeptical and localized opposition appeared in the communities closest to the most viable shale gas leases. Energy companies, especially SWN Resources and Corridor Resources, which actually had viable fracked shale gas wells and operational natural gas extraction already, were taken aback by the loud and angry public protests. Initially, these criticisms were centred on the environmental concerns with the extraction process, and various groups such as the Conservation Council of New Brunswick sought to encourage the government to be more forthcoming and clear about the risks versus rewards in shale gas extraction. In the time it took the government to develop a communications strategy, local citizens along with independent environmental and First Nations activists had begun to help organize communities against further shale gas exploration.

Despite a limited consultation process with the public and Indigenous groups, and despite promising to introduce the most rigorous regulatory regime for shale gas extraction in North America, protests escalated in places like Sussex and especially near Rexton and Elsipogtog First Nation in Kent County, where SWN Resources was testing on Crown land near First Nations communities (see also Coates and Poelzer in this volume). While opposition to shale gas was not as commanding a voice against the government as was opposition to the NB Power deal, it stymied the government in moving forward on other economic fronts as the protests filled the political media bandwidth. Having to invest time and energy into courting public opinion, Alward kept trying to roll out a policy process that addressed all of the stakeholder concerns. However, the public remained skeptical of both the perceived economic benefits from a multi-decade gamble and the continued lack of transparency by the government and energy companies about the risks involved. Compounding matters was the creation of the Energy Institute of New Brunswick, an arm's length entity that most New Brunswickers assumed was not for gathering government-created data and information but rather a shill for the energy lobby.

The low point for both those for and against shale gas development was the protests that escalated to violence in 2012 near Rexton; they resulted in police cars burned, people injured, many peaceful protestors arrested, and government communications befuddled by the whole episode. This brought negative national focus and attention on the province. Further, the protests tended to shine a light not on the government's handling of shale gas but on its lack of consultation with First Nations communities (Wyatt and Baker 2014, 222). It demonstrated that after a year of trying to force the public to commit to hydrofracking, the government had failed to get the social licence and public support necessary to proceed. By then, the opposition parties had begun to call for a shale gas exploration moratorium after the next election.

In his second budget speech in March 2012, Higgs noted that the government had reduced the annual deficit by nearly $180 million and blamed the previous government for the lack of more fiscal discipline (Department of Finance 2012). The budget also did not feel like it had taken the PC government's initial budget rhetoric to heart and showed limited progress in combatting the structural deficit. The 2012–13 fiscal year still had a projected deficit of over $400 million. Scant mention was made of the significant deficit reduction that had been the fiscal hallmarks of the first year.

To make matters worse for the Alward government, devastating economic news came in June 2012 when Standard & Poor's (S&P) downgraded the credit rating for the province from AA minus to A plus. The downgrade stressed that the long-term economic and demographic projections did not look good and, coupled with the high debt-to-GDP ratio of New Brunswick, a rate drop was necessary as a wake-up call to government. This placed New Brunswick on the watch list of credit-rating agencies, during the height of Eurozone austerity concerns (Saillant 2014, 1, 137). It also forced the New Brunswick government to demonstrate some fiscal discipline in 2012. The S&P downgrade also took into account persistent problems since Shawn Graham had become premier. Provincial economic growth, which had been in the 2–3% range for much of the 1990s and early 2000s had fallen off to just around 1% annually. Further, provincial unemployment, which had fallen in the McKenna and Lord years, had climbed back into persistent double-digit levels and hovered around 10–11%.

Given how bad it looked within a neoliberal paradigm, Higgs and Alward attempted to make the most of a crisis opportunity. Since the 2007–08 crisis, the issue of the solvency of public pension plans was of great concern to New Brunswick retirees. After watching American state governments deal with these problems in ham-handed and combative ways, New Brunswick's leading public-sector unions came together to work on the problem collectively. In collaboration with the Alward government, they introduced the Public Sector Shared

Risk Plan pension model in 2012 that had been developed through a task force made up of a pension lawyer, an economist, and an actuary. With the support of the unions and government, a hybrid pension model was developed that adversely affected retirees but secured them a base pension benefit and adjusted cost-of-living increases to the health of the pension fund (Office of the Premier 2012; Goar 2013). It was rolled out slowly, making the adjustment to changes incremental over time. While retirees, particularly in Fredericton, were unhappy, the government was less exposed because the New Brunswick public was generally satisfied with how this was handled. The fact that the consultative task force utilized input from the unions to develop a solution that could have been a lot more austere and draconian showed that the government was taking at least some of its fiduciary responsibility seriously. Each major fiscal initiative was reacting to neoliberal forces, however, and not responding to the major challenge – to grow the provincial economy in transformative ways.

In his third budget, Higgs again presented a poor economic picture, with less than 1% annual growth again. For fiscal year 2013–14, the deficit was projected to rise to close to $480 million as a result of declining government revenues (Department of Finance 2013). Part of the blame was placed on the federal government's zero increase in transfer payments. New Brunswick relies on between $2.5 and $3 billion of its total budget from federal government transfer payments, and over half of that is from equalization payments. Each fiscal year, between 33% and 38% of the budget comes from the federal government. The Harper government's enforcement of transfer payment and equalization formulas, without annual adjustments that account for structural provincial problems and with neglect of the challenges facing smaller have-less provinces, had lowered that rate to just 32.8% of the budget by 2013–14. That put New Brunswick's transfer payment level at even below inflation adjustments as a result of federal government stinginess. If transfer payment levels returned to 37%, the adjustment would wipe out the structural deficit (Campbell 2014).

Again, Higgs's concerns and the government plan to address these economic problems revolved around budget tinkering, with small changes to tax rates and seasonal updates to different sectors of the economy. The budgets were essentially visionless and void of the sweeping reforms demanded to improve the long-term viability of the economy. While the fiscal responsibility ethos was apparent and the pension and deficit reduction files came into line with the austerity measures hinted at by the S&P downgrade, the government still lacked any kind of long-term vision.

The election year 2014–15 budget would be Higgs's last as Alward's finance minister. It came on the heels of repeated warnings from the Auditor General Kim MacPherson, whose office continued to be skeptical of government's focus to pay down its debt (Office of the Auditor General 2013). Like the two previous budgets, forecasted deficits were lower than actual deficits as the no-growth economy continued to reduce government revenues. The 2013–14 fiscal year had a $564 million deficit, while Higgs forecast a 2014–15 fiscal deficit of just under $400 million (Department of Finance 2014a). All told, the Progressive Conservative government, despite focusing on debt reduction, left office with accumulated provincial debt at around $12 billion.

The 2014 Auditor General's Report pointed out that New Brunswick had one of the highest increases in net provincial debt in Canada between 2006 and 2014 with a 69% increase in just eight years. It also had one of the largest increases in net debt per capita and net debt as a percentage of GDP over the same time period. McPherson's point was not only that New Brunswick was in difficult economic shape but that over the same period, other provinces with similar economic struggles coming out of the 2007–08 crisis, such as Manitoba and Nova Scotia, did not have the same level of net debt increases (Office of the Auditor General 2014, 10–18). While most provinces have struggled with debt management since the crisis, including Alberta, which had eliminated its provincial debt up to that point, New Brunswick seems acutely problematic in the aftermath with chronic problems in finding new sources of provincial revenues to offset rising deficits (Atkinson et al. 2013, 91–3). Even without the crisis, economic and demographic trends had put the New Brunswick fiscal system on a "structurally imbalanced" trajectory in every economic scenario leading up to 2025–26 (Ruggeri, Goodwin, and Zou 2004, 121). The 2007–08 crisis simply exacerbated that trajectory.

Even with as prudent a fiscal manager as Higgs, Alward's government allowed the total provincial debt to increase at the same rate that the Graham government did. The problem was the same as in the Lord and Graham years; without a successful strategy for economic investment and attracting private-sector jobs to the province, all New Brunswick's government offered were austerity reactions to

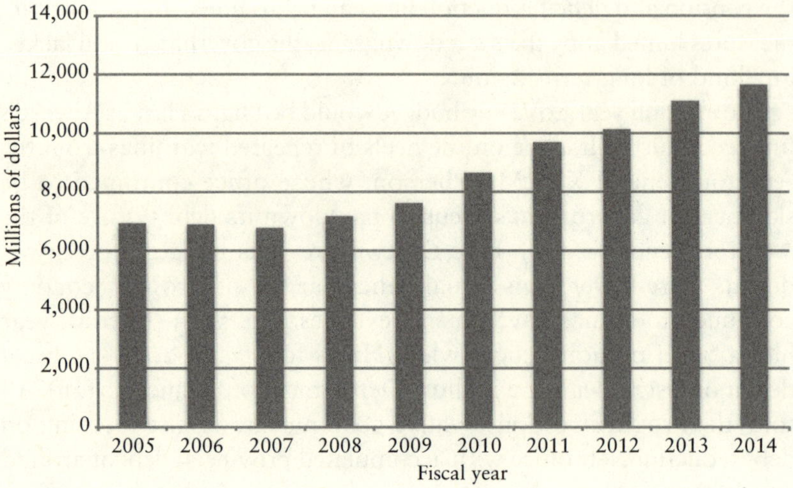

Source: 2014 Report of the Auditor General of New Brunswick

Figure 7.1 Province of New Brunswick, net debt

international economic forces, as opposed to real economic solutions. Higgs should be commended for trying to control spending and for bringing more openness to the budget process, especially with the introduction of the *Fiscal Transparency and Accountability Act* in 2014 that made cabinet ministers responsible for overspending by imposing monetary fines and requiring all parties to account for their campaign promises by having each spending promise independently verified (Department of Finance 2014b). In the end, however, despite their justified criticisms of the Graham government for the imprudent fiscal decisions during the global economic crisis that returned New Brunswick to structural deficits, the Alward government's fiscal record was no better than Graham's.

The Alward legacy was more a muddling-through legacy than a series of blunders. Shale gas industry development became the focus of their "Just Say Yes!" 2014 election strategy. Without an economic achievement record to defend and with only the promise of potential future revenue from an industry that the public was unconvinced would lead to wealth and far more likely would lead to environmental degradation, Alward was defeated by the youngest political leader of a major party in New Brunswick history. To add insult to his signature campaign issue, not only did the Liberal Party campaign on a hydro-fracking moratorium but also Energy Minister Craig Leonard, who was responsible for championing the shale gas initiative, was defeated

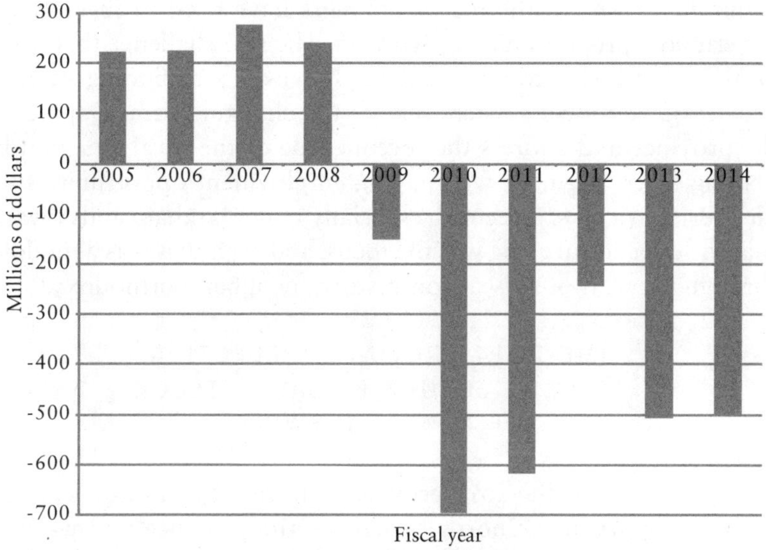

Source: 2014 Report of the Auditor General of New Brunswick

Figure 7.2 Province of New Brunswick annual surpluses and deficits

in the Fredericton South constituency by the leader of the Green Party of New Brunswick, David Coon. Coon became the first Green politician elected east of British Columbia.

Both the Graham and Alward years can be considered watered-down versions of McKenna's neoliberal policies. While neither government tried to do anything dramatic in terms of decreasing the public-sector labour force, each strategic review led to the paring down of non-partisan positions in government. These deficit-era budgets neither dramatically shifted social services funding in major ways, nor did they attempt to overhaul or change systems that the public saw as broken.

While many in the labour community have been critical of New Brunswick's economy as a whole, often labelling it as a stereotypical "company" province owned and operated by the Irvings, that characterization cannot be applied to the government itself. Each of the provincial leaders have tended to move away from corporate influence when it comes to government workers and programs. The budgets of the Graham and Alward years, despite being unsuccessful in terms of fiscal discipline or economic development and revenue enhancement strategies, did try to insulate the most popular government spending programs. None of the recent premiers have tried to severely cut government programming or workers. The real challenge that Lord, Graham, and Alward never solved, however, was finding ways to provide government services that fit the changing demographics of the province and address the revenue side of the fiscal equation by helping to create more well-paying employment opportunities for New Brunswickers. It seemed, especially under Graham and Alward, that the expenditure side was the focus, and even that was a muddle-through in terms of a fiscal conservative neoliberal orthodoxy.

THE 2014 PROVINCIAL ELECTION AND THE FUTURE FISCAL OUTLOOK OF NEW BRUNSWICK

Brian Gallant won the 2014 provincial election by shrewdly consolidating support in the northern part of the province and winning almost every Francophone-majority riding. He held enough southern and central New Brunswick seats to form the government. The youngest premier elected with a majority government in Canadian history has had difficulty in even trying to govern. The public had rejected the policies of both major parties in two consecutive elections and had ushered in an era of a province with the most government turnover in the country. Prior to McKenna's departure, only Alberta had a more stable provincial political environment. Up until McKenna retired, New Brunswick had only three governments over forty years. Since 1999, the province has had four different governments in fifteen years (Gillies 2014).

One of the potential upsides to Gallant's election, however, was that he could be less wedded to partisan constituencies within his own party because, like Bernard Lord, he had not been around long enough to be co-opted by party interests, especially the traditional business base of the Liberal Party. That could have given him more room to maneuver in challenging the economic status quo. Four years later, outside-the-box thinking has not really happened, as the signature economic policy the Liberals promised in the 2014 campaign – besides the shale gas moratorium – was a new $900 million infrastructure project which was seen as a sop to traditional Liberal supporters. Gallant also faced a potential labour market cliff because young New Brunswickers are leaving the province at high rates. Further, a demographic crunch with low birth rates, and with both low immigration and low interprovincial migration to New Brunswick, has flatlined provincial population growth. Gallant has struggled to find solutions that are not simply small adjustment ideas or tinkering around with programs. The challenges to the New Brunswick economy require more than free tuition for lower-income families or a new provincial Youth Employment Fund. Gallant now presides over a New Brunswick economy that has stagnant real GDP growth, the lowest of all ten provinces (Office of the Auditor General 2014, 19), and net debt per capita that is approaching, or has become, the highest in Canada (Office of the Auditor General 2015b, 16–17).

Structural economic problems continue to plague the province. Diversification is difficult when very few companies control sectors of the economy. In forestry, for example, the major player J.D. Irving practically stacked the deck in its favour when the Alward government agreed in 2014 to a new, twenty-five-year Forestry Management Agreement Practices Plan that increased the allowable cut dramatically and offered few incentives for independent woodlot owners and non–J.D. Irving mill operators (CBC News 2014a). The current government, like the previous one, may spend as much time undoing or considering undoing previous government policies than investing time and resources into designing new ones of their own.

The Liberal government, like its predecessors, has embraced neoliberal government-spending reductions, rolling out a government-wide strategic program review weeks upon taking office and then massively increasing the target for provincial cuts and efficiencies from $250 million to $600 million (CBC News 2015). Gallant, as well as his minister responsible for strategic program review Victor Boudreau and the new finance minister Roger Melanson, then talked fiscal-discipline talk; the premier even suggested new approaches to health services, including the potential of repurposing underutilized hospitals and investing in more cost-effective community health centres. A sweeping fiscal discipline and economic development statement in the first year would have gone a long way to changing the trajectory of discussion about New Brunswick's fiscal future. However, the government was restrained with their first budget, opted for minimal cuts across most sectors, and passed a budget with a deficit of over $400 million for fiscal year 2015–16. They then followed this with a year-long strategic program review process, looking at spending reductions, finding efficiencies, and considering further revenue enhancement options. Presented in 2016, the strategic program review, which had primed the public for tolls on provincial highways and at borders, as well as potential changes to health care and education, resulted only in an increase in the harmonized sales tax.

The strategic program review process in 2015 and 2016 highlighted the major problem facing New Brunswick. Governments are very reluctant, given the policy failures of the Graham and Alward governments, to embark on big-picture strategies. They instead toil in neoliberal tinkering with the budget and with programs. Shuffling deckchairs on a sinking economic ship does little in the long run for economic revival, and it has the potential in the 2018 election to lead to a third consecutive one-term government in the province. New Brunswick's austerity issue is really one of small-picture pessimism, almost waiting for an economic crunch so destabilizing that it forces transformative change. That helps make the distinction between, for example, large provincial economies such as Alberta's in the wake of the plunge in world oil prices and New Brunswick's, and it also helps explain why neoliberal policies in an austerity era affect the New Brunswick economy in less immediate and dramatic ways.

The Auditor General has reiterated her office's concerns about continued problems with the fiscal management of the province. While McPherson offered limited praise for the previous government in terms of controlling spending, the revenue enhancements that should have accompanied this discipline never materialized (Office of the Auditor General 2015a). Revenue enhancements, through increases in both income and sales taxes, are only one side of the challenge, and the economic growth side needs to be addressed. Taxing their way out of a structural deficit likely will not work. Net debt reduction targets need to be implemented and carried out, at least in the next two years, to then propose a series of innovative policies before the next provincial election to get the economy going. Further, the provincial government is acutely aware of its reliance on credit markets and staving off credit rating downgrades in this neoliberal era of structural deficits (see Hanniman 2013). Servicing debt interest obligations and paying attention to fiscal health will likely remain priorities over innovative economic growth solutions.

Beyond an actual economic and business investment strategy that pays off with increased employment opportunities and new growth in the private sector, the New Brunswick government also needs to challenge the federal government on two fronts. First, because the province has less than 3% of the Canadian population, New Brunswick issues are ignored in Ottawa, and were particularly disregarded by the Harper government whose base of support was out west, despite most of the New Brunswick federal caucus being Harper Conservatives until the 2015 election. This is likely to continue under Justin Trudeau and the Liberals, despite the province being in political lockstep federally and provincially in 2016 through to the 2018 provincial election. The federal politicians still play into Harper's "culture of defeat" attitude toward Atlantic Canadian economies and rarely challenge or fight for needed changes to federal government initiated economic development programs that have now ceased being priorities in Ottawa (CBC News 2002). Donald Savoie (2001, 192–3) has characterized it as a "history of victimization," as New Brunswick's federal politicians blame failed federal government programs as the reasons for continued economic decline. Further, outside of the Maritime provinces (see also Sweeney in this volume), politicians from have-more provinces have tended to argue that these have-less provinces need to pick themselves up by their bootstraps and revitalize their economies rather than relying on the benefits of equalization and of simply being a part of Canada (Savoie 2006, 197). The alterations to employment insurance and the aforementioned scaling back of transfer payments are two areas where New Brunswick federal politicians need to find more backbone.

Second, politicians in New Brunswick must seize the issue of equalization and transfer payments based on formulas that significantly hurt smaller provinces with stagnant growth, like New Brunswick, Nova Scotia (Clancy in this volume), and Prince Edward Island (Conrad in this volume). Executive federalism mechanisms, such as First Ministers' Conferences as well as one-on-one meetings with the prime minister, need to be venues for challenging the status quo and forcing the federal government to meet its obligations under section 36 of the *Constitution Act, 1982* that includes equal opportunity for New Brunswickers, and investment and economic development to support that opportunity through new and effective government programs. At this point, few federal politicians listen to New Brunswick, so acting more aggressively in interprovincial negotiations and demanding changes from the federal government, like Quebec does, would do little damage to the province's reputation. Further, the province has a case to be made in intergovernmental relations that the current formula developed for equalization payments has not been enforced by the Harper or Trudeau governments to the letter and spirit of what the Section 36 principle of equalization was designed to do.

As for the provincial labour force, both public and private sector, the future looks grim. At some point, the government is going to get into the business of choosing which smaller communities receive services and which do not. That will likely speed up the rural-to-urban migration in the province. It also puts more pressure on the large centres to retain jobs and employment opportunities for an increased population. Going forward, executive leaders in New Brunswick, starting with Brian Gallant, need to consider their position not just as a fiscal and economic steward but as an innovator in forcing New Brunswickers to challenge their deep-seeded, small "c" conservatism when it comes to rethinking the province as a whole. One of the largest shifts occurring in New Brunswick is the rural-to-urban and northern-to-southern migration throughout the province, with Moncton and its suburban growth being the prime beneficiary. While rural northern communities and cities decline in population, there is a huge potential upside to this change as more equitable distribution of services and efficiencies that did not exist previously will become options for future governments. While the public might want to frame this as the provincial government picking and choosing which rural communities to abandon, a better way of looking at it is as the government investing more strategically in three growing cities rather than eight small centres and hundreds of rural communities all competing for a slice of a shrinking pie. Intraprovincial demographic shifts are but one area a visionary leader could turn into a major positive.

REFERENCES

Atkinson, Michael M., Daniel Béland, Gregory P. Marchildon, Kathleen McNutt, Peter W.B. Phillips, and Ken Rasmussen. 2013. *Governance and Public Policy in Canada: A View from the Provinces*. Toronto: University of Toronto Press.

Campbell, David W. 2014. "Federal Transfer Payments to NB: Declining Influence." *It's The Economy, Stupid*. http://davidwcampbell.com/2014/11/federal-transfer-payments-to-nb-declining-influence/.

CBC News. 2002. "Harper Plans to Battle 'Culture of Defeatism' in Atlantic Canada." 30 May. http://www.cbc.ca/news/canada/harper-plans-to-battle-culture-of-defeatism-in-atlantic-canada-1.306785.

– 2008a. "Balanced Budget Target 'At Risk' with Deficit: NB Auditor General." 3 December. http://www.cbc.ca/news/canada/new-brunswick/balanced-budget-target-at-risk-with-deficit-nb-auditor-general-1.754142.

– 2008b. "N.B. Government Projects $285M Deficit, Blames Global Economic Turmoil." 3 December. http://www.cbc.ca/news/canada/new-brunswick/n-b-government-projects-285m-deficit-blames-global-economic-turmoil-1.723165.
– 2010. "Atcon Faces Bankruptcy Filings by Bank." 25 February. http://www.cbc.ca/news/canada/new-brunswick/atcon-faces-bankruptcy-filings-by-bank-1.923296.
– 2011. "N.B. Takes Cue from U.S. Shale Gas Industry." 26 January. http://www.cbc.ca/news/canada/new-brunswick/n-b-takes-cue-from-u-s-shale-gas-industry-1.1072319.
– 2014a. "J.D. Irving Pushing Forestry Deal with Media Blitz." 22 May. http://www.cbc.ca/news/canada/new-brunswick/j-d-irving-pushing-forestry-deal-with-media-blitz-1.2650523.
– 2014b. "Brian Gallant Ready to Make Unpopular Decisions to Save Economy." 20 December. http://www.cbc.ca/news/canada/new-brunswick/brian-gallant-ready-to-make-unpopular-decisions-to-save-economy-1.2886658.
– 2015. "Victor Boudreau Pushing to Save $600M in Program Review." 15 January. http://www.cbc.ca/news/canada/new-brunswick/victor-boudreau-pushing-to-save-600m-in-program-review-1.2902029.
Desserud, Donald A. 2011. "The 2010 Provincial Election in New Brunswick." *Canadian Political Science Review* 5 (1): 99–116.
– 2015. "The Political Economy of New Brunswick: Selling New Brunswick Power." In *Transforming Provincial Politics: The Political Economy of Canada's Provinces and Territories in the Neoliberal Era*, edited by Bryan M. Evans and Charles W. Smith, 110–34. Toronto: University of Toronto Press.
Gillies, Jamie. 2014. "New Brunswick's Trend of Electing Young Premiers." CBC News, 21 September. http://www.cbc.ca/news/canada/new-brunswick/new-brunswick-votes-2014/jamie-gillies-new-brunswick-s-trend-of-electing-young-premiers-1.2772086.
Goar, Carol. 2013. "How New Brunswick Became a Pension Trailblazer." *Toronto Star*, 21 August. http://www.thestar.com/opinion/commentary/2013/08/21/how_new_brunswick_became_a_pension_trailblazer_goar.html.
Goodwin, Michael, and Joe Ruggeri. 2004. "Demographic, Economic and Fiscal Developments, 1984–2003." In *Government Budgeting and Fiscal Sustainability in New Brunswick*, edited by Joe Ruggeri. Fredericton: Policy Studies Centre, University of New Brunswick.
Haan, Michael. 2014. "New Brunswick Should Be 'Nervous' about Future Outmigration." CBC News, 11 September. http://www.cbc.ca/news/

canada/new-brunswick/new-brunswick-votes-2014/new-brunswick-should-be-nervous-about-future-outmigration-1.2762040.

Hanniman, Kyle. 2013. "Provinces in the Credit Markets: Market Discipline and the New Classic Federalism." In *How Ottawa Spends 2013–2014*, edited by Bruce Doern and Christopher Stoney, 31–46. Montreal and Kingston: McGill-Queen's University Press.

Lee, Philip. 2001. *Frank: The Life and Politics of Frank McKenna.* Fredericton: Goose Lane Editions.

Marotte, Bertrand. 2010. "Hydro-Québec Agrees to Revise N.B. Power Deal." *Globe and Mail*, 19 January. http://www.theglobeandmail.com/report-on-business/industry-news/energy-and-resources/hydro-quebec-agrees-to-revise-nb-power-deal/article1207451/.

McCarthy, Shawn. 2010. "Danny Williams Still Upset over NB Power Deal." *Globe and Mail*, 21 January. http://www.theglobeandmail.com/news/politics/danny-williams-still-upset-over-nb-power-deal/article4188515/.

McHardie, Daniel. 2009. "N.B. Budget Cuts Hundreds of Millions in Taxes." CBC News, 17 March. http://www.cbc.ca/news/canada/new-brunswick/n-b-budget-cuts-hundreds-of-millions-in-taxes-1.776697.

McKenna, Frank. 2014. "Good Governments Do Not Allow Mob Rule." *Halifax Chronicle Herald*, 4 November. http://thechronicleherald.ca/opinion/1248701-mckenna-good-governments-do-not-allow-mob-rule.

Milne, William J. 1996. *The McKenna Miracle: Myth or Reality?* Toronto: University of Toronto Monograph Series on Public Policy and Public Administration.

New Brunswick. Department of Finance. 2006. *Budget 2006–2007: Investments for People*. Fredericton: Department of Finance, 28 March. http://www2.gnb.ca/content/dam/gnb/Departments/fin/pdf/Budget/2006-2007/FinalEnglish.pdf.

– 2007. *Budget 2007–2008*. Fredericton: Department of Finance, 12 March. http://www2.gnb.ca/content/dam/gnb/Departments/fin/pdf/Budget/2007-2008/FinalEnglish.pdf.

– 2008. *Budget 2008–2009*. Fredericton: Department of Finance, 18 March. http://www2.gnb.ca/content/dam/gnb/Departments/fin/pdf/Budget/2008-2009/Speech0809_E.pdf.

– 2009a. *Budget 2009–2010: Leadership for a Stronger Economy*. Fredericton: Department of Finance, 17 March. http://www2.gnb.ca/content/dam/gnb/Departments/fin/pdf/Budget/2009-2010/Speech_2009-2010-e.pdf.

– 2009b. *Budget 2010–2011: Creating Opportunities Today for Self-Sufficiency Tomorrow*. Fredericton: Department of Finance, 1 December. http://www2.gnb.ca/content/dam/gnb/Departments/fin/pdf/Budget/2010-2011/Budget_Speech-e.pdf.
– 2011. *Budget 2011–2012: New Direction, New Brunswick*. Fredericton: Department of Finance, 22 March. http://www2.gnb.ca/content/dam/gnb/Departments/fin/pdf/Budget/2011-2012/Budget_Speech_2011-2012-e.pdf.
– 2012. *Budget 2012–2013: Rebuilding New Brunswick Together*. Fredericton: Department of Finance, 27 March. http://www2.gnb.ca/content/dam/gnb/Departments/fin/pdf/Budget/2012-2013/Budget_2012-13_Final-E.pdf.
– 2013. *Budget 2013–2014: Managing Smarter for a Brighter Future*. Fredericton: Department of Finance, 26 March. http://www2.gnb.ca/content/dam/gnb/Departments/fin/pdf/Budget/2013-2014/Budget_2013-14_Final-E.pdf.
– 2014a. *Budget 2014–2015: Putting Our Resources to Work*. Fredericton: Department of Finance, 4 February. http://www2.gnb.ca/content/dam/gnb/Departments/fin/pdf/Budget/2014-2015/2014-2015Budget.pdf.
– 2014b. "New Accountability Legislation for Election Costing and Budgeting Announced." 7 May. http://www2.gnb.ca/content/gnb/en/news/news_release.2014.05.0512.html.
New Brunswick. Office of the Auditor General. 2013. "Auditor General Concerned That Provincial Government's Structural Deficit Persists." Fredericton: Auditor General of New Brunswick, 5 December. http://www.agnb-vgnb.ca/content/agnb-vgnb/en/media/releases/renderer.2013.12.1253.html.
– 2014. *Report of the Auditor General 2014*. Fredericton: Auditor General of New Brunswick. http://www.agnb-vgnb.ca/content/dam/agnb-vgnb/pdf/Reports-Rapports/2014V1/Agrepe.pdf.
– 2015a. "Auditor General Concerned about Continued Growth of New Brunswick's Net Debt." Fredericton: Auditor General of New Brunswick, 22 January. http://www.agnb-vgnb.ca/content/agnb-vgnb/en/media/releases/renderer.2015.01.0041.html.
– 2015b. *Report of the Auditor General 2015*. Fredericton: Auditor General of New Brunswick. http://www.agnb-vgnb.ca/content/dam/agnb-vgnb/pdf/Reports-Rapports/2015V3/Agrepe.pdf.
New Brunswick. Office of the Premier. 2012. "New Pension Model Introduced." Fredericton: Office of the Premier, 31 May. http://www2.gnb.ca/content/gnb/en/news/news_release.2012.05.0477.html.

Poitras, Jacques. 2004. *The Right Fight: Bernard Lord and the Conservative Dilemma*. Fredericton: Goose Lane Editions.

Ruggeri, Joe. 2004. *Government Budgeting and Fiscal Sustainability in New Brunswick*. Fredericton: University of New Brunswick Policy Studies Centre.

Ruggeri, Joe, David Goodwin, and Yang Zou, 2004. "Fiscal Balances and Fiscal Sustainability." In *Government Budgeting and Fiscal Sustainability in New Brunswick*, edited by Joe Ruggeri. Fredericton: Policy Studies Centre, University of New Brunswick.

Saillant, Richard. 2014. *Over the Cliff? Acting Now to Avoid New Brunswick's Bankruptcy*. Moncton: Canadian Institute for Research on Public Policy and Public Administration.

Saillant, Richard, and David Campbell. 2014. *Shale Gas in New Brunswick: Towards a Better Understanding*. Moncton: Canadian Institute for Research on Public Policy and Public Administration.

Savoie, Donald J. 2001. *Pulling Against Gravity: Economic Development in New Brunswick During the McKenna Years*. Montreal: Institute for Research on Public Policy.

– 2006. *Visiting Grandchildren: Economic Development in the Maritimes*. Toronto: University of Toronto Press.

– 2010. "New Brunswick: Let's Not Waste a Crisis." *Journal of New Brunswick Studies* 1: 42–53.

Toronto Star. 2009. "Hydro-Quebec to Get Most of NB Power's Assets." 29 October. http://www.thestar.com/business/2009/10/29/hydroquebec_to_get_most_of_nb_powers_assets.html.

Workman, Thom. 2003. *Social Torment: Globalization in Atlantic Canada*. Halifax: Fernwood Publishing.

Wyatt, Stephen, and Janelle Baker. 2014. "First Nations and Shale Gas in New Brunswick: Partners or Bystanders?" In *Shale Gas in New Brunswick: Towards a Better Understanding*, edited by Richard Saillant and David Campbell. Moncton: Canadian Institute for Research on Public Policy and Public Administration.

CHAPTER EIGHT

Provincial Fiscal Strategies and Public-Sector Management in Nova Scotia

PETER CLANCY

This book explores a series of themes across provincial and territorial experience. In this chapter, we ask what patterns distinguish fiscal policy and public-sector management in Nova Scotia.[1] In particular, it is important to assess the shape of neoliberal politics in Nova Scotia. Neoliberalism combines several threads, including a sustained attack on the public sector aimed at curtailing the provincial state in favour of the market domain, cutting taxes and using the ensuing deficits as a rationale for dismantling further programs, and launching a frontal challenge to the unionized public-sector workforce. If so, the neoliberal impulse in Nova Scotia is more uneven and less fully expressed than elsewhere. However, Thomas Edsall (2012) is certainly correct in arguing that we live in a prolonged era of austerity, which throws up a variety of political narratives. In this broader sense, the neoliberal signature is amply evident in Nova Scotia.

The province of Nova Scotia is no stranger to public-sector experiments. Consider some modern examples. In 1997, the Liberal government of John Savage cut the ribbon on the new Highway 104 toll road connecting northern Nova Scotia to points east and west (Highway 104 n.d.). This was one of only a handful of such user-pay highway projects completed in that era (others included Ontario's Highway 407, BC's Coquihalla Highway, and New Brunswick's Route 2). In 2000, the Nova Scotia Conservative government of John Hamm legislated a new fiscal rule that mandated balanced budgets (Nova Scotia 58th General Assembly 2000). Eight years later, the Rodney

MacDonald Conservatives suffered a non-confidence defeat while attempting to undo that fiscal rule (Nova Scotia 60th General Assembly 2009). The ensuing election brought the New Democratic Party (NDP) to power. For fiscal guidance in the post-crisis period, Premier Darrell Dexter appointed an independent "wise persons" panel to advise on fiscal options and announced a three-month public consultation on how the province's finances could be brought "back to balance" (Beale et al. 2009). Three years later NDP finance minister Graham Steele resigned from cabinet, in large part due to the premier's unilateral decision to settle a labour negotiation with public-sector workers at a higher than planned level (Steele 2014). Finally, the Stephen McNeil Liberals had barely taken office in 2013 when they cancelled a planned cut to Nova Scotia's 15% harmonized sales tax (HST), in the name of revenue protection (Doucette 2013). Such vignettes only begin to capture the range of public-sector adjustment mechanisms.

This suggests that Nova Scotia has an extensive policy repertoire for fiscal politics, program delivery, and public employment. The province's experience is rich in other ways as well. In the past two decades, all three major parties have spent time in office. In addition, the province has been ruled by four majority and three minority governments since 1993. This period encompasses several business cycles as well as the cathartic 2008 financial crisis. In sum, Nova Scotia offers a rich and variable fiscal laboratory. Part of the argument below is that the period of fiscal experimentation stretches further back than might be expected. The province's first modern fiscal crisis arose in the early 1990s, at a time that some recall as "the Savage Years" (Clancy et al. 2000). It had a signal impact on the party system and provincial fiscal culture as well as public-sector management strategies.

Nova Scotia is a small province with a distinct economic makeup and a distinct public-sector profile. The province is highly sensitive to federal fiscal transfers and to business cycles, and as a result it "imports" certain neoliberal forces as well as generating others at home. However, this chapter argues that Nova Scotia experiences them in particular ways that are mediated through provincial structures. For example, the early 2000s collision between the federal–provincial equalization system and the rise of offshore petroleum played a particularly deep role, reflected in provincial budgeting almost from the point that the Sable Offshore Energy Project's gas (from the offshore field) began to flow in 2000. Other examples will be presented in the pages below, including the rival choices on preferred tax/expenditure mixtures, perspectives on budget surplus or deficit management, and public-sector labour relations.

THE PROVINCIAL ECONOMY

Before turning to the politics and policies of fiscal management, it is important to consider the provincial economy. Nova Scotia's is a small regional economy in the Canadian context. In 2012, the provincial gross domestic product or GDP was $38.4 billion and amounted to a very modest 2.1% of national GDP. The 2000s saw a faltering in rates of aggregate growth. In the six years prior to the crash, GDP growth ranged from 0.3% in 2006 to 2.1% in 2008 and the story since the crash is not dissimilar (Finance and Treasury Board 2014). This also has important implications for provincially sourced revenues, as seen below.

What of the Nova Scotia economy more generally? The consumer and labour markets are based on a small aggregate population of less than one million that has been declining (throughout the study period) by 0.5% per year. It is also an aging population, which carries implications for health service provision and income sources, not to mention public expectations. One projection suggests that by 2036 the provincial labour force could decline by 100,000 workers (Ivany 2014, 12). For decades, a pronounced internal population shift has been under way, from rural and small towns toward the greater Halifax region. That metropolitan area now accounts for more than one-third of all residents and more than half of provincial GDP (Greater Halifax n.d.).

One recent study identified two features that help define the particularity of the provincial economy. First, the 2008 crisis was more muted in its impact on Nova Scotia than it was on the country as a whole. Real GDP declined by 1.4% in Nova Scotia in 2009 compared to 4.8% for Canada (Sharp and de Avillez 2012). This is consistent with other reports that the provincial business cycle fluctuates within a narrower band than the national business cycle. On another scale, the Nova Scotia public sector (including all three levels) is almost double the size of the national public sector, in percentile terms. For Nova Scotia, the public-sector share of GDP is 10.8% compared to 5.7% for Canada (ibid.). This underlines the potential amplified impact of federal, provincial, or municipal measures aimed at restructuring or downsizing. Another salient contrast is between the trade union density in private-sector employment (under 15%) and public-sector employment (over 70%).

The internal structure of the economy also deserves mention. It has been suggested that Nova Scotia should be treated as a "two-gear economy." This contrasts the greater Halifax region, which powers the province with over 2.5% growth, with the rural economy that imposes a compensatory drag. This generates a tension between the region that is driving tax revenues and the region that depends on public expenditures for stabilization in the face of lagging growth. At the same time, the mounting public-service claims of the metropolitan region imply the likelihood of an inter-regional transfer. As a result, "the politics and policy of this new resource shift will be complicated and will not unfold in a straight line" (Hodgson 2013).

FISCAL VARIABLES

Macroeconomic conditions are integral to fiscal strategy as attested by the assessments offered in every budget speech. Indeed, to the extent that the province claims a role in business cycle management (a point taken up in more detail later in the chapter) such aggregate data will be primary points of reference. At the same time, ministers of finance must also deal with the challenges of fashioning budgets as balance sheets. Here, the central categories are total expenditures; total revenues; and the resulting surpluses, balances, deficits, or borrowing needs.

Consider expenditures first. A central fact is the preponderant share taken up by three program sectors. The health envelope accounts for over 40% and shows no sign of slowing its growth. Not only is it a part of social policy that affects all citizens (as users of health services), but it is an area of great voter sensitivity. Consequently, when expenditure control measures are applied to the health sector, with implications for access to family physicians, surgical wait times, rural hospital service availability, and health union contract negotiations, the entire electorate is engaged. The education envelope comes second at 12% and covers systems from early childhood and primary to grade twelve. Here, the number of school enrollees has been declining ever since 1972 with present enrolment at only 55% of the peak level (Clancy et al. 2000, 146). As a result, the challenge takes a different form, managing a school system with surplus classroom capacity in some regions and rising enrolments elsewhere. The education envelope covers one of the most organized labour forces in the provincial sector, with a history of successful collective bargaining. Third in magnitude is the community and social services envelope, which accounts for about 9% of estimated 2014–15 spending. Fourth is the debt service envelope, also at 9% (Department of Finance 2014). Several dozen smaller envelopes, each accounting for 4% or less of total spending, deliver additional services.

On the revenue side, Nova Scotia's own-source revenues amount to two-thirds of all revenues. The largest streams include personal income tax (over one-third) and harmonized sales tax (over one-quarter) with corporate income tax adding another 7%. The residual third of Nova Scotia revenues involves federal government transfers. Of these, equalization payments constitute over half of the total while the Canada Health Transfer and Canada Social Transfer make up another third. Federal transfer payments are obviously a crucial stabilizer of Nova Scotia public finances. This element has become increasingly tenuous over the past two decades as federal austerity programs, first by Jean Chrétien and Paul Martin and later by Stephen Harper and Jim Flaherty, have hit both transfers and direct federal spending in Nova Scotia. In particular, the provincial equalization transfer peaked in 2008–09 before falling by 24% by 2010–11 (Feehan 2014, 8).

Another essential element on the revenue side is the significance of tax expenditures. This refers to the use of tax deductions and tax credits to incentivize behaviour deemed to be in the public interest. This is sometimes described as "giving without taking" (McLaughlin and Proudfoot 1981). Since the result is to reduce the revenue receipts that would otherwise flow to the province, such measures can be realistically viewed as expenditures in disguise. A recent study of Nova Scotia tax expenditures put the total level for 2009 at $909 million, an amount almost equal to the community and social service expenditures of that year (Department of Finance 2011; 2008). In 2014, the Broten report on tax reform proposed the elimination of a wide swath of these tax expenditures as part of a revenue-tightening initiative. However, there has been little evidence of support for this at either political or administrative levels (Broten 2014).

The third key element in the fiscal trinity is the aggregate net budgetary position – the surplus, deficit, or balance. Nova Scotia's fiscal coordinates have fluctuated here. In the 1990s, the province faced continued deficits, with record levels in 1993 and again in 2000. This changed with the surplus of 2002–03 and continued to have a surplus until the financial crisis. Since then, the province has again recorded a string of net deficits. Figure 8.1 offers further details on this point. At the time of writing, the estimated deficit for 2014–15 was $279 million.

In assessing deficit positions, the distinction between the cyclical and structural components of a budget deficit is important. The former captures the deficit share that is due to a business cycle downturn, when tax receipts decline and expenditure programs expand due to a slumping economy. When economic growth returns, this component disappears. The structural share of a deficit is the shortfall that remains when an economy recovers, and it implies a revenue–expenditure imbalance of a different order. One recent estimate suggested that the cyclical share was at most 25% of the provincial deficit (O'Neill 2009, 25–6).

As noted earlier, Nova Scotia's current interest payments to service provincial debt is the fourth-largest expenditure envelope. Accumulated debt service is a category that connects the political past with the present. Its significance can be expressed in several ways, including in absolute terms (billions), in terms of the annual cost of interest obligations, or of total debt as a percentage of GDP. Each taps into a separate field of meaning. Almost all governments have accumulated high aggregate debt (Alberta excepted) so the absolute level expressed in billions of dollars, despite its shock value, may not be particularly telling (see Brownsey as well as Sabin in this volume). More pertinent is debt service spending as a share of annual budget spending, since debt service is a statutory obligation and represents a diversion of funds from current service funding. In this millennium, the annual debt service payment has dropped from the 20% range to a 9% share of annual expenditures. On the measure of total debt as a share of Nova Scotia GDP, it fell from 49% in 2000 to 36% in 2013 (CCPA 2014b). Both measures point to a degree of discipline in debt management.

The modern public sector is administration-driven, which means that civil service workers play an essential role. In any province, this includes workers at all three levels of government. The Nova Scotia profile departs from the national trend in several respects. It joins the neighbouring Atlantic provinces in hosting a public sector that is larger, as a share of GDP, than the Canadian norm. As mentioned

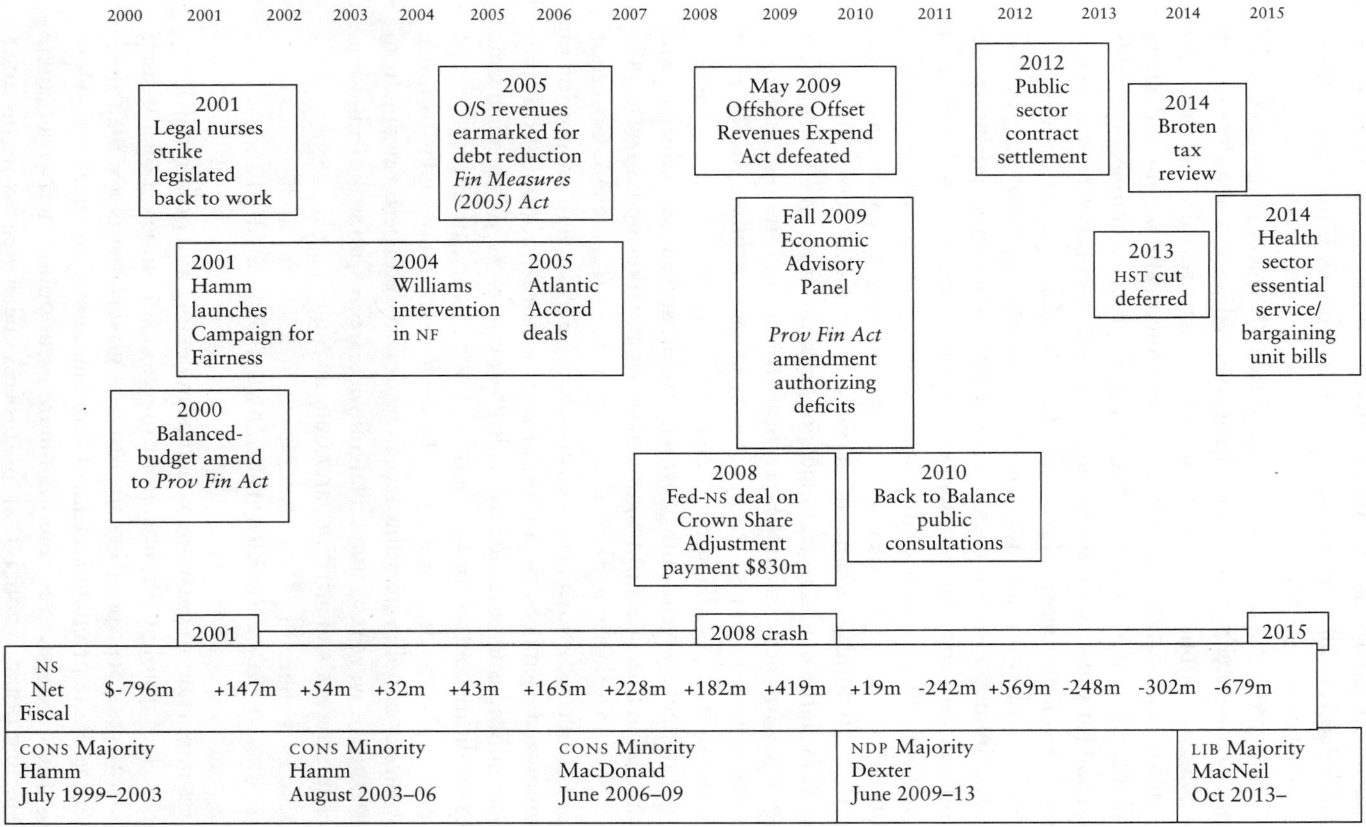

Figure 8.1 Major fiscal events in Nova Scotia

previously, Sharp and de Avillez (2012) report that the Nova Scotia public sector (all levels) is almost double that of Canada, at 10.8% as compared to 5.7% in the 1997–2008 period. Second, it is one of the few provinces where federal public employment surpasses that of the province. Expressed as a ratio of civil service employees per 100,000 of population, recent Nova Scotia data reveal 1,443 in federal employment, 1,036 in provincial employment, and 950 in municipal. Third, the provincial share of total public-sector employees (30%) is typical for Canadian jurisdictions, while federal employment is higher (at 42%) and municipal is lower (at 28%) (Eisen 2009).

This underlines the fact that the Government of Nova Scotia has direct influence on less than a third of total civil-service positions and indirect influence on another (municipal) third. Halifax's role as a regional administrative centre for the Government of Canada is underlined in the size of the federal share. Specifically, there were more than 24,000 federal government employees in Nova Scotia in 2012. However, the cumulative impacts of Ottawa's 2007–10 expenditure reviews, 2010 operational expenditure freeze, and strategic and operating review begun in 2011, amount by one estimate to 1670 job losses by 2014–15 (Bourgeois et al. 2012, 23–5).

In budgetary terms, the provincial public service has a dual significance. First, the cost of wages and benefits makes up just over 58% of Nova Scotia's annual expenditures in 2014 (Lieutenant Governor 2014). Second, Nova Scotia's public service has a high proportion of unionized members. As a result, the expenditure allotment on civil-service wages is governed by multi-year contracts. At the same time expenditure controls or cuts must, out of necessity, affect employment levels and, as such, pose a direct challenge to the unionized workforce. A variety of policy instruments can be drawn upon here, ranging from negotiated wage restraint, unilateral wage freezes, no strike legislation, hiring freezes and attrition, and outsourcing.

FISCAL NARRATIVES AND POLICY CHOICE

It is important to grasp the way that budgeting and program delivery processes unfold over time. In this section, a number of overarching narratives corresponding to different governments are identified. (Some of the prominent elements are highlighted in figure 8.1.) How do these perspectives help illuminate fiscal politics in Nova Scotia? The first point to note is that this process began well before the 2008 financial crisis, with trial experiments stretching back several decades. This should not be surprising given that neoliberal pressures were stirring in Canada as early as the 1980s (Swartz and Panitch 1985; Calvert 1984; McBride and Shields 1993). In Nova Scotia, John Buchanan (1978–90) led what might be described as the last of the "traditional" postwar governments (Kavanagh 1988). It was distinguished by a clientelistic style of expenditure politics that was underpinned by the adroit use of federal transfer programs, both social and economic (Clancy et al. 2000, chapter 1). During a short tenure as premier in 1991–93, Conservative Donald Cameron tried to escape from this syndrome, launching a number of new measures under the rubric of fiscal reform but driven by a need to differentiate from the Buchanan years. They included the privatization of Nova Scotia Power and the disposal (either by sale or by closure) of the provincially owned Sydney Steel Corporation, along with a two-year public-sector wage freeze.

Two more durable fiscal narratives were fashioned by subsequent premiers. First, the 1993 election brought the Liberals to power under the leadership of John Savage. The combined force of the early 1990s recession and Cameron's pre-election stimulus meant that the Liberals inherited a record $650 million deficit. This left Nova Scotia among a subset of beleaguered provinces that were negatively rated by both credit raters and bond buyers. Perhaps the most severely affected was Saskatchewan (MacKinnon 2003; see also Smith in this volume). In response, the Liberals produced a comprehensive multi-year control scheme known as "Government by Design." Over the next four years, the Savage government acted on multiple fronts, raising the sales tax and adding an income surtax, entering into public–private partnerships (P3) on capital account projects, imposing a public-sector wage freeze, and eliminating selected programs. The ensuing political dislocation was felt at many levels – the Liberal Party, the public-sector unions, and program clientele groups among them (MacLeod 2006). Although the budget was balanced by 1997, the government's popularity plummeted, and John Savage resigned in the hope that new leadership could sustain his legacy. In the ensuing leadership campaign, the heir-apparent Finance Minister Bernie Boudreau was defeated by federal backbench member of Parliament Russell MacLellan, a candidate who had no prior executive experience but promised a more traditional form of leadership.

The Savage government has been described as a neoliberal experiment. Yet, it would be a mistake to view it through the lens of Mike

Harris in Ontario (see Evans and Fanelli in this volume). The Nova Scotia Liberals saw fiscal stabilization as a necessary step to releasing the powers of positive government. The inner cabinet was far more familiar with Osborne and Gaebler's *Reinventing Government* (1993) than they were Hayek's *The Road to Serfdom* (1944). The strategy sought to fracture the iron grip of clientele interests and create new regional administrative structures in education, health and rural enterprise development. The most glaring failure of the Savage Years was one of political legitimation, an absence of empathy for the compounded social dislocations. It can be argued, however, that this period began the process of transforming provincial fiscal culture, breaking with traditional practices and elevating awareness, and catalyzing public debate.

Following the MacLellan minority government interregnum, a new Conservative era opened in 1999 under John Hamm. Like Savage, Hamm was sensitive to the structural imbalance signified by deficit politics in the province. His responses, however, were quite different. For one, he came to power with an alternative fiscal agenda. Inheriting a set of public accounts that were basically in balance, Hamm sought to lock in future surpluses and begin a pay down on public debt. What made it more than a moral injunction was the decision to legislate budget rules to that effect. The *Provincial Finance Act* was amended in 2000 to require a balanced budget (Nova Scotia 58th General Assembly 2000). Subsequent amendments in 2004 and 2005 gave statutory expression to the Hamm government's Debt Reduction Plan, designating minimum annual contributions to debt pay down and requiring that all extraordinary revenues be deposited in a debt retirement fund (Nova Scotia 59th General Assembly 2004; 2005; Department of Finance 2005). These were notions that could have been lifted directly from market-oriented lobby groups like the Atlantic Institute for Market Studies (AIMS) or the Canadian Taxpayer Federation, both exponents of balanced budget fundamentalism. It was the Nova Scotia expression of the "rule-governed" approach to budgeting that enjoyed wide currency among provinces at the time (Simpson and Wesley 2012).

The second fiscal thread that ran through the Hamm years was the pursuit of maximum revenue benefits from provincial petroleum production. It was inaugurated in a series of speeches beginning in 2001 and challenged the federal government's application of a discriminatory transfer rule. The "campaign for fairness," as it was known, challenged Ottawa's provision to claw back Nova Scotia offshore revenues through the equalization scheme (Hamm 2000; 2001a; 2001b). Not only was this manifestly unfair, Hamm argued, but it was contrary to the spirit of benevolent federalism. This thread of fiscal populism was well received within the province. However, the case fell on deaf ears federally. Success came only after Newfoundland premier Danny Williams joined the fray (see Sweeney in this volume), pressuring the Martin Government in Ottawa into concessions during the 2004 election. The Atlantic Accords of 2005 brought comfort to both provinces (Clancy 2011, chapter 8). For Nova Scotia, the fiscal reward took several forms. The equalization-offset provision resulted in a decade of annual payments for petroleum revenues. There was also a separate deal to pay Nova Scotia \$830 million for an unfulfilled "Crown share adjustment" in an earlier Canada–NS petroleum agreement. Most significantly, these arrangements boosted provincial revenues during the peak period of Sable gas production and helped the Conservatives to post substantial budget surpluses for four additional years up to 2009. Yet what an offshore boom delivered, an offshore slump could take away. The planned twenty-five-year project lifespan was abandoned in 2010 after it became clear that Sable gas output was in decline. Only the more modest Deep Panuke field was under development, and Nova Scotia's revenues declined almost simultaneously with the financial crisis.

For years after 2005, Nova Scotia enjoyed the revenue benefits from the Atlantic Accord and budget surpluses followed until 2008–09. However, the principled pursuit of the budget surplus Holy Grail began to fade after Hamm's retirement. A long-standing practice, known to insiders as "March Madness," involved bringing forward program proposals toward the close of the fiscal year to spend down the surplus. One of the most egregious examples was the 2008–09 adjustment to fund the following year's university block transfer in advance (Deloitte and Touche 2009, chapter 2).

THE GREAT SLUMP: A SPECIAL "DISTURBANCE" OR A NORMAL "PUNCTUATION" TO THE NS "EQUILIBRIUM"?

Opportunities for new fiscal narratives arose in the wake of the 2008 crisis. Less than a year after the collapse of Lehman Brothers investment bank and the global credit crunch, Nova Scotia elected its first New Democratic Party government. In many respects, the financial crash and the accompanying recession were less severe in Nova Scotia than might have been expected. Of course, there were major impacts on consumption and provincial tax receipts. However, the Nova Scotia slump registered as a -1.6% GNP fall in 2009 compared to -4.8% for Canada at large (Sharp and de Avillez 2012). Nova Scotia's real GDP registered 2.1% in 2008 and recovered to 3.0% in 2010, a performance linked to the federal stimulus program. It was after 2010 that provincial growth slowed again with GDP shifts of 0.6% in 2012, -0.1% in 2012, and 0.3% in 2013. It was in these years that two of the three major forest-processing complexes were closed and offshore-petroleum spending wound down.

The politics of the post-crisis slump are a different matter. While it was not immediately evident, the Conservative leadership shift of 2006, from John Hamm to Rodney MacDonald, marked a major transition. First, MacDonald lacked the debt control conviction of his predecessor. Instead, his commitment to budget surpluses was opportunistic – accepted but only so long as petroleum revenues and the millennial growth wave permitted. Once the banking dominoes began to fall in 2008, there was little sense of strategy. The MacDonald Conservatives further muddied the fiscal waters in early 2009, with three successive finance ministers in only three months. The spring legislative session unfolded without a budget debate. Indeed, the government was defeated on a bill that would have brought fiscal flexibility by rescinding the Hamm budget rules (Nova Scotia Legislature 2009). The June election took place without a 2009–10 budget in place.

As majority winners in June 2009, the Dexter New Democrats were not shy in staking out their own fiscal narrative. It included a blunt disclosure of an inherited fiscal straightjacket, a determination to bring the public accounts into balance over a four-year span, and a guarantee of early implementation of the NDP's rather modest campaign commitments. The accounting firm Deloitte was commissioned to audit the provincial accounts, and an Economic Advisory Panel (EAP) of four non-government policy experts was commissioned to advise on fiscal strategies.

The Deloitte report warned that escalating expense claims (including the pressures of an aging population) combined with flat revenue trends (with the expiry of one-time offshore and equalization adjustment provisions) "are creating the largest financial management challenge for the [Government of Nova Scotia] for the decade ahead" (Deloitte and Touche 2009, 12). Under prevailing assumptions, the 2012–13 projected annual deficit was $1.3 billion. There was another perhaps more deeply ominous message in the Deloitte report. The period of revenue surplus from offshore oil and gas was on the wane. Not only was Sable gas output in decline but also the offshore payments stipulated by the 2005 Atlantic Accord would expire in a few short years. In other words, another fiscal hole loomed ahead in the Nova Scotia accounts.

The Economic Advisory Panel warned that a deep deficit position could not be remedied in the short term. Instead, it proposed a sustained four-year fiscal tightening to culminate in a balanced budget in 2012–13. The EAP further outlined three main pathways – augmented revenue, curtailed expenditures, and expanded economic output – and advised the pursuit of all three (Beale et al. 2009). The initial NDP fiscal approach reflected this advice. The 2009–10 budget acknowledged Deloitte's "new normal" of flat revenues and rising expenditures. The deficit was estimated at $592 million. NDP election commitments, with an estimated cost of $32 million, were also factored in. As well, the *Provincial Finance Act* was amended to permit offshore petroleum revenues to be channeled into the operating budget.

The following year, the NDP presented its first signature budget. This was framed in terms of an extended public consultation titled "Getting Back to Balance," from which the finance minister claimed a mandate for a three- to five-year road to a budget balance (Department of Finance 2009). Expenditure cuts of more than a billion dollars were outlined, which were linked to wage restraint, pension plan changes, and normal cuts. On the revenue side, the HST was raised from 13% to 15%, occupying the sales tax "space" that had been vacated by the Harper Conservatives in 2006 and 2008. The forecast deficit fell to $222 million. The overall thrust here was moderately countercyclical in the sense of combining a stimulative deficit and a full-term budget-balancing timetable. It acknowledged the deficit constraint without elevating it to obsessive levels. This may have been an instance of Dexter's professed goal of "governing like [Manitoba NDP premier Gary] Doer and not like [Ontario NDP premier Bob] Rae" (Clancy 2015, 92; see also Camfield in this volume).

However, there was an implicit cost in terms of new programs forgone, and not all commentators accepted this formula. In its *Alternative Nova Scotia Budget* series, the Canadian Centre for Policy Alternatives (CCPA) called for a very different fiscal mix that elevated equity as a distributional principle. This applied both to the tax side, where high-income rates would be incrementally raised, and on the expenditure side, where low income support programs would be enhanced along with "good job"–generating measures (CCPA 2014a, 13–48, 117–25). This formed part of a general critique of the Dexter government for accepting a "third way" approach to capitalist politics, in effect a "friendly" form of neoliberalism (Fodor 2010).

Up to the halfway point of its term, the Dexter government polled well above 40% in public support. In October 2011, Irving Shipbuilding Inc.'s Halifax Shipyard won a massive $25 billion naval construction contract that presaged a decade of heavy industry production after 2015 (Canadian Press 2011). At the same time, there was mounting pressure in rural areas as several large industrial employers announced closures. The government spent much of 2011–12 searching for new buyers for the Port Hawkesbury and the Liverpool pulp and paper mills, succeeding in the former case but not the latter. For Port Hawkesbury, the grant/loan financial assistance package exceeded $100 million over multiple years. In 2012, it became known that Nova Scotia had also provided some $260 million in forgivable loans over a decade to enhance the Irving shipyard's successful bid. While such measures may have been pivotal in levering major investments, their magnitude contrasted strikingly with the fiscal controls that were being applied to public sector.

This contributed to the negative GDP growth of 2012 and the announced 1%+1% (sequential) cuts in the HST, to begin in 2014. Some major public-sector union contracts were also up for renegotiation in 2012. Here, internal differences over the level of the government's final offer led to the resignation of Finance Minister Graham Steele (Steele 2014, chapter 10). By this time the Dexter government's fortunes had turned. For reasons that remain difficult to explain, by the fall of 2012, the NDP and the Liberals switched positions in voter preference. Certainly, there was little evidence that fiscal differences played a significant role, though the New Democrats were doubtless linked to the persistent deficits.

For their first year in office, after the October 2013 election, the McNeil Liberals were searching for a fiscal strategy. Certain aspects recalled the Dexter accession four years earlier. The new government pointed to a deficit inheritance, estimated at $482 million for 2013–14. More than half of this involved a one-time pension adjustment. Furthermore, the Liberals noted that GDP was little more than flat at 1.4%, with tightening revenues from virtually all sources (Minister of Finance 2014). One early decision was to cancel the NDP's planned 2% HST cut until a surplus was achieved. Another was a 1% across-the-board program cut, with exemptions for health and education (i.e. for two-thirds of the overall spending program). February 2014 also saw the release of the Ivany report on the state of the provincial economy, with a warning that Nova Scotia stood at the verge of long-run economic decline (Ivany 2014, vi, 16). On fiscal policy, Ivany confirmed what was increasingly evident, that the prolonged twentieth-century era of federal transfer stabilization would no longer hold, and uncertain times loomed. As if to confirm this prognosis, the spring of 2014 saw reports of at least a half-dozen small rural municipalities facing financial foreclosure, with another half dozen in the queue that followed (Campbell 2014; Beswick 2014; Delaney 2014). Around the same time, Finance Minister Diana Whalen appointed a one-person tax commission to review all revenue sources and report by year-end (Bundale 2014). This produced a plan for strengthening revenues by closing tax expenditures while at the same time shifting the proportionate reliance on income taxes and sales taxes, in favour of the latter.

Like the NDP earlier, McNeil faced major public-sector negotiations in year one. The backdrop was the three-year 2%-2.5%-3% pay-raise deal agreed by Dexter in the previous settlement. In 2014, the Liberals drew a red line and argued the fundamental need to restrain public-sector settlements going forward (Minister of Finance 2014). This was justified as the core of the government's deficit reduction program, given that almost 60% of the Nova Scotia budget covered wages and salaries. McNeil argued that Nova Scotia's prior settlement ran well ahead of the national pattern of 1.2 to 2.1% per year, promising "tough conversations" in the upcoming round to enable the province to achieve "the right wage pattern" (Canadian Press 2014; Doucette 2014).

The previous spring, in the face of strike action, the Liberals enacted essential-service legislation that covered unionized Capital District Health Authority workers and designated them an essential service. This occurred in the face of mass public-sector protests. There was a greater ramification of this contract showdown, however. After consolidating nine regional health authorities into one, the Liberals indicated that they wished to rationalize the previous fifty union bargaining units in the provincial health sector down to one for each of four bargaining units (nurses, health care workers, administrative support, and service support). This legislation also met mass protests in late September 2014 (Enxuga 2014). Without question, the Liberals sought to simplify the bargaining process by restructuring the bargaining units, though whether this led necessarily to lower contract settlements remained to be seen.

As the Liberal government's term of office deepened, there were several other fiscal measures of note. First, in the spring of 2015 the universities were warned that serious operating budget deficiencies would not be tolerated. A new statute "respecting accountability of sustainability of universities" provided that, in such circumstances, a provincially appointed panel would design a "revitalization plan," while strikes or grievances by unionized workers would be prohibited (Laroche 2015). Second, a new Pharmacare premium formula was announced early in 2016. This formula sought to save the government $10 million by more than doubling the annual premium paid by middle-income seniors. The presentation of this policy was confusing and contradictory, sowing resistance across the public, and the proposal was quickly withdrawn. Third, the McNeil government engaged a consultant to investigate highway twinning and toll road prospects on eight sections with high stress traffic. This included a "willingness to pay" survey that suggested prospective tolls of six to ten cents per kilometre (CBCL Ltd 2016). Following the release of this report, a second study stage, which included public consultation was launched, with a flexible horizon that might conceivably stretch past the next election.

Nova Scotia's fiscal straightjacket is evidently more enduring than the 2008 crisis alone. Put differently, the structural roots of the current slowdown are deeper. To answer the question posed in the heading of this section, the financial crisis can be seen as a slightly abnormal punctuation on a longer-term fiscal equilibrium. Even without 2008's financial crisis, the province would have struggled with mounting deficits given the petroleum revenue decline and federal equalization adjustments. Certainly, the crisis flattened the trading sector and tilted marginal enterprises into failure. However, it also brought stimulus through capital spending. In addition, the two-gear economy became increasingly difficult to manage.

PUBLIC-SECTOR LABOUR RELATIONS

In Nova Scotia, the first step away from patronage-based appointments was the beginning of a civil service commission in the 1930s. However, it was not until the 1950s that the first civil-service association was formed, and not until the 1970s that trade union consciousness was evident. Not coincidentally, it was in that decade that the Regan government sought first voluntary and later compulsory wage restraint. The modern Nova Scotia bargaining regime took form in the 1970s under the *Civil Service Collective Bargaining Act*. It was a no-strike, no-lockout deal that sent disputes to arbitration if necessary. The public-sector employees' association evolved into the Nova Scotia Government Employees Union (NSGEU) by 1983, by which time the number of provincial employees had doubled in two decades to more than ten thousand (Wagar 2001, 37–41).

The 1990s saw the first sustained break from a cost-of-living bargaining pattern. This coincided with the fiscal tensions noted in earlier sections. Cameron's 1991 restraint act suspended collective bargaining on compensation for two years. This was followed by Savage's 1993 legislation imposing five unpaid leave days on the provincial public service, defined broadly to include the municipal sector. The following year saw more aggressive measures in the form of a 3% pay cut for all public servants earning greater than $25,000 per year, along with a wage freeze under all signed contracts until 1997 (ibid., 45–50).

Of equal importance were the institutional changes that created regionalized authorities in education, health, and municipal government. As a result, about 40% of the NSGEU membership shifted from labour relations under jurisdiction of the *Civil Service Act* to the *Trade Union Act*. When collective bargaining resumed in 1997, contract settlements reflected wage adjustments of 2% in each of two years, in effect locking in the losses imposed by the sequence of freezes, caps, and cuts.

After "normal" operations resumed, it became clear that the health sector would remain a leading target for special bargaining rules. This was partly due to its unparalleled importance as a budget envelope and partly due to the question of its status as an "essential service." In 2001 for example, facing the prospect of a strike by health care workers the Hamm Conservatives passed legislation that suspended the right to strike for three years. Shortly later, in the face of considerable protest, these provisions were withdrawn and a process of final offer arbitration was agreed to. In that particular bargaining round, the union offer was selected for registered nurses while the employer offer was selected for the other units. However, a precedent had fleetingly been established.

By the early 2000s, three bargaining models could be discerned in provincial health union bargaining across Canada (Haiven and Haiven 2002, 25–6). A permanent strike ban applies in some provinces while a regulated strike system (with compulsory emergency provisions during a strike) applies in others. Nova Scotia was part of a third group of unregulated strike systems in which essential service provisions were voluntarily agreed upon by employers and unions.

Over the past decade in Nova Scotia, governments have proposed at different times to replace the unregulated strike model with each of the others. During the MacDonald Conservatives' government, the health minister proposed in 2007 to outlaw health sector strikes (Haiven and Haiven 2007). Under conditions of minority government, however, this was never likely to happen. More recently in 2014, the McNeil Liberals enacted a series of three bills aimed at restructuring the health sector bargaining framework as well as imposing essential service regulations (Haiven 2014; Bush 2014).

As it turned out, this was only the beginning. The McNeil government continued its hard fiscal stance on public-sector settlements into 2015, offering the teachers (Nova Scotia Teachers' Union or NSTU) and government employees (NSGEU) a multi-year wage freeze followed by annual increments of 1.0%, 1.5%, and 0.5%. After the teachers rejected a draft settlement, the Liberal government responded in December with the *Public Services Sustainability Act*. By its terms, the government embedded the increments described above and capped the terms of potential arbitration awards at the same level. Finance Minister Randy Delorey indicated that the statute would only be proclaimed if a prospective contract exceeded these terms. This measure recalled the wage limits imposed by the Savage government in the 1990s. In the face of this bill, the NSGEU leadership reversed its earlier support for a draft settlement and declined to schedule a membership vote. In effect, the two unions continued to work under expired contracts while escalating their opposition to the Liberal government. Early in 2017, after the teachers rejected a third contract offer, the McNeil government legislated to impose the contract. At the time of writing, the tensions continue, though it should be noted that the McNeil government was polling at 56% voter intention levels at the close of 2016.

CONCLUSION

In Nova Scotia, questions of structured approaches to fiscal, programming and employment strategies well pre-date the 2008 financial crisis. This is because the core conditions of fiscal crisis (cyclical slump, deep tax expenditures, statutory program obligations, and deficit) took hold much earlier. In contemporary Nova Scotia, governments have displayed moderation in the intensity of fiscal policies but experimentation with a range of policy tools.

The Savage Liberals confronted very modern contradictions and fashioned equally modern responses to forces that resurfaced, variously, over the next generation. The Hamm Conservatives took office during relatively buoyant times when the allocation of surplus rather than the struggle with deficits drove fiscal choice. They chose to entrench a set of rules aimed at constraining the choices of future governments in the service of market orthodoxy. In less than a decade, this prescription broke down, however, in the face of renewed contradiction. The MacDonald Conservatives strained and eventually failed in their efforts to overcome fiscal contradictions. In the face of the 2008 crisis and recession, the NDP struck a compromise course. It plotted a four-year plan toward a balanced budget (a target not ultimately achieved) through a combination of tax hikes and spending cuts (including negotiated wage restraint). However, the Dexter New Democrats came to power with a modest program for social change and the cost of new commitments was slight; this inevitably disappointed broad swaths of the party base. When voters swept that government aside in 2014, they backed a Liberal Party whose fiscal program differs little from its predecessor. Once again, a four-year plan has been outlined to eliminate a near-record deficit, which suggests that sizeable deficits are politically legitimate within a rhetoric of fiscal control. Once again, the usual policy suspects are rounded up including incremental tax hikes, spending freezes, and wage restraint. They are applied selectively, however, rather than comprehensively.

It is difficult to discern a "hard" neoliberal ideology at work in Nova Scotia in the past several decades. In the two sustained phases of deficits, 1991–97 and 2009–present, the tendency was to combine revenue and expenditure measures in multi-year plans to close the fiscal gap. The John Hamm majority comes closest, in both rhetoric and action, to a neoliberal stance. Nova Scotia's fiscal predicament was exacerbated, in both deficit phases, by transfer austerity from Ottawa. What is missing, however, is the classic neoliberal formula that runs from tax cuts to deficit discovery to swinging expenditure cuts and the curtailment of public-sector scope. Savage and Dexter both strained to co-ordinate revenue and program measures. This is the policy band in which the Nova Scotian state tends to operate.

It appears that, in the real world of Nova Scotia's fiscal management, choices are tightly constrained. A provincial government presiding over a small economy with a larger than average public sector and a dampened business cycle has demonstrated caution in its approach. The diminished scale of federal transfers on the revenue side further underlines the province's vulnerability to outside forces. While the 2008 financial crisis may not have been as immediately disruptive as elsewhere, its refracted impacts continue to grow, in fiscal planning in Ottawa and in shifting patterns of business investment and corporate strategy. Since 2011, governments have counted on the naval shipbuilding contract and Muskrat Falls (Labrador) hydro as megaprojects that could fuel a decade of new growth, boosting revenues to substitute for the demise of Sable gas. Unless or until this materializes, provincial authorities will continue to struggle with over $200 million deficits and to juggle $50 million policy measures in order to keep that deficit within a politically sustainable range. Whether or not the Nova Scotian public is fully aware of such considerations, the political legitimacy of budget policy may rest upon the perception that measures are, in some sense, balanced or proportionate among the interests of multiple social groups.

The fiscal policy discourse within the province will continue to outline a wider set of choices. On the right, the AIMS calls for flat tax schemes and a phasing out of equalization in favour of enhanced provincial tax room. Chambers of Commerce press for more immediate budget balances, lower corporate and small business taxes, and spending restraint in health and education. On the left, the CCPA Nova Scotia argues in favour of tackling social inequality far more aggressively than the New Democrats sought, shifting policy attention from the fiscal deficit to the social deficit where affordable, focusing on housing and child care, and broadening access to early learning and higher education. Also figuring in this debate are the Ivany report, which insists that the traditional fiscal infrastructure is unsustainable (though stopping short of positive advocacy), and the Broten report on tax reform, which suggests a relative shift from income tax toward sales tax in future revenue raising and throwing in a carbon tax for good measure.

The election of the Justin Trudeau Liberals in Ottawa shows little sign of altering this picture. Nova Scotia will press for larger immigration allotments, in the hope of expanding workforce growth, and for infrastructure stimulus support for a variety of capital projects. Nevertheless, the outcome of the health transfer deliberations may prove the most consequential issue for provincial finances. The evidence above suggests that while partisan contrasts can be found among elements of fiscal strategies since the early 1990s, these contrasts are neither as deep nor as exclusive as can be found elsewhere. In practice, Nova Scotia governments may have recently maneuvered within a relatively narrow band of choice since the mid-2000s. This may continue until the next political shock, whatever its source, forces more abrupt responses.

NOTE

1 I wish to acknowledge financial support for this project from the Centre for Regional Research at St Francis Xavier University. Mr Isaac Turner contributed significantly as research assistant on the project.

REFERENCES

Beale, Elizabeth, Tim O'Neill, Lars Osberg, and Donald J. Savoie. 2009. *Addressing Nova Scotia's Fiscal Challenge*. Panel of Economic Advisors Report to Premier Darrell Dexter. Halifax: November.

Beswick, Aaron. 2014. "Which Towns Might Be Next?" *The Chronicle Herald*, 6 March.

Bourgeois, Michael, Joanne Hussey, Christine Saulnier, and Sara White. 2012. *Public Disservice: The Impact of Federal Job Cuts in Atlantic Canada*. Halifax: Canadian Centre for Policy Alternatives Nova Scotia, November.

Broten, Laurel C. 2014. *Charting a Path for Growth: Nova Scotia Tax and Regulatory Review*. Halifax: Province of Nova Scotia, November. http://www.novascotia.ca/finance/docs/tr/Tax_and_Regulatory_Review_Nov_2014.pdf.

Bundale, Brett. 2014. "N.S. Aims to Reform Tax System." *The Chronicle Herald*, 27 February.

Bush, David. 2014. "A Major Blow to the Right to Strike in Nova Scotia." *New Socialist*, 13 April.
Calvert, John. 1984. *Government Limited: The Corporate Takeover of the Public Sector in Canada*. Ottawa: Canadian Centre for Policy Alternatives.
Campbell, Frances. 2014. "Dissolving Springhill – A Town Asks Why." *The Chronicle Herald*, 6 March.
Canadian Press. 2011. "Irving Shipyard Wins $25b Shipbuilding Deal." 20 October.
– 2014. "NS Premier Says Public Sector Wages Not Supported by Economy." 11 December.
CBCL Ltd. 2016. *Highway Twinning Feasibility Study: Preliminary Screening/Assessment*. Halifax: CBCL Ltd, July.
CCPA. 2014a. *Nova Scotia Alternative Budget*. Halifax: Canadian Centre for Policy Alternatives Nova Scotia, 19 March.
– 2014b. *Ten Nova Scotia Fiscal Facts*. Halifax: Canadian Centre for Policy Alternatives Nova Scotia, 3 April.
Clancy, Peter. 2011. *Offshore Petroleum Politics: Regulation and Risk in the Scotia Basin*. Vancouver: UBC Press.
– 2015. "Nova Scotia: Fiscal Crisis and Party System Transition." In *Transforming Provincial Politics: The Political Economy of Canada's Provinces and Territories in the Neoliberal Era*, edited by Bryan M. Evans and Charles W. Smith, 77–109. Toronto: University of Toronto Press.
Clancy, Peter, James Bickerton, Rodney Haddow, and Ian Stewart. 2000. *The Savage Years: The Perils of Reinventing Government in Nova Scotia*. Halifax: Formac Books.
Delaney, Gordon. 2014. "Fiscal Cliff Looms at Bridgetown." *The Chronicle Herald*, 21 March.
Deloitte and Touche. 2009. *Province of Nova Scotia Financial Review: Interim Report*. Halifax: Deloitte & Touche LLP, 7 August. http://www.novascotia.ca/finance/site-finance/media/finance/final_report.pdf.
Doucette, Keith. 2013. "Nova Scotia Books in No Shape for Legislated Cut to HST: Finance Minister." *Canadian Press*, 17 December.
– 2014. "Public Sector under Siege." *The Chronicle Herald*, 31 December.
Edsall, Thomas. 2012. *The Age of Austerity: How Scarcity Will Remake American Politics*. New York: Doubleday.
Eisen, Ben. 2009. *Manitoba's Public Sector Is Larger, More Expensive than Most*. Backgrounder 80, Frontier Centre for Public Policy. CANSIM 281-0024 and 281-0027.

Enxuga, Shay. 2014. "NS Liberals vs. Workers Round 2: The Battle over Bill 1." *RankandFile.ca*, 3 October.

Feehan, Jim. 2014. *Canada's Equalization Formula: Peering Inside the Black Box … and Beyond*. School of Public Policy, University of Calgary, SPP Research Papers 7 (24) September.

Fodor, Matt. 2010. "The Dexter NDP: Old Wine, New Bottle?" *Relay: A Socialist Project Review*. Bulletin 294, January.

Greater Halifax Partnership. n.d. "Latest Economic Data." www.greaterhalifax.com.

Haiven, Larry, and Judy Haiven. 2002. *The Right to Strike and the Provision of Emergency Services in Canadian Health Care*. Ottawa: Canadian Centre for Policy Alternatives, December.

– 2007. "A Tale of Two Provinces: Alberta and Nova Scotia." The Right to Strike in Nova Scotia Series. Halifax: Canadian Centre for Policy Alternatives Nova Scotia, October.

Haiven, Larry. 2014. "Bill 37 – Cutting Nova Scotia's Unions Off at the Knees." *RankandFile.ca*, 3 April.

Hamm, John F. 2000. *Remarks to the Nova Scotia Chamber of Commerce*. Halifax: 24 October.

– 2001a. *Newsmaker Breakfast Series*. Ottawa: 7 February.

– 2001b. *Remarks to the Metropolitan Halifax Chamber of Commerce*. Halifax: 17 January.

Hayek, Friedrich A. 1944. *The Road to Serfdom*. Chicago: University of Chicago Press.

Highway 104. n.d. http://www.highway104.ns.ca.

Hodgson, Glenn. 2013. "Nova Scotia's Two-Gear Economy: The Shape of Things to Come." Ottawa: Conference Board of Canada, 25 July. http://www.conferenceboard.ca/economics/hot_eco_topics/default/hot-topics-in-economics-blog/2013/07/25/nova_scotia_s_two-gear_economy_the_shape_of_things_to_come.aspx.

Ivany, Ray. 2014. *One Nova Scotia: Shaping Our New Economy Together*. Nova Scotia Commission on Building Our New Economy. Halifax: February.

Kavanagh, Peter. 1988. *John Buchanan: The Art of Political Survival*. Halifax: Formac Books.

Laroche, Jean. 2015. "Nova Scotia Universities Face Increased Financial Scrutiny with New Bill." CBC News. 22 April.

MacKinnon, Janice. 2003. *Minding the Public Purse*. Montreal and Kingston: McGill-Queen's University Press.

MacLeod, Jeffrey. 2006. "Nova Scotia Politics: Clientelism and John Savage." *Canadian Journal of Political Science* 39 (3): 553–70.

McBride, Stephen, and John Shields. 1993. *Dismantling a Nation: Canada and the New World Order*. Halifax: Fernwood Publishing.

McLaughlin, Kevin, and Stuart B. Proudfoot. 1981. "Giving without Taking: A Primer on Tax Expenditures." *Canadian Public Policy* 7 (2): 328–37.

Nova Scotia 58th General Assembly. 2000. *Financial Measures (2000) Act* (Bill 46). 1st session. http://nslegislature.ca/legc/bills/58th_1st/1st_read/b046.htm.

Nova Scotia 59th General Assembly. 2004. *Financial Measures (2004) Act* (Bill 62). 1st session. http://nslegislature.ca/legc/bills/59th_1st/1st_read/b062.htm.

– 2005. *Financial Measures (2005) Act* (Bill 177). 2nd session. http://nslegislature.ca/legc/bills/59th_1st/3rd_read/b177.htm.

Nova Scotia 60th General Assembly. 2009. *Offshore Offset Revenues Expenditure Act* (Bill 240). 2nd session. http://nslegislature.ca/legc/bills/60th_2nd/1st_read/b240.htm.

Nova Scotia. Department of Finance. 2005. *Debt Reduction and Offshore Offset Agreement*. Halifax: Province of Nova Scotia. https://www.novascotia.ca/finance/docs/DebtReductionPlan2005.pdf.

– 2008. *Nova Scotia Budget Highlights 2008–09*. http://www.novascotia.ca/finance/site-finance/media/finance/highlights.pdf.

– 2009. *A Guide: Getting Back to Balance*. Halifax: Province of Nova Scotia.

– 2011. *Overview of the Nova Scotia Tax System*. Halifax: Province of Nova Scotia, April. https://www.novascotia.ca/finance/site-finance/media/finance/Overview_of_NS_Tax_System_2011-04-04.pdf.

– 2014. *Budget 2014–15 Highlights*. Halifax: Province of Nova Scotia. http://www.novascotia.ca/finance/site-finance/media/finance/budget2014/Budget_Highlights.pdf.

Nova Scotia. Finance and Treasury Board. 2014. "Current Economic Environment – Highlights." Halifax: Province of Nova Scotia, 11 December. http://www.novascotia.ca/finance/statistics/topic_news.asp?id=10388&fto=22v&rdval=2014-12.

Nova Scotia. Legislature. 2009. *Proceedings*. 1 May and 4 May.

Nova Scotia. Lieutenant Governor. 2014. *Speech from the Throne*. Halifax: Province of Nova Scotia, 25 September. http://0-nsleg-edeposit.gov.ns.ca.legcat.gov.ns.ca/deposit/b10451638_Sep2014.pdf.

Nova Scotia. Minister of Finance. 2014. *Budget Address 2014–15*. Halifax: Province of Nova Scotia, April. http://www.novascotia.ca/finance/site-finance/media/finance/budget2014/Budget_Address.pdf.

O'Neill, Tim. 2009. "Assessing the Fiscal Challenges Facing the New Government." In *Addressing Nova Scotia's Fiscal Challenge*. Panel of Economic Advisors Report to Premier Darrell Dexter. Elizabeth Beale, Tim O'Neill, Lars Osberg, and Donald J. Savoie, 25–56. Halifax: November.

Osborne, David, and Ted Gaebler. 1993. *Re-inventing Government: How the Entrepreneurial Spirit Is Transforming the Public Sector*. New York: Plume Books.

Sharp, Andrew, and Ricardo de Avillez. 2012. *A Detailed Analysis of Nova Scotia's Productivity Performance, 1997–2010*. Ottawa: Centre for the Study of Living Standards Research, June.

Simpson, Wayne, and Jared Wesley. 2012. "Effective Tool or Effectively Hollow: Balanced Budget Legislation in Western Canada." *Canadian Public Policy* 38 (3): 291–313.

Steele, Graham. 2014. *What I Learned about Politics: Inside the Rise – and Collapse – of Nova Scotia's NDP Government*. Halifax: Nimbus Publishing.

Swartz, Don, and Leo Panitch. 1985. *From Consent to Coercion*. Toronto: Garamond Press.

Wagar, Terry H. 2001. "Provincial Government Restructuring in Nova Scotia: The Freezing and Thawing in Labour Relations." In *Public-Sector Labour Relations in an Era of Restraint and Restructuring*, edited by Gene Swimmer, 36–65. Toronto: Oxford University Press.

CHAPTER NINE

Austerity in the Garden Province of Prince Edward Island

PATRICIA CONRAD

Prince Edward Island (PEI) is characterized as the Garden Province and the Gentle Isle. It is Canada's smallest province in size and population. A significant proportion of its residents are distributed throughout small bucolic communities, clusters of countryside farms, and the urban centres of Charlottetown and Summerside. Approximately 55% of Islanders live in rural areas. This feature contributes to the preservation of a lifestyle that typifies traditional values and conservative ways of being (Randall et al. 2015). These values and ways are manifested in Islanders' strong ties to the land and pastoral ways of life that contribute to PEI's high degree of social cohesiveness.

Regardless of where the population is situated, PEI governments of all stripes must ensure access to a certain level of publicly funded services. All have grappled with how to equitably provide public services to a dwindling rural population. The harsh reality facing PEI governments is a need to fund infrastructure and deliver services such as health care, which must adhere to the same standards as its larger counterparts through terms and conditions set out in the *Canada Health Act*. The challenge facing PEI is how to meet these requirements with a much smaller tax base and less capacity to raise government revenue within a mix of additional constraining factors including geography, population base, and natural resources.

Notwithstanding its natural beauty, community cohesiveness, and reputation as a rejuvenating retreat from the fast pace and complexities of Canada's crowded urban centres, PEI is vulnerable on a number of fronts (Rural Development PEI 2010). From an economic perspective, the largely resource-based economy located mostly in rural areas is generally blamed for PEI's languishing fiscal performance (Prince Edward Island Minister of Finance, Energy, and Municipal Affairs 2012). Other challenges include a poor industrial base, susceptibility to weather patterns that affect its food production capabilities, a high proportion of elderly residents, and an unhealthy population. These impose an ongoing reliance by PEI's governments on federal transfers such as equalization payments and federally sponsored social programs such as Employment Insurance (EI).

Describing the Canadian interpretation of decentralization – the one austerity instrument used by provincial governments to control health care spending – provides a backdrop for discussing reforms to the PEI health system. Figure 9.1 illustrates the evolution of health care reform milestones for the province of PEI from the early 2000s through to 2015. This chapter will highlight the relationship between health reforms implemented by successive PEI governments, beginning in the 1990s, and the extent to which decentralization as representative of a neoliberal tactic can curtail growth in health care spending. It outlines how regionalization – the made-in-Canada version of European decentralization – was the only austerity mechanism permitted under the *Canada Health Act*. Of specific interest is the success of regionalization in controlling health care costs through creating meso-level organizations where budgets of various sectors, such as home care and hospitals, were amalgamated into one administrative structure. Provinces were persuaded by Canadian health reformers to believe that this structure would create capacity to shift or reallocate resources from more expensive hospital-based beds to less costly home care and community-based care settings in contrast to predictions by E.E. Schattschneider's scope of conflict theory as discussed in *The Semisovereign People* (1960).

Governments driven by the need to reduce or control spending have relied on neoliberal public policy instruments (see Evans and Fanelli's introduction to this volume). According to McGregor (2001), neoliberal ideology provides a platform for governments to implement austerity measures aimed at extenuating their fiscal challenges. The instruments available include decentralizing delivery of government services to other levels of government, creating free markets through deregulation and privatization of government services, and promoting individualism and the pursuit of self-interest through a free market orientation (McGregor 2001). McGregor (2001) notes that the contradictions of neoliberal approaches become particularly evident when

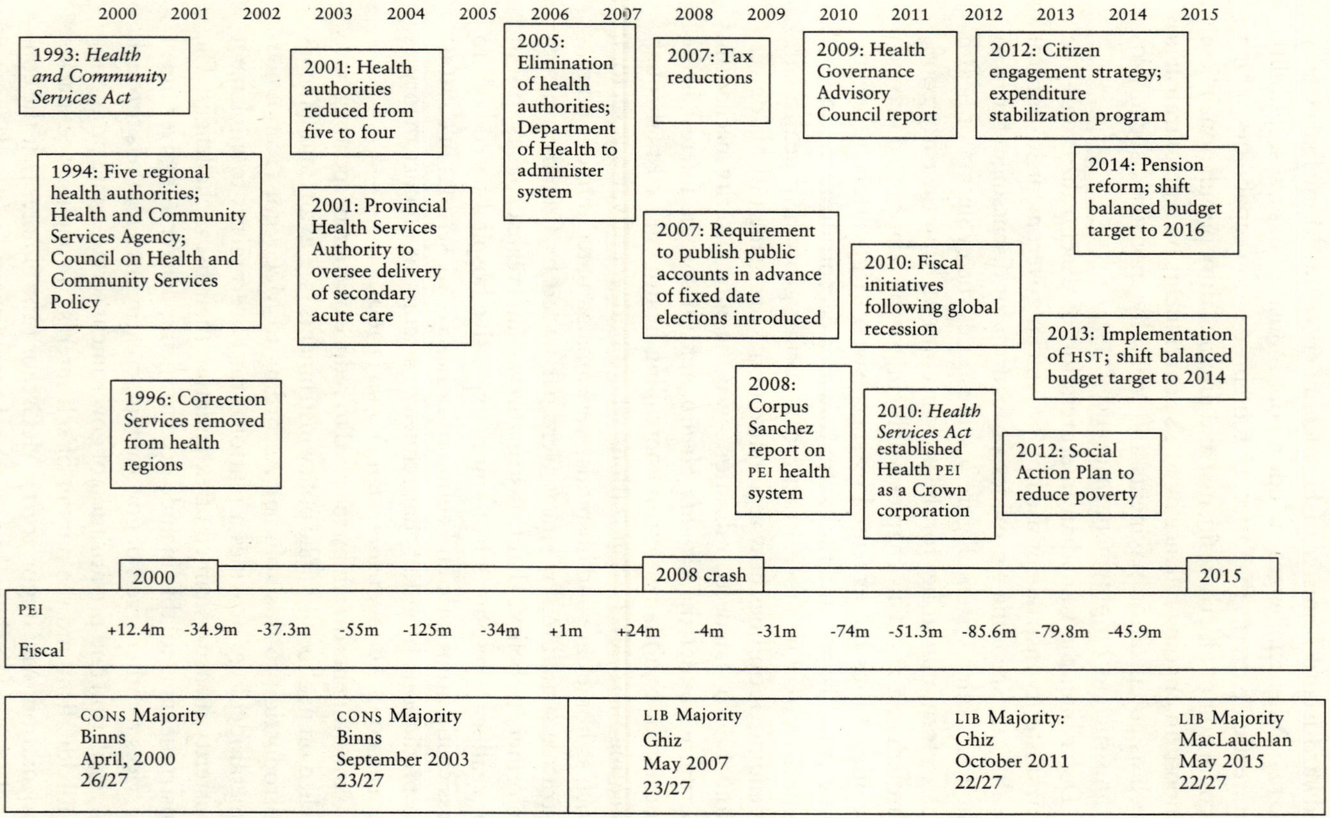

Figure 9.1 Major health and fiscal policy events in PEI

applied to a popular public program such as health care. One significant problem that affects the applicability of a neoliberal ideology to Canadian health care is an assumption that neoliberalism treats all goods and services as private. A neoliberal approach fails to acknowledge the existence of public goods and to distinguish between the nature of public and private goods especially in relation to how these different goods are established and sustained (ibid.).

Many countries take the position that health care is a public good, which ensures that access to health services is not compromised by a patient's inability to pay; under this model, health care is financed by redistributing government revenue raised through taxation (Deber 2002; 2000). Since governments in Canada take the position that health care is a public good, Deber (2002; 2000) contends this viewpoint implies it will be regarded differently than how an open market views the production and acquisition of private goods. Since one role of government is to ensure that public goods are equitably distributed, many governments employ safeguards to achieve equity, some of which include the use of physicians (and in some instances nurse practitioners) as gatekeepers who control access to medically necessary treatment. Looking at health care as a private good can constrain access because to obtain a private good one must have financial resources to pay, and in this situation those with no financial resources will be denied needed care.

Some contextual factors that define Canadian health care include the division of delivery responsibilities between the Canadian federal and provincial governments and the conditions to which provinces must adhere in the delivery of health care as enshrined in the *Canada Health Act,* such as accessibility, universality, public administration, portability, and comprehensiveness. These conditions underpin the federal funding transfers to the provinces provided through the Canada Health Transfer. The amounts are determined by the Canadian federal government and, in turn, the provinces use these and provincial finances to fund the delivery of health care services. The Canadian perspective of health care as public good, therefore, affects the extent to which austerity measures can be applied to this health policy arena.

The explicit inclusion of numerous terms and conditions in the *Canada Health Act* directs the delivery of health care by imposing certain limits on the extent to which provincial governments can apply austerity mechanisms. For instance, reorganizing the governance and delivery of health care through decentralization was the predominant policy tool used by provincial governments during the 1990s in their attempts to alter the trend of escalating health care expenditures through reallocating resources from more expensive hospital care to less costly home care services. As this chapter will show, the instrument of regionalization – the made-in-Canada version of decentralization – has failed to achieve this policy goal.

The Canadian efforts by provincial health reformers were increasingly influenced by European interpretations and implementations of neoliberal reforms. Within the European context, neoliberalism took the form of "internal markets" created through unravelling the *purchase* of health services from *delivery mechanisms* (Saltman and Figueras 1997; Saltman et al. 1998; Saltman and van Otter 1992). Across Canada, regionalization differed from the European model of decentralization in various ways. For example, provincial models of regionalization did not create a split between the purchasing and delivery mechanisms. Rather, most Canadian provinces assigned governance and delivery of health care to an intermediate-level, arm's-length organization whose mandate included both delivery and purchasing of health care (Church and Barker 1998; Eyles et al. 2001a; 2001b). The exception was the province of Ontario, where local health integrated networks (LHINS) were established as non-profit, community-based organizations funded by the Ministry of Health and Long-Term Care to plan, fund, and coordinate services delivered by hospitals. In this instance, LHINS were not directly involved with health care delivery, making Ontario's approach closest to the European model of decentralization. Furthermore, the Canadian regionalization model differed from its European predecessor in that it involved both devolution and centralization (Lewis and Kouri 2004). This made-in-Canada construct had two distinct elements: decentralization and consolidation. First, it featured devolution of governance and delivery of numerous services, such as public health, home care, long-term care, and mental health care, from provincial governments to regional health boards. Second, the centralization component amalgamated the governance of acute care hospitals under regional health boards and away from what were previously autonomous governance and delivery organizations (ibid.). A common feature shared by all provincial models was that prescription drugs and physicians were not decentralized but continued to be directly managed by provincial governments (Lomas 1997).

Beginning in the 1990s, each provincial government was explicit about expected outcomes for regionalization in that it was viewed as the one way in which the growth of health care expenditures could be controlled (see Whiteside in this volume). Hence, governments set up regions with the idea that consolidating hospitals would rationalize the number of hospital beds needed and care would move into less costly home- and community-based settings (Lomas and Rachlis 1996). The extent to which PEI achieved this policy goal will be critically evaluated by discussing the capacity of PEI's model of regional governance to facilitate this shift. For example, did the inclusion of home care into the regional basket of health and community services by the PEI government result in the home care sector gaining a higher share of the regional health budget? How did PEI expenditures for home care (and its subsequent share of health spending) compare with the other Maritime provinces, notwithstanding the differences in the regional models each implemented? With these questions in mind, this analysis will conclude by exploring how new pressures to find cost savings post-2008 were influenced by the socio-political characteristics and beliefs held by Islanders about health, and how these pressures affected health care reforms following the economic downturn in 2008. These are centred on the failure of the PEI regionalization experiment to achieve one of its key policy goals of increasing home care budgets.

As shown in figure 9.1, there were numerous attempts by successive PEI governments to redesign the governance and organization of health care. However, depending on the government of the day's ideology about the governance and delivery of health care, the pendulum swung back and forth between centralization and decentralization. Centralized planning and control was the dominant belief of the PEI Conservative Party. This approach was subsequently reformed by the Liberal Party following their election to government in the early 1990s. Health care reform under the Liberals centred on designating health regions. PEI was the first jurisdiction in Canada to implement its population-based model, which Lomas and Rachlis (1996) describe as the most progressive approach of all the Canadian regionalization models.

In 2005, the PEI Conservatives recentralized health care to within government control by eliminating the regional health boards. Following the defeat of this Conservative government in 2007, the Liberals hired the consulting firm Corpus Sanchez International to conduct a review of health care, and their report identified governance as a critical issue that the government needed to fix. Subsequently, an advisory body was formed to recommend a governance approach for health care. Following the release of a report by the Health Governance Advisory Council in 2009, a single health authority that encompassed the entire Island as one region was implemented. This move by the Liberal government coincided with emerging evidence about the ineffectiveness of the PEI health regions in their attempt to substantially shift resources from hospitals to home care (Conrad 2008). Furthermore, PEI was once again at the forefront of a trend, as it was the first province to "de-regionalize" the governance and delivery of health care (Lewis 2008). The resulting inability of health regions to curb hospital costs highlights the complications encountered when jurisdictions applied the neoliberal instrument of decentralization as the panacea.

CONTEXTUALIZING PEI: THE INFLUENCE OF SOCIO-ECONOMIC FACTORS

The province of PEI is situated on the east coast of Canada in the Gulf of St Lawrence. It is the smallest of the ten Canadian provinces and three territories, both in physical size (5,660 square kilometres) and in population (146,283). The island is 224 kilometres long and is linked to New Brunswick via the Confederation Bridge, which opened in 1997. It is connected to Pictou in northern Nova Scotia and to the Magdalene Islands in Quebec through daily ferry service from Wood Islands and Souris, respectively. The province is divided into three counties, the largest being Queens County in the centre of the island, while Prince County is on the western side and the much less populated Kings County is on the eastern side.

The island has the third-highest rate of bilingualism in Canada; 12.7% of the population self-identify as speaking both English and French (Prince Edward Island Statistics Bureau 2011a). PEI has the lowest Aboriginal population in Canada with a rate of 1.5%. Only Newfoundland and Labrador (see Sweeney in this volume) has a lower rate of visible minorities at 1.1% versus PEI's rate of 1.4% (Astles, Foster, Lye, and Prada 2013).

As of 2014, 17.3% of the PEI population was over the age of sixty-five, compared to 15.3% for Canada (Chief Public Health Officer 2014). Many of these older Islanders live in rural areas. The rural population is eroding through a continual exodus of younger people, largely due to government initiatives targeting economic development in urban centres. This scenario is a double-edged sword for the PEI government. On one hand, growing an urban-based economy is a key strategy for increasing government revenues, while on the other, providing health and community services safely, efficiently, and effectively to rural areas with shrinking populations must be accommodated. This latter situation is not unique to PEI as health systems everywhere are struggling to solve these same issues (Corpus Sanchez 2008).

PEI has always depended on the land and the sea as the basis for its primary industries of agriculture, fisheries, forestry, and tourism (Randall et al. 2015). Its economy is considered to be weak in the absence of a strong industrial or manufacturing base (Prince Edward Island Minister of Finance 2012). Most of the predominant activity of this resource-based economy has been in rural areas. More recently, through the Island Prosperity Strategy (Prince Edward Island Lieutenant Governor 2008), the PEI economy has been diversifying as a result of government support aimed at growing industries such as aerospace, biosciences, information technology, and renewable energy. These efforts have resulted in a depopulating of the rural areas as younger Islanders pursue attractive employment opportunities in these emerging economic sectors (PEI Rural Action Plan 2010). Furthermore, the location of federal government agencies, including the Tax Centre in Summerside and Veterans Affairs in Charlottetown, has been a key supplier of employment. Coupled with the growth of urban-based industries, these public-service agencies have assisted the two cities to expand their importance to all Islanders as they evolve into employment and service centres for rural and urban citizens (PEI Rural Action Plan 2010).

As table 9.1 shows, PEI has substantial (and consistent) part-time employment, which includes seasonal workers in the farming, fishing, and tourism sectors (Randall et al. 2015). For example, 5% of workers employed in PEI's agricultural sector is much higher than the national rate at 1.7% (ibid.). As of June 2015, PEI's unemployment rate was 10.4% and this slight decrease is largely attributed to the cyclical nature of PEI's economy (Prince Edward Island Statistics Bureau 2015). This trend in unemployment has serious implications for the fiscal stability of PEI because it translates into a substantial reliance on federally sponsored Employment Insurance to supplement workers' seasonal incomes. PEI is second only to Newfoundland and

Table 9.1
PEI selected labour market statistics, 2004–15

Year	Unemployment rate (percent)	Participation rate (percent)	Total employment (thousands)	Full-time employment (thousands and percentage of total employment)	Part-time employment (thousands)
2004	11.3%	67.8%	66.7	55.6 (83.4%)	11.0
2005	10.9%	68.1%	67.7	56.3 (83.2%)	11.4
2006	11.1%	68.3%	68.0	57.3 (84.2%)	10.7
2007	10.2%	67.8%	68.4	56.8 (83.0%)	11.6
2008	10.9%	68.2%	69.0	57.7 (83.6%)	11.3
2009	11.9%	67.5%	68.1	56.5 (83.0%)	11.6
2010	11.4%	67.6%	69.7	57.1 (82.0%)	12.6
2011	11.0%	68.1%	71.9	59.9 (83.3%)	12.0
2012	11.2%	68.6%	73.0	60.4 (82.7%)	12.7
2013	11.6%	69.7%	74.1	61.0 (82.3%)	13.2
2014	10.6%	68.7%	74.0	62.1 (84.0%)	11.9
2015	10.4%	67.6%	73.2	60.8 (83,1%)	12.4

Source: Prince Edward Island Department of Finance 2015.

Labrador in the number of EI recipients per hundred residents who reside outside metropolitan areas (Randall et al. 2015).

The economic downturn of 2008 gave rise to successive provincial deficits (see figure 9.1: $31 million in 2009, $74 million in 2010, $51.3 million in 2011, and so on), which added to the net provincial debt. In response, the Liberal government of Robert Ghiz (first elected in 2007 and re-elected in 2011) set the stage during the 2012 Budget Address by introducing methods by which the operating cost of government services would be reduced. Given that the capacity of the PEI government to generate additional revenue is limited, various means aimed at reducing expenditures were outlined: consolidating back office functions (these consist of administrative and support roles such as records management, procurement, information technology, and so on), introducing group purchasing, non-replacement of retiring public-sector employees, and freezing MLA salaries (Prince

Edward Island Minister of Finance 2012). The 2013 Budget Address continued to build on the previous measures and introduced others that consisted of the following: implementing the Harmonized Sales Tax, introducing pension reforms, and amalgamating the school boards to form one provincial board. Pension reform became one of the more contentious cost-cutting proposals, which resulted in protests staged by the PEI unions that were strongly supported by Islanders. Despite these public demonstrations, the pension legislation was subsequently passed in December 2013 (Wright 2013).

Approximately 30% of PEI's combined labour force, encompassing the public and private sectors, is unionized (McKenna 2015). Within this overall rate, a vast majority of unionized workers (83%) are employed in the public sector, while 17% work in the private sector (ibid.). According to McKenna (ibid.), PEI unions (and Islanders in general) are not known for taking aggressive actions; however, the PEI Union of Public and General Employees did strongly react to the pension reform announced in the 2013 provincial budget (Wright 2013). This action by the unions was uncharacteristic because the PEI labour movement generally lacks a culture of militancy (McKenna 2015).

The PEI reductions to government spending and the accompanying reforms to the public sector happened largely outside health care. In 2014, the year for which we have the most recent data, there was a loss of 900 public-service positions in education and general government services, as shown in table 9.2. In contrast, the numbers of nurses and physicians have been steadily increasing, although the population growth for PEI was minimal during the years from 1995 onward. Table 9.2 shows a loss of positions in the overall public-service sector through to 2014 and corresponds with the 300 positions per year that was a target announced in the 2012 budget. In contrast, the number of employees within the health sector up to 2014 remained relatively stable or grew slightly compared with the numbers in the mid-2000s. Despite minimal reductions in health care positions between 2004 and 2008, there had been substantial upheaval and destabilization among the workforce when approximately 4,000 employees were transferred to the health regions in 1995. Beginning in 2005, following the elimination of the health regions, these employees were subsequently returned to employment with the PEI provincial government.

Table 9.2
PEI labour market statistics for public service and health sectors, 1995–2014

Year	*Changes in health, education, and public administration positions (1)*	*Number of employees in health and social assistance sector (2)*	*Number of nurses (3)*	*Number of physicians (4)*
1995	NA	NA	NA	158.00
1996	NA	NA	NA	160.00
1997	NA	6,343	NA	151.00
1998	NA	6,577	1,277	159.00
1999	NA	7,506	1,232	149.00
2000	NA	7,953	1,255	148.00
2001	NA	7,663	1,270	157.00
2002	Gain of 500 positions	7,730	1,293	163.00
2003	NA	7,806	1,373	164.00
2004	Gain of 500 positions	8,910	1,377	178.00
2005	Loss of 400 positions	8,975	1,433	178.40
2006	Loss of 800 positions	8,543	1,428	186.00
2007	Gain of 900 positions	8,510	1,435	195.60
2008	NA	8,666	1,479	206.00
2009	Gain of 400 positions	9,148	1,406	210.75
2010	Gain of 1600 positions	9,348	1,472	218.45
2011	Gain of 400 positions	9,320	1,517	216.35
2012	Gain of 300 positions	9,132	1,555	219.35
2013	NA	8,684	1,571	224.40
2014	Loss of 900 positions	8,793	NA	222.59

NA – Data not available
Sources:
(1,3,4) Prince Edward Island Department of the Provincial Treasury 2002, 2003, 2004, 2005, 2006, 2007, 2008; Prince Edward Island Department of Finance and Municipal Affairs 2010, 2011; Prince Edward Island Department of Finance, Energy, and Municipal Affairs 2012, 2013, 2014.
(2) Prince Edward Island Department of Finance 2015.

The growth in the number of nurses and physicians relative to PEI's population growth can in part be explained by the additional federal funding each provincial government was guaranteed in the 2004 Health Accord. A significant portion of this funding was targeted to reducing wait times in selected medical procedures such as hip and knee surgery, which in the case of PEI and other jurisdictions translated into the hiring of additional nurses and physicians. Furthermore, the Robert Ghiz government continued to bolster the expansion of human resources in the health sector beginning in 2008 by implementing a robust plan to increase the supply of physicians because government recognized Islanders had limited to access to family physicians.

The cost-cutting measures introduced by the Ghiz government following the economic downturn of 2008 appear to have had minimal effect on the health care workforce. In fact, spending aimed at increasing the number of doctors and nurses working in PEI was largely due to the 2004 Health Accord, which assured additional federal funding over the ten-year timeframe of this federal government agreement.

SHIFTING THE GOVERNANCE AND DELIVERY OF HEALTH CARE

Islanders' life expectancy is 80.2 years, with males expected to live to 78 years while the female lifespan is 83 years (Chief Public Health Officer 2014). PEI has higher-than-average rates of common conditions such as arthritis, asthma, obesity, and diabetes. The Island population has a higher number of heart attacks per 100,000 at a rate of 251 compared with 206 for Canada (ibid.). A similar scenario exists for strokes at 145 per 100,000, while the Canadian rate is significantly lower at 119 (ibid.). These health conditions, along with high unemployment, high alcohol consumption, and low income are indicators that Islanders are less healthy than the Canadian average (ibid.). These results illustrate what is commonly known as the East–West health gradient; that is, beginning on the East Coast and heading westward, the farther one goes, the healthier the population.

Overall, the lower socio-economic status of Islanders, coupled with PEI's performance on various health status indicators, reveals that it is an unhealthy province. The high incidence of acute illnesses and chronic health conditions create challenges for the PEI health system. The conundrum facing the PEI government is how to achieve a balance between the delivery of acute care diagnostics and treatments while at the same time increasing prevention and promotion, managing chronic disorders, and making enhancements to home care (Conrad 2008). To achieve these policy goals, the strategy of regionalizing the delivery of health care was predicated on shifting (or reallocating) resources from acute care hospitals to home care and community-based primary health services through newly formed meso-level governance and delivery organizations (Lomas and Rachlis 1996). Alternatively, provincial governments have an option of increasing funding to home care if regional health boards fail to reallocate resources from acute care hospitals (Conrad 2008). Because home care is not an insured service under the *Canada Health Act*, the sector is dependent on the availability of provincial government funding, which, inevitably, could be compromised by a province's fiscal situation. This dilemma is not unique to PEI. Accommodating the competing needs between maintaining institutionalized acute care and increasing the availability of community-based home care significantly complicates priority setting and resource allocation efforts within all health systems (Lomas 1997).

In the early 1990s, as health reforms rolled out across Canada, the PEI Liberals under the leadership of Joe Ghiz introduced a comprehensive review of all government operations (Armstrong and Armstrong 2008). Various ministry-led Task Forces (for the Ministries of Health, Education, Tourism, and Agriculture) were formed, and the Task Force on Health issued a report in March 1992 called *Health Reform: A Vision for Change*. Since this Task Force was comprised of only government officials, this review was unlike other provincial health reform commissions where citizen participation was a key element. In spite of this difference, every provincial commission including PEI has recommended the governance and delivery of health care be consolidated under a regional structure (Eyles et al 2001a; 2001b; Lomas 1997; Lomas and Rachlis 1996; Crichton et al. 1997).

A large number of reasons were identified by the PEI Task Force as to why changes to the health system were needed. These included a lack of emphasis on health promotion and home care; fragmented administrative structures, each with its own mandate and funding; the evolution of health care services in the absence of needs-based planning and evaluation of effectiveness; rising health care costs and increasing utilization; a lack of community and individual responsibility for and involvement in planning and decision making; and difficulties in co-ordinating health services across a continuum of care (Crichton et al. 1997). All of these were situated alongside the financial constraints facing the PEI government, which had one of the highest percentages of GDP spent on health in Canada.

Prior to restructuring the health system, PEI had approximately twenty-three independent boards and government departments with responsibilities for the delivery of health care and social services (Eyles et al. 2001). Each board and department operated independently and developed their own budgets in isolation. Health reformers viewed this fragmentation as one way in which historical funding patterns became entrenched. In addition, these disconnected entities perpetuated a planning and funding gridlock that restricted the movement of resources across sectors and within program areas (Eyles et al. 2001a; 2001b; Lomas 1997; Lomas and Rachlis 1996).

Premier Joe Ghiz's government of the early 1990s championed a population-based health perspective, which emphasized the social determinants of health (Lomas and Rachlis 1996). PEI's blueprint for health reform integrated the planning and delivery of health care across a continuum of care that included hospitals, public health, home care, nursing homes, and mental health and addictions, along with community services comprised of income assistance, public housing, corrections, and child welfare. All were amalgamated under a comprehensive regional structure (ibid.). Of all the provincial regionalization models, PEI's featured the broadest scope of services (ibid.). It was considered forward thinking and leading edge because of this. Owing to its broad range of services, which included human services aligned with the social determinants of health as well as medical care, the PEI approach was characterized as a population health model. Under this philosophical framework, access to a range of prevention and community services such as public health and housing was viewed as being just as important as access to medical care in relation to an ability to effect health status (Eyles et al. 2001a; 2001b).

The comprehensiveness of the PEI model was a deliberate decision by the Liberal government to focus on population health. It was also based on the premise that health regions with a broad range of health and human services would be well positioned to redistribute funding from hospitals to community-based services such as home care, health promotion, and disease prevention (Lomas and Rachlis 1996). This model assumed that the close proximity of regional decision makers (the community representatives appointed to the five regional health boards by the provincial government) to the communities they represented would assist them in having a better understanding of local needs – in contrast to a centralized planning model situated within government, where Charlottetown-based bureaucrats made decisions in isolation of knowledge about the priorities of local communities. Finally, the PEI government recognized that divesting politically difficult decisions to the health regions, such as downsizing acute care hospitals, would insulate them from the political fallout arising from decisions aimed at containing rising health care costs through rationalizing and reducing beds (Eyles et al. 2001a; 2001b; Lomas and Rachlis 1996; Crichton et al. 1997).

In addition to forming five health regions, PEI also implemented two central agencies. The Health and Community Services Agency (a Crown corporation) had a mandate to plan the health system, make funding decisions, and allocate budgets. The Health Policy Council was created to provide strategic policy advice to the minister of health. These restructurings reduced the size of the provincial civil service, as over 4,120 employees were reassigned to either the Provincial Agency (120 staff) or to one of the regional health authorities (Prince Edward Island Health and Community Services System 1997).

The Canadian health reform literature suggests that forming health regions to govern and deliver health services by consolidating separate program budgets under one administrative structure would result in a reallocation of resources, thereby adding more funding to home care and other community-based health and social programs (Eyles et al. 2001a; 2001b; Lomas 1997; Lomas and Rachis 1996; Crichton et al. 1997). In contrast, the scope of conflict theory as popularized by E.E. Schattschneider (1960) predicted that the larger the "scope" or array of health and other types of services assigned for regional administration, the greater the potential for conflict and competition. This theory also assumes that the health sectors that enter this arrangement with the highest budgets (such as acute care hospitals), will enjoy a powerful advantage over those actors (such as home care or public health), who enter with a smaller share of overall health spending.

The governments of Nova Scotia (Clancy in this volume) and New Brunswick (Gillies in this volume) each implemented different regionalization models during the mid-1990s. Initially, New Brunswick (NB) began its reform efforts at a slower pace and in a controlled fashion, as health boards were only assigned responsibility for hospitals. Later, the NB government devolved the delivery of the Extra-Mural Program (EMP) which provided acute or hospital replacement home care services (Eyles et al. 2001a; 2001b). Accompanying the decision to assign home care for regional administration was the caveat that the EMP budget would continue to be decided by government officials within the Health Department. The health regions could decide to add resources to the EMP budget; however, this central government oversight would protect the EMP budget from cannibalization by the hospital sector and ensure that the EMP share of provincial health spending was preserved (Conrad 2008).

Nova Scotia (NS) was one of the last provinces to regionalize health care; however, the Liberal government did not assign home care for administration by the health regions. This decision was made primarily out of fear that the nascent and fragile status of home care in Nova Scotia would be left vulnerable if combined for regional administration with other sectors, such as acute care (Conrad 2008). Prior to regionalizing health care, the NS government had been gradually allocating additional funding to the provincial home care program. However, Nova Scotia bureaucrats, similarly to their New Brunswick counterparts, voiced concerns that the home care budget would be under attack by the more powerful acute care hospital sector if it were included in the basket of services to be governed and delivered by the health regions (ibid.).

As Canadian provinces developed plans in the early 1990s to reform their health systems, evidence about home care as a cost-effective and viable alternative to more expensive hospital-based acute care was emerging (ibid.). This new knowledge led to a comparative policy analysis of regionalization models in the Maritimes that sought answers to the following policy questions: How does the home care share of the overall health budget compare with that of hospitals? Does putting home care under regional administration result in a different pattern of resource allocation compared with keeping the administration of home care centralized (ibid.)?

REALLOCATING RESOURCES TO HOME CARE: WIN, LOSE, OR DRAW?

Over a ten-year period, the hospital share of the PEI health budget (table 9.3) decreased from 54.3% in 1990–91 to 48.4% in 2000–01, while during that same time period, the home care share increased from 1.7% to 2.2% (CIHI 2007). Between 1990–91 and 2000–01, the overall Canadian percentage change in provincial government home care spending increased by 157% while the share of government health budgets allocated to home care grew from 3.1% in 1994–95

Table 9.3
Comparison of home care and hospital share of provincial government health expenditures, Maritime provinces and Canada, current dollars

HOME CARE SHARE OF PROVINCIAL GOVERNMENT HEALTH EXPENDITURES (1)				
Year	*PEI*	*Nova Scotia*	*New Brunswick*	*Canada*
1990–91	1.7%	1.4%	4.1%	n/a
2000–01	2.2%	5.4%	7.6%	n/a
HOSPITAL SHARE OF PROVINCIAL GOVERNMENT HEALTH EXPENDITURES				
Year	*PEI*	*Nova Scotia*	*New Brunswick*	*Canada*
1990–91 (2)	54.3%	58.8%	52.6%	49.2%
2000–01 (2)	48.4%	50.0%	51.4%	43.4%
2012 (3)	29.9%	30.8%	33.5%	29.2%
2013 (3)	31.0%	30.9%	33.1%	29.6%
2014 (3)	31.4%	30.4%	33.2%	29.6%

Sources:
(1) Conrad 2008, Table 8-2, 204.
(2) Canadian Institute for Health Information 2007, Table C2.2, 48.
(3) Canadian Institute for Health Information 2014, Table 6, 44; 2013, Table 6, 46; 2012, Table 6, 67.

to 4.2% in 2002–03 (ibid.). However, it does not appear that PEI followed this national trend. For example, the gain in home care's share of health spending was much smaller than the corresponding decrease in the hospital share of health spending. Accordingly, it is assumed that the PEI health regions did not use the savings from rationalizing and reducing hospitals beds to fund more home care. How savings from acute care were actually spent is unclear. One plausible explanation is that, since all provinces including PEI were confronted with very challenging fiscal situations, the savings generated by the regional health boards through the downsizing of acute care were given back to provincial governments and used to reduce annual government deficits.

Prior to restructuring health care, the PEI per capita expenditure for home care was $24.11 in 1990–91. As shown in table 9.4, this was not the lowest per capita spending among the Maritime provinces. Nonetheless, by 1998–99 PEI's per capita amount at $35.43 had fallen behind Nova Scotia and New Brunswick at $82.32 and $122.99

Table 9.4
Comparison of provincial government per capita home care expenditures, Maritime provinces and Canada, 1990–91, 1998–99, 2003–04, constant dollars

Year	*PEI*	*Nova Scotia*	*New Brunswick*	*Canada*
1990–91 per capita (1)	$24.11	$22.84	$67.84	$35.06
1998–99 per capita (1)	$35.43	$82.32	$122.99	$90.22
Change between 1990–91 and 1998–99	47%	260%	82%	157%
2003–04 per capita (2)	$46.21	$105.24	$156.35	$91.14
Change between 1998–99 and 2003–04	30.4%	27.8%	27.2%	1.0%
Change between 1990–91 and 2003–04	91.2%	361%	130.4%	160%

Sources:
(1) Canadian Institute for Health Information.
(2) Canadian Institute for Health Information.

respectively. Furthermore, there was a substantial gap between PEI's per capita spending ($35.43) and the Canadian per capita spending at $90.22. Finally, although PEI's growth in its per capita rate did increase by 47% between 1990–91 and 1998–99, this was the smallest gain in home care spending among the Maritime provinces. Clearly, the spending on home care in PEI had not kept pace with the home care spending in New Brunswick and Nova Scotia. It is suggested this outcome could be attributed to the inclusion of home care in the broad and comprehensive scope of services administered by the PEI health regions and is in line with the assumptions predicted by Schattschneider's scope of conflict theory (Conrad 2008).

The first wave of PEI health reform involving implementation of health regions in the 1990s was intended to curtail growth in health spending (among other policy goals) by rationalizing acute care hospital beds and reallocating the savings to less costly home care programs (Lomas 1997; Lomas and Rachlis 1996). Table 9.4 compares the percentage changes in home care spending by the governments of PEI, New Brunswick, and Nova Scotia. In reviewing these results, the first observation is that both PEI and Nova Scotia spent less than the Canadian average for home care in 1990–91, whereas New Brunswick spent considerably more (recognizing its per capita included only expenditures for the EMP program). PEI's increases at 47% in 1998–99, at 30.4% in 2003–04, and an overall 91.2% gain between 1990–91 and 2003–04 are the lowest of the Maritime provinces and much lower than the average growth rates for Canada. In analyzing this trend, it would appear a history of entrenched spending for hospitals did matter (Conrad 2008). Furthermore, it would seem that the views held by regional health board towards home care also counted, especially in relation to its position relative to the status enjoyed by PEI's hospitals and their accompanying visibility and prominence within Island communities (ibid.).

The protections for home care budgets implemented through two distinct policy decisions by government officials in Nova Scotia and New Brunswick were successful (ibid.). Recall that New Brunswick decentralized the delivery of home care but kept decision making about resource allocation centralized with the Health Department, which created a protective mechanism for the EMP budget. In a similar manner, the Nova Scotia government decided to not devolve home care to the health regions as a mechanism to protect previous funding increases. Clearly, these two distinct actions ensured the home care share of health spending in both provinces was not eroded by the more powerful acute care sector. Meanwhile home care in PEI had to compete for its share of the regional budget and the decisions by the regional health boards caused only marginal growth (ibid.). This disappointing outcome was not what the PEI government had expected, because a key element of its reform strategy involved the expansion of the home care budget by reallocating savings through reducing the number of hospital beds and a concomitant decline in acute care spending (ibid.).

RESTRUCTURING HEALTH CARE: THE PENDULUM SWINGS BACK TO THE CENTRE

The Joe Ghiz Liberal government, which was the original architect of PEI's regionalization model, was defeated in 1996. The newly formed Progressive Conservative government led by Premier Pat Binns (who maintained power for a ten-year period through to 2007), initiated a series of regressive health system reforms. The first modification came in 1996 with the repatriation of correctional services to government control. This was followed by the dissolution of the Health and Community Services Agency and the return of approximately 120 staff to the Health Department (PEI System Evaluation Project 1997). Following the re-election of the Binns government in 2000, more extensive changes to the health system were made. They began with reducing the number of health regions from five to four. This was followed by centralizing the delivery of secondary and specialized acute care to a newly created organization called the Provincial Health Services Agency (ibid.).

The Conservatives were re-elected to a third term in 2003. Although the Binns government was disillusioned with the performance of the PEI health regions, it took almost two years after its re-election before it disbanded the health regions (Kelly 2002). This radical approach was characterized by Lewis (2008) as "de-regionalizing" the governance and delivery of health care. Although the four regional health authorities were eliminated; however, the community-based advisory boards were maintained as a way of engaging with local citizens.

The move by Binns to recentralize the administration of health care within the government bureaucracy coincided with emerging empirical evidence about the effectiveness of regionalization in achieving its policy goals in the Canadian context (Lewis and Kouri 2004). A major problem that bedeviled the PEI government (and others) was determining the optimal size of a health region; that is, what is the number of residents who need to reside within a defined geographical area to safely and economically deliver health services? Finding the answer appeared to be an insurmountable challenge for the small province of PEI given that the size of the Island's entire population approximated the number of residents (100,000) that Canadian regionalization researchers had determined as the optimal size for a health region (ibid.). Clearly, this evidence reinforced the position taken by the Binns government, as it came to the realization that none of the four PEI health authorities was of sufficient size to be an efficient and effective mechanism for health care delivery from the perspective of an economy of scale.

In addition to size, Canadian research about regionalization also exposed other problems health regions had encountered in attempting to fulfill the policy goals advanced by the provincial governments. For example, regions were blamed for being unresponsive to local needs (Philippon and Braithwaite 2008). They also pointed out that health regions were inclined toward propagating local empires as they competed with each other in their quest for additional power and resources. Instead of breaking down the barriers and silos that existed prior to their development, it appears as if most health regions perpetuated parochialism (ibid.). Finally, many health regions were uncooperative and protectionist through an unwillingness to participate in system-wide planning efforts initiated by provincial governments that were aimed at finding solutions to increase access and eliminate regional disparities (ibid.).

These findings seemed to substantiate the largely anecdotal evidence used by Binns in PEI and other provinces to justify recentralizing health care. The PEI Conservatives did, however, distinguish themselves as the first provincial government to recentralize the governance and delivery of health care. Once again, PEI – the smallest Canadian province – was at the forefront of a trend that eventually spread to other Canadian jurisdictions, as they followed PEI's lead in either creating a single provincial authority (such as in Alberta, Nova Scotia, and Saskatchewan) or reducing the number of health regions (such as in New Brunswick and Manitoba).

In 2007, PEI voters returned the Liberal Party to power under the leadership of Robert Ghiz (son of former premier Joe Ghiz). Building on the mounting evidence about the ineffectiveness of health regions, especially for smaller jurisdictions such as PEI, coupled with the Liberal's concern about growing access problems to primary health care along with other acute care services, the government introduced a new vision for the PEI health system centred on building a "One Island Health System" (Prince Edward Island Lieutenant Governor 2009). Throughout the Throne Speeches and Budget Addresses beginning in 2008, this vision was featured in statements such as "Together with Islanders we will build a sustainable, integrated health care system, one that shifts emphasis and culture toward wellness and primary care, placing patients, the community as a whole and sustainability above all considerations. That remains our priority" (Prince Edward Island Lieutenant Governor 2008).

In an effort to support this renewed vision (which did not emphasize home care to the extent the Liberal reforms of the 1990s had), the Robert Ghiz government commissioned Corpus Sanchez International – a consulting firm – to undertake a study of the PEI health system. The firm released a report in 2008 that harshly criticized the "deregionalization" implemented by the Binns Conservatives because this decision made elected politicians responsible for operational decision making instead of independent health administrators and community representatives. A major criticism by Corpus Sanchez

(2008) was that the PEI Cabinet and Treasury Board were the "default operators of the PEI health system," which impeded planning and, more importantly, blurred the lines of authority and accountability. A number of management and administrative positions had been eliminated by this decision and these cuts had seriously eroded the ability of government staff to pursue strategic policy development for the PEI health system. More importantly, from an accountability perspective, a separation no longer existed between the government's role in policy setting and service delivery (ibid.). The Corpus Sanchez report (ibid.) also recommended that PEI should reduce its focus on a hospital-centric model of health care delivery, which had continued to persist largely because regionalization had failed to shift resources to home care and other community-based services (Conrad 2008). However, instead of focusing solely on home care, the Liberal reform efforts centred on building "a robust primary health system" aimed at reducing PEI's reliance on hospital beds.

The Liberals did follow the advice of Corpus Sanchez and, in 2008, announced the Health Governance Advisory Council. This group had a mandate to design a governance model for the PEI health system based on "theory and best practices" (Health Governance Advisory Council 2009). The Council subsequently recommended forming a corporate entity that would be at arm's length from government. The Liberals adopted this approach and passed the *Health Services Act* on 1 April 2010, which established Health PEI as a Crown corporation that would oversee health care delivery for the entire province. This move entrenched the policy decision of having one board govern and deliver health care. Furthermore, this structure enabled the Department of Health to resume its role in health system planning and policy development.

THE HOME CARE CONUNDRUM

The 2011 Budget Address, as well as subsequent budgets, announced new (albeit much smaller) investments by the PEI government in new home care initiatives such as the Frail Seniors Pilot Project and the Palliative Care Home Care Drug Pilot Project. These spending decisions were aimed at bolstering home care spending, which signalled that Robert Ghiz's Liberal government did consider the home care sector as one way of meeting the needs of PEI's growing elderly population.

Patricia Conrad's 2008 comparative policy analysis reveals that allocating resources centrally is a more effective way to grow home care than by shifting resources under a regionalization model. Various factors appear to have influenced why the PEI home care sector lagged behind New Brunswick, Nova Scotia, and Canada following the implementation of health regions. Although one of the main policy goals underlying regionalization was its potential to reallocate resources between health care sectors (Lomas 1997), Conrad's 2008 analysis does not extend to a discussion of other factors as described by other policy studies (McKenna 2015; Randall et al. 2015; MacKinnon 2011; Kelly 2002).

Islanders are devoted church attendees, which goes hand in hand with a rural lifestyle (Randall et al. 2015; MacKinnon 2011; Kelly 2002). There is also a close relationship between religion and political affiliation; that is, the Catholics have Liberal Party leanings and tend to reside on the western side of the Island, while the Protestants, with their inclination towards the Conservative Party, reside on the eastern side (McKenna 2015). Religion in PEI is not as influential in the political arena as it once was; however, it does perpetuate a strong attachment to the foundational values associated with rurality, including traditionalism, hard work, community solidarity, and sanctity of the family farm (MacKinnon 2011). It is suggested these beliefs continue to influence Islanders' desire to preserve the status quo (McKenna 2015). Others have characterized a close connection between rural life, parochialism, and conservatism (McKenna 2015; Randall et al. 2015; Kelly 2002). These observations reinforce the assertion that Islanders' attachment to traditional values could have contributed to a reluctance by regional health board members (community representatives appointed by the PEI government) to reallocate resources to home care – which they viewed as a drastic measure in contrast to maintaining the status quo.

MacKinnon (2010) suggests Islanders' parochial attitudes are gradually changing; however, the enduring values underlying these attitudes continue to perpetuate an insular culture, where change is generally eschewed (or is very slow moving) in favour of preserving the status quo. For example, abortion services were not available on PEI (ibid.). A decision announced by the provincial government on 31 March 2016 specified that abortion services would be provided by Health PEI. Up until this decision, PEI was the only jurisdiction in Canada where women needing an abortion had to travel outside their home province to obtain this service (ibid.). The unavailability of abortion services is a striking illustration of how PEI's beliefs and values have exerted influence over the Island's health care policies.

Home care, unlike hospital care, is largely "invisible" (Conrad 2008). Its fledgling status as a viable actor is largely attributed to its lower share of health spending. The dominant view held by Islanders, particularly those appointed to the regional health boards, is that their community hospitals, which reflect both community pride and a desire to maintain a hospital-centric system, appears to have influenced these regional decision makers and their reluctance to support the growth of home care through reallocating resources from acute care (ibid.).

Jonathan Lomas and Michael Rachlis (1996) maintain that physicians enjoy an elevated status as policy influencers. Conrad (2008) suggests the Island physicians used this power within the communities they practice and live to reinforce the importance of hospitals throughout PEI's experimentation with regionalization during the 1990s and onward. According to Lomas (1997), physicians are self-interested actors. It seems plausible the PEI physicians realized they would be adversely affected by the downsizing of hospital beds because they perceived that growth in home care would affect the income they previously earned through providing hospital-based medical care (Conrad 2008). Consequently, they used their influence over regional health board members, by reinforcing the importance of community hospitals in meeting the needs of local citizens, hence reinforcing a hospital-centric model of health care. The status quo would be preserved! John Church and Paul Barker (1998) suggest that regional decision making was most likely dominated by experienced health care administrators whose knowledge and expertise could have intimidated lay board members. Accordingly, the PEI regional health board members undoubtedly deferred to these better-informed actors who had greater resources and knowledge at hand with which to exercise power over these lesser informed, locally appointed citizens. This confluence of factors is offered as a plausible explanation for the slow growth of the home care sector during the first wave of PEI health reform that began in the 1990s. As a consequence, it is argued these philosophical, societal, institutional, and political impediments played a major role in eroding the potential of health regions to reallocate resources to home care.

The PEI situation stands in stark contrast to New Brunswick. From the outset, the Extra-Mural Program was supported (and embraced) by physicians; this allegiance is largely attributed to the role Dr Gordon Ferguson (a physician) played as the driving force behind its development as a "hospital-in-the-home program" (New Brunswick Extra-Mural Program 1992). The lack of early engagement with physicians by the PEI home care program no doubt played a role in fortifying their skepticism towards home care (Conrad 2008).

Although the PEI reforms of the 1990s were aimed at growing home care spending, for the reasons previously described hospitals largely retained a substantial share of health care spending. However, further monitoring of outcomes for home care is obstructed by the unavailability of standardized national expenditure data. Tracking changes to home care spending for the years following the global economic crisis of 2008 has been problematic. In the early 2000s, the Canadian Institute for Health Information (CIHI) changed the way expenditure data was reported for home care and spending for this sector was subsequently included within a category comprised of spending for numerous health care sectors. This decision by CIHI has complicated the ability to monitor the national and provincial home care share of health spending and the per capita expenditures from 2008 onwards. CIHI did, however, conduct two independent studies on home care in 2007 and 2001 respectively: *Public-Sector Expenditures and Utilization of Home Care Services in Canada: Exploring the Data* and *Home Care Estimates in National Health Expenditures Feasibility Study.* These were the major sources of home care expenditure data as previously shown.

The PEI government posted budget surpluses in 2006 and 2007 (see figure 9.1) and appeared to be on a path to fiscal stability prior to the setback caused by the economic events of 2008. Following the return of the Liberals to power in 2007, the budgets up to 2012 had announced needed investments in health, education, and economic development (Prince Edward Island Minister of Finance 2011). In 2012, the government outlined a three-year fiscal plan – a roadmap that would lead to balanced budgets in the future, assuming that revenues increased faster than government expenditures (Prince Edward Island Minister of Finance 2012). The fiscal plan was based on the following assumptions: revenues will increase at traditional economic growth levels; health expenditures will grow at 3% per year; other departments will maintain expenditures at current levels, while absorbing compensation and inflationary increases; pension plans will be modified to minimize dramatic changes to obligations;

federal infrastructure funding will be maintained; and some flexibility will be required for unforeseen circumstances (Prince Edward Island Minister of Finance 2013).

It was not until the 2012 budget that the PEI government was persuaded by numerous annual reports by the Auditor General and other key external stakeholders that it needed to introduce sweeping measures to curb expenditure growth. These included various measures aimed at maximizing the efficiency of government operations through back office consolidations, salary freezes, downsizing the public service through attrition, and pension reform. Despite these, the Robert Ghiz government promised to maintain services that Islanders most need (that is, education and health care) and to retain "some" capacity for making new investments (Prince Edward Island Minister of Finance 2012).

The 2013 provincial budget continued along these lines and projected that revenues would grow by 3.1% annually, while expenditures would be capped at 1.5%, with the exception of health and education. In 2014, government departments were directed to continue to hold their spending to the 2013 levels, while Health PEI projected moderate growth in spending to meet the needs of patients. The provincial debt continued to grow, but the Ghiz government was not prepared to move quickly to a balanced budget at the expense of "comprising the programs and services, especially in health care and education that are necessary for the well-being of Islanders" (Prince Edward Island Minister of Finance 2014). This approach was supported by pre-budget consultations held with Islanders – a new citizen engagement strategy introduced in 2012 (see figure 9.1).

As the following list of selected health investments illustrates, growth in the home care share of PEI health spending continued between 2009 and 2014 through annual increases:

- 2009: The government increased the allocation to home care by $2.2 million, which represented a 25% increase over the 2008 allocation (Prince Edward Island Minister of Finance 2009).
- 2010: More investment in home care was announced through an increase of $1.3 million (ibid., 2010).
- 2011: More investments were targeted to grow home care and community-based primary health care (ibid., 2011).
- 2012: The PEI health care system received a funding increase of 4.1% and was capped at a growth rate of 3.5% in subsequent

years as part of the government's fiscal plan. This cap was put in place despite a guaranteed federal transfer under the 2004 Health Accord. This move by the PEI government suggests that funding for health care was purportedly used to offset general government expenditures. Nevertheless, the government rationalized its decision by saying, "while PEI's spending cap is higher than several other jurisdictions, it represents a significant drop from the levels of the past several years, and it will be challenging to attain given the many needs and cost pressures facing the system" (ibid., 2012).

- 2013: The government reported the total annual investment in health care had increased by $192 million since 2007. This increase supported access to new medications, strengthened home care, the addition of twenty-one physicians, and improvements to nursing homes. The government pledged the expenditure stabilization program would exclude health and education, regardless of recessionary pressures (ibid., 2013).
- 2014: Government indicated that it "could get to a balanced budget more quickly, but not without compromising the programs and services, especially in health care and education, that are necessary to the well-being of Islanders." During pre-budget consultations, Islanders made it clear this budget should not be balanced through service reductions (ibid., 2014).

CONCLUDING REFLECTIONS

PEI has enduring vulnerabilities that transcend the global economic crisis of 2008. These include the size of its population and corresponding tax base coupled with an economy primarily based on natural resources. Compared with many Canadian provinces, PEI has a weak industrial base, a higher unemployment rate, and a higher proportion of its population that is older and sicker. Taken together, these have dire consequences for PEI's fiscal situation. On the other hand, these circumstances have propelled innovation and bold decision making by PEI governments. It was the first Canadian jurisdiction to implement two bold innovations in the health policy arena – regionalization and de-regionalization – each of which restructured the governance and delivery of health care purportedly to improve outcomes and to control costs.

Health care is predominantly insulated from the use of neoliberal austerity measures in that this policy arena differs from others for which Canadian provincial governments are responsible. The *Canada Health Act* establishes protections that limit the extent to which austerity instruments can be applied. This national legislative framework takes the position that health care is a public good. Since neoliberalism assumes that all goods are private and paid for by those who consume them, austerity instruments can only go so far in their applicability to health care within the Canadian context.

It follows that restructuring the delivery of health care through decentralization (or regionalization, which is the made-in-Canada version) was the only austerity instrument used by provincial governments in their efforts to control health spending through using home care. Conrad (2008) observes that regionalization in PEI did not achieve its expected outcome of controlling health care spending by reallocating resources to home care and other less costly services, despite early predictions by Canadian health reformers that it would solve the health care spending crisis. Conrad's (ibid.) finding for PEI was predicted by Schattschneider's (1960) scope of conflict theory. This theory, when considered in the health care context, postulated that consolidating budgets of weaker health care actors, such as home care, with more powerful actors, such as acute care under a single administrative structure could create a situation where the more powerful actor could cannibalize the resources of the weaker actor. In the case of PEI, the failure of the health regions in reallocating resources to home care is attributed to various factors including PEI's socio-economic characteristics, political beliefs, and community values in tandem with home care's status as a nascent sector. These, coupled with regional board members' preference for and attachment to community hospitals as the preferred model for health care delivery, played a central role. Conrad (2008) argued these factors wielded a tremendous influence over the extent to which the government-appointed health board members were prepared to reallocate resources, despite being surrounded by aging and chronically ill Islanders with a need for enhanced home care and community-based services as way of coping with their functional impairments. Another reason that confounded regionalization as a cost control strategy was the introduction of the Health Accord in 2004 by the federal government. This ten-year agreement provided guaranteed annual funding to the Canadian provinces and territories. Consequently, this additional funding saved them from directing health regions to implement drastic cuts to health care budgets following the economic crisis of 2008.

Most Canadian provinces during the 1990s, with the exception of Ontario, followed the early lead of PEI in restructuring health care through forming health regions. The Joe Ghiz Liberal government was the first jurisdiction to set up Canada's most comprehensive basket of health and community services for administration by PEI's five health regions. In 2005, the Binns Conservative government once again led Canada with its bold step to "de-regionalize" the governance and delivery of health care. Regionalization was the only austerity measure available to provinces and territories that could be applied under the *Canada Health Act* in their quest to control rising health care costs. However, as the case of PEI has shown, regionalization was constrained in its attempt to reallocate resources from more expensive hospitals to less costly home care. One explanation is that the PEI citizens whom the government had appointed to the regional health boards were reluctant to challenge the status quo. In their role as board members, they showed a strong attachment to community hospitals and overall support of these settings as the vehicle through which health care should be delivered. This was strongly influenced by the views of physicians, who also supported the preservation of acute care hospital budgets. Entrenched spending and historical funding patterns in the hospital sector were also influential in maintaining the status quo. These reasons, coupled with the ensuing power struggles among established and emerging health actors as they competed for resources in PEI's regionalized governance and delivery model, were clear impediments to reallocating resources to home care.

REFERENCES

Armstrong, Pat, and Hugh Armstrong. 2008. *About Canada: Health Care*. Nova Scotia: Fernwood Publishing.

Astles, Philip, Trevor Foster, Jeannette Lye, and Gabriela Prada. 2013. *Paving the Road to Higher Performance: Benchmarking Provincial Health Systems*. Ottawa: Conference Board of Canada. http://www.conferenceboard.ca/cashc/research/2013/pavingtheroad.aspx.

Canadian Institute for Health Information. 2001. *Home Care Estimates in National Health Expenditures Feasibility Study*. Ottawa: Canadian Institute for Health Information. http://s3.amazonaws.com/zanran_storage/secure.cihi.ca/ContentPages/29102874.pdf.

– 2007. *Public-Sector Expenditures and Utilization of Home Care Services in Canada: Exploring the Data*. Ottawa: Canadian Institute for Health Information, 22 March. https://secure.cihi.ca/free_products/trends_home_care_mar_2007_e.pdf.

– 2012. *National Health Expenditure Trends, 1975 to 2012*. Ottawa: Canadian Institute for Health Information. https://secure.cihi.ca/free_products/NHEXTrendsReport2012EN.pdf.

– 2013. *National Health Expenditure Trends, 1975 to 2013*. Ottawa: Canadian Institute for Health Information. https://secure.cihi.ca/free_products/NHEXTrendsReport_EN.pdf.

– 2014. *National Health Expenditure Trends, 1975 to 2014*. Ottawa: Canadian Institute for Health Information. https://www.cihi.ca/en/nhex_2014_report_en.pdf.

Church, John, and Paul Barker. 1998. "Regionalization of Health Services in Canada: A Critical Perspective." *International Journal of Health Services* 28 (3): 467–86.

Conrad, Patricia. 2008. "Do Regional Models Matter? Resource Allocation to Home Care in the Maritime Provinces." PhD diss., University of Toronto, Toronto, ON.

Corpus Sanchez International. 2008. *An Integrated Health System Review in PEI: A Call To Action: A Plan For Change*. http://www.gov.pe.ca/photos/original/doh_csi_report.pdf.

Crichton, Anne, Ann Robertson, Christine Gordon, and Wendy Farrant. 1997. *Health Care: A Community Concern? Developments in the Organization of Canadian Health Services*. Calgary: University of Calgary Press.

Deber, Raisa B. 2000. *Getting What We Pay For: Myths and Realities about Financing Canada's Health Care System*. Ottawa: Health Canada, 11 April. http://www.pnhp.org/docs/atrevised3.pdf.

– 2002. *Delivering Health Care Services: Public, Not-for-Profit, or Private?* Ottawa: Commission on the Future of Health Care in Canada, Discussion Paper No. 17. http://www.publications.gc.ca/collections/Collection/CP32-79-17-2002E.pdf.

Eyles, John, Michael Brimacombe, Paul Chaulk, Greg Stoddart, Tina Pranger, and Olive Moase. 2001a. "What Determines Health? To Where Should We Shift Resources? Attitudes towards the Determinants of Health among Multiple Stakeholder Groups in Prince Edward Island, Canada." *Social Science and Medicine* 53 (12): 1611–9.

Eyles, John, Greg Stoddart, John Lavis, Tina Pranger, Laurie Molyneaus-Smith, and Colin McMullan. 2001b. *Making Resource Shifts Supportive of the Broad Determinants of Health: The Prince Edward Island*

Experience. Ottawa: Canadian Health Services Research Foundation. http://www.fcass-cfhi.ca/Migrated/PDF/ResearchReports/OGC/eyles_report.pdf.

Health Governance Advisory Council. 2009. *Final Report*. PEI: Charlottetown. http://www.gov.pe.ca/photos/original/health_adv_09.pdf.

Kelly, Katherine. 2002. "Regional Health Boards in Prince Edward Island: Negotiating Authority, Credibility, and Accountability." Master's thesis, University of Prince Edward Island, Charlottetown, April.

Lewis, Steven. 2008. "De-regionalizing Alberta: The Road to Reform or Collateral Political Damage?" *Longwoods Healthcare Blog*. http://longwoodsblog.blogspot.ca/2008/05/de-regionalizing-alberta.html.

Lewis, Steven, and Denise Kouri. 2004. "Regionalization: Making Sense of the Canadian Experience." *Healthcare Papers* 5 (1):12–33.

Lomas, Jonathan. 1997. "Devolving Authority for Health Care in Canada's Provinces: 4. Emerging Issues and Prospects." *Canadian Medical Association Journal* 156 (6): 817–23.

Lomas, Jonathan, and Michael Rachlis. 1996. "Moving Rocks: Block Funding in Prince Edward Island as an Incentive for Cross-Sectoral Reallocations among Human Services." *Canadian Public Administration* 39 (4): 581–600.

MacKinnon, Wayne. 2010. *Muddling Through: The Prince Edward Island Legislative Assembly*. Canadian Study of Parliament Group. http://cspg-gcep.ca/pdf/PEI_MacKinnon-e.pdf.

– 2011. "The Prince Edward Island Assembly." *Canadian Parliamentary Review* 34 (2): 8–18.

McGregor, Sue. 2001. "Neoliberalism and Health Care." *International Journal of Consumer Studies*. 25 (2): 82–9.

McKenna, Peter. 2015. "Politics on Prince Edward Island: Plus ça change." In *Transforming Provincial Politics: The Political Economy of Canada's Provinces and Territories in the Neoliberal Era*, edited by Bryan Evans and Charles Smith, 49–76. Toronto: University of Toronto Press.

Milne, David A. 1982. "Politics in a Beleaguered Garden." In *The Garden Transformed: Prince Edward Island 1945–1980*, edited by Verner Smitherman, David Milne and Satadal Dasgupta, 39–72. Charlottetown: Ragweed Press.

New Brunswick Extra-Mural Program. 1992. *The Hospital without Walls Newsletter.*

Philippon, Donald, and Jeffrey Braithwaite. 2008. "Health System Organization and Governance in Canada and Australia: A Comparison of

Historical Developments, Recent Policy Changes and Future Implications." *Healthcare Policy* 4 (1): 168–86.

Prince Edward Island Chief Public Health Officer. 2014. *Promote, Prevent, Protect – PEI CPHO Report and Health Trends 2014: Keep Moving on Life's Journey*. https://www.princeedwardisland.ca/sites/default/files/publications/cpho_trends_14.pdf.

Prince Edward Island Department of Finance. 2015. *41st Annual Statistical Review for 2014*. Charlottetown: PEI Statistics Bureau, Department of Finance. https://www.princeedwardisland.ca/en/topic/historical-annual-statistical-reviews.

– 2016a. *PEI Unemployment Rate, June 2016*. Charlottetown: PEI Statistics Bureau, Department of Finance, Economics, Statistics and Fiscal Relations. http://www.gov.pe.ca/photos/original/pt_lfs.pdf.

– 2016b. *42nd Annual Statistical Review for 2015*. Charlottetown: PEI Statistics Bureau, Department of Finance. https://www.princeedwardisland.ca/en/topic/historical-annual-statistical-reviews.

Prince Edward Island Department of Finance, Energy, and Municipal Affairs. n.d. *2011 Census: Population and Dwelling Counts*. PEI Statistics Bureau, Department of Finance and Municipal Affairs, Economics, Statistics and Fiscal Relations. http://www.gov.pe.ca/photos/original/2011Census.pdf.

– 2012. *38th Annual Statistical Review for 2011*. Charlottetown: PEI Statistics Bureau, Department of Finance, Energy and Municipal Affairs. https://www.princeedwardisland.ca/en/topic/historical-annual-statistical-reviews

– 2013. *39th Annual Statistical Review for 2012*. Charlottetown: PEI Statistics Bureau, Department of Finance, Energy and Municipal Affairs. https://www.princeedwardisland.ca/en/topic/historical-annual-statistical-reviews.

– 2014. *40th Annual Statistical Review for 2013*. Charlottetown: PEI Statistics Bureau, Department of Finance, Energy and Municipal Affairs. https://www.princeedwardisland.ca/en/topic/historical-annual-statistical-reviews.

Prince Edward Island Department of Finance and Municipal Affairs. 2010. *36th Annual Statistical Review for 2009*. Charlottetown: PEI Statistics Bureau, Department of Finance and Municipal Affairs. https://www.princeedwardisland.ca/en/topic/historical-annual-statistical-reviews.

– 2011. *37th Annual Statistical Review for 2010*. Charlottetown: PEI Statistics Bureau, Department of Finance and Municipal Affairs.

https://www.princeedwardisland.ca/en/topic/historical-annual-statistical-reviews.

Prince Edward Island Department of Fisheries, Aquaculture and Rural Development. 2010. *Rural Action Plan: A Rural Economic Development Strategy for Prince Edward Island*. Charlottetown: Rural Development PEI, Department of Fisheries, Aquaculture and Rural Development. http://www.gov.pe.ca/photos/original/FARD_REDS.pdf.

Prince Edward Island. Department of Health. 2005. *Meeting the Needs of Islanders: An Action Plan for Health Human Resources on Prince Edward Island*. Charlottetown: Government of Prince Edward Island. http://www.gov.pe.ca/photos/original/Health_HHR05.pdf.

Prince Edward Island Department of the Provincial Treasury. 2002. *28th Annual Statistical Review for 2001*. Charlottetown: Economics, Statistics and Federal Fiscal Relations Division, Department of the Provincial Treasury. https://www.princeedwardisland.ca/en/topic/historical-annual-statistical-reviews.

– 2003. *20th Annual Statistical Review for 2002*. Charlottetown: Economics, Statistics and Federal Fiscal Relations Division, Department of the Provincial Treasury. https://www.princeedwardisland.ca/en/topic/historical-annual-statistical-reviews.

– 2004. *30th Annual Statistical Review for 2003*. Charlottetown: Economics, Statistics and Federal Fiscal Relations Division, Department of the Provincial Treasury. https://www.princeedwardisland.ca/en/topic/historical-annual-statistical-reviews.

– 2005. *31st Annual Statistical Review for 2004*. Charlottetown: Economics, Statistics and Federal Fiscal Relations Division, Department of the Provincial Treasury. https://www.princeedwardisland.ca/en/topic/historical-annual-statistical-reviews.

– 2006. *32nd Annual Statistical Review for 2005*. Charlottetown: Economics, Statistics and Federal Fiscal Relations Division, Department of the Provincial Treasury. https://www.princeedwardisland.ca/en/topic/historical-annual-statistical-reviews.

– 2007. *33rd Annual Statistical Review for 2006*. Charlottetown: Economics, Statistics and Federal Fiscal Relations Division, Department of the Provincial Treasury. https://www.princeedwardisland.ca/en/topic/historical-annual-statistical-reviews.

– 2008. *34th Annual Statistical Review for 2007*. Charlottetown: Economics, Statistics and Federal Fiscal Relations Division, Department of the Provincial Treasury. https://www.princeedwardisland.ca/en/topic/historical-annual-statistical-reviews.

Prince Edward Island Executive Council Office. n.d. Island Geography. https://www.princeedwardisland.ca/en/information/executive-council-office/island-geography.

Prince Edward Island Health and Community Services System. 1997. *PEI System Evaluation Project, Volume 1*. Charlottetown: Government of Prince Edward Island, June. http://www.gov.pe.ca/photos/original/hss_sys_eval.pdf.

Prince Edward Island Health Task Force. 1992. *Health Reform – A Vision for Change*. Charlottetown: Island Information Services.

Prince Edward Island Lieutenant Governor. 2008. *Speech from the Throne: One Island Community: One Future*. Charlottetown: Legislative Assembly of Prince Edward Island, 4 April. http://www.assembly.pe.ca/speech/2007/index.php.

– 2009. *Speech from the Throne: One Island, Working Together*. Charlottetown: Legislative Assembly of Prince Edward Island, 12 November. http://www.assembly.pe.ca/speech/2009/index.php.

Prince Edward Island Minister of Finance, Energy, and Municipal Affairs. 2009. *Budget Address 2009*. Charlottetown: Department of Finance, 16 April. https://www.princeedwardisland.ca/en/publication/2009-budget-address.

– 2010. *Budget Address 2010*. Charlottetown: Department of Finance, 23 April. https://www.princeedwardisland.ca/en/publication/2010-budget-address.

– 2011. *Budget Address 2011*. Charlottetown: Department of Finance, 6 April. https://www.princeedwardisland.ca/en/publication/2011-budget-address.

– 2012. *Budget Address 2012*. Charlottetown: Department of Finance, 18 April. https://www.princeedwardisland.ca/en/publication/2012-budget-address.

– 2013. *Budget Address 2013*. Charlottetown: Department of Finance, 27 March. https://www.princeedwardisland.ca/en/publication/2013-budget-address.

– 2014. *Budget Address 2014*. Charlottetown: Department of Finance, 18 April. https://www.princeedwardisland.ca/en/publication/2014-budget-address.

Randall, James E., Don Desserud, and Katharine MacDonald. 2015. *Prince Edward Island*. In *State of Rural Canada Report*. http://sorc.crrf.ca/wp-content/uploads/2015/09/SORC2015PE.pdf.

Saltman, Richard B., and Josep Figueras. 1997. *European Health Care Reform: Analysis of Current Strategies*. Geneva: World Health Organization Regional Publications.

Saltman, Richard B., Josep Figueras, and Constantino Sakellarides. 1998. *Critical Challenges for Health Care Reform in Europe*. Buckingham: Open University Press.

Saltman, Richard B., and Casten von Otter. 1992. *Planned Markets and Public Competition: Strategic Reform in Northern European Health Systems*. Philadelphia: Open University Press.

Schattschneider, Eric E. 1960. *The Semisovereign People: A Realist's View of Democracy in America*. New York: Holt, Rinehart and Winston.

Wright, Teresa. 2013. "P.E.I. Pension Reforms Pass as Legislature Closes." *The Guardian*, 6 December. http://www.theguardian.pe.ca/news/local/pei-pension-reforms-pass-as-legislature-closes-96115/.

CHAPTER TEN

Newfoundland's Boom: A Study in the Political Culture of Neoliberalism

ROBERT C.H. SWEENY

Once again, Newfoundland and Labrador is the odd one out. Our comedic genius Andy Jones simply calls it the "N factor" – for whatever reason, things always seem to work out differently in Newfoundland. Historians and social scientists do not enjoy the same artistic licence; we are expected to explain the unusual. In the context of this collection, the Newfoundland experience requires a lot of explaining. While all the other provincial and territorial governments faced challenging conditions brought on by the worst crisis since the 1930s, between 2005 and 2011 Newfoundland and Labrador was transformed by the greatest boom in Canadian economic history. Everywhere else, people and their governments experienced the maniacal swing from a speculative boom to a spectacular bust. In Newfoundland, median income soared by 43%. Note that I said median, not average. Almost everyone saw significant improvement in their market-based incomes. In marked contrast to the experience elsewhere, the new forms of inequality characteristic of this period were not created by the market place. Instead, provincial policies generated marked increases in after-tax inequality. The redistributive function of the state was quite literally turned on its head.

To understand and hopefully explain this remarkable transformation, I have divided this chapter into four analytical parts. First, I establish the general parameters by examining the changes in provincial revenue streams and the rapidity and extent of changes to taxable incomes. Second, I evaluate the major provincial policy initiatives and demonstrate how they embodied a neoliberal worldview. Third, I address how a combination of leadership and language was remarkably successful in reframing the basic issues facing this island society and its mainland colony of Labrador.[1] Finally, I discuss how the evolving local political culture (and I admit this is perhaps just academic jargon for the N factor) related to the Tory brand of populist nationalism. In a brief epilogue, I reassess this relationship in light of the exceptional difficulties the provincial Liberals have had in governing since their election in the fall of 2015.

"HAVE-NOT" NO MORE

It is a measure of how much Newfoundland is a distinct society within English Canada that even the most basic terms of the conversation require translation. In his 1982 election victory speech Brian Peckford, Progressive Conservative premier from 1979 to 1989, said that the people were united in the belief that one day the status of being a "have-not" province in the federation "would be no more." That day did not come until 3 November 2008.

Figure 10.1 shows that a dramatic increase in primarily nonrenewable resource revenue over the late 2000s largely explains this signal change in Newfoundland's relationship to the rest of Canada. It is understandable but misleading to think of this as being an oil boom. In fact, 2008 was actually the last of a run of seven years in which annual provincial oil production significantly surpassed a hundred million barrels. It was a boom in royalties and associated offshore revenue, a boom that followed the production and sale of most of the province's then-known oil reserves that explains the change in status. As this suggests, it was largely the result of politics, not economics, and this is central to understanding the significance of a particular form of populist nationalism to our story.

The Atlantic Accords of 1985 and 2005 with the federal government established the rules for the joint management of offshore oil production. From the perspective of provincial revenues, the most important aspects of these agreements were first that they extended provincial tax regimes to cover all aspects of the offshore so, for example, provincial sales tax applied; second, they had varying offsetting provisions so that every dollar of provincial oil revenue was not immediately deducted from federal equalization payments.[2] Nonetheless, as is so evident in figure 10.1, federal transfers declined precipitously over the decade.

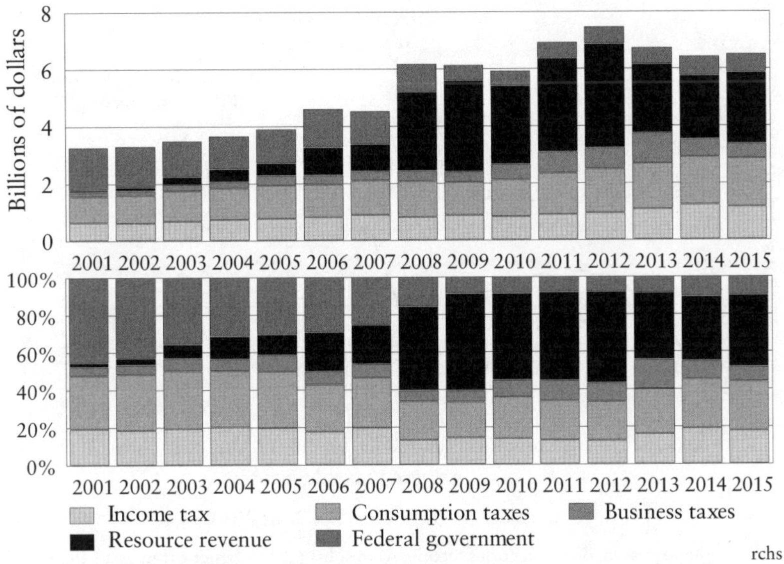

In the early years the declining role of federal transfers is the main story, but that was soon overshadowed by the increase in non-renewable resource revenue, whose exceptional and relatively short-term boom coincided with the onset of the global economic crisis in 2008. *Sources*: Newfoundland and Labrador Department of Finance, *Public Accounts 2001–13* and *Budget Estimates 2014*.

Figure 10.1 Newfoundland and Labrador provincial revenues, 2001–15

In Newfoundland and Labrador, the provincial government has negotiated separate royalty regimes for each new oil field as it comes online, but they share a common set of features. First, and this is also highly visible in figure 10.1, oil companies pay only minimal, tier one royalties until they have made back everything that they had invested in the field, plus interest, which in a rather revealing turn of phrase is called "reaching payout." Then tier two royalties kick in, initially at a relatively low level, but they increase if oil prices rise to historically high levels.[3] A combination of having reached "payout" on Hibernia, the first and largest field, with historically high oil prices explain most of the exceptional revenues from 2008 to 2012.[4] The logic here is the same as in the related mineral royalties negotiated for the large nickel, cobalt, and silver deposit at Voisey Bay in coastal Labrador and with the more recent iron ore projects in western Labrador. The provincial government minimizes royalty payments, but in exchange maximizes employment opportunities

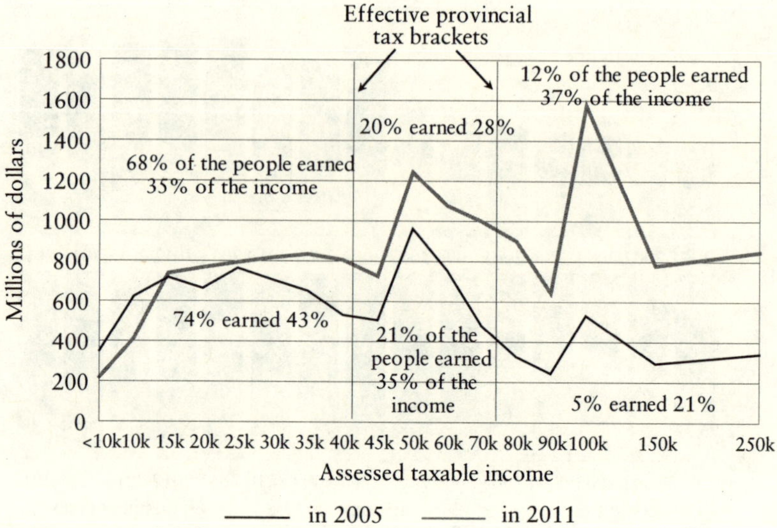

In all but the lowest income categories, people were substantially better off in 2011 than in 2005, with the greatest gains being achieved in the top tax bracket.
Sources: Canada Revenue Agency, *Final Tables 2007* and *2013*.

Figure 10.2 Taxable incomes by income category in 2005 and 2011

and technological transfers to the province. Rent for non-renewable resources is kept low to encourage growth in corporate profits, personal incomes, and consumer spending.

It is a strategy that can be said to have worked. By the end of the boom, in 2012, revenues from consumption taxes, income taxes, and business taxes surpassed total provincial revenues prior to the boom. And this was achieved despite considerable cuts to both income and business tax rates. The problem, of course, is that there is no long-term plan for when the resources are no more. The type of legacy fund that the Norwegian government has established, for example, simply does not exist (Campbell 2013).

The provincial income tax regime has only three brackets, with the highest being reached at taxable incomes over $64,000. In this "have-not" province back in 2005, access to such rarified income levels was achieved by only one in twenty taxpayers. By contrast, better than one in ten in the three "have" provinces earned at least this amount.[5] It is a mark of how rapidly the boom transformed the income structure of the province that, by 2011, one in eight taxpayers were in the top

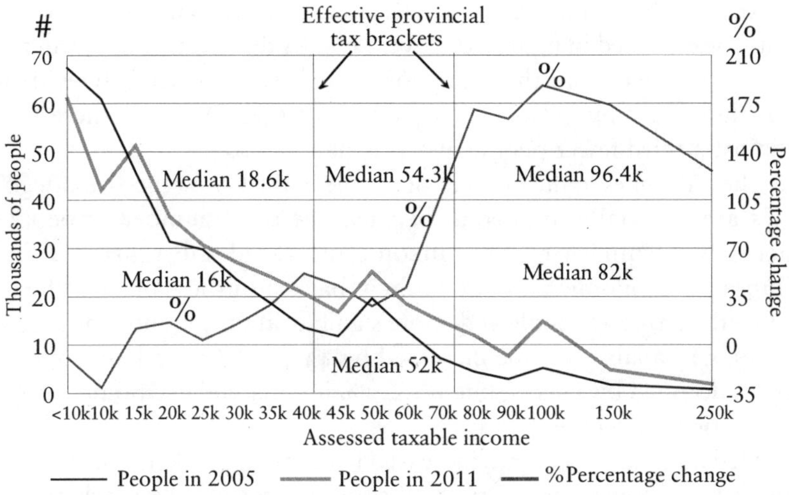

The 31% drop in those earning between $10,000 and $15,000 contrasts sharply with the doubling of the number of people in all of the higher-income categories.
Sources: Canada Revenue Agency, *Final Tables 2007* and *2013*.

Figure 10.3 Number of people in each income category in 2005 and 2011 and the proportional change

bracket. The transformation is even more visible at the extremes. In 2005, the taxable income earned by the 67,340 people earning less than $10,000 each slightly exceeded the taxable income of the 840 people who earned more than $250,000. By 2011, the highest-income earners had almost tripled their earnings, while the lowest category saw their taxable income drop by almost half.

Figure 10.2 indicates that, in all but the lowest income categories, people were substantially better off in 2011 than in 2005. Furthermore, one in fourteen people's earnings had improved so much that they had risen into a new tax bracket. This absence of any apparent blockage is significant. The shift into the middle bracket was more than matched by the shift into the top bracket. It was there that the greatest increases in income were achieved.

The widespread nature of this upward movement is confirmed by examining the transformation in terms of people, as in figure 10.3, rather than in terms of income as in figure 10.2. In all but the lowest income categories, the numbers of people increased substantially. In each of the income categories above $60,000 the number of people more than doubled and for those earning between $100,000 and

$150,000 they almost tripled. The declines in income in the lowest categories, noted in figure 10.2, were in part due to large drops in the number of people in these categories. This was particularly evident for those earning between $10,000 and $15,000, where there was almost a third fewer people in 2011 than in 2005.

These declines in the number of people in the lowest income categories are especially important because the total number of people actually earning a taxable income increased substantially. The improved economic conditions drew back into the paid workforce more than 26,000 people and, more significantly, the number of people earning a taxable income increased by 43,000.[6] Overall, unemployment declined by a sixth, but at 12.7% it remained five points above the national average.

Median taxable incomes increased in each tax bracket: 16.25% for those in the lowest bracket; 4% for those in the middle bracket; and 17.6% for those in the top bracket. The appearance of only a modest change in the middle bracket is deceptive, as undoubtedly the 29,000 newcomers in the top bracket came overwhelmingly from the middle bracket, and were in turn replaced by the 28,000 taxpayers who had moved out of the lowest bracket.

Overall, the short-term boom in provincial revenues was closely aligned with, but not caused by, the generalized increase in personal incomes. The boom in revenues was royalty-based, while the general economic upturn was not by any means limited to the resource sector. Between 2005 and 2011, capital investments increased by 59%, provincial gross domestic product (GDP) by 54%, both personal income and housing starts by 39%, retail sales by 33%, new car sales by 24%, and even the value of fish landings rose by 14%. Only pulp and paper production, once the lifeblood of much of central Newfoundland, fared badly with a 69% collapse in metric tonnes of newsprint shipped.[7] In 2011, for the first time in its history, the average weekly wage in the province surpassed the Canadian average (Statistics Canada 2011). This rapidly changing economic situation opened up possibilities for new policy choices.

THE POLITICS OF POLICY CHOICES

Understanding the political implications of this multi-faceted boom requires a little history. A single government, the Progressive Conservatives, was in power throughout the boom. In 2004, in their first budget since coming to office in 2003, the Tories stressed the difficult fiscal situation facing the province. They alleged that the Liberals, under Brian Tobin and Roger Grimes, had set the province on course toward a completely unmanageable debt load. Their solution was to suspend all electoral promises; impose immediate cuts to the civil service, which involved the loss of 400 unionized positions and 20 office closures across the province; and announce planned reductions in program spending that were to total $534 million by 2007, with the loss of an additional 4,000 public-sector jobs. The funds freed up were to be used to pay down the debt. As part of the stringency plan, the province imposed a three-year wage freeze on public and para-public sectors.

This was the context in which the Progressive Conservatives, led by one of the province's wealthiest businessmen, Danny Williams, developed their long-term growth strategy. It was also fully two years into the short-lived oil boom of over a hundred million barrels a year and shortly after the first of the agreements on Voisey Bay. In short, the broad parameters of the royalty regime were already in place. The question thus became: Could the province negotiate a better deal, not with the resource companies but with Ottawa?

After a high-stakes public relations spat,[8] which saw a histrionic Williams order that all Canadian flags be removed from provincial buildings, a deal was struck in January 2005 and signed in St John's on Valentine's Day. This was not a love-in but the anniversary of the *Ocean Ranger* disaster, when eighty-nine men lost their lives in the sinking of an oil rig off the coast of Newfoundland in 1982.[9] Of particular importance, given the Harper government's subsequent reneging on the deal, was that the 2005 Accord guaranteed an advance payment of $2 billion on future equalization payments. This was explicitly designed so that the province could pay down its debt. It was used to fund the teachers' pension plan, from which the province had taken repeated contribution "holidays" over the lean years in the late 1990s and early 2000s. In exchange, the teachers' union signed on to the wage freeze.

Modest surpluses in 2005 and 2006 gave way to massive surpluses in 2007 and 2008, totaling more than $3.8 billion. Unquestionably, the roll-out of the strategic choices made in these years was affected by the effective cancellation of the 2005 Atlantic Accord in the 2007 federal budget. How much this unilateral federal change would cost the province was a matter of substantial debate. The best available analysis at the time placed the total cost to the province by 2019 at $4.5 billion in lost revenues (Locke 2007). For 2009, the provincial government estimated the loss at $414 million, which allowed it to cast the blame for that year's $295 million deficit onto the federal government.[10] A more likely candidate was the province's own changes to income tax, but no matter how you cut it, these were very large figures in a province of only half a million people. Their principal effects were rhetorical in the first instance and, over the longer term, they changed the political culture of the province. They confirmed that the province not only should not but could not rely upon the federal government.

The first hint of a new policy direction came in 2005, with the unveiling of the poverty reduction strategy. It promised that the province that had long seen the highest poverty rates in the country would have the lowest by 2015. To achieve this lofty goal, an allocation of 0.58 of 1% of the provincial budget was made in 2006. By 2010, this "government-wide approach to promoting self-reliance, opportunity and access to key supports for persons vulnerable to poverty"[11] had seen its budget increase to 2.17% of provincial expenditures and, drawing on eight departments, was administering more than eighty initiatives. Most were programs that to some extent involved serving people living in poverty, such as the programs for domestic violence prevention or repairs to public housing, but they did precious little to eradicate poverty.[12] In 2011, the National Household Survey (NHS) found that the overall poverty rate had increased, with a particularly disturbing rise in childhood poverty. Indeed, almost one in four children born since the strategy was first announced was living in poverty.[13]

The framing of systemic social problems as issues to be overcome through individual initiative also characterized provincial education policy. This is perhaps most evident in the contrasting approaches to adult basic education (ABE) and post-secondary education. Both were developed by the Department of Advanced Education and Skills, a ministry whose very name reflected the influence of Organisation for Economic Co-operation and Development (OECD) thinking on labour markets.[14]

The province's chronic problems of illiteracy were well known and of very long standing. A major international study conducted in 2003 ranked Newfoundland as the worst-performing province in all four basic forms of literacy (HRSDC 2005, 31–2). When linked to the 2006 census, this study revealed that, in all but a handful of the province's census districts, concentrated in St John's and vicinity, the majority of the adult population was functionally illiterate.[15] The first Poverty Reduction Strategy in 2006 allocated $1.2 million in subsidies to private colleges for Adult Basic Education programs. Since then, community-based non-governmental organizations have been contracted by the provincial government to offer these services. These organizations all rely upon volunteer teachers and staff. The only financial support available for someone needing ABE is that provided by the federal Employment Insurance program. By 2012, the functional illiteracy rate of people sixteen and over in the province was 56.8%, the worst of any province in the country (HRSDC 2013).

Improving access to higher education, on the other hand, has been accorded top priority. Although he did like to claim responsibility, this was a policy choice that predated Danny Williams's government. Along with the rest of English Canada, Newfoundland imposed substantial increases to university tuition in the 1990s. First under Brian Tobin and then much more aggressively under Roger Grimes, the rise was halted and, quite exceptionally for Canada, turned back. Williams frequently said he wanted to emulate the Irish "Tiger" model of neoliberal development, including their tuition-free universities, but his government did not continue Grimes's rollbacks. It did, however, maintain the freeze while increasing the annual budgetary allocation to Memorial University of Newfoundland (MUN), the public and only university in the province.

At $2,644, Newfoundland now has the lowest annual tuition in the country (CCPA 2014). This has encouraged an increasing number of students, many from elsewhere in Atlantic Canada, to attend Memorial. Between 2005 and 2011, the number of full-time-equivalent students increased by 21%, while the proportion of people twenty-five and over with a university degree in the province increased 31%. Meanwhile, government funding of Memorial increased by 134% and its funding of the public College of the North Atlantic increased by 81%. Both of these unprecedented and ongoing investments have taken place against a decline in the number of college-aged students within the province. This support did not come without strings attached, and a serious crisis was only narrowly avoided in 2010 when the minister of education interfered in the hiring process for a new university president. Furthermore, it has been the government, rather than the university or the college, that has made the strategic decisions about which fields should be accorded priority; not surprisingly, they chose oil and gas in the 2000s and the trades and professional schools since then.

Spending on health care, by far the largest single budgetary item, did not see anything like the largesse afforded higher education. The operating budget for primary health care barely kept pace with inflation, increasing a mere 13% between 2005 and 2011. But there was a major shift in thinking within the department that saw significantly higher compensation for physicians, up 48%, and a massive increase in capital expenditures of 493%. This exceptional figure of course reflected the cutbacks during the early years of the Williams administration; nonetheless, spending on sophisticated medical equipment and facilities became much more common, even if it was still highly concentrated in St John's.

These policy choices in differing areas were of a piece. They all reflected an emphasis on the individual, who the government was to facilitate in his or her advancement or treatment. There was, however, a corollary: a marked reticence to address systemically rooted problems, indeed a denial that such problems existed, because the government believed that the market was the best arbiter. As they phrased it when unveiling their flagship reform of income tax in 2007, the government should "leave the money in the pockets of those who earned it." This explicit renunciation of the redistributive role of provincial income tax, dramatically illustrated in figure 10.4, was justified by the need to be competitive. Initially, these cuts aimed at reducing rates to below those prevailing anywhere else in Atlantic Canada (see Clancy in this volume).[16] By the final stage of the reform, in 2010, the government had repositioned the province as one of the lowest-taxed jurisdictions in the country.[17]

The idea that everything not only can, but should, be valued by the market is the core principle of neoliberalism (see Evans and Fanelli's introduction to this volume). This worldview believes that an idealized set of market relations are the appropriate framework to guide not just fiscal policy, but all human relations (see Camfield in this volume). Dardot and Laval have encapsulated this particularly clearly in their succinct definition of neoliberalism as governing by competition.[18] So in figure 10.4, we are not just seeing what happens when a government adopts a less progressive tax regime but the logical outcome of subjugating all other values to those of the marketplace.

This ideological choice has proved exceptionally costly for the province. Revenues forgone by the province by 2013 totalled

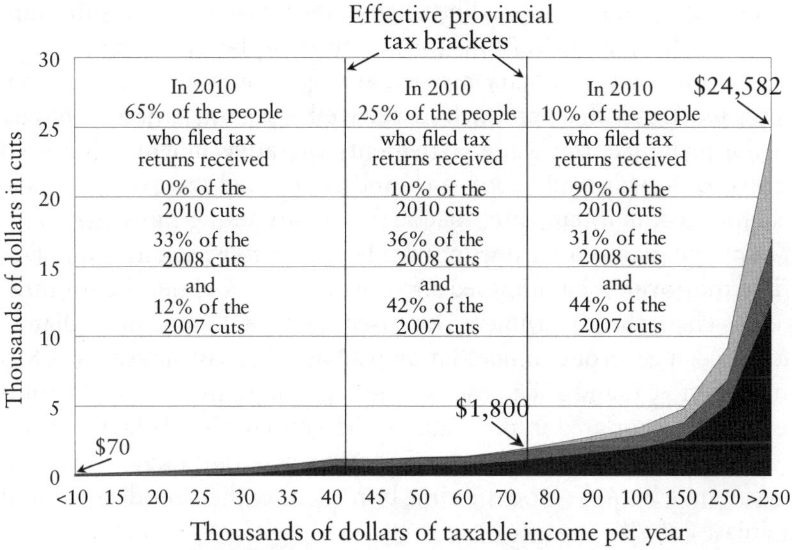

The government's 2007 promise to "leave the money in the pockets of those who have earned it" translated into a wildly disproportionate distribution of the tax cuts by 2010.
Sources: Canada Revenue Agency, *Final Tables 2009, 2010*, and *2012* and Newfoundland and Labrador Department of Finance, *Budget 2007, 2008*, and *2010*.

Figure 10.4 Per capita distribution in 2010 of the tax cuts of 2007, 2008, and 2010

$2.7 billion. Currently, the cost rises by $460 million a year, but as the proportion of revenues earned by the top bracket continues to expand, so too does the scale of the give-away. When combined with the numerous cuts to corporate and business taxes, also justified by the need to be competitive, the cost at the time of writing exceeds $510 million annually. Or put another way, if left unchecked, by 2019 the Williams tax cuts would cost the province $1.3 billion more in lost revenues than the worst-case scenario for Harper's cancellation of the 2005 Atlantic Accord (see Gillies in this volume). Despite the devastating effect of Williams's decisions on the public purse, no one suggested the provincial flag be lowered to even half-mast.

There is a widespread misconception that neoliberalism means restricting the role of the government in the economy. In fact, neoliberal governments don't just intervene in the economy, they actively and continuously interact as major economic players in their own right and, through myriad policies, directly affect the private sector.

What is different about neoliberal governments is that they subordinate all major policy decisions to the values of the marketplace.

The quite extraordinary provincial wage policy over the past ten years illustrates this approach rather well.[19] As the largest employer in the province, the wage settlements the government – imposed (2005–07), proposed (2008–11), and negotiated (2012–15) – have each served as a template for collective bargaining more generally. Yet, at first glance there does not really appear to be a coherent policy. First, the government imposed a freeze on wages and salaries for three years. Then, the government proposed, and the unions immediately accepted, a generous compensation package that saw increases of 8% in the first year and 4% in each of the following three years. The third template, negotiated in the wake of the first large-scale layoffs since 2004, had no increases for the first two years (although somewhat sweetened by a $1,400 signing bonus) and then modest annual increases of 2% and 3%.

The logic of this policy is to do away with a key element of the decades-old social contract with public servants and replace it with an alternate, market-based solution. Since the 1960s, when public-sector unions led by the postal workers struggled for and won regular cost-of-living adjustments, public servants in Canada have largely been protected from the uncertainties of inflation. This policy jettisons that understanding in favour of "what the market will bear." Real incomes are only assured when surpluses permit. Otherwise, public servants can expect to subsidize the government through their declining real wages. This transformation of an acquired right of workers into a discretionary option for management was highly political. It contributed to a cult of leadership – "Danny's [Williams] generous offer" – while further compromising the independence of the civil service, itself an anathema to neoliberals.

A similar market-based reasoning explains the changes to the provincial minimum wage. Until 2011, Newfoundland had the highest proportion of its people working at or below the minimum wage in Canada (Yalnizyan 2013). For decades, the provincial minimum wage had been among the lowest in Canada and was allowed to lag behind inflation. This contributed to continued out-migration, but it did not become a serious issue for the government until the economy began to heat up. To have a "competitive" minimum wage in 2005, the government announced a series of regular increments that would take it from $6 to $8 an hour by 2008 when a new announcement increased it by steps to $10 an hour by 2010. This 66% increase in only five years is why there was such a significant decline in the number of people earning between $10,000 and $15,000 a year in figure 10.3. Then, the crisis elsewhere removed that "competitive" pressure and so the increases stopped. In response to a government-appointed review that recommended tying the minimum wage to the consumer price index, the government has announced only derisory increases, which "raised" the minimum wage to $10.50 an hour in October 2015, making Newfoundland's minimum wage the lowest in Canada.

LANGUAGE AND LEADERSHIP

Newfoundland was the first province or state in English-speaking North America with its own dictionary. As this suggests, here language matters. There is a rich oral tradition of songs, storytelling, and recitations. People like to talk, indeed rant, as Rex Murphy and Rick Mercer have respectively taught the rest of the country. Newfoundland also has a more recent, but firmly established, tradition of strong political leadership. Joey Smallwood, Brian Peckford, Clyde Wells, Brian Tobin, and Danny Williams were not just provincial premiers, but major actors on the Canadian political scene. Can you even name five post-war premiers of Manitoba, Saskatchewan, New Brunswick, PEI, Nova Scotia, or even Alberta?

The relationship between language and leadership is not new, nor is it without its own large scientific literature. It is not, however, something that often comes up in discussions of the neoliberal transformation of our country. But understanding everything from free trade agreements to attack ads requires, I would argue, careful attention to this relationship. Here, I am interested in how language has been used to reinforce a particular form of political leadership. I will argue that, in Newfoundland, the success of a neoliberal discourse of populist nationalism has seriously compromised our ability to democratically discuss the basic issues we face.

The titles of the provincial budgets encapsulate the Progressive Conservative's primary messaging over these eleven years. The public relations framing of these important political statements makes it almost impossible to distinguish a fiscally poor year, say 2004, from an exceptionally good year like 2008. How could anyone possibly know that the reality behind "Protecting Our Future" was suspension of all electoral promises, years of layoffs, public service cuts, and

Table 10.1
Titles of the Newfoundland and Labrador provincial budgets, 2004–14

Year	*Title*
2004	Protecting Our Future
2005	A New Future … A Renewed Pride
2006	The Right Choices: Momentum for Growth and Prosperity
2007	Vision. Action.
2008	Securing a Sustainable Future
2009	Building on Our Strong Foundation
2010	The Right Investments – For Our Children and Our Future
2011	Standing Strong: For Prosperity. For Our Future. For Newfoundland and Labrador.
2012	People and Prosperity: Responsible Investments for a Secure Future.
2013	A Sound Plan, A Secure Future
2014	Shared Prosperity, Fair Society, Balanced Outlook

Despite the idiosyncratic capitalization and punctuation, there can be no doubt about the messaging: building a secure and prosperous future is job number one for this government.
Sources: Newfoundland and Labrador Department of Finance, *Budgets 2004–14*.

a looming debt crisis? Equally opaque is "Securing a Sustainable Future," which meant the $1.8 billion surplus would finance the largest tax cuts in the province's history, cost-of-living adjustments for the civil service, and exceptional increases in managerial salaries. None of this had anything remotely to do with the environment, which in 2008 was still what the word "sustainable" brought to mind for most people.

The longer the Tories were in power, the more understandable their desire to stay "on" message, as it was increasingly their management of the economy that might be called into question. Nonetheless, the positive language used to frame the record deficits of 2009 and 2010 is astounding. No sense of the scale or importance of the problems facing the society was permitted. This atemporal, feel-good approach even prevailed in the 2014 budget, in which for the first time all of the government's own indicators clearly showed the boom was definitively over. Led by a collapse in capital spending and a one-third decline in housing starts and aided by rising unemployment and declining non-renewable resource revenues, the government predicted in 2014 that, in constant dollars, the provincial GDP would shrink 10% by 2017. This they called "Shared Prosperity, Fair Society, Balanced Outlook."

The language used to explain the situation to the people exhibited a similar opacity. The word cloud in figure 10.5 shows the 200 most frequently used content words in the eleven Tory budgets.[20] Four different ministers of finance delivered these speeches, and yet there is a remarkable uniformity of language. The 200 words in this cloud were only 3% of the 5,967 different words used by the ministers, but they constituted 14% of the 102,972 words spoken. By privileging a particular vocabulary, the government set the tone and parameters for political conversations in the province. Thus, the singular lack of specificity to these content words is important, for as the folk musician Fergus Brown O'Byrne observed of a preliminary version of this graph, "for a list of content words, it is strikingly void of content."

In French, we call this langue de bois,[21] a term that has been translated as political cant, but I think Wikipedia comes much closer to the mark with "language that uses vague, ambiguous, abstract, or pompous words in order to divert attention from the salient issues." Clearly, *Newfoundlanders* and *Labradorians need* a *strategy* of *investments* that will *provide* and *support funding* of *health care*, *infrastructure*, and *services*, because *commitment* to such *public* and *strategic initiatives*, *plans,* and *projects* will *develop strong economic opportunities*; *ensure development*; *create growth*; and *increase income*, *work,* and *employment* to *benefit people*, *communities*, *industry*, *seniors*, *women,* and *students*, even *children*, in a word the *public.* Who can be against this? Well, anyone interested in a serious political conversation about what the province should do with its windfall revenue. It is well-nigh impossible to identify, let alone discuss, any of the specific problems facing Newfoundland and Labrador that are hidden by this word cloud. Crises in forestry and fishery, depopulation and aging of the outports, illiteracy, unemployment, non-renewable resource dependency, inadequate royalties, the dramatic shortage in affordable housing, and increased dependency on remittances are just some of the many highly problematic issues upon which "budget speech" is silent.

There are only two areas of actual concern that can be discerned in this cloud of verbiage: poverty (eighty-eight references) reduction (eighty-six) and violence (fifty-five) against women (forty-nine). As the near twinning in the frequency of their citings suggests, both were

For a word to appear in the graphic, it had to have been used more than forty times over the eleven years. Consult the notes for details on the selection process.

Source: Newfoundland and Labrador Department of Finance, *Budget Speech 2004 – Budget Speech 2014*.

Figure 10.5 Budget speech: Two hundred most commonly used content words in the provincial budgets, 2004–14

identified as policy concerns relatively early on and became the subject of targeted programs. Here, the ministers refer to their programs, rather than the problems themselves. Conceptually, this is important. For a problem or issue to be discussed, it must have first been transformed into an area of policy concern and then become the subject of a program, strategy, or project. Almost none of the specific issues that so desperately need an open and frank discussion have received such treatment by the government. In this discourse, a problem is only real if the government has a solution for it. This subordinates democratic discussion of policy options to the exigencies of political marketing. It reduces complex social problems to the level of branding and successful product placement.

The government's emphasis could change with an evolving context, as can be seen in table 10.2. Particular content words were more in evidence in certain years than others. Despite the similarities in their titles, the discourse of the agenda-setting budget speech of 2004, which warned of a looming debt crisis, did use quite a different vocabulary than in 2008, a year of record-breaking surplus. It also used it more forcefully; the first six words on that year's list were all uttered thirty or more times. The open-ended vocabulary of 2008 and the looking-past-current-problems language of 2013 also conveyed important political messages. In each case, we are dealing with a conscious use of language not just to orient politics, but to circumscribe problems so that citizens are effectively discouraged from engaging in meaningful conversations.

These three years illustrate an important technique in the successful use of language in support of a neoliberal leadership. In each of the three years, a key word that most people would have associated with green politics was used: "environment" in 2004, "sustainable" in 2008, and "sustainability" in 2013. In each case, however, it meant something qualitatively different. The environment that mattered in 2004 was the financial environment. What was to be sustained in 2008 was the boom. The issue of sustainability in 2013 referred to the continued viability of government services despite the wild variations and long-term decline in non-renewable resource revenues.[22]

The importance of this shift in meaning for the very legitimacy of the neoliberal project as a whole would be difficult to overemphasize. The economic transformation of Newfoundland and Labrador is inextricably and causally connected to the current global

Table 10.2
Key content words and context, 2004, 2008, and 2013

2004 *$406m deficit*	*2008* *$1.8b surplus*	*2013* *$726m deficit*
social	sustainable	secure
deficit	investment	sound
debt	opportunities	child
fiscal	allocating	responsible
revised	initiatives	sustainability
revenue	infrastructure	long-term
summary	communities	
protecting	strategy	
provide	students	
financial		
business		
corporation		
environment		

These words appeared at least ten times in that year's budget speech *and* at least twice as frequently that year as in the other two years. The order of the words reflects the frequency of use; in each year, the top words on the list appeared at least thirty times in the speech.

Sources: Newfoundland and Labrador Department of Finance, *Budgets 2004, 2008,* and *2013*.

environmental crisis and so represents a fundamental change in how people, both on the island and in Labrador, relate to nature.

Newfoundland is the oldest English-speaking colony in the Americas. It was, for its first four hundred years, primarily based on the systematic exploitation of resources from the sea: whales, cod, and seals. For a little more than a century, there was a world-scale pulp and paper industry; *The Times* of London was long published on Newfoundland newsprint. For most of the last two centuries, the peoples of Labrador trapped furs. All of those historically rooted relationships with nature were, at least in principle, renewable.

No such argument can be even remotely advanced for the current boom. All of the new projects – from Hibernia to White Rose and Terra Nova, from the open-pit nickel mine and its proposed underground extension at Voisey Bay to the Long Harbour hydromet facility (an innovative method of metal refining), and from the gravity-based system for Hebron being built at Bull Arm to the new iron ore mines of western Labrador – are major contributors to global warming in their own right, and the non-renewable resources they transform into commodities will go on destroying the earth's ecosystem for decades.

In a profound and terrible irony, these new carbon-based industries are not just transforming the economy of Newfoundland. They are, with breathtaking rapidity, acidifying the ocean itself. Shellfish, which are all that is left of Newfoundland's once-great fishery, will be among the first of the many victims of this irreversible transformation (Curran and Azetsu-Scott 2012; Roberts 2011). In this context, avoiding a societal debate on the ethics and environmental impact of current developments is quite literally vital to the legitimacy of the entire neoliberal project. A similar critique might be made of provincial resource strategies from Quebec's *Plan du Nord* to Ontario's Ring of Fire, and certainly of the tar sands of Alberta and Saskatchewan, but here in Newfoundland and Labrador the composition and distribution of the population poses unique challenges.

Not only is Newfoundland the most culturally uniform jurisdiction in Canada,[23] it is also the most widely dispersed (see also Conrad in this volume). Fewer than one in five people live in the province's only city, and fully two-thirds of the population still live either in small, former one-industry towns or in the hundreds of outports scattered along the tens of thousands of kilometres of coastline. People here still live close to nature in a way that, save for the North, has not been the case on the mainland since before the Second World War. They no longer, however, live in viable communities. Twenty-five years on from the cod moratorium, local economic life in rural Newfoundland is at best episodic, seasonal, and dependent on the vagaries of tourism. Furthermore, it has until recently been heavily underwritten by remittances from the men of the community working high-paying jobs in the tar sands or on the province's own massive capital works projects, while the women struggle to get by on service jobs in the regional centres (Cadigan 2013). People no longer attend school, shop, or worship where they live. In 2009, some of my first-year students from outport Newfoundland began to report that they did not have a home town; now, a third confess they do not know the meaning of the term.

Although the causes of this widespread cultural and social dislocation predate the current economic transformation of the province, it has nevertheless been profoundly affected by it. The remarkable and unprecedented growth in market incomes for most people has been fuelled by the retail revolution of the super–box stores. The near worldwide triumph of individualistic consumerism is one of neoliberalism's signal achievements, but in the Canadian context, the extent of the cultural transformation it has wrought is perhaps greatest in Newfoundland. Provincial government policy choices have made a major contribution to this broader transformation. Indeed, fundamental changes to the redistributive function of the state are arguably the most important political result of the emerging neoliberal consensus.

Three differing policy choices by the provincial government have resulted in a rolling back of the redistributive function of the state. First, in concert with the Harper government, the provincial Tories chose to significantly reduce their commitment to social transfers. In English-Canada, social assistance, old-age pensions, guaranteed income supplements, employment insurance, and worker's compensation are the major social transfers. In 2005, they amounted to 17.3% of total assessed income in Newfoundland. By 2011, after six years of unprecedented growth in the provincial economy, social transfers amounted to only 12.6% of total income and this despite the introduction of the Universal Child Care Benefit. Expenditures on the two transfers exclusively under provincial responsibility, social assistance and worker's compensation, plummeted from $490 million to $313 million. If the two levels of government had chosen to simply maintain their existing level of commitment to social transfers, an additional $750 million would have been directed to help the most vulnerable.

Social transfers to those in need are not the only type of transfer. Through tax credits and deductions, governments also make what might be called anti-social transfers; these are programs that specifically benefit those in the higher tax brackets. In Canada, they include subsidies to private pensions and retirement savings plans,[24] large scale write-offs of both capital gains and borrowing costs. In 2005, these anti-social transfers within Newfoundland totalled $503 million, with 38% going to the top income earners, 41% to the middle bracket, and only 22% to the 78% of people who were in the lowest tax bracket. Under Stephen Harper's Conservatives, these anti-social transfers expanded to include a privileged treatment of highly gendered pension inequities within families,[25] and a variety of programs from mineral exploration to security options. In 2011, again only for Newfoundland, these anti-social transfers totalled $911 million, or 45% of that year's better-known social transfers, with the top income earners pocketing 54%, the middle bracket 32%, and the bottom bracket 13%. By 2014, the final year of Tory rule in both Ottawa and St John's, anti-social transfers totalled $1,207 million, with the distribution even more skewed in favour of the wealthy: 62% went to the top bracket, 24% to the middle bracket, with only 14% of this extraordinary largesse going to the 60% of tax filers who were in the bottom bracket (CRA 2007, 2013, 2016).

Many of these measures are primarily or exclusively federal responsibilities, but as Quebec has shown a province does not have to follow Ottawa's lead. Other choices are possible (Noël 2013). Just across Newfoundland's longest shared border, effective anti-poverty measures, early childhood education, accessible daycare, support for young families, pharmacare, addressing the problems of illiteracy and high school drop-outs – all financed through a more progressive tax regime – were the policy choices until very recently.

The third set of policy choices rolling back the state's redistributive role concerns income tax. With Alberta's abandonment of a flat tax (see Brownsey in this volume), all Canadian provinces now have a progressive tax regime whereby those who can afford it are expected to shoulder a greater share of the load. Table 10.3 shows how quickly Newfoundland is moving away from this guiding principle of fairness. In 2005, middle-income earners contributed marginally more to provincial coffers than their share of the total taxable income, while those in the top bracket paid a premium of almost $300 million. By 2011, the tax cuts introduced by the Danny Williams government, and to lesser degree those of the federal government, had effectively eliminated the premium paid by middle-income earners and cut that paid by the wealthiest by a third. Overall, provincial income taxes declined from 8.4¢ to 6.9¢ of the taxable dollar. As was the case with social transfers, these choices came at a substantial cost. These reductions in the progressivity of the tax regime meant a loss in 2011 of an additional $414 million that would have been available to help those most in need.

The scale of the Williams tax cuts was so large, it is difficult to fathom. Once again, the extremes are most revealing of the ethical choices being made. Between 2005 and 2011, the average total income

Table 10.3
Reducing the progressive nature of the income tax regime in Newfoundland, 2005–11

	Tier one < $42,000		*Tier two < $70,000*		*Tier three > $70,000*	
	Pre-tax	*After-tax*	*Pre-tax*	*After-tax*	*Pre-tax*	*After-tax*
2005	43%	55%	35%	26%	21%	19%
2011	35%	40%	28%	25%	37%	36%

In 2005, middle-income earners paid 4% and those in the top bracket 14.5% more in income taxes. By 2011, middle-income earners no longer paid a premium, while the wealthy had their share cut by a third.

Sources: Canada Revenue Agency, *Final Tables 2007* and *2013*.

of those earning more than $250,000 a year increased by $40,350.[26] If they had merely earned that amount, after personal exemptions, they would have owed $7,400 in provincial and federal income tax. But because they had earned on average not $40,350, but eleven times more ($445,780) they pocketed all of the increase, tax-free, and paid $18,075 less in tax than they had in 2005. As this object lesson in the deep pockets of neoliberalism suggests, inequality has grown in the face of abundance and it has done so largely as a result of the conscious political choices of the Progressive Conservative government, aided and abetted by the Conservatives in Ottawa. By 2011, their choices had resulted in an annual loss to public revenues of approximately $1.25 billion from Newfoundland and Labrador alone. This would have been more than enough to make substantial headway on reducing illiteracy, eradicating poverty, addressing the chronic shortage in affordable housing, and beginning the move to clean energy.

THE CHANGING CONTEXT OF POPULIST NATIONALISM

"We got it! We got it!" This is how, on a cold January day in 2005, pumping his fist into the air, Danny Williams announced to a fawning crowd at the St John's airport that he had successfully negotiated a new Atlantic Accord. Not "I did it," but "we got it." This is the language of leadership typical of populist nationalism: inclusive, simple, and direct. As we have seen, this is not the type of language that generally characterized his government, but his mastery of it is one of the key reasons he was such a successful politician.

The appeal of populist nationalism is an appeal to a particular political identity, one that transcends the divisions of class and gender by privileging race and ethnicity. It is a collective identity, and here in Newfoundland, just as in Quebec, there are the necessary historic roots for this type of political mobilization. It generates a particular political culture that bonds leaders to their electorate in potentially powerful ways. It helps explain why so many politicians from both of these historically oppressed nations within Canada have so often punched well above their weight within the federation. It is not, however atemporal; context matters.

Earlier attempts at imposing a neoliberal agenda, most notably by the Clyde Wells government in the 1990s, were singularly unsuccessful. The turning point was the Liberals' failed privatization of Newfoundland Hydro. It was blocked by a coalition of civil-society groups led by Greg Malone, the comedian of CODCO fame. As this suggests, populist nationalism in Newfoundland has, since the cultural renaissance of the 1970s, always had a strong cultural component.[27] Danny Williams was well aware of this and was always careful to ensure that provincial cultural funding was protected and, when possible, increased. His successors have paid the cost for not being so mindful, because branding neoliberalism as a genuinely Newfoundland product is essential to its success.

Ironically, it has been the widespread misapprehension of what was to be Danny Williams's legacy project of Muskrat Falls that perhaps best illustrates the difficulties of building a populist nationalist consensus on these shifting cultural and economic sands. A little background is necessary. In the late 1960s, a provincial Crown corporation, Hydro-Québec and the Rothschild-owned Brinco[28] signed two agreements for the development and subsequent sale of the power from Churchill Falls in western Labrador. Since the oil shock of 1973, the fixed price agreed to in the 1966 agreement has generated exceptional profits for Hydro-Québec. They are currently estimated to be $1.7 billion a year. In 2016, a twenty-five-year renewal of the initial agreement kicked in, but at an even lower price, as a result of a subsequent 1969 agreement.[29]

Understandably, the search for a way to renegotiate the upper–Churchill Falls agreements with Hydro-Québec has been the holy grail of Newfoundland politics for forty years. The hydroelectric potential of the lower Churchill River is only a little over a third of that of the upper, but it had long been thought of as the way to address the inequity. Premiers Bouchard and Tobin even announced a memorandum of understanding to that effect in 1998. Premier Williams's approach was different; building on the widespread animosity towards Quebec, he opted for an end run around Hydro-Québec. Just months before retiring, he announced an agreement had been struck to develop the Muskrat Falls portion of the lower Churchill River with Emera, the owner of Nova Scotia Power. Undersea cables would bring power to the island and then on to Nova Scotia.

Early objections to the Muskrat Falls project took three forms. First, the lack of transparency fed into a widely shared apprehension of the potential debt load the province was taking on. In a sense, the premier who first warned of the danger of a debt crisis was hoisted on his own petard. Second, there was a popular fear that cost overruns would lead to marked increases in domestic electricity rates. Having long been told that the values of the marketplace are the most reliable political guide, it is hardly surprising that instead of reacting as proud Newfoundlanders standing strong, people acted like the price-conscious consumers the neoliberal revolution in retailing has taught them to be. Third, the long-simmering disaffection in Labrador was raised to a boil, with the announcement that none of the power would be used to service the many isolated communities of the "Big Land" that are still dependent on expensive and unreliable oil-fired generators.[30]

Since these early objections, the debate has continued to grow. What was initially estimated to cost $6 billion dollars has since ballooned to $11.4 billion. Sam Marshall, the Dwight Ball appointee as CEO of Nalcor, described it as a "boondoggle," but one too large to stop. Aboriginal land defenders did, in the fall of 2016, almost succeed in stopping it, through a combination of hunger strikes and a non-violent occupation of the construction site in Labrador. They were objecting to the mercury poisoning that will result from the dam's reservoir. In a dramatic about-face after weeks of confrontation, the government announced it would strip much of the vegetation in the area to minimize this threat. The concerns now focus on the long-term costs for ordinary households. It may be that the project, now scheduled to deliver first power in 2020, will require a near doubling in the price of a kilowatt hour to consumers.

The Muskrat Falls debate illustrates a key aspect of populist nationalism. If the real problems facing the nation are not openly discussed within the realm of electoral politics, then the ability of politicians to mobilize effectively is seriously undermined. The populist character means that for any such mobilization to be effective over the longer term it must be seen to be actually addressing the problems people face in their daily lives. The language of obfuscation that has characterized Tory policies, combined with a denial of the systemic nature of so many of the problems we face, has created a mistrust in government that ironically makes any organized opposition to further neoliberal inroads all the more difficult.

Newfoundland and Labrador have had four premiers in as many years, three Tories and a Liberal: Kathy Dunderdale, Tom Marshall, Paul Davis, and Dwight Ball. I have to name them, because there really is no reason for anyone outside the province to have heard of them. The inability of these erstwhile leaders to assume the position sadly confirms the main points of my analysis of populist nationalism during the boom. The transformations wrought by the boom were not merely, perhaps not even primarily, economic. Profound cultural and political changes have made the building of a meaningful consensus all the more difficult, while the earlier policy choices continue to limit the possibilities of any genuinely alternative political order.

Premier Kathy Dunderdale paid the political price for failing to establish the feasibility of Muskrat Falls. Despite winning a majority government, she was forced to resign within the year. Her insistence on dialogue and co-operation with the Harper government in Ottawa to procure a federal guarantee of debt repayment on this project further compounded the problem. No doubt, there was a deeply rooted misogyny at work here. For a brief moment, all three parties in the House of Assembly were headed by women, and Dunderdale's insistence that talking is better than fighting was widely condemned by the almost exclusively male "commentariat" as being a betrayal of Williams's legacy. Apparently, all true Newfoundlanders rant and roar.

Indeed, the appeal of this machismo is a widespread political phenomenon of our time, as it is closely linked to the deindustrialization of advanced capitalist countries and the resultant loss of working-class masculine identities. In Newfoundland, this phenomenon has had its own particularities; the exclusively male preserve of forestry has collapsed and the fishery has not just been eviscerated but largely emasculated. The increasing numbers of male household heads working long-distance commutes to the tar sands add to this crisis in masculinity. For a time, consumerism masked the seriousness of these gender dynamics, a fact recognized by the Finance Department's close tracking of that revealing economic indicator: new truck purchases. As the economic tide reversed, however, these tensions revealed how difficult it becomes to create a socially inclusive consensus when all the policies stress the importance of individual initiative and self-reliance.

Tom Marshall tried his best. Poaching selective policies from a resurgent NDP, his finance minister Charlene Johnson – youngest woman ever elected to the House of Assembly – tried to fashion a new-look Tories: grants instead of student loans, full-day kindergarten, modest increases in income support, and tax breaks for seniors and the working poor. At less than 1% of the province's $7.9 billion in expenditures, these new policies offered great political bang for the buck (Sweeny 2014a). Marshall's resurrection of the anti-poverty strategy of the late 2000s also suggested a more caring government. Much to their credit, Marshall and Johnson were able to amicably solve the multi-billion dollar liability of the public pension plans. They worked fast, because they knew they had little time. Marshall was an interim leader and Johnson's one and only budget provided the first clear indication that the economy had stalled.

Meanwhile, a quite different Conservative politic was being fashioned by newcomer Paul Davis. If Marshall had raised the hope of a return to a more socially aware Red Toryism, Davis made it clear he was banking on oil and gas to address the provincial debt. The first premier not to have a university degree since Joey Smallwood, Davis had spent nineteen years in the ranks of the Royal Newfoundland Constabulary (RNC). Opposed by the party establishment, Davis fell one vote short of a majority in a run-off second ballot before eking out a slim majority in the third. He immediately appointed his former commanding officer at the RNC to head his staff. Not surprisingly, stopping crime received higher priority than education. MUN, the province's only university, had $49.8 million slashed from its budget (Sweeny 2015). He further alienated the powerful legal profession by renaming the Department of Justice the "Department of Public Safety" and appointing an unelected friend as the new minister. Lobbying by the Canadian Bar Association resulted in the name being restored within a matter of weeks, but the damage was done.

Davis had honed his political skills as a RNC media relations officer from 2006 to 2010. As premier, his public pronouncements regularly failed that most basic of tests – if you want to know if something meaningful is being said, simply negate it and then ask yourself: would anyone ever say this? If not, then the affirmative is a meaningless platitude (Sweeny 2014b). Thus, the deterioration in the level of public discourse shown in the Tory budgets reached new and disturbing levels, but the worst was yet to come.

TO CONCLUDE, BUT NOT TO FINISH

Weather in Newfoundland is extremely variable, and so we all understand that forecasts are just that. Only "come from aways" believe them.[31] So the gathering storm shown in table 10.4 was largely ignored. The first budgets of each premier from 2012 to 2016 has indicated not just that the boom is over, but that the situation is likely to deteriorate quite rapidly. This change, it needs to be stressed, predates the collapse in the price of a barrel of Brent crude, the baseline used to price Newfoundland oil production. Anybody paying attention would have known that the party was over.

The apparent stability in GDP foreseen by the Dunderdale administration simply disappears when inflation, running at 2% per year, is taken into account. The decline from 2014 in GDP was considerably larger than these current dollar figures might suggest. The optimism foreseen by the Marshall administration, while perhaps necessary to negotiate both a resolution of the pension issue and the remaining collective agreements in the public sector, is in retrospect remarkable. I stress the importance of hindsight here, for it was not the medium-term growth that drew attention but the assessment that, by 2017, in constant dollars the province's GDP would lose a tenth of its value (Sweeny 2014a). For Davis's finance minister Ralph Wiseman, the actual situation in 2015 must have been sobering. The previous year's forecast of GDP was off by a whopping $5.6 billion. Even this proved, however, to be too optimistic, for in 2016 when Dwight Ball's finance minister Kathy Bennett looked back at the previous year's GDP it was a further $2.8 billion less than that estimated by Wiseman. The last time the provincial GDP was this low in current dollars was back in 2010, while in constant dollars one has to go back to 2007.

The initial estimates linked the slowdown to the end of a quite remarkable series of large-scale projects in the resource sector. Indeed, part of the initial appeal of the Muskrat Falls development was that it would soften the predicted shortfall in capital spending by the private sector. Under both Dunderdale and Marshall, the impact on household spending was assumed to be real, but slight. The

Table 10.4
Deteriorating provincial economic indicators

Indicator	*Premier*	*2012*	*2013*	*2014*	*2015*	*2016*	*2017*	*2018*	*2019*
Gross domestic product (billions of dollars)	Dunderdale	31.6	34.6	33.7	33.9				
	Marshall		36.2	37.7	38.5	37.8	37.8		
	Davis			35.1	32.9	34.6	35.0	36.0	38.3
	Ball				30.1	29.6	30.3	30.6	31.1
Household disposable income (billions of dollars)	Dunderdale	15.7	16.8	17.1	17.7				
	Marshall		16.8	17.4	17.9	17.8	18.0		
	Davis			17.5	17.5	17.5	17.9	18.1	18.7
	Ball				17.1	17.2	16.5	16.1	16.3
Capital investment (billions of dollars)	Dunderdale	10.0	11.8	12.0	11.5				
	Marshall		12.3	12.6	12.4	9.7	7.5		
	Davis			12.1	12.4	10.9	10.4	8.5	8.7
	Ball				10.9	11.0	9.6	7.2	6.9
Labour force (thousands of people)	Dunderdale	263.3	267.6	265.9	267.1				
	Marshall		262.8	263.4	262.5	256	251.1		
	Davis			270.9	268.3	262.8	260.6	256.9	259.3
	Ball				270.8	268.1	261.5	255.6	253.2
Unemployment rate (%)	Dunderdale	12.5	11.5	11.8	11.6				
	Marshall		11.4	11.4	11.4	12.3	12.6		
	Davis			11.9	12.4	13.1	13	13.3	12.7
	Ball				12.8	12.8	15.2	18.3	19.8

Each of the four successive governments recognized that the party was over, but their forecasts of the severity of the crisis have grown dramatically.

Sources: Newfoundland and Labrador Department of Finance, *Provincial Economic Indicators*, 2013, 2014, 2015, and 2016.

Marshall-Johnson administration did foresee this slowdown in capital spending as causing an upturn in unemployment, a situation foreseen to worsen over the medium term by the Davis-Wiseman administration, before improved consumer spending led to a slight decline in unemployment. Nothing, however, prepared us for the doom and gloom of the Ball-Bennett administration. Despite there being 17,700 fewer people in the active labour force, they are planning for one in five workers to be unemployed by 2019. I stress the word planning, for the new Liberal government is marketing this dramatically worsening of the situation as "the way forward," sacrificing the hard-won gains of working people to slay the deficit.

It is perhaps too generous to describe the collective fumbling of the Ball-Bennett administration since their election in October 2015 as following a plan. They had abandoned all of the planks of their electoral platform by the 2016 spring budget, which introduced an exceptionally regressive deficit reduction surtax: 11% on those on earning $35,000, but only 1.2% on those with incomes above $250,000. Six weeks later, as Dwight Ball plummeted to a 17% approval rating in the polls, the levy on those earning less than $50,000 was eliminated, leaving middle-income earners paying proportionally four times the rate of the highest income earners. Half the province's libraries were slated to close, while the provincial portion of the harmonized sales tax increased 20% and a temporary 16¢ per litre tax on gas was introduced.

These draconian measures did little to reduce the projected deficit, because the Dwight Ball administration completely reversed its policy on Muskrat Falls. Opposed to the $6 billion project when in opposition, the Liberals endorse it now that the price tag has edged north of $11 billion. They increased their financing of the project by $553 million, bringing the charge to the public purse in 2016 to a whopping $1.3 billion, or $2,650 for every person in the province.

Kathy Bennett, who inherited the provincial franchise for McDonald's, showed that fast-food millionaires also are adept at pulling fast ones. Although her budget declared that the announced cuts to public services would reduce (she actually said "impact") the deficit by $282 million in the current fiscal year, in fact, half the funds resulting from the announced cuts will be redirected to other programs within the same ministries. Her own ministry, finance, saw its available funding for new programs increase by $46 million, almost all of which has been slated for a discretionary fund of loans and grants to subsidize private ventures consistent with government policies. In simpler times, we called this a "slush fund." Meanwhile, according to the Provincial Estimates, a further $153 million in unannounced cuts were to be made in 2016 alone (Sweeny 2016).

Creative use of language has always been an important political skill. As we have seen, during the boom, successive provincial budgets devalued language. Indeed, by the end of the Tory reign with Premier Davis, the very idea that public statements should be meaningful was seriously open to question. This obfuscation damages democracy, because words are the very currency of public debate. A variation on Gresham's law – bad currency drives out good – applies here too.

It is unparliamentary to accuse a sitting member of lying to the House; fortunately, I am not subject to this rule. For more than a decade, provincial politicians have been skating very close to a line that was clearly crossed by Kathy Bennett in her budget speech. It was either completely incompetent or dishonest, take your choice, but there can be no doubt it does very serious damage to the credibility of government and to the accountability of public officials. Cumulative quantitative changes can and do lead to qualitative transformations. In the Brexit referendum and Donald Trump's presidency, we have seen societies with much longer democratic traditions than Newfoundland fall victim to similar attacks on truth.

Thus, although the recent economic history of Newfoundland sets it apart from its fellow provinces, and indeed much of the advanced capitalist world, it has not escaped this more general collapse in public discourse. This shared experience underscores the significance of the cultural and political transformations of our digital age. The gender, class, and spatial politics of identity are all changing remarkably rapidly. Here, new-found wealth has made for a new-found pride, but it is no longer rooted in a strong sense of coming from a particular place within Newfoundland. This new identity is temporally located, not rooted, in a virtually imagined and socially networked sense of Newfoundland's unique position in a post-modern North Atlantic world. Thus, culture will continue to shape the nature of politics, but in new and unforeseeable ways – all the more so, given the loss of meaning detailed in this chapter. The only certainty is that our relationship to the environment will be a defining aspect of that future.

NOTES

1 Representing almost three-quarters of the territory, but only one in twenty residents, Labrador has had a long and highly costly relationship with Newfoundland. For a harrowing account of who has paid the highest costs over the past two and a half centuries see Sider (2014).

2 The offsetting provisions in the 1985 Atlantic Accord foresaw a gradual reduction in equalization payments during the twelve years after first oil. First oil flowed from the Hibernia field in November 1998 and so that offset would have run until 2011, but the improvement in the general economic situation in the province was so rapid that the province was no longer eligible for equalization three years earlier than expected. The 2005 Atlantic

Accord replaced these earlier offset provisions and ensured equalization payments would not be affected by anticipated oil revenues for at least eight years. The Conservative government abrogated this agreement in their 2007 budget, which resulted in the legendary (at least in Newfoundland) ABC campaign – vote "Anybody But Conservative" – that the provincial Progressive Conservatives led against their federal party in the 2008 election.

3 Understandably this has been the subject of considerable debate among economists, most notably pitting Wade Locke of Memorial University (2004; 2010) against Jack Mintz and Duanjie Chen of the University of Calgary (2010; 2012.)

4 The subsequent decline reflects lower Hibernia oil production and that the two newer fields of Terra Nova and White Rose took time to reach "payout" as well as down time for repairs to the floating storage production offloading units used in these newer fields.

5 In 2005, 9.5% of British Columbia's taxpayers, 11.7% of Ontario's taxpayers, and 14.2% of Alberta's taxpayers earned a taxable income in excess of $75,000 (Canada Revenue Agency, *Final Tables 2007*).

6 Elsewhere in Canada, such increases would largely have been the result of immigration. In Newfoundland and Labrador, according to the National Household Survey, only 2,220 people born outside the country immigrated to the province between 2006 and 2011. The long-term effects of the cod moratorium declared in 1992, which devastated the economy of rural Newfoundland, explains where the people came from. They had always been there but had largely given up looking for work.

7 All figures based on statistics provided in the provincial budget documentation, 2005 to 2017, Department of Finance, Government of Newfoundland and Labrador.

8 For a detailed commentary on these negotiations, and indeed on almost any issue in recent provincial political history, consult *The Sir Robert Bond Papers*, the perceptive and highly informative blog of Edward Hollett, which has been "afflicting the comfortable since 2005."

9 The official announcement that all hands were lost came the following day, but in popular memory and culture the loss is indelibly linked to Valentine's Day, as the storm had peaked late on the fourteenth. The disaster is the subject of two of the most iconic cultural works in recent Newfoundland history: the song "Atlantic Blue" by Ron Hynes and the novel *February* by Lisa Moore.

10 Department of Finance Government of Newfoundland and Labrador, *Budget 2009*. While in the budget debates, Premier Williams spoke of lost revenues totalling $1.6 billion by 2011.

11 Department of Advanced Education and Skills, Government of Newfoundland and Labrador, *Poverty Reduction,* http://www.swsd.gov.nl.ca/poverty/index.html.

12 A spreadsheet listing all projects funded under this strategy is available online at *Budget 2014 – Detailed Spending,* http://www.swsd.gov.nl.ca/poverty/index.html.

13 In 2005 the provincial government, using Statistics Canada's low income cut-off measure of inequality set the overall poverty rate at 12.2% and the childhood rate at 16.7%. In 2011 the NHS, using the more broadly accepted low income after tax measure, found the overall provincial rate to be 17.9% and the childhood rate to be 22.5%, but for children under six it was 24.2%. The NHS was not a mandatory survey, so it seriously under-represents smaller communities and those living in poverty in larger urban centres. Thus, the situation is likely to be worse than the NHS reported, but as these problems apply across the country, it probably gives us a fairly reliable image of the relative position of the province. For Canada as a whole, overall poverty stood at 14.9%, childhood poverty at 17.3%, and for those under six at 18.1%.

14 Since the mid-1990s, the Organisation for Economic Co-operation and Development has consistently argued that the labour market changes brought on by trade liberalization and the export of manufacturing employment to the Global South was a good thing for advanced capitalist economies as it meant a shift to a higher skilled labour force by OECD member countries. For an extended discussion of how this affected both federal and provincial policy, see Keith Banting and John Myles (2013).

15 The International Adult Literacy Survey established a five-level scale to measure literacy, with the ability to draw basic inferences from a text being the key distinguishing mark between levels two and three. To be functionally literate means scoring at least at level three. Canadian Council on Learning, *Prose Literacy Map of Canada.*

16 The aim to reduce Newfoundland's rates to below any of those prevailing in the Maritime provinces actually dictated the new rates. Nova Scotia taxed 8.79% on the first $29,550, so the Williams government reduced its rate for the lowest bracket to 8.7%. Prince Edward Island then became the target to beat, because it had the lowest rates on both the middle (13.8%) and the top tax brackets (16.7%), so Newfoundland's rates were cut to 13.8% and 16.5% respectively. Since PEI taxed its lower-income earners at higher than 8.7%, the effective tax rate for middle-income Newfoundlanders became lower than that of islanders.

17 The further round of cuts in 2010 only benefited those in the upper two brackets and reduced rates to 12.7 for the middle bracket and 13.2% for the top bracket. This meant Newfoundland had the lowest increase, at 0.5%, between brackets of any province. Alberta, with its flat tax of 10%, had no brackets, but for the vast majority of its taxpayers their provincial taxes would be higher than those prevailing in Newfoundland since 2008.

18 For Pierre Dardot and Christian Laval, neoliberalism is "l'ensemble des discours, des pratiques, des dispositifs qui déterminent un nouveau mode de gouvernement des hommes [*sic*] selon le principe universel de la concurrence" (Hébert 2014, 1).

19 For a more orthodox explanation of these wide variations see Scott Lynch (2013).

20 In this exercise, the focus is on words with specific content, so articles, most adjectives and adverbs, proper nouns, and numbers are excluded. I have also eliminated a number of words that, while having a particular and meaningful content, appeared exceptionally frequently due to the nature of the document. These include millions (mentioned 1,138 times), year (809), new (611), Labrador (565), province (434), Newfoundland (423), program (380), budget (262), Mr Speaker (252 each), years (232), provincial (202), province's, (149) program's (131), centre (102), year's (61), government's (49), and department (47). These eighteen words account for 6% of all words spoken in the eleven budget speeches. The most frequently used words that were retained for inclusion in the word cloud were health (350) and investment (350).

21 In his history of the term, Christian Delporte defined it as "Un ensemble de procédés qui, par les artifices déployés, visent à dissimuler la pensée de celui qui y recourt pour mieux influencer et contrôler celle des autres" (Robitaille 2012).

22 Indeed, it was the subject of a ten-year "sustainability plan" released as a companion piece to the budget itself.

23 According to the National Household Survey of 2011, immigrants only account for 1.8% of the province's population and most of that is from the UK or the US. People who self-identified as visible minorities were 19.1% of Canadian population, but only 1.4% in Newfoundland and Labrador. From July 2012 to June 2013, the province attracted 680 of the country's 262,947 immigrants (Statistics Canada 2013).

24 For the costs to Newfoundland in 2008 of registered pension plans and registered retirement savings plans see Sweeny (2011).

25 For an analysis of the cost of pension-splitting with specific reference to Newfoundland see Sweeny (2012). For a more general discussion see Macdonald (2011).

26 They also more than doubled in number from 840 to 1,900.

27 The local printer and apparel manufacturer Living Planet's best-selling line features in silhouette a crowd of young men and women holding aloft musical instruments, where one would expect guns, under the title of Newfoundland Liberation Army.

28 The Rothschilds had, for more than a century, been among the most powerful banking families in Europe and their participation in the project was, in the view of the Smallwood government, a guarantee of its long-term solvency.

29 The best primer on this controversy is James Feehan (2008).

30 This is not just an inconvenience but a potentially life-threatening problem as ice prevents refuelling these communities when break-up comes late. The government's attitude was strongly reminiscent of one of the earliest Canadian assessments of Labrador: "the day will yet arrive when the hitherto desolate shores of Labrador, north, east, and west, will possess a resident population capable of contributing largely to the comfort and prosperity of more favoured countries" (Hind 1863). Former premiers Tobin and Williams both immediately joined a board of directors of an iron ore company exploiting western Labrador upon their retirement from formal politics.

31 A "come from away" is an Irish turn of phrase to refer to someone who does not come from the immediate area; in Newfoundland and Labrador it has been shortened to CFA and adapted to mean anyone not born in the province.

REFERENCES

Banting, Keith, and John Myles, eds. 2013. *Inequality and the Fading of Redistributive Politics*. Vancouver: University of British Columbia Press.

Cadigan, Sean. 2013. "Oil: Boom, Bust and Bull." Public lecture, History Department, Memorial University of Newfoundland, 27 March.

Campbell, Bruce. 2013. *The Petro-Path Not Taken: Comparing Norway with Canada and Alberta's Management of Petroleum Wealth*. Ottawa: Canadian Centre for Policy Alternatives.

Canada Revenue Agency. 2007–2017. *Final Tables 2005–2016*.

Canadian Centre for Policy Alternatives. 2013. *Tuition in Canada*. Ottawa: Canadian Centre for Policy Alternatives.

Canadian Council on Learning. 2010. "Prose Literacy Map of Canada." *Learning, Teaching, and Leadership*. https://drsaraheaton.wordpress.com/2010/03/08/ccls-interactive-prose-literacy-map-for-canada/.

Curran, Kristian, and Kumiko Azetsu-Scott. 2012. *Ocean Acidification: State of the Scotian Shelf Report. Dartmouth*. NS: DFO and the Bedford Institute of Oceanography.

Feehan, James. 2008. "The Churchill Falls Contract: What Happened and What's to Come?" *Newfoundland Quarterly* 101 (4): 35–8.

Hébert, Guillaume. *La gouvernance en santé au Québec*. Montréal: IRIS, 2014.

Hind, Henry Youle. 1863. "Preface." In *Explorations in the Interior of the Labrador Peninsula*. London: Longman, Roberts & Green.

Hollett, Edward. 2005. The Sir Robert Bond Papers. http://bondpapers.wordpress.com.

HRSDC (Human Resources and Skills Development Canada). 2005. *Building on Our Competencies: Canadian Results of the International Adult Literacy and Skills Survey*, 2003. Ottawa: Catalogue no. 89-617-XIE.

– 2013. *Indicators of Well-Being in Canada*.

Locke, Wade. 2004. *Exploring Issues Related to Local Benefit Capture in Atlantic Canada's Oil and Gas Industry*. ACOA Working Paper.

– 2007. "Cutting through the Gordian Knot – An Objective Assessment of the Equalization Implications for Newfoundland and Labrador of the 2007 Federal Budget." Public Lecture, Faculty of Arts, Memorial University of Newfoundland, 4 April.

– 2010. *Do Newfoundland and Labrador Royalties Subsidize Offshore Oil and Gas Investments? An Independent Assessment of the Claims made in Mintz and Chen (2010) and Mintz (2010)*. St John's: Harris Centre Working Paper.

Lynch, Scott. 2013. "The Paradox of Plenty and the Curse of Resource Rent Volatility: The Perils of Boom Bust Budgeting." Paper presented at the Economics Department, Memorial University of Newfoundland.

Macdonald, David. 2011. *Robin Hood in Reverse: The Real Numbers behind Income Splitting*. Ottawa: Canadian Centre for Policy Alternatives.

Mintz, Jack, and Duanjie Chen. 2010. *Taxing Canada's Cash Cow: Tax and Royalty Burdens on Oil and Gas Investments*. Calgary: School of Public Policy.

– 2012. *Capturing Economic Rents from Resources through Royalties and Taxes*. Calgary: School of Public Policy.

Newfoundland and Labrador Department of Advanced Education and Skills. 2006–2014. *Poverty Reduction Strategy Progress Reports*. St John's: Government of Newfoundland and Labrador. http://www.cssd.gov.nl.ca/publications/index.html.

Newfoundland and Labrador Department of Finance, 2005–2017. *Budgetary Documents*. St John's: Government of Newfoundland and Labrador. http://www.fin.gov.nl.ca/fin/budget/budget.html.

Noël, Alain. 2013. "Quebec's New Politics of Redistribution." In *Inequality and the Fading of Redistributive Politics*, edited by Keith Banting and John Myles, 256–82. Vancouver: University of British Columbia Press.

Roberts, Callum. 2011. *The Ocean of Life: The Fate of Man* [sic] *and the Sea*. New York: Viking Books.

Robitaille, Antoine. 2012. "Mots et maux de la politique." *Le Devoir*, 3 December.

Sider, Gerald. 2014. *Skin for Skin: Death and Life for Inuit and Innu*. Durham: Duke University Press.

Statistics Canada. 2011. *Earnings, Average Weekly, by Province and Territory*. Ottawa, Government of Canada.

– 2012. *National Household Survey*. Ottawa, Government of Canada.

– 2013. *Components of Population Growth*. Ottawa, Government of Canada.

Sweeny, Robert. 2011. "RRSPs." *The Independent*, 28 February.

– 2012. "Promoting Gendered Inequality." *The Independent*, 8 March.

– 2014a. "A Good News Budget?" *The Independent*, 15 March.

– 2014b. "Words Matter." *The Independent*, 20 September.

– 2015. "On a Rock in a Hard Place: MUN and the Davis Budget." *The Independent*, 19 May.

– 2016. "Estimating the Damage." *The Independent*, 6 May.

Yalnizyan, Armine. 2013. "Boost the Minimum Wage, Boost the Economy." *The Progressive Economics Forum*, February.

CHAPTER ELEVEN

Nunavut: Conceived in Austerity

JACK HICKS

In 1993, two decades of ethno-political mobilization resulted in a comprehensive land claim agreement between Inuit and the Canadian state. The Nunavut Land Claims Agreement (NLCA) resulted in division of the Northwest Territories (NWT); the creation of a third territory in the Canadian Arctic; the establishment of a new public[1] territorial government to deliver the programs and service of most direct importance to the 37,000 Nunavummiut[2] (education, health, housing, and social services); the creation of powerful representative Inuit organizations (foremost among them Nunavut Tunngavik Inc. [NTI]); and a number of other measures.[3]

It is important that we are clear on the depth of the social challenges that Nunavut faces. "Some 85 percent of Nunavummiut are Inuit. Nunavut has a fast-growing, and very young, population. Government consequently faces unrelenting pressure to provide adequate housing, education, and employment opportunities. The territory is beset by serious social problems, ranging from unemployment and overcrowded, substandard housing to high rates of violent crime and suicide" (Hicks and White 2015, 6). While 7.7% of all Canadians encounter food insecurity (meaning an inability to acquire sufficient good-quality food) during the year, the comparable figure in Nunavut is 31.6%. Of the Inuit households with children aged three to five, 70% are food insecure, and 25% of pre-school aged children are "severely food insecure" (Egeland et al. 2010). The territory is short 3,500 public housing units (Nunavut Housing Corporation 2016), a deficit that only increased federal funding can address. During a recent coroner's inquest into the death by suicide of an eleven-year-old boy, testimony by family members and RCMP officers revealed that there were up to twenty-three other people staying in the home where the child lived (Eggertson 2015; Skura 2015). Four out of every ten Nunavummiut rely on social assistance, with community-level rates ranging from 15% in the capital, Iqaluit, to 74% in Gjoa Haven (Department of Family Services 2016). Elevated rates of early childhood adversity – including childhood maltreatment (Perroud 2016) – and widespread substance abuse contribute significantly to mental distress (Bell 2012; 2013; *Nunatsiaq News* 2015d) and impact educational attainment, labour force participation, and overall well-being (George 2010) over the life course. Rates of violence are among the highest in the country, both suicide and tuberculosis continue to be significant public health issues, and overall life expectancy trails the national average by ten years.

The Government of Nunavut (GN) and the twenty-five municipal governments also face critical shortfalls in other essential infrastructure: roads, ports, airports, water/sewage treatment and waste management, high-speed communication networks, and energy (Nunavut 2010). As Liberal candidate Hunter Tootoo[4] said during the 2015 federal election campaign, "Nunavut greatly suffers from a significant infrastructure deficit as a result of a decade of neglect and underfunding" (*Nunatsiaq News* 2015a).

It would be more accurate to say "decades" of neglect and underfunding, as both Liberals and Conservatives have always governed the Arctic "on the cheap." Due to climate, distance, and the small population, doing anything in the Arctic is far more expensive than doing it in the South. Ottawa has long viewed the Arctic – the Eastern and Central Arctic in particular – with alarm. In short, it was viewed as a financial sinkhole. For decades, the Canadian state maintained sovereignty over the North at the lowest possible cost – often to the detriment of the well-being of the primarily Indigenous population. The result was that, when the time came to create a political jurisdiction to accommodate (and arguably to constrain) Inuit aspirations for self-determination, one of the resulting territory's parents – the Government of the Northwest Territories (GNWT) – was such an emaciated entity that the new government's birth weight was guaranteed to be low (see Coates and Poelzer in this volume).

Canadians often think of "austerity measures" as something introduced in the 1980s or 1990s, after a few decades of Keynesianism, when reasonably well-developed provincial governments cut back their expenditures by several percentage points (see Evans and Fanelli's introduction to this volume). However, the Eastern and Central Arctic never had a period of "normal" Keynesian welfare state development prior to the period of fiscal restraint introduced by the Chrétien/Martin Liberals in the mid-1990s – the precise historical moment when Nunavut was being designed and implemented (see also Sabin in this volume).

FINANCING THE CREATION OF NUNAVUT

After the NLCA was signed and the ball started rolling toward the division of the NWT and the creation of Nunavut, prominent *Globe and Mail* columnist Jeffrey Simpson looked north – and did not like what he saw. Mixing constitutional development and the settlement of land claims in the north with the assertion by Indigenous people of their right to self-determination, Simpson penned a column entitled "Paying for Native Self-Government: If Nunavut's the Model, It's a Big Tab" (Simpson 1993). The column expressed the lack of knowledge that even the self-proclaimed national newspaper had about the cost of having ownership of the Arctic. The bulk of the projected per-resident cost of Nunavut was not the result of the new territorial government headquarters, but the cost of maintaining twenty-five isolated communities across a land mass the size of Western Europe and providing their residents with basic services. Having sovereignty over the Arctic costs Ottawa a lot of money; Simpson had not been aware of just how much.

John Amagoalik, often referred to as "The Father of Nunavut," replied to Simpson in a letter to the editor that "Nunavut represents what Canadians badly need 500 years after the arrival of Columbus in the New World: a workable, sensible and significantly scaled model of the restructuring of political institutions to respect and reconcile the rights and opportunities of aboriginal and non-aboriginal Canadians" (Amagoalik 1993). Amagoalik also noted that "the mining industry, which has been pursuing a number of promising new ventures in the Arctic, supports completion of the land claim as soon as possible." In other words, invest in the Arctic and its people and you might see a decent return on your investment.

To understand the context in which Nunavut was created, it is imperative to understand that the planning for the division of the NWT (see Coates and Poelzer in this volume) and the creation of a Government of Nunavut took place during the period of "the far-reaching cuts imposed on the provinces and territories by federal Finance Minister Paul Martin's 1995 budget. This was exacerbated by the effects of fiscal retrenchment in Ontario regarding the formula finance payments, the mainstay of the [Government of the Northwest Territory]'s budget" (Hicks and White 2015, 118; see also Evans and Fanelli in this volume).

John Todd,[5] NWT minister of finance at the time, subsequently confirmed that, for the first two or three years of the Nunavut Implementation Commission's (NIC)[6] work, the GNWT was preoccupied with the financial aspects of division and did not pay much attention to issues of organizational design. The "big issues" about which the GNWT was most concerned – whether Ottawa would provide enough funding for Nunavut infrastructure, other "incremental costs," the disposition of the Workers' Compensation Board, and the NWT Power Corporation – were beyond NIC's mandate. Todd explains this focus with reference to the very difficult and unprecedented financial situation the GNWT faced, which involved "a horrendous exercise in making cuts; the GNWT had never done anything like that before" (Hicks and White 2015, 118). This reflected a blunt fiscal reality: the federal government had made it clear that, if the GNWT expected to get the funding it wanted for division, it had better get its financial house in order. The financial crunch facing the GNWT was not entirely of its making, but territorial politicians felt they had no option but to reduce spending in response to substantial reductions in the transfer payments it received from Ottawa (Hicks and White 2015, 118). As a concrete example of how the Chrétien/Martin Liberal cuts affected the creation of Nunavut, the GNWT sold off many of its staff housing units. While this policy may have been a logical decision in the Western NWT, to both raise cash and encourage home ownership, it made no sense in the East – where every single staff housing unit was going to be needed due to the increase in the size of the civil service. Thus, "NIC pressed the GNWT to suspend its policy [of selling off staff housing units] until division occurred. While for a variety of reasons the pace of implementing the policy may have slowed, the actual policy remained in place" (ibid., 122).

Things became heated. In April 1996, the Iqaluit Chamber of Commerce issued a press release stating, "Finance Minister John Todd has launched an attack on Nunavut with his recently announced roll back of GNWT public service benefits" (van Rassel 1996). The manner in which the rollbacks were structured were said to have penalized employees in the Eastern and Central Arctic more than employees in the Western Arctic. Todd replied angrily: "It's part of a cabinet decision and part of an overall strategy to reduce the deficit to make damn sure that the kids in Nunavut and everybody else in 1999 don't inherit a $300–400 million deficit. Is that what the Chamber of Commerce wants?" (van Rassel 1996).

Moreover, the federal government's austerity policies had a huge impact in the size and details of the financing package put in place to support the creation of the GN (Hicks and White 2015, 146–51). NTI president Jose Kusugak warned in 1996 that "Nunavut must not be set up to fail as a result of inadequate financing" (ibid., 152). Some wondered if that was not precisely what was happening.

HUGE CHALLENGES

The creation and initial development of the GN was challenging, to put it mildly, for all who were a part of the process. A key design feature of the GN was decentralization: the placement in small communities of jobs and "headquarters functions" that would more conventionally be placed in the capital city. Nunavut's first premier, Paul Okalik, was determined to see decentralization happen "come hell or high water" (Rodrigue 2000). And he did: the great majority of the government jobs located outside Iqaluit are still there, and while the GN may be "a centralized government with jobs spread all over the place" (Hicks and White 2015, 301) the fact is that hundreds of well-paying positions are located in communities that desperately need the jobs. Article 23 of the NLCA requires all levels of government in Nunavut to achieve "representative levels" (i.e. the proportion of Inuit in the total population – 85%) of Inuit employment, an obligation that the GN is far from meeting. And "[a]s of November 2014, Inuit hires in decentralized positions stood at 55%; across the GN, it remained at 50%" (ibid., 306–7).

A frank review of the strengths and weakness of the GN after its first decade took place in the form of the *Qanukkanniq?* (How are we doing?) "report card," in which a newly elected government tried to gauge the strengths and weaknesses of the GN at the beginning of its mandate (Bell 2009). The ability of Premier Eva Aariak to address the weaknesses identified in the report was severely hampered by the discovery of a $110 million cost overrun in the government's most important housing construction program (*Nunatsiaq News* 2010).

Faced with the choice between completing hundreds of desperately needed social housing units (and incurring a huge deficit) and not completing those social housing units, the Cabinet decided to complete the social housing units. This meant several years with essentially no discretionary funds, and increased reliance on the Conservative federal government of Stephen Harper. The GN has serious capacity deficiencies – both in financial and human resources. A remarkable percentage of government jobs are vacant at any given point in time, in part because of the shortage of housing.

The Government of Nunavut's historical role at this point in the development of capitalism in the Canadian Arctic is to be a "developmental state" – to educate and train a healthy Inuit workforce for employment in both the public and the private sectors. The GN struggles with these responsibilities. For example, when the territory was created in 1999 the hamlet of Igloolik had a vibrant Head Start program for pre-school children (and other programs for their parents) while the neighbouring hamlet of Hall Beach did not. Eighteen years later, there is still no Head Start program in Hall Beach – or in most other Nunavut communities. In the Kitikmeot region, the school attendance rate is less than 60% – starting with grade one. The territory's high school graduation rate is far lower than the national norm.

Like previous Nunavut governments, the Cabinet led by Premier Peter Taptuna (from 2013 to 2017) pinned many of its hopes on "devolution" from the federal government. Devolution in the Nunavut context means "the process of transferring control over Nunavut's public (Crown) lands and resources to the Government of Nunavut. Devolution will allow Nunavummiut to make decisions on how public lands and resources are used and developed. An agreement will be negotiated between the Government of Nunavut, the Government of Canada and Nunavut Tunngavik Incorporated that sets out the process for this transfer" (Nunavut, Department of Executive and Intergovernmental Affairs, n.d.). Devolution would not only give the GN more control over non-renewable resource development in the territory (by the assumption of almost all province-like powers), it also holds the prospect of significant royalties should significant development occur – royalties that, under the existing arrangements, would flow to Ottawa.

"Devolution is a long-term goal," Taptuna told *The Globe and Mail* in early 2015. "You're not going to see royalties rolling in after an agreement is signed. We still have to develop our natural resources by putting in infrastructure" (Rennie 2015). Devolution, resource development, and the resulting royalties could ease the GN's intense financial pressures. This is certainly the long-term goal and assumption underwriting territorial government policy. The Government of Nunavut is, and always has been, "open for business." As Taptuna noted, "Nunavut enjoys Canada's lowest personal tax rates and no sales tax. Our business and corporate taxes are among the lowest in Canada. Investors that partner with Inuit or Nunavut based businesses can potentially access financing, loans and wage subsidy programs. The territory is also working with industry to support responsible development" (Taptuna 2014).

Readers desiring a comprehensive overview of Nunavut's economy, and the challenges it faces, would be well advised to consult the *2013 Nunavut Economic Outlook – Nunavut's Next Challenge: Turning Growth into Prosperity,* prepared by Impact Economics for the multistakeholder Nunavut Economic Forum (Impact Economics 2013). It provides a wealth of detail and analysis that space does not permit this chapter to present, except to note that responsible non-renewable resource development would appear to be the only viable option for growth and employment in Nunavut in the coming decades. Indeed, facilitating *responsible* non-renewable resource development was one of the goals of the Inuit leaders who negotiated the NLCA – thereby negotiating Nunavut into existence.

In December 2014, the Conference Board of Canada (2016, n.p.) confidently asserted that "Over the next few years, Nunavut will see a number of mining projects advance to the construction stage as some projects, like the [Baffinland Iron Mines Corp's] Mary River project, move into production and others progress." Since those words were penned, the ongoing global economic crisis, which began in 2008 and has been mutating ever since (Roberts 2016), has resulted in a plunge in prices for iron ore and other major industrial commodities. The lack of confidence among global investors and the downturn in China (which sharply lowered global demand for iron and steel) now ripping through global world markets have darkened Nunavut's economic future as much as that of any resource-dependent economy. Even the Mary River iron ore project, originally envisioned to be massive, has been scaled back (Sopinsky 2012). The bright spot on the mining front is gold, as Nunavut will soon have at least three operating gold mines.

In addition to the challenges posed by global markets, the GN's intentions to generate significant revenue through extraction will likely face challenges from many Nunavummiut. The pace, scale, and types of extraction implied in the GN's strategy is likely to face stiff opposition from many communities, whose long-term well-being may suffer from the effects of mineral development. While there is widespread support for mining development in principle, hunting and other land-based activities remain crucially important to Inuit – both culturally and economically. The sharing of "country food" through family networks and community freezers is often the only source of healthy food for vulnerable community members who would otherwise be unable to acquire it through the market. Some proposals for resource development pose threats to the long-term viability of important wildlife populations through habitat destruction, as well as the health of Nunavummiut through toxic contamination.

There are numerous examples of recent community-based and grassroots campaigns opposing particularly destructive resource development proposals, including the Hamlet of Clyde River's legal challenge to offshore seismic surveys (Bernauer 2014; 2016), the Baker Lake hunters' opposition to the proposed Kiggavik uranium mine (Bernauer 2012; Rogers 2015; Nunavummiut Makitagunarningit 2015), and the Hamlet of Grise Fiord's opposition to coal exploration in the High Arctic (Dolphin 2013). There has also been significant political organizing on a regional basis to ban oil and gas development in Lancaster Sound (*Nunatsiaq News* 2010) and mining in caribou calving grounds (Bernauer 2015). The fact that many of these campaigns have been successful illustrates that communities are capable of saying no to a specific project if they do not feel that it would be in their long-term best interest. It is important to note that the GN has either remained neutral or sided with the interests of capital in many of these struggles, putting the harvesting sector (and the well-being of the many Nunavummiut who rely on it) at risk in favour of potential increases in government revenue in the future. In review processes, GN officials frequently use technical discourses to discount opposing (often "community") views.

Turning political issues into technical debates is a deeply political act, usually carried out to forward a political and economic agenda – the logic of private capital accumulation. Ellen Wood (2006, 25) could have been speaking of the GN when she wrote that the essential role of the state under capitalism involves "creating and sustaining the conditions of accumulation at arm's length, maintaining the social, legal and administrative order necessary for accumulation." The GN

Table 11.1
Nunavut fiscal and economic indicators

	*Federal cash transfers**	*Own-source revenue**	*Own-source as % of total revenue**	*Program expenditures**	*Surplus (deficit)**	*Net debt**		*GDP growth***	*Employment rate****
1999–00	677	64	8.67%	670	72	-33	1999	4.2%	
2000–01	704	94	11.74%	736	62	-7	2000	6.4%	
2001–02	695	84	10.75%	776	2	25	2001	2.3%	
2002-03	759	100	11.68%	847	12	43	2002	-0.1%	
2003-04	803	95	10.63%	891	7	100	2003	4.7%	55.9
2004-05	881	88	9.05%	914	55	94	2004	-0.6%	54.3
2005-06	978	100	9.28%	969	109	12	2005	1.0%	58.9
2006-07	1,176	94	7.42%	1,124	146	-88	2006	8.1%	63.4
2007-08	1,042	134	11.41%	1,155	21	-75	2007	14.3%	54.3
2008-09	1,115	145	11.53%	1.283	(23)	-17	2008	-7.0%	53.0
2009-10	1,201	146	10.83%	1.283	63	-2	2009	18.5%	55.9
2010-11	1,278	166	11.52%	1,425	19	37	2010	5.4%	54.9
2011-12	1,359	155	10.21%	1,458	55	-22	2011	2.2%	56.9
2012–13	1,463	157	9.71%	1,498	122	-215	2012	10.5%	58.5
2013–14	1,574	180	10.25%	1,605	149	-276	2013	-1.4%	54.2
2014–15	1,616	179	9.96%	1,686	109	-295	2014	-0.5%	53.8
2015–16	1,658	204	10.96%	1,763	99	-320	2015	1.8%	56.3
2016–17 Interim	1,683	202	10.72%	1,871	4	-248	2016		54.8

Sources:
* Finance Canada, Fiscal Reference Tables September 2017 (millions of dollars), www.fin.gc.ca/frt-trf/2017/frt-trf-17-eng.asp
** Statistics Canada, CANSIM Table 384-0038 Gross domestic product, expenditure-based, provincial and territorial (expenditure-based, chained 2007 dollars)
*** Statistics Canada, CANSIM Table 282-0100, Labour Force Survey estimates (LFS), by territories, sex, and age group (15 years and over, September)

is very much a "servant state" in the service of private capital, and it appears to be carrying out its role quite successfully: albeit from a very low base, Nunavut led the country in terms of the average rate of capital accumulation between 2007 and 2013 (McCormack and Workman 2015, 149–50). That being said, the overall percentage of the adult population that is employed has remained essentially unchanged since 1999 – as have the extreme disparities in employment rates between ethnicities (the Inuit rate is just under 50%, the non-Inuit rate over 85%) and communities (some isolated communities have employment rates as low as 30%).

Of greater complexity is the nature of and role of NTI and the regional Inuit associations, which have consistently taken industry-friendly positions that are often not much different than those of the GN (see, for example, *Nunatsiaq News* 2016; Bell 2017).

AUSTERITY POST-DIVISION? NOT SO MUCH

At the time of writing, the Legislative Assembly of Nunavut has met for more than 675 days and has generated almost 45,000 pages of Hansard. The word "austerity" has only been uttered twice. The first time was a passing reference to a capable SAO (the senior administrative officer of a municipal government) who was lauded for his "fiscal austerity and good planning." The second time was by GN finance minister Keith Peterson who in 2014, in response to a question about the creation of an air quality specialist position, noted, "I believe it has always been a position that has been needed. The Department of Environment has asked for it several times. Due to austerity measures and priority items, it just didn't make it to the main estimates and getting approval" (Hansard 6 November 2014, 1633).

The Legislative Assembly of Nunavut is run on a non-party basis, so the majority of the members (MLAs) are usually not "opposition" members as such – although there have been cases of Regular Members (those MLAs not selected for cabinet) voting as a block to force a change in government policy, with all cabinet members voting in favour of the status quo. Not only have successive Nunavut governments not called for what are usually understood as "austerity measures," the Regular Members have not critiqued government policy in those terms. It is a remarkably apolitical legislature, with MLAs never questioning the government's neoliberal agenda or proposing alternative approaches to addressing fundamental questions.

Fiscal transfers from the federal government to the GN have increased steadily since 1999 – including under the Conservative government of Stephen Harper. Even though Nunavut's basic operations, maintenance, and capital needs are arguably not being met, such is the level of both fiscal need and fiscal dependence that federal government has had no option but to send more cash to the GN with each passing year. It's the price of having sovereignty over the Arctic, and the demands of a young and rapidly growing population.

The GN's fiscal situation has limited both the quality and quality of public services in the territory but is less the result of austerity measures than of deficiency in structural capacity. There have been no significant staff layoffs, little confrontation with the main public-sector union, limited expenditure reductions, few new user fees, no termination of business subsidies or tax breaks, limited increase in contracting out, and equally limited selling off of public assets. In the years since the establishment of the "headquarters" functions of the GN, there has been no decrease in the size of the public sector as a percentage of the total workforce, of public-sector expenditures as a percentage of territorial GDP, or of union density. The GN's budget has increased from $740 million in 1999–2000 to $2 billion in 2017–18.

No wonder young university graduates from the South who land a job with the GN often feel like they've won the lottery – they have the kind of secure government job (with good benefits, including a decent pension plan) that their classmates can scarcely dream of. No wonder also that there are few young Inuit willing to publicly challenge government policy – the social layer most capable of doing so is employed by government departments or Inuit organizations, and has mortgages to pay.

For the majority of the Inuit population however, life is far less pleasant or secure. As an editorial in the territory's pugnacious newspaper *Nunatsiaq News* put it in early 2015, as a federal election loomed:

> There are two Nunavuts. One group, representing more than half the population, is poor and deprived, excluded from the economic growth the territory has enjoyed over the past three or four years. Many, though not all, live in small hamlets. Trapped by long-term structural unemployment and a dysfunctional school system, they face a bleak future: excluded, marginalized and too often forgotten.
>
> The other Nunavut is affluent and comfortable. This group enjoys rising incomes, increasing net worth and expanding opportunities. Most of these people are located in Iqaluit and some of the larger communities.

The editorial concluded,

> Nunavut needs a new social contract: a root and branch reform of all its social programs that encourages more people to work

> and to keep what they earn instead of having it clawed back or taxed. (Bell 2015)

What Nunavummiut have experienced since 1999 is a limited expansion of the public service (population growth and regulatory requirements have made some new hiring a necessity), "prudent" growth in government spending (with the occasional unofficial spending freeze, broken to a certain extent by absolute necessity), small budget surpluses every year but one,[7] social programs seemingly incapable of addressing widespread social suffering, and considerable interest in private–public partnerships (P3s) as a means by which to raise capital for infrastructure development.

BEYOND NICKELS AND DIMES: PUBLIC MONEY FOR P3S

P3s were an established manner of financing infrastructure before Nunavut – and the Government of Nunavut – came into existence. The federal government's decision that much of the new infrastructure (primarily office buildings) required to set up the new government be built by the Nunavut Construction Corporation (NCC) became a bone of contention in the already difficult relationship between Ottawa and Yellowknife over the creation of the GN. NTI negotiated arrangements with the federal government, which infuriated the GNWT:

> Exacerbating the animosity over infrastructure was NTI's siding with the federal government against the GNWT's insistence that it was better placed to manage infrastructure design and construction. NTI's position reflects its view that the federal government offered greater prospects for favouring Inuit-owned firms – most notably the Nunavut Construction Corporation (NCC), which was wholly owned by the Inuit "birthright" economic development corporations, which, in turn, were owned by NTI or regional Inuit associations – in the awarding of contracts and jobs. Additional friction arose because the GNWT took the position that, as a public government, its responsibility was to see that all Northern businesses, not just those that were Inuit-owned, were given favourable treatment. Nonetheless, Ottawa did convey to the NCC responsibility for financing, constructing, and managing the infrastructure needed for the GN. (Hicks and White 2015, 90)

The willingness of the various affected federal departments to agree to such a large, high-risk, and completely unorthodox procedure – allocating without tender contracts for construction of tens of millions of dollars of infrastructure to NTI through NCC – was nothing short of remarkable, given that NTI had no experience in such an undertaking and that the NCC had essentially zero equity. Rarely, if ever, had standard government procedures been superseded in risk-averse Ottawa in such fashion. The normally conservative Department of Finance proved uncommonly open to innovative approaches for ensuring that necessary infrastructure would be in place on time. Indeed, while the bureaucrats from Finance, Indian Affairs and Northern Development, and Public Works all had very different mandates and perspectives, they found a common interest in being at the forefront of a historic development that was clearly a top government priority. As for the politicians, one official involved in the process commented: "The [federal] ministers liked it because it meant no further major expenditures immediately; the ministers spoke: 'here's the budget, there isn't any more so make it work'" (ibid., 149–50).

The president of the NCC was Tagak Curley – one of the key Inuit politicians from the earliest days of the Nunavut proposal, a prominent Liberal, a strong proponent of private-sector development, a former GNWT minister of economic development and tourism, and later a GN cabinet minister and candidate for premier of Nunavut.

The GNWT had built a new Legislative Assembly building using P3 funding, and had the support of the influential Northern business community[8] – but not the main public-sector union[9] – to fund more infrastructure though P3s (Wilkin 1998). When the GN came into existence in 1999, it inherited five P3 projects already under development or consideration. The first P3 agreement for a $10 million health facility in the community of Arviat with the Arviat Development Corporation (ADC), was announced in the Legislative Assembly by GN finance minister (from 1999 to 2004) Kelvin Ng on 19 May 1999. The ADC was one of the "birthright development corporations" established under the tutelage of the Evaz Group, a Rankin Inlet–based corporation spearheaded by businessman and politician John Todd. The ADC later went bankrupt (Hansard 7 December 2009, 1041), and the Assembly passed a supplementary appropriation of $4.4 million to allow the GN to purchase the building (Hansard 1 June 2010, 2022). Other projects considered for P3 arrangements were larger health facilities in Iqaluit, Rankin Inlet and Cambridge Bay, and a residence for Nunavut Arctic College campus in Cambridge Bay (Hansard 12 April 2000, 1403).

In October 2000, Ng took what one MLA described as "an about turn" on P3s. Ng told the Legislative Assembly that after initially "aggressively pursuing" P3s the government had concluded, "There was no perceived long-term advantage for us in continuing to pursue public private partnership financing concept that would differentiate between conventional capital leasing arrangements. So, we have made a decision, basically to go back to more conventional methods of financing in respect to those three health facilities and any future capital facilities that might be provided by the private sector" (Hansard 20 October 2000, 2368). This statement by Ng did not settle the matter, as some politicians and bureaucrats continued to see P3s as a way to access capital for badly needed investments.

Debate continued when MLA Tagak Curley brought the matter up in the Assembly in May 2004. After GN finance minister (from 2004 to 2005) Leona Aglukkaq noted that "We always need more money, we know that, we are short funding for health, we are short funding for infrastructure development, housing, what-have-you," Curley stated, "I just want to stress to the minister that there should be public-private partnerships considered. Some people always think that if it's taken over by the private company that it's going to be more expensive, but to me it's not like that" (Hansard 31 May 2004, 55). Curley's frustration with the level of federal funding was apparent. In November 2004 he stated, "What I wanted to say was that the federal government's strategic infrastructure fund for Nunavut … I wonder why they are nickel and diming us in Nunavut. The Yukon government and the Northwest Territories government, while they have so many millions and millions of dollars yet they are asking for infrastructure funding, but in Nunavut, even where there is an infrastructure fund, they just seem to be giving us nickels and dimes" (Hansard 22 November 2004, 227).

With regard to housing, Curley has made the following statements:

> Federal funding for housing in Nunavut will continue to be extremely limited … [We are] frustrated and disappointed that the Federal Government has not announced a new funding agreement for housing in Nunavut. (Hansard 22 November 2005, 354)

> Recognizing that there is a housing crisis in Nunavut, [I] urge the minister to investigate every avenue to increase the housing stock including private–public partnerships, federal infrastructure funding, partnerships with Inuit organizations, and joint initiatives with other Government of Nunavut departments. (Hansard 31 May 2004, 64)

GN Finance Minister (from 2005 to 2007) David Simailak[10] replied, "P3s are definitely one very good possibility for what you want to do in Nunavut. There is no way that we could come up with the money ourselves to do what we need to do. There is no way that the federal government is going to fund all that we need to do in Nunavut" (Hansard 22 November 2004, 232). Simailak suggested that P3 funding might facilitate the rather fanciful Bathurst Inlet Port and Road Project (Hansard 1 November 2007, 2229; George 2009), and MLA Keith Peterson suggested using P3s to build a trades school (Hansard 26 November 2004, 482) and social housing (Hansard 12 March 2008, 3837). MLA John Ningark wondered if the government couldn't work out a P3 arrangement whereby NTI would provide financial support for Inuit wishing to purchase equipment for hunting so as to "better the conditions of people who cannot afford or don't have access to nutritional food" (Hansard 18 March 2009, 125). This suggested a less-than-complete understanding of the concept of public–private partnership funding which, with the very best of intentions, Ningark tried to put to use to address widespread poverty and food insecurity.

MLAs had requested the government develop a formal policy on P3s in 2004. Keith Peterson raised the matter again in the Legislative Assembly in November 2007, and Tagak Curley did so again in March 2008. By this point, GN officials were attending national P3 conferences organized by the federal government. GN finance minister (in 2008) Louis Tapardjuk tabled a Public–Private Partnership Policy on September 17, 2008. The policy stated that "a cooperative approach to building infrastructure through public–private partnerships can be an appropriate, efficient and effective use of Nunavut's resources to deliver services" (Nunavut, Government of Nunavut 2013). The Department of Finance was to be the lead department, and a committee of three deputy ministers was to evaluate proposals.

In March 2010, the Standing Committee on Oversight of Government Operations and Public Accounts noted, "The Department of

Finance's 2009–10 business plan does not make any reference to the GN's new P3 Policy. During the minister's appearance before the standing committee, members were advised that the government continues to consider the potential of using P3 approaches in its capital planning process" (Hansard 16 March 2010, 1596). The Standing Committee made almost identical comments the following year (Hansard 8 March 2011, 409), and again the year after that (Hansard 7 March 2012, 2307). A revised GN P3 Policy was released in April 2013 (Nunavut 2013).

In 2016, the Nunavut Housing Corporation announced its intention to "engage with Regional Inuit Associations (RIAS) and their associated business arms on potential public–private partnerships or private investment opportunities for housing developments, to block land development, and the development of Inuit-owned lands (IOLS) within municipal boundaries, with priority given to approaches that also support innovation, community economic development, and building local capacity" (Nunavut Housing Corporation 2016, 35). It would seem that, in the absence of adequate core funding from the federal government, the GN is intent on using P3S as a way to meet its most basic infrastructure needs.

Including for a Taj Mahal of an Airport in Iqaluit

Improvements to the Iqaluit International Airport have been described as Nunavut's "largest and most urgent infrastructure need" (Hansard 30 October 2012, 3121), although that title is debateable given the territory's acute shortage of social housing.

P3 funding for an expansion of the Iqaluit International Airport[11] was included in the Department of Economic Development and Transportation's proposed 2012–13 Capital Estimates. In its review of the proposed capital plan, the Standing Committee on Community and Economic Development simply stated that its members "look forward to ongoing updates on the status [of the project]" (Hansard 24 October 2011, 1284). No questions were asked or objections made.

A request for qualifications (RFQ) for a new, state-of-the-art airport in Iqaluit was released in June 2012, and in September of that year Nunavut MP Leona Aglukkaq announced that the federal Crown corporation PPP Canada would provide $77.3 million toward the estimated total project cost of $300 million – by far the biggest capital project undertaken since the creation of the territory (PPP Canada n.d.). Aglukkaq stated that P3 projects "provide better value" for the government's money (George 2012).

A consortium called Arctic Infrastructure Partners "was selected as the preferred proponent to design, build, finance, operate and maintain the Iqaluit International Airport Improvement Project" in July 2013 (Department of Economic Development and Transportation 2013). The consortium consists of investment banking firm InfraRed Capital Partners Ltd., the Montreal-based construction company Bouygues Building Canada Inc., a subsidiary of Bouygues called Colas Canada Inc., and The Winnipeg Airports Authority.

According to the *Iqaluit International Airport Improvement Project – Project Report* the P3 approach is something of an economic miracle, saving the GN almost $100 million over the life of the project: "The net present cost (NPC) of the 30-year Project Agreement is estimated to be $418.9 million. The NPC of delivering the same project using a Design Bid Build approach rather than the partnership approach is estimated to be $518.7 million. The GN is achieving value for taxpayers' dollars of $99.8 million by procuring the project as a partnership" (Nunavut 2014). No independent assessment of this math has been prepared.

Two MLAs from smaller communities have inquired if P3 funding might make expansion of the airports in their communities possible as well. GN Minister of Economic Development and Transportation Peter Taptuna responded that to access the $77.3 million from P3 Canada for the Iqaluit airport expansion, "we have taken the majority of the capital infrastructure money that we do put up from this government. Doing it in that manner, through that process, saves our funds for doing other projects and infrastructure buildings within the smaller communities" (Hansard 6 September 2013, 4737).

Such is the magnitude of the territorial and municipal government's infrastructure shortfall – estimated by the GN to be $6 billion (Varga 2014) – that in February 2013 the GN minister of community and government services (CGS) told the MLAS that a P3 model "is being examined by CGS to address solid waste infrastructure for communities. The feasibility of the P3 model for other infrastructure initiatives will continue to be examined" (Hansard 27 February 2013, 3429). P3 approaches to funding hydroelectric development have also been discussed within the government (Hansard 12 March 2013, 3958), but no other announcements of P3 projects in Nunavut have been made.

The only public voice of concern over the potential for greater P3 funding for infrastructure funding in Nunavut has come from *Nunatsiaq News* editor Jim Bell, who in 2013 called the airport expansion a "grandiose plan" without a solid justification:

> The GN says "Several major exploration projects on Baffin Island are expected to develop into mines in the near future, such as the Mary River iron ore deposits, and Chidliak diamond project."
>
> The near future? Really? The developers of the Chidliak diamond project near Iqaluit, Peregrine Diamonds Ltd. and De Beers, have dug up some interesting samples. But they have yet to prove their isolated site contains a viable resource and they have yet to produce a credible feasibility study. It's foolish for the GN to predict this uncertain project will become a producing mine any time soon.
>
> As for the Mary River project, Baffinland's current scaled-back scheme would cut its production by about 80% from the company's original plan. Given the current weakness of global steel prices, this project must also be deemed uncertain until proven otherwise …
>
> There's only one question we can answer with certainty. That question has to do with why the GN chose to use a private-public partnership, or "P3."
>
> Governments turn to P3s for the same reason poor people turn to Money Mart. It's their only option. And after the GN managed in 2012 to pry a $77.3 million handout from [PPP Canada], a federal agency, construction of this huge project became inevitable. (Bell 2014)

The editorial also cautioned against "private Inuit associations and birthright corporations" being able to access P3 funding to promote mining-related ventures in the same way that the editorial suggested that the public government has:

> If the federal government believes it's good policy to provide handouts to private businesses, including private aboriginal businesses, that's their prerogative. But it's not in the public interest to use scarce funds that would otherwise go to public

> governments for public infrastructure. The federal government could accomplish the same objectives by either creating new aboriginal business programs or by putting more money into existing ones. (Bell 2014)

An alternative use of the "scarce funds" that Bell referred to could be to address urgent social needs, one of the most pressing being suicide prevention.

But No Funding for Suicide Prevention

Suicide has been an urgent public health matter in the Arctic since the 1970s. Claims by academics that Indigenous leaders were "resisting this despoliation of their human capital" (Coates and Powell 1989, 16) were not accurate. The GNWT never developed a suicide prevention strategy, despite an internal government report which warned that "We may have an epidemic on our hands in the future, if we do not take care and tackle the problem now" (Westcott et al. 1989). Powerful GNWT cabinet ministers from the Eastern Arctic (e.g. Dennis Patterson, John Todd, and Tagak Curley) could have ensured that action was taken, if evidence-informed suicide prevention had been a priority for them. It wasn't, and by the time the new Nunavut territory and government came into being, the suicide rate among young Inuit males was nearly 500 per 100,000 – almost forty times the rate for young men across the country (Hicks 2009; 2015).

Right from its establishment in 1999, the senior officials of the GN's new Department of Health and Social Services did not see suicide as their particular responsibility – "it's society's problem," one GN deputy minister told me – and, as a result, suicide prevention activities did not receive much attention from the new government. There were modest efforts here and there, such as a poster campaign with messaging such as "Suicide is not the Inuit way." GN health and social services minister Ed Picco promised that his government's campaign will be a "multi-year, multi-faceted program" that would cost "a million dollars" (Bell 2001). It was not a multi-faceted program, it was a media campaign – and no spending of that magnitude occurred. Frustrated, the members of the Legislative Assembly held a debate on the subject on 5 March 2003 – perhaps the first time a legislature anywhere held a debate on suicide and suicide prevention.

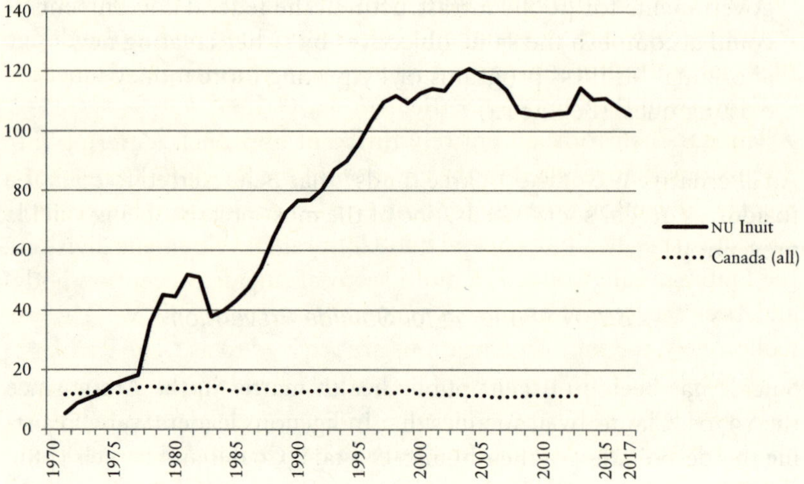

Note: Rates for Nunavut Inuit are five-year rolling averages
Sources:
- data on deaths by suicide from 1 January 1969 to 31 March 1999 obtained from the Department of Justice, Government of the Northwest Territories
- data on deaths by suicide from 1 April 1999 to 31 December 2016 obtained from the Office of the Chief Coroner of Nunavut
- demographic data: special Census tabulations prepared by Statistics Canada, October 2016
- rates for Canada from CANSIM table 102-0551, accessed 2017 July 1

Figure 11.1 Crude rate of death by suicide by Nunavut Inuit and all Canadians, 1972–2017

In the fine print of a 2004 overall strategy document, the new (i.e. second) government stated that it would develop "a suicide prevention strategy with a focus on wellness." By January 2007 the ever-vigilant *Nunatsiaq News* was noting that "government officials have been unable to confirm whether any plans exist to honour this commitment" (Thompson 2007) and editorializing that the government's efforts to date had been a "made-in-Nunavut failure" (Bell 2007). Premier Paul Okalik responded to the criticism by taking responsibility for suicide prevention away from his Health Minister Leona Aglukkaq and directing one of his political staff, Pat Angnakak, to prepare a strategy. Written in just a few months, Angnakak's strategy was sharply criticized in the media – and then quietly but quickly shelved.

It is important to note that the process of developing the first suicide prevention strategy ignored the GN's obligation under Section 32.1.1

of the NLCA to "[provide] Inuit with an opportunity to participate in the development of social and cultural policies, and in the design of social and cultural programs and services, including their method of delivery, in the Nunavut Settlement Area."

The GN then took an entirely different approach, entering into discussions that resulted in the creation of the Working Group for a Suicide Prevention Strategy for Nunavut – a partnership between the GN, NTI (specifically its Social and Cultural Development division), the Embrace Life Council (a multi-sectoral suicide prevention body) and, later, the Royal Canadian Mounted Police (RCMP)'s "V" Division. Collectively, the four organizations are referred to as "The Partners."

The Working Group met weekly, reviewed a wide range of literature, examined strategies from other jurisdictions (several Canadian provinces, Greenland, Alaska, Australia, New Zealand, Scotland, and Wales), and were briefed on the work of the psychological autopsy study that was under way in the territory (Chachamovich et al. 2013; 2015). The members of the Working Group were struck by research results demonstrating that approximately two-thirds of suicide attempts are attributable to abusive or traumatic childhood experiences, an attributable risk fraction "an order of magnitude rarely observed in epidemiology and public health data" (Dube 2001, 3095). Improving the socio-emotional well-being of children in Nunavut became one of the Working Group's highest priorities.

In April 2009, the Working Group released a lengthy discussion paper in both Inuktitut (the Inuit language) and English. Consultation sessions across all twenty-five Nunavut communities engaged more than 500 people. The consultations "took many forms. Some were as informal as conversations, email exchanges, or drop-in sessions; others were more structured, involving "town hall" sessions with the general public, or meetings with key stakeholders and community members" (Bobet 2009). NTI had insisted on this wide-ranging consultative process, and it paid almost all the costs – approximately $250,000. This contribution reflected the key role that Natan Obed, NTI's director of health and social development, played in the Working Group.

The Partners reviewed the results of the consultation, continued their internal discussions, and finalized a draft strategy. It was NTI staff who insisted on the unambiguous name "Nunavut Suicide Prevention Strategy." The draft was approved by the GN Cabinet, the NTI Board of Directors, the Embrace Life Council Board of

Directors, and the RCMP. In October 2010, the Partners released the Nunavut Suicide Prevention Strategy (NSPS) (Nunavut, Nunavut Tunngavik Inc., Royal Canadian Mounted Police, and Embrace Life Council 2010).

The NSPS presents a compelling hypothesis regarding the roots of the level of social suffering seen in Nunavut communities today. Shortly after the Second World War, federal government policies resulted in the coerced relocation of Inuit from seasonal camps into settled communities controlled by non-Inuit administrators. The rules that had governed historical Inuit society were replaced by the rules of a non-Inuit colonial government – with respect to education, justice, housing, and other domains:

> The cumulative effects of this massive disruption of Inuit society produced dramatic results. The first and all subsequent generations of children who have grown up in the communities embody a fundamental transition in Inuit society, away from a traditional Inuit lifestyle and towards a mix of Inuit and southern values. The generations of Inuit who have been raised in communities since have struggled with the delicate balancing act of living concurrently in two very different cultures ...
>
> The trauma experienced first-hand by Inuit in the settlement transitional period has had an immense impact on all following generations, as many Inuit who were negatively affected in this period did not ever heal. This unresolved trauma compromised their ability to cope with stress in a healthy manner. Negative behaviour often followed in the form of alcohol abuse, sexual, physical, and emotional abuse, child neglect, and violent crime. It is important to note that elevated suicide rates emerged within the first generation of Inuit youth who grew up in the communities. In the absence of an adequate healing process, a continuous cycle of trauma has been created, which has been passed from generation to generation. This is referred to as the intergenerational transmission of historical trauma. (Nunavut, Nunavut Tunngavik Inc., Royal Canadian Mounted Police and Embrace Life Council 2010, 6)

The Inuit adults who were coerced into living in settled communities were not the ones who began dying by suicide at elevated rates; it was the first generation of children who grew in settled communities.

The NSPS was premised on the understanding that a cohort of the population that endured elevated rates of childhood adversity can suffer elevated rates of suicidal behaviour over the life course.[12]

The NSPS contains eight "commitments": take a more focused and active approach to suicide prevention; strengthen the continuum of mental health services, especially in relation to the accessibility and cultural appropriateness of care; better equip youth to cope with adverse life events and negative emotions; deliver suicide-intervention training on a consistent and comprehensive basis; support ongoing research to better understand suicide in Nunavut and the effectiveness of suicide prevention initiatives; communicate and share information with Nunavummiut on an ongoing basis; invest in the next generation by fostering opportunities for healthy development in early childhood; and provide support for communities to engage in community-development activities.

The NTI vice-president with responsibility for social issues said he believed "the plan reflects a combination of Inuit input and knowledge and best suicide prevention practices from around the world" (Windeyer 2011). The Partners then prepared and released a detailed implementation plan (called the "Action Plan") for the strategy (Nunavut, Nunavut Tunngavik Inc., Royal Canadian Mounted Police and Embrace Life Council 2011). Premier Eva Aariak told the media that "My government recognizes that suicide in this territory is not only a serious issue, but an urgent crisis that cannot continue" (Windeyer 2011). GN health and social services minister Tagak Curley "told reporters the action plan contains about $1 million in new spending" (ibid.).

In fact, the NSPS went unfunded. An email sent by Peter Ma, the GN's deputy minister of health and social services,[13] documented that he had removed the "resources required" column from the final version of the Action Plan. Keith Peterson, who had replaced Curley as GN minister of health and social services, did not submit a request to the Cabinet for funds to implement the NSPS. It is not clear whether Curley deliberately misled the public or whether Curley was misled by his officials, but Peterson clearly did not feel bound by his predecessor's public statement.

It gradually became apparent to the other Partners – and to the media and the public – that the GN's implementation of the NSPS was less than energetic. In 2013, Nunavut suffered its worst-ever year for death by suicide, both in numbers (forty-five) and in rate (for Inuit residents, 154 per 100,000). Nunavut's anguished chief coroner urged GN "social envelope" ministers and deputy ministers to declare "a state of emergency," and after that failed to happen she later called a discretionary coroner's inquest into the territory's high rate of death by suicide.

Meanwhile, the other Partners lobbied the GN to allow an independent evaluation of the implementation of the NSPS. The evaluation report was detailed and critical, noting that the lack of dedicated resources had undermined implementation efforts: "To date the resourcing of the Strategy and AP has not been effective as there are no common funds or resources available to the Implementation Committee and the Partners collectively" (Aarluk Consulting 2015, 125).

The coroner's inquest was held in September 2015 and was closely covered by the media (*CBC News* 2015) and discussed among the public. The testimony, and the questioning of witnesses was intense and often emotional. The coroner's jury released a strong suite of recommendations including that the GN "shall immediately declare Suicide as a Public Health Emergency," appoint a minister responsible for suicide prevention with dedicated staff, and work with the other Partners to prepare a revised Action Plan, among other measures. The coroner's jury, in effect, declared that the emperor had no clothes.

And so, it came to pass that, on 23 October 2015, Premier Peter Taptuna rose in the Legislative Assembly and told the speaker, "Mr Speaker, today, we declare suicide as a *CRISIS* in Nunavut" (*Nunatsiaq News* 2015b). Taptuna named the world's first minister responsible for suicide prevention – former premier Paul Okalik – with an assistant deputy minister position filled by a senior Inuit official, Karen Kabloona, created to manage a secretariat supporting the portfolio.

By any reasonable definition of "priority," suicide prevention was clearly not a priority for the GN during its first sixteen and a half years – during which time almost 500 Nunavummiut died by suicide (Hicks 2015). It took the humiliation of damning recommendations from a coroner's jury to force the Taptuna Cabinet to take suicide prevention seriously, and to allocate funding for implementation of the NSPS (Ducharme 2016). The good news is that the revised NSPS implementation plan, developed in true partnership between the Partners and launched in 2017 (Nunavut, Nunavut Tunngavik Inc., Royal Canadian Mounted Police, and Embrace Life Council 2017), is a tremendous step forward – demonstrating what could have possible years earlier if the political and bureaucratic will had been there.

CONCLUSION: NUNAVUT AS NEOLIBERALISM

The specific manner and timeframe in which capitalist development has unfolded in the Canadian Arctic has resulted in the development of state structures – and state spending – playing an even more crucial role than they have in southern Canada. However, like most of Indigenous Canada, the Central and Eastern Arctic never experienced the investment in physical and social infrastructure that non-Indigenous parts of the country benefited from during the years of postwar Keynesian spending. The Inuit experience of "combined and uneven development" (Makki 2015) has been a transition from highly autonomous life "on the land" to life under essentially neoliberal governments – first the GNWT, and then the GN. The transition to life in communities itself and the poor living conditions that many Inuit now experience – and have no choice but to raise their children in – have both contributed significantly to the serious social problems that Inuit society now suffer.

The point of exploring the Nunavut P3 story and the GN's failure (hopefully now finally being rectified) to fully implement the Nunavut Suicide Prevention Strategy has been to demonstrate that while there was public money – both federal and territorial – available to build a "Taj Mahal" of an airport in Iqaluit (Rohner 2016), there has not been anywhere near that kind of money available for tackling the intergenerational transmission of historical trauma and the resulting social suffering. The availability of public money for infrastructure spending but not for strengthened health and social services is profoundly ideological, rendering absurd the GN's depiction of itself as an apolitical and/or managerial body.

It could be said that the GN has followed a fiscally conservative path, but more fundamentally, the GN has followed a politically conservative path – with neoliberal economic and social policies. So great is the desire of the political/managerial elite to be seen as a "normal" government running a "normal" jurisdiction that it has not found the courage to tackle the social suffering that limits its future. While "austerity" rarely enters the political vocabulary in Nunavut, a sense of restraint and an unspoken acceptance of the "limitation of the possible" is never far from the surface.

Nunavut faces some of the most daunting challenges of any government in Canada, with by far the weakest of any government at the provincial/territorial level. That being said, the GN's limitations are as much intellectual and political as they are fiscal. Neither politicians nor senior officials in Nunavut seem to grasp that it is in the interest of capital that the territorial state aggressively attend to the basic health and education needs of the population before, or least in advance of, large-scale non-renewable resource development.

Addressing historical trauma and sharply elevated rates of death by suicide would have required vision and leadership, while implementing P3 policies just required copying what other governments were already doing. It's not as if there was a debate in the Legislative Assembly on the social costs and benefits of expanding the Iqaluit International Airport versus tacking the social determinants of elevated rates of suicidal behaviour. There was no such debate. There was no debate whatsoever about the cost of the prestige airport – it simply got approved – while the countless hours of discussion about suicide did not result in any significant spending. The Canadian state (and most provinces) made an ideological turn to P3 financing; so, the GN did as well. Canada is one of the few developed countries not to have taken suicide prevention seriously (Matsubayashia and Ueda 2011; World Health Organization 2014; Eggertson 2016) and (until very recently) neither has the GN. Like father, like son.

Both mining and P3s seem to be part of the territory's political DNA; aspects of the desire – especially of the political/managerial elite – to develop a stronger private sector and reduce "dependence" on the federal government. Devolution would make both mining and P3s more likely, and all three things may eventually come together as a package. The representative Inuit organizations may be capable of levering their veto over devolution for a role in P3 projects as "private" partners.

Nunavut may be isolated in many ways, but it is far from immune to the political effects of global economic stagnation. It remains to be seen how the Inuit of Nunavut will respond over time if the territory and government they voted for in the division plebiscite of 1993 turns out to be little more than a politically correct form of neoliberalism, with the fiscally constrained elected leaders of the day spending their time chasing P3 funding to build desperately needed water/sewage treatment, waste management, public housing, facilities for the aged, etc. rather than designing and implementing interventions to improve the educational and health outcomes of their young and rapidly growing population.

It also remains to be seen if the many promises made to Indigenous peoples by the Liberal party during the 2015 federal election campaign result in increased investment by the federal government to address the deficits in physical and social infrastructure which characterize so many Indigenous communities in Canada – including Nunavut.

NOTES

1 Meaning that, as in the provinces, both Inuit and non-Inuit can run for elected office and vote in elections. Nunavut is therefore *not* a form of Inuit self-government, although the great majority of the members of the Legislative Assembly are Inuit.

2 The Inuktitut term for "residents of Nunavut" – both Inuit and non-Inuit.

3 For a detailed account of the creation of Nunavut see Hicks and White (2015).

4 Tootoo won the election and was appointed minister of fisheries and oceans but resigned from Cabinet and from the Liberal caucus after just a few months in office (Fife 2016).

5 John Todd, a wily businessman from Rankin Inlet, was president of the Liberal Party's Northwest Territories riding association and minister of finance in the GNWT. For most of the 1990s he was arguably the most influential politician in the NWT. An editorial in *Nunatsiaq News* upon his departure from territorial politics in 1998 called him "one of Nunavut's great builders" (Bell 1998). He was also a faithful Liberal who dutifully implemented Martin's cuts in the NWT.

6 The NIC was the federal government commission created under the *Nunavut Act* to advise Canada, the GNWT and NTI on the design and implementation of a Nunavut government.

7 The GN itself has no debt, but does use a modest amount of debt to finance the operation of three territorial corporations responsible for power, housing, and business development corporations.

8 "But there's not enough cash for the government to do it all on its own, so the practical question is to have it or not to have it," said David Connelly, president of the NWT Chamber of Commerce (quoted in Wilkin 1998).

9 "It's another pork-barrel," said Union of Northern Workers president Jackie Simpson. "But this trough is deeper and wider than any that has been conceived before. P3 is nothing more than the wholesale transfer

of our public assets – our public legacy – into private hands" (quoted in Bourgeois 1998).

10 Simailak was another prominent Liberal from the Kivalliq region and was also the head of an Evaz-driven "birthright corporation." He later resigned from Cabinet for conflict of interest regarding his business interests (Bell 2008).

11 A master plan for the Iqaluit International Airport was prepared in 1999, and a revised plan in 2009.

12 A recent example of this approach can be found in Parkinson et al. 2016, which found that "The risk of suicide increased in Scotland for those born between 1960 and 1980, especially for men living in the most deprived areas, which resulted in a rise in age-standardised rates for suicide among young adults during the 1990s. This is consistent with the hypothesis that exposure to neoliberal politics created a delayed negative health impact."

13 Obtained by the author through an Access to Information request.

REFERENCES

Aarluk Consulting. 2015. *Final Report on the Evaluation of the Nunavut Suicide Prevention Strategy and Action Plan.* Aarluk Consulting Inc., June. http://www.scribd.com/doc/281185450/NSPS-Evaluation-FINAL-Report-June-2015.

Amagoalik, John. 1993. "Benefits of Nunavut Outweigh the Costs: Creating Self-Government in the Arctic Territory Will Accomplish What 12 Years of Constitutional Negotiations Failed to Do." *The Globe and Mail*, 15 February.

Bell, Jim. 1998. "Nunavut Will Miss John Todd." *Nunatsiaq News*, 25 June. http://www.nunatsiaqonline.ca/archives/nunavut980630/editorial.html.

– 2001. "Health Department Launches Anti-suicide Campaign: Nunavut Health Minister Ed Picco This Week Unveiled a Multi-media Suicide Prevention Campaign Aimed at Helping Nunavummiut Help Each Other." *Nunatsiaq News*, 23 February. http://www.nunatsiaqonline.ca/archives/nunavut010228/nvt10223_06.html.

– 2007. "A Made-in-Nunavut Failure." *Nunatsiaq News*, 19 January. http://www.nunatsiaqonline.ca/archives/2007/701/70126/opinion Editorial/editorial.html.

– 2008. "Simailak Facing $5,000 Fine for Ethical Breaches: Sleaze Probe Turns Up Numerous Contraventions." *Nunatsiaq News,* 19 September. http://www.nunatsiaqonline.ca/archives/2008/809/80919/news/nunavut/80919_1533.html.

– 2009. "Blunt Report Recommends Sweeping Changes to GN: 'The Expectations Most People Had of Nunavut Have Not Yet Been Met.'" *Nunatsiaq News*, 1 October. http://www.nunatsiaqonline.ca/stories/article/961_blunt_report_recommends_sweeping_changes_to_gn/.
– 2012. "Nunavut Study Reveals Widespread Mental Distress, Suicidal Thoughts, Childhood Sexual Abuse." *Nunatsiaq News*, 2 October. http://www.nunatsiaqonline.ca/stories/article/65674nunavut_study_reveals_widespread_mental_distress_suicidal_thoughts/.
– 2013. "Suicide in Nunavut: Child Abuse, Pot Smoking, Mental Disorders the Biggest Factors." *Nunatsiaq News*, 6 June. http://www.nunatsiaqonline.ca/stories/article/65674suicide_in_nunavut_child_abuse_pot_smoking_mental_disorders_the_bigges/.
– 2014. "A Bad Idea: 'It's Not in the Public Interest to Use Scarce Funds That Would Otherwise Go to Public Governments.'" *Nunatsiaq News*, 20 August. http://www.nunatsiaqonline.ca/stories/article/65674a_bad_idea/.
– 2015. "Nunavut Needs a New Social Contract: 'Those at the Top Are Doing Better and Those at the Bottom Are Doing Worse.'" *Nunatsiaq News*, 9 January. http://www.nunatsiaqonline.ca/stories/article/65674nunavut_needs_a_new_social_contract/.
– 2017. "Nunavut Inuit Orgs Team Up to Denounce Protected Areas." *Nunatsiaq News*, 21 February. http://www.nunatsiaqonline.ca/stories/article/65674nunavut_inuit_orgs_team_up_to_denounce_protected_areas/.
Bernauer, Warren. 2012. "The Uranium Controversy in Baker Lake." *Canadian Dimension* 46 (1). https://canadiandimension.com/articles/view/the-uranium-controversy-in-baker-lake.
– 2014. "A Call to the South from Baffin Island: Mobilizing against Offshore Extraction." *Briarpatch Magazine*, 1 September. https://briarpatchmagazine.com/articles/view/a-call-to-the-south-from-baffin-island1.
– 2015. "The Nunavut Land Claims Agreement and Caribou Habitat Management." *Canadian Journal of Native Studies* 35 (1): 5–32. https://www.questia.com/library/journal/1P3-3911633181/the-nunavut-land-claims-agreement-and-caribou-habitat.
– 2016. "Clyde River Report: Trudeau's Promises Unravel in Legal Battle over Indigenous Rights." *Canadian Dimension* 50 (4): 32–5. https://canadiandimension.com/articles/view/trudeaus-promises-unravel-in-legal-battle-over-indigenous-rights.
Bobet, Ellen. 2009. "Towards the Development of a Nunavut Suicide Prevention Strategy: A Summary Report on the 2009 Community

Consultations." Report prepared for the Working Group for a Nunavut Suicide Prevention Strategy. http://www.tunngavik.com/wp-content/uploads/2010/04/towards-the-development-of-a-nunavut-suicide-prevention-strategy-eng.pdf.

Bourgeois, Annette. 1998. "Todd Unveils Business–Government Partnership Policy: The GNWT Says the Only Way to Build Most Capital Projects in the Future Will Be through Creative Partnerships between Government and Business." *Nunatsiaq News*, 16 January. http://www.nunatsiaqonline.ca/stories/article/todd_unveils_business-government_partnership_policy/.

CBC News. 2015. "Day by Day at Nunavut's Suicide Inquest." 20 September. http://www.cbc.ca/news/canada/north/day-by-day-at-nunavut-s-suicide-inquest-1.3235940.

Chachamovich, Eduardo, Jack Haggarty, Margaret Cargo, Jack Hicks, Laurence J. Kirmayer, and Gustavo Turecki. 2013. "A Psychological Autopsy Study of Suicide among Inuit in Nunavut: Methodological and Ethical Considerations, Feasibility and Acceptability." *International Journal of Circumpolar Health* 72 (1). https://www.ncbi.nlm.nih.gov/pubmed/23539438.

Chachamovich, Eduardo, Jack Haggarty, Margaret Cargo, Rod McCormick, Laurence J. Kirmayer, and Gustavo Turecki. 2015. "Suicide among Inuit: Results from a Large, Epidemiologically Representative Follow-Back Study in Nunavut." *Canadian Journal of Psychiatry* 60 (6): 268–75. http://www.ncbi.nlm.nih.gov/pmc/articles/PMC4501584/.

Coates, Ken S., and Judith Powell. 1989. *The Modern North People, Politics and the Rejection of Colonialism*. Toronto: James Lorimer.

Conference Board of Canada. 2016. *Economic Outlook for the Territories in 2015 Is Encouraging*. Ottawa: Conference Board of Canada. http://www.conferenceboard.ca/press/newsrelease/14-12-16/economic_outlook_for_the_territories_in_2015_is_encouraging.aspx.

Dolphin, Myles. 2013. "Town Stands against Coal Company: Public Consultation Meeting Follows Letter of Opposition." *Northern News Services*, 22 July.

Dube, Shanta R., Robert F. Anda, Vincent J. Felitti, Daniel P. Chapman, David F. Williamson, and Wayne H. Giles. 2001. "Childhood Abuse, Household Dysfunction, and the Risk of Attempted Suicide throughout the File Span: Findings from the Adverse Childhood Experience Study." *Journal of the American Medical Association* 286 (24): 3089–96. http://www.facmed.unam.mx/cainm/publicaciones/biblio/2/2.pdf.

Ducharme, Steve. 2016. "Nunavut MLAS Vote $4.5M for Suicide Prevention." *Nunatsiaq News*, 9 June. http://www.nunatsiaqonline.ca/stories/article/65674nunavut_mlas_vote_4.5m_for_suicide_prevention/.

Egeland, Grace, Angela Pacey, Zirong Cao, and Isaac Sobol. 2010 "Food Insecurity among Inuit Preschoolers: Nunavut Inuit Child Health Survey, 2007–2008." *Canadian Medical Association Journal* 182 (3): 243–8. http://www.cmaj.ca/content/182/3/243.full?sid=46dabcaa-a7ef-40ac-859c-ec1200522470.

Eggertson, Laura. 2015. "Nunavut Suicide Inquest: The Tragedy of an 11-Year-Old's Death." *Canadian Medical Association Journal* 187 (15): 1118. http://www.cmaj.ca/content/187/15/1118.full?sid=65cd2556-f93d-423c-b6fd-eeb6867a29b2.

Fife, Robert. 2016. "Hunter Tootoo's Messy Love Triangle Helped Spur Resignation from Cabinet." *The Globe and Mail*, 12 September. http://www.theglobeandmail.com/news/politics/hunter-tootoos-messy-love-triangle-helped-spur-resignation-from-cabinet/article31822441/.

George, Jane. 2009. "The BIPAR Is Back, Kitikmeot Leader Says." *Nunatsiaq News*, 29 October. http://www.nunatsiaqonline.ca/stories/article/729_the_bipar_is_back_kitikmeot_leader_says/.

– 2010. "Charlie Lyall: Drugs and Booze Destroy Inuit Job Training Efforts at Doris North Gold Mine: Thirty-Six of 40 Nunavut Trainees Fail Drug Test." *Nunatsiaq News*, 4 October. http://www.nunatsiaqonline.ca/stories/article/98789_charlie_lyall_drugs_and_booze_destroy_inuit_/.

– 2012. "Ottawa to Give Nunavut up to $77.3 Million for $300-Million P3 Airport at Iqaluit." *Nunatsiaq News*, 12 September. http://www.nunatsiaqonline.ca/stories/article/65674feds_give_77.3_towards_300_million_iqaluit_airport_p3_project/.

Hicks, Jack. 2009. "Toward More Effective, Evidence-Based Suicide Prevention in Nunavut." In *Northern Exposure: Peoples, Powers and Prospects in Canada's North*, edited by Frances Abele, Thomas J. Courchene, F. Leslie Seidle, and France St-Hilaire, 467–95. Montreal: Institute for Research on Public Policy.

– 2015. "Statistical Data on Death by Suicide by Nunavut Inuit, 1920 to 2014." Report prepared for Nunavut Tunngavik Inc. http://www.tunngavik.com/blog/2015/09/15/pdf-statistical-data-on-death-by-suicide-by-nunavut-inuit-1920-to-2014/.

Hicks, Jack, and Graham White. 2015. *Made in Nunavut: An Experiment in Decentralized Government*. Vancouver: UBC Press.

Impact Economics. 2013. *2013 Nunavut Economic Outlook – Nunavut's Next Challenge: Turning Growth into Prosperity.* Prepared for the Nunavut Economic Forum. http://neds2.ca/wp-content/uploads/2014/10/2013_Nunavut_Economic_FINAL_Jan_28_2014.pdf.

Makki, Fouad. 2015."Reframing Development Theory: The Significance of the Idea of Uneven and Combined Development." *Theory and Society* 44 (5): 471–97. http://link.springer.com/article/10.1007/s11186-015-9252-9.

Matsubayashia, Tetsuya, and Michiko Ueda. 2011. "The Effect of National Suicide Prevention Programs on Suicide Rates in 21 OECD Nations." *Social Science & Medicine* 73 (9): 1395–1400. https://doi.org/10.1016/j.socscimed.2011.08.022.

McCormack, Geoffrey, and Thom Workman. 2015. *The Servant State: Overseeing Capital Accumulation in Canada.* Halifax: Fernwood Publishing.

Nunatsiaq News. 2010a. "Nunavut Housing Trust Fiasco: Everything That Could Go Wrong Did Go Wrong, Review Finds." 8 October. http://www.nunatsiaqonline.ca/stories/article/89789_nunavut_housing_fiasco_everything_that_could_go_wrong_did_go_wrong/.

– 2010b. "Nunavut Judge Grants Temporary Injunction against Seismic Testing." 8 August. http://www.nunatsiaqonline.ca/stories/article/98789_nunavut_judge_grants_temporary_injunction_against_seismic_testing.

– 2015a. "Nunavut Liberal Candidate Praises Port, Dumps on Aglukkaq." 31 July. http://www.nunatsiaqonline.ca/stories/article/65674nunavut_liberal_candidate_praises_port_dumps_on_aglukkaq/.

– "Nunavut Premier Declares Suicide a 'Crisis,' Names Minister to File." 23 October. http://www.nunatsiaqonline.ca/stories/article/65674 nunavut_premier_declares_suicide_crisis_names_minister_to_file/.

– 2015c. "Nunavut Review Board Says No to Kiggavik Uranium Mine: Absence of Definite Start Date Raises Too Many Ecosystemic, Socio-economic Questions, NIRB Says." 8 May. http://www.nunatsiaqonline.ca/stories/article/65674breaking_nunavut_review_board_says_no_to_kiggavik_uranium_mine.

– 2015d. "Poor Health Associated with Mental Distress among Inuit: StatsCan." 18 November. http://www.nunatsiaqonline.ca/stories/article/65674poor_health_unmet_health_care_needs_top_causes_of_mental_distress_amon/.

– 2016. "Nunavut Government, Inuit Org Go to Bat for Rejected Mine Project." 1 September. http://www.nunatsiaqonline.ca/stories/

article/65674nunavut_government_inuit_org_go_to_bat_for_rejected_mine_project/.

Nunavummiut Makitagunarningit. 2015. "Nunavummiut Makitagunarningit Responds to Review Board's Rejection of AREVA's Kiggavik Proposal." Media release, 12 May. https://makitanunavut.wordpress.com/.

Nunavut. Department of Economic Development and Transportation. 2012. "RFQ Issued for Iqaluit International Airport Improvement Project." Iqaluit: Government of Nunavut, 29 June. http://www.gov.nu.ca/edt/news/rfq-issued-iqaluit-international-airport-improvement-project.

– 2013. "Iqaluit International Airport Improvement Project Moves Forward with Selection of Preferred Proponent." Iqaluit: Government of Nunavut, 3 July. http://www.gov.nu.ca/edt/news/iqaluit-international-airport-improvement-project-moves-forward-selection-preferred.

Nunavut. Department of Executive and Intergovernmental Affairs. 2012. *Building Our Infrastructure*. Iqaluit: Government of Nunavut. http://gov.nu.ca/eia/documents/nunavut-infrastructure. Accessed 12 November 2016.

– n.d. *Devolution*. Iqaluit: Government of Nunavut. http://www.gov.nu.ca/eia/information/devolution. Accessed 10 November 2016.

Nunavut. Department of Family Services. 2016. *Reducing Dependence. Supporting Communities. Report in the Review and Reform of Income Assistance and Economic Development*. Iqaluit: Government of Nunavut, June. http://gov.nu.ca/sites/default/files/iareport2016en.pdf.

Nunavut. Government of Nunavut. 2013. "Public–Private Partnership Policy." Iqaluit: Government of Nunavut, 8 April. http://gov.nu.ca/sites/default/files/files/Public-private%20Partnership%20Policy.pdf.

– 2014 January. *Iqaluit International Airport Improvement Project – Project Report*. Iqaluit: Government of Nunavut, January. http://gov.nu.ca/sites/default/files/iqaluit_international_airport_improvement_project_report.pdf.

Nunavut, Government of, Nunavut Tunngavik Inc., Royal Canadian Mounted Police, and Embrace Life Council. 2010. *Nunavut Suicide Prevention Strategy*. http://www.tunngavik.com/files/2010/10/2010-10-26-nunavut-suicide-prevention-strategy-english1.pdf.

– 2011. *Nunavut Suicide Prevention Strategy Action Plan: September 1, 2011 – March 31, 2014*. http://www.tunngavik.com/files/2011/09/nsps-action-plan-eng4.pdf.

– 2011. *Inuusivut Anninaqtuq Action Plan 2017–2022*. http://inuusiq.com/wp-content/uploads/2017/06/Inuusivut_Anninaqtuq_English.pdf.

Nunavut Housing Corporation. 2016. *The Blueprint for Action on Housing Implementation Plan for the GN Long-Term Comprehensive Housing and Homelessness Strategy.* http://assembly.nu.ca/sites/default/files/TD%20187-4(3)%20EN%20Blueprint%20for%20Action%20on%20Housing.pdf.

Nunavut. Legislative Assembly. *Hansard.* http://assembly.nu.ca/hansard.

Parkinson, Jane, et al. 2016. "Recent Cohort Effects in Suicide in Scotland: A Legacy of the 1980s?" *Journal of Epidemiology and Community Health* 71 (2): 194–200. http://jech.bmj.com/content/71/2/194.

Perroud, Nader. 2016. "Childhood Maltreatment." In *Understanding Suicide: From Diagnosis to Personalized Treatment*, edited by Philippe Courtet, 361–70. Springer International Publishing.

PPP Canada. n.d. "Iqaluit International Airport Improvement Project (Iqaluit, NU)." http://www.p3canada.ca/en/about-p3s/project-map/iqaluit-international-airport-improvement-project/. Accessed 12 November 2016.

Rennie, Steve. 2015. "Nunavut Premier Seeks Devolution Pact, Eyes Control over Land, Resources." *The Globe and Mail*, 3 February. http://www.theglobeandmail.com/news/national/nunavut-premier-seeks-devolution-pact-eyes-control-over-land-resources/article22777248/.

Roberts, Michael. 2016. *The Long Depression.* Chicago: Haymarket Books.

Rodrigue, Michaela. 2000. "MLAs Atack Government over Decentralization." *Nunatsiaq News*, 21 January. http://www.nunatsiaqonline.ca/stories/article/mlas_attack_government_over_decentralization/.

Rogers, Sarah. 2015. "Nunavut Review Board Decision on Uranium Mine 'Not What We Expected,' Areva Says." *Nunatsiaq News*, 11 May. http://www.nunatsiaqonline.ca/stories/article/65674nirb_decision_on_uranium_mine_not_what_we_expected_areva/.

Rohner, Thomas. 2016. "Welcome to the Taj Mahal of Nunavut Airports." *Nunatsiaq News*, 17 August. http://www.nunatsiaqonline.ca/stories/article/65674a_peek_at_iqaluits_fancy_new_300-million_airport/.

Simpson, Jeffrey. 1993. "Paying for Native Self-government: If Nunavut's the Model, It's a Big Tab." *Globe and Mail*, 4 February.

Skura, Elyse. 2015. "Nunavut Suicide Inquest: Mother of 11-Year-Old Boy Testifies." *CBC News*, 15 September. http://www.cbc.ca/news/canada/north/nunavut-suicide-inquest-day1-1.3228326.

Sopinsky, John. 2012. "Mary River: The Most Ambitious Mining Project in the Arctic." *The Globe and Mail*, 3 December. http://www.theglobeandmail.com/report-on-business/industry-news/energy-and-resources/

mary-river-the-most-ambitious-mining-project-in-the-arctic/article5939723/.

Taptuna, Peter. 2014. "Economic Development in Nunavut." *Resources Quarterly*, 13 June. http://www.resourcesquarterly.com/economic-development-in-nunavut/.

Thompson, John. 2007. "Two Suicides Gloomy Start to New Year: No Sign from GN on Promise for Prevention Strategy." *Nunatsiaq News*, 17 January. http://www.nunatsiaqonline.ca/archives/2007/701/70119/news/nunavut/70119_03.html.

Varga, Peter. 2014. "Future Oil Royalties Could Pay for Infrastructure, Nunavut Premier Says." *Nunatsiaq News*, 2 December. http://www.nunatsiaqonline.ca/stories/article/65674future_oil_royalties_could_pay_for_infrastructure_nunavut_premier_says.

van Rassel, Jason. 1996. "Todd Angrily Denies He's Attacking Nunavut." *Nunatsiaq News*, 26 April. http://www.nunatsiaqonline.ca/archives/back-issues/week/60426.html#3.

Westcott, David, Sharon Freitag, Sergio P. Barrero, and Luis Barreto. 1987. "Review of Mortality Due to Suicide in the N.W.T. 1975 to 1986." Report prepared by staff of the GNWT Department of Health and Social Services, and tabled in the Legislative Assembly 13 February 1989.

White, Patrick. 2011. "The Trials of Nunavut: Lament for an Arctic Nation." *The Globe and Mail*, 1 April. http://www.theglobeandmail.com/news/national/nunavut/the-trials-of-nunavut-lament-for-an-arctic-nation/article547265/.

Wilkin, Dwayne. 1998. "More Public–Private Partnerships Coming: Business Leaders Look Forward to New Opportunities Building and Leasing Back Government Building Projects." *Nunatsiaq News*, 30 January. http://www.nunatsiaqonline.ca/stories/article/more_public-private_partnerships_coming/.

Windeyer, Chris. 2011. "Nunavut Unwraps Anti-suicide Action Plan: 'An Urgent Crisis That Cannot Continue.'" *Nunatsiaq News*, 12 September. http://www.nunatsiaqonline.ca/stories/article/65674nunavut_unwraps_long-awaited_anti-suicide_action_plan/.

Wood, Ellen Meiksins. 2006. "Logics of Power: A Conversation with David Harvey." *Historical Materialism* 14 (4): 9–34.

World Health Organization. 2014. *Preventing Suicide: A Global Imperative*. http://www.who.int/mental_health/suicide-prevention/world_report_2014/en/.

CHAPTER TWELVE

Fiscally Conservative Governance without Austerity: Devolution, Aboriginal Self-Government, and the Northwest Territories

KEN COATES AND GREG POELZER

Canada's Northern territories present a fiscal and governance paradox within the Canadian political system. Although constituting nearly 40% of Canada's geographical expanse, Canada's Northern territories do not have the same constitutional status as the ten provinces and retain a fiduciary relationship with the federal government, a dynamic that is very distinct from their provincial counterparts. At the same time, all three territories have made significant strides over the past four decades to becoming province-like political units through devolution, with Yukon the most fully devolved, Nunavut the least, and the Northwest Territories (NWT) in between. Moreover, Aboriginal people and politics matter more than anywhere else in Canada, as Aboriginal people constitute 20% of the population in Yukon, 50% in the Northwest Territories, and 85% in Nunavut. In all three territories movements toward Indigenous self-determination have introduced transformative political dynamics and have led to complex governance arrangements that have few parallels south of sixty.

Historically best understood as Canada's colonies, the geographically large, resource rich, and sparsely populated Yukon, Nunavut, and Northwest Territories continue to rely heavily on the Government of Canada. In fact, they are heavily subsidized province-like governments, reliant on large-scale, dependable fiscal transfers that have, for the past three decades, protected the territories from many of the vicissitudes of the resource-dependent economy of the Far North and have enabled the emergence of globally innovative, political institutions. The language of neoliberalism that has been so pronounced across Canada in recent decades (see Evans and Fanelli's introduction to this volume) found voice in the Yukon Party government in Yukon (see Sabin in this volume). This was primarily expressed through a strongly pro-development strategy and struggles around consultation with Indigenous peoples, but it did not figure prominently in the Northwest Territories or Nunavut where the greatest emphasis was on devolution and the incorporation of Indigenous priorities into government.

Drawing on the case of the Northwest Territories, this chapter argues that the politics of austerity that figured in many provinces did not play out in parallel ways in the Territories. Simply put, the Northwest Territories did not experience comparable fiscal pressures nor implement austerity measures like those undertaken in provincial jurisdictions. Devolution in the forms of quests for greater regional autonomy and Aboriginal self-determination, as well as the federal government's response to these demands, is central to understanding fiscal relations, service delivery, and employment in the territorial North. There were, as will be seen, small changes in user fees, shifts in taxation systems, a general maintenance of the public sector, and limited government programmatic changes. The Government of the Northwest Territories, despite being heavily reliant on federal government subsidies and still in the process of securing control of their resources, followed a fiscally conservative path, eschewing major stimulus programs, rejecting a major expansion in territorial services, and maintaining small territorial surpluses throughout the national recession. This fiscally prudent approach and the unique demographic situation of the Northwest Territories reflect broader polity-building projects: regionally, the construction of an increasingly autonomous and more self-reliant territorial government; locally, the realization of self-governing First Nations. Both of these projects involved the development of new institutions of multi-level governance and intergovernmental relations. The proponents of these polity-building projects succeeded in establishing two significant policy instruments to help strengthen political autonomy and, in the long term, to buffer territorial and Aboriginal government from future economic downturns. The first instrument is the creation of a sovereign wealth fund called the NWT Heritage Fund (Northwest Territories Department of Finance 2010). The second is resource-revenue sharing, between the federal government and territorial government on one hand, and between Aboriginal governments and federal or territorial governments on the other hand.

Even as territorial and Aboriginal governments increase their own source revenue, it is unlikely that future federal governments will significantly reduce their levels of fiscal support, at least for the foreseeable future. Climate change, global demand for natural resources, and broader security issues have all garnered increasing international attention to the Arctic region. Ironically, the relative (compared to most jurisdictions in the Circumpolar North) underdevelopment of basic transportation and communications infrastructure in much of the Canadian North, along with scarce environmental surveillance and management resources and limited social, health, and educational capacity fosters a sense of insecurity on Canada's hold in the Arctic region. Among other reasons, this latter phenomenon is likely to strengthen the federal government's continued support for high levels of fiscal transfers rather than weaken it. Thus, contrary to some narratives that view devolution as part of a broader austerity agenda of a neoliberal federal government, where fiscal reductions are offloaded onto the territorial this chapter views devolution as a process driven by territorial residents and Aboriginal communities seeking greater control over their own lives. The combination of Northern polity building and the federal government's fiduciary responsibility help explain the paradox of Northern Canada in an era of austerity.

POLITICAL TRANSITIONS THE NORTHWEST TERRITORIES

The Northwest Territories, along with its territorial neighbours, have experienced dramatic political transitions in recent decades. Before 1967 and the relocation of the territorial capital from Ottawa to Yellowknife, the Northwest Territories was operated as a colony of Canada. The Government of Canada had a minimal presence in the NWT providing rudimentary health care and social services, maintaining a police presence but little in the way of a northern military establishment. The federal government ramped up its expenditures after the Second World War, part of a national social-welfare initiative designed to address the poverty and isolation of Aboriginal Peoples, including widespread suffering among the Inuit in eastern Arctic and northern Quebec. There was a small military presence, primarily by accepting a network of American Distant Early Warning Line radar stations across the Arctic. On the social front, the federal government was active throughout the postwar era, including relocating some Inuit to the high Arctic islands, expanding residential schools in the region, requiring Aboriginal people to move into government-built communities in areas selected for administrative convenience, supporting corporate investments in resource developments through Roads to Resources and other programs, and adding to the Northwest Territories' limited regional and community infrastructure.

As late as the 1970s, the NWT did not have a fully elected government; federal officials maintained control over territorial finances. In 1975, responding to growing pressure from northern residents for greater engagement, the federal government set up the first fully elected, fifteen-member Territorial Council, later renamed the Legislative Assembly. Shortly after, the territorial government became involved in major land claims issues (including the division of the Northwest Territories itself and the groundbreaking Inuvialuit claim in 1984), established new financial relationships with the Government of Canada, supported Aboriginal self-government accords, started an extensive process of devolving federal powers to the territorial administration, and gaining control of land and natural resources in 2014. The transition was, in retrospect, fast and effective, as the NWT changed from a federally controlled jurisdiction to a self-governing territory in little more than a generation. The key devolution step involving land and resources occurred in the aftermath of the recession of 2008–10 at a time of steadily improving economic prospects. The territory continued its effort to rebound from the closure of the NWT's most important mine at Pine Point in 1988, pinning its hopes on the development of a high-profile diamond industry and promising opportunities in the oil and gas sector.

Devolution was a contentious issue in the NWT. It involved the transfer of federal government responsibilities to the Government of the Northwest Territories. The process took several decades, lagging behind the process under way in the Yukon but moving more quickly than in Nunavut (see Hicks in this volume). Territorial residents worried that the transfer of authority over non-renewable resources, a key and symbolic step in this undertaking, would result in job losses, declining federal attention to the North, and potentially higher taxes and reduced government services. Gabrielle Slowey (2015, 348), assessing the progress of devolution, argued that "devolution means that the Government of Canada's embedded neoliberalism is simply being reproduced at the local level. As a result, devolution only transforms the GNWT into another colonizing government." The suggestion that devolution simply imported neoliberal models and approaches into the territory understates the degree to which residents of the territory valued political autonomy and administrative independence from the Government of Canada and intended to use incremental political power to adjust governance and economic systems to address regional aspirations. Where Slowey was right is the GNWT's fiscal prudence and concern about adding to the existing regional dependence on the federal government. Stephanie Irlbacher-Fox and Stephen Mills (2007) viewed the process differently, seeing it as a sign of the political maturity of the Northwest Territories and emphasizing the importance of securing control over land and resources to underwrite regional autonomy.

The territorial administration did not adopt Canadian political and administrative norms, working instead to ensure that territorial governance reflected the jurisdiction's cultural diversity. The NWT legislature eschewed party politics and standard premier–cabinet government. In this system, members of the territorial legislature are elected to represent communities/regions and are not bound by party loyalties. The speaker, premier, and cabinet ministers are selected by elected members after the territory-wide vote. Those not selected for cabinet, referred to as Regular Members, serve as an unofficial opposition. The consensus-style government is extremely responsive to local and community influences, limits the influence of political ideology, and eliminates partisan politics. Overall, the NWT system operates under the strengths and limitations of the "politics of smallness," where personalities matter a great deal and where the electorate remains strongly connected to the routine affairs of government. In general, the NWT political arrangements ensure that elected officials have an appreciation of community-level economic and social transitions and are not constrained in speaking in defence of constituency interests in a manner that is not commonplace in systems governed by political parties.

FISCAL RELATIONSHIPS WITH THE GOVERNMENT OF CANADA

The financial cornerstone of the Northwest Territories' governance system is its fiscal relationship with the Government of Canada (an

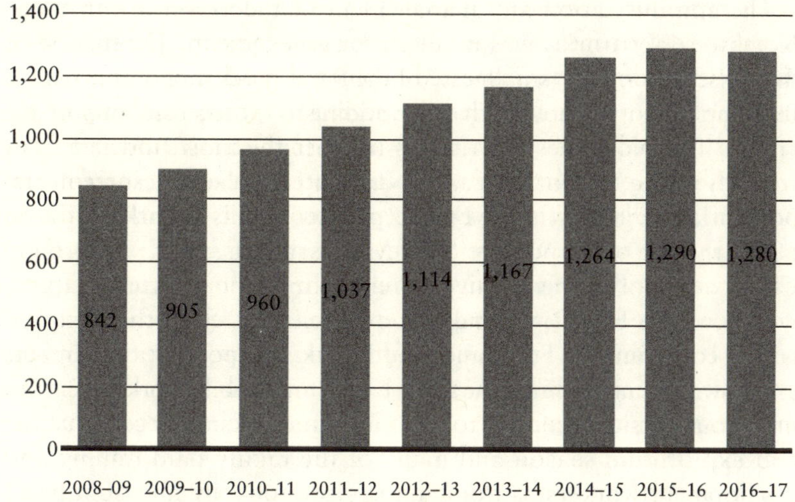

Figure 12.1 Total federal support to NWT by fiscal year, millions of dollars

arrangement that has shifted due to the territorial government assuming control over natural resources and lands). Under Territorial Formula Financing (TFF) arrangements, the Government of Canada provides substantial annual allocations to the Government of the Northwest Territories to cover standard provincial governments operations, from health care and education to economic development and community infrastructure. The GNWT also receives specific funding from the Canada Health Transfer and the Canada Social Transfer, but these are comparatively small contributions. In 2006–07, for example, the health arrangements brought $23 million to the territory while another $9 million came by way of the social transfer. The TFF, in contrast, delivered $789 million to the GNWT. The total federal transfers to the territory amounted to over $18,000 per person, well under Nunavut ($28,500), more than the Yukon ($17,000), and much more than the national per capita allocations to provincial governments ($1,300). In 2006–07, of course, the federal government received all royalty revenue from Northwest Territories developments, funding that in the provincial south stayed with the regional government. For 2017–18, by way of comparison, the health transfers to the GNWT jumped to $45 million. The social transfer reached $17 million. The total TFF exceeds $1,232 million.

The administration and management of the Government of the Northwest Territories was influenced, as well, by the population of the jurisdiction. The "smallness" of the NWT is a demographic reality. Put simply, people know each other, adding to the intensity of political affairs. The Northwest Territories (neither the most northerly, nor westerly of the Yukon, NWT, and Nunavut) has the largest territorial population, with just over 44,000 people. This is slightly less than 6% of the size of the population of Mississauga, a suburb of Toronto. Close to half of the people live in Yellowknife, the territorial capital, with 3,700 in Hay River and 3,000 people in each of the next two largest communities, Fort Smith and Inuvik. The population numbers are, however, misleading. The NWT has a very mobile workforce, with numerous outsiders coming to the North for the summer construction and exploration season and many of the highly paid mining and development workers working in the North on a fly-in/fly-out basis. The major projects, including the diamond mines and the oil and gas developments near Norman Wells, rely heavily on the movement of workers in and out of the North. Importantly, increasing the regional population and limiting the reliance on the recruitment and use of transient resource workers has not always been a territorial priority, with the government sometimes emphasizing the need to improve the quality of life for Aboriginal residents rather than having to cope with the challenges of rapid but cyclical resource-based population change.

The Northwest Territories remains unique among the three territories in the balance between the Indigenous and non-Indigenous population and the diversity of the Aboriginal communities in the jurisdiction. The territory, with half the population (over 21,000 in total) being Aboriginal, includes significant numbers of Inuit (20% of all the Aboriginal people), Metis (17%), and First Nations people (61%). The Yukon, in contrast, is almost 80% non-Aboriginal while Nunavut is close to 85% Inuit. In the Northwest Territories, the non-Indigenous population is centred in the three largest communities. They also dominate the resource camps, while the smaller communities remain predominantly Aboriginal.

Between 2007, the year before the latest financial crisis, and 2014, the northern economy experienced dramatic gyrations tied to the uncertainties and fluctuations of global resource markets. In the first part of the twenty-first century, the prospects for the NWT's resource sector looked promising. The long-debated Mackenzie Gas Project, although still subject to environmental assessment and approval,

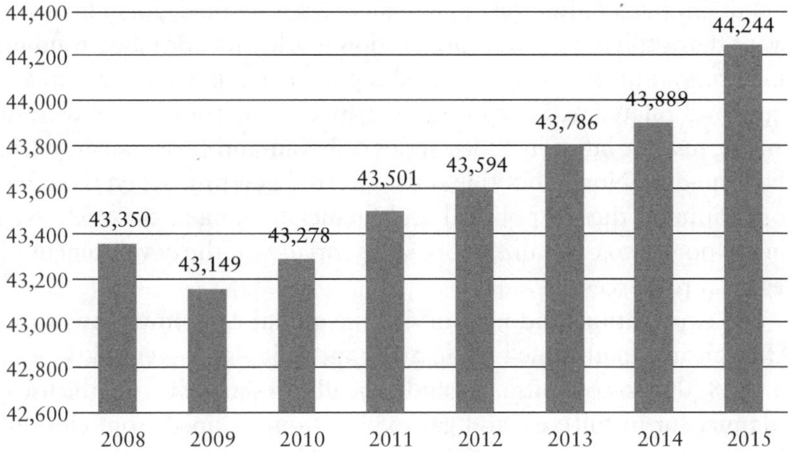

Figure 12.2 NWT territorial population estimates

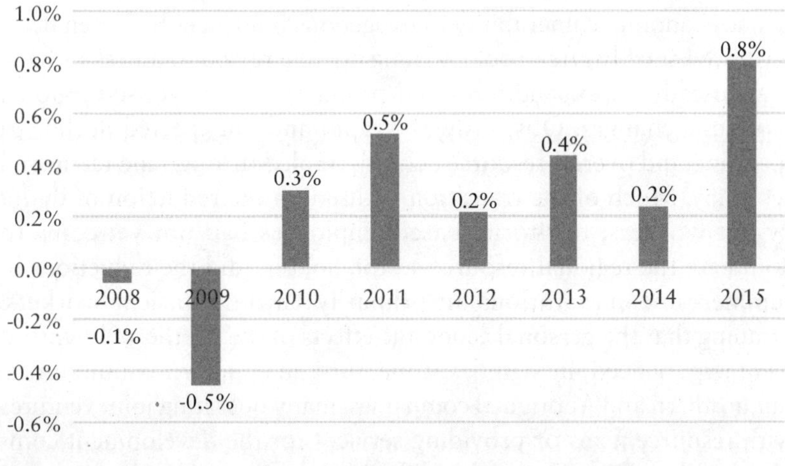

Figure 12.3 NWT territorial population estimate percentage change

seemed on track for development, with the important difference that Aboriginal people stood to own 30% of the project. The high-profile diamond mines continued to lead the territorial economy, but oil and gas development in the Sahtu district and the Mackenzie River delta loomed on the horizon. Continuing mineral exploration throughout the territory held additional promise for economic expansion. The economy, however, suffered from a dramatic decline in exploration and development after the 2008 fiscal crisis, a seminal global financial event that stalled industrial production worldwide, dried up funding for exploration, and resulted in a sharp reduction in resource employment and related activity in the Northwest Territories. This was, of course, just the latest in a long series of boom-and-bust transitions in the Canadian North, but this shift occurred at a time when the territory thought, due to political and financial changes, the NWT was finally poised to capitalize more substantially on the development of regional resources.

The expectations did not survive the global economic downturn. After hitting an all-time high in 2005 and enjoying a secondary peak in 2008 (due to commitments and expenditures made before the fiscal calamity hit in full), oil and gas exploration dropped from close to $400 million in 2008 to slightly more than $100 million in 2012. Mineral exploration followed a similar trajectory, surging to over $190 million in 2007 before collapsing to a meagre $44 million in 2009 (by far the lowest in the twenty-first century).

The economic vulnerability to exogenous influences had been demonstrated starkly after 2008. Mining and energy companies cut back dramatically on expenditures and production in response to global economic changes. Obviously, the rapid and unexpected decline in spending and overall resource activity rippled through the territorial economy. Much of the transition focused on the reduction of fly-in/fly-out workers; territorial-based employees had not yet come to dominate the regional resource sector. So, too, did the reductions in summer-time explorations hit primarily on the transient workers, meaning that the personal economic effects of the northern downturn were experienced, in significant measure, in southern communities. But northern and Aboriginal companies, many operating joint ventures with resource firms or providing services for the development companies, likewise suffered through sharp declines in private-sector production and exploration activities.

Even in the midst of the global recession, the Northwest Territories appeared to be an unusually promising jurisdiction, belying any need for emergency austerity measures. As one observer wrote of this time,

> In light of a decision in late 2010 by the National Energy Board to approve the development of the Mackenzie Valley Pipeline (and subsequent approval by Cabinet), it now appears that the project will go ahead, assuming that the companies backing it

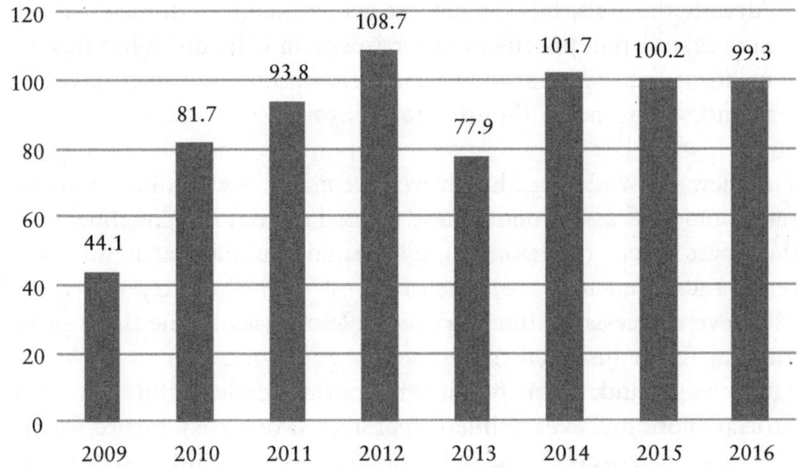

Figure 12.4 NWT mineral exploration and deposit appraisal expenditures, millions of dollars

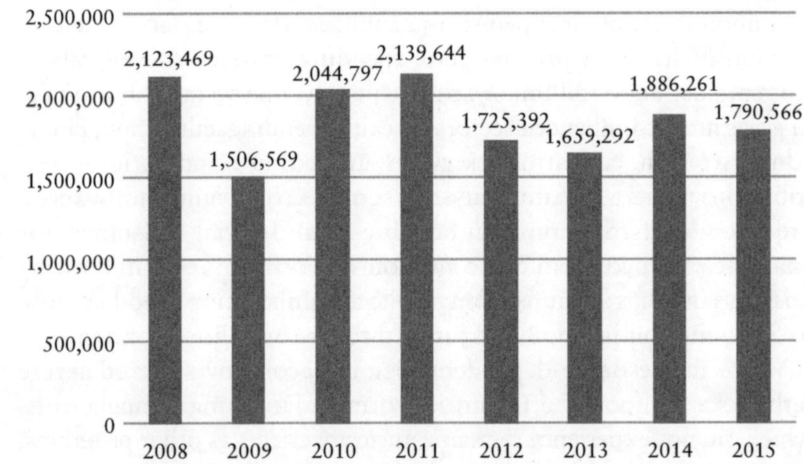

Figure 12.5 NWT mineral production, dollar value

proceed with development. Consequently, the economic prospects for the GNWT are strong. The NWT's geological resources are vast and include an array of minerals, including gold and diamonds, as well as hydrocarbon potential in oil and natural gas.

> Already the NWT has the highest per capita gross domestic product (GDP) of all provinces or territories in Canada. What this means is the NWT has the potential to become the first "have" territory in Canada. (Slowey 2015, 357–9)

This view was widely held; however, events did not unfold as forecast. Environmental assessment delays slowed the natural gas pipeline to the point where the sponsoring firms concluded that it was non-economical. But in 2010, when the rest of the country was mired in a severe recession, the Northwest Territories seemed somewhat immune to the financial crisis.

On the ground, it was possible to see the steady decline of the territorial economy, even while forecasters saw a rosy future for the territory. The effects of the global financial crisis could be seen across the Northwest Territories' resource economy. The territorial GDP peaked at $4.5 billion in 2007 but dropped dramatically to $3.6 billion by 2009 and to $3.5 billion in 2011 (before rebounding to close to $3.6 billion in 2013). Diamond mining, which reached over $1 billion in 2007, dropped to $521 million by 2012. Construction, previously driven by private-sector spending, cratered as well, falling from almost $400 million in 2007 to just over $180 million in 2011. In government-influenced sectors – health spending, education, public administration, educational services, and cultural industries – contributions to GDP remained at or, in some sectors, significantly above pre-2008 levels. Spending on health care and social assistance, for example, jumped from $220 million in 2007 to $238 million by 2013. GDP contributions from public administration stood at close to $500 million in 2008 and jumped to $540 million by 2013.

While the resource-dependent regional economy suffered severe setbacks after 2008, the Territorial Formula Financing arrangements, which did not experience the same austerity effects as other programs, provided a crucial buffer for the Government of the Northwest Territories after 2008. Federal funding stood at $880 million in 2007–08 jumped to over $960 million by 2010–11. Growth continued thereafter, increasing to $1,114 million in 2012–13 and $1,264 million by 2014–15. While the increased allocations to the Government of the Northwest Territories were not substantial – Ontario (see Evans and Fanelli in this volume) experienced comparable growth due to its slide from "have" to "have-not" fiscal status and Alberta's (see Brownsey in this volume) allocations grew substantially as a result

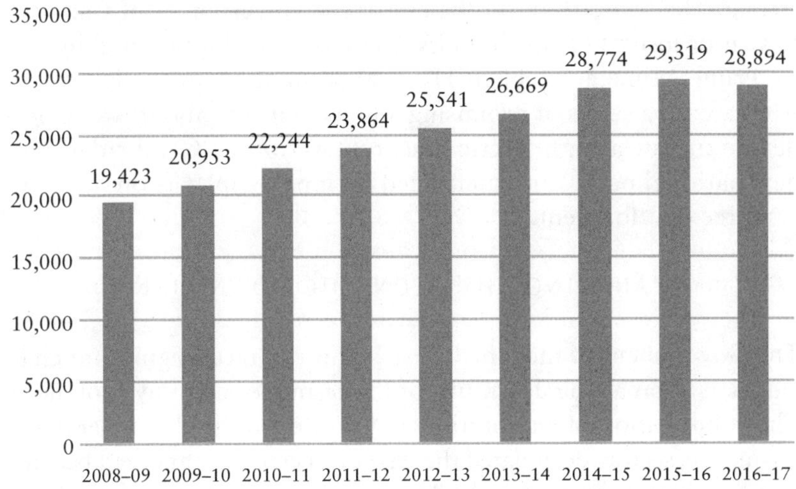

Figure 12.6 NWT per capita allocation, dollars

of population growth – the territory continued to receive significant sums from the Government of Canada.

While direct transfers to the Government of the Northwest Territories remained stable throughout the national recession, direct federal spending on territorial projects suffered due to austerity. Major commitments, such as the government's plan to expand Arctic research capabilities in the Far North, were reduced or delayed as the national government wrestled with economic struggles across the country. A series of high-profile promises, from an Arctic port to major defence commitments (primarily in Nunavut), were slowed or postponed until more fiscally auspicious times (Coates et al. 2008).

Clearly, the Northwest Territories (along with the other two territories) was not singled out for intense fiscal austerity. Given the comparatively small size of the federal commitment to the North, the economic vulnerability of the area, and the important governance developments under way in the region, the Government of Canada opted not to impose sweeping cuts. The sensitive negotiations with Aboriginal groups – on land claims settlements and implementation, self-government, resource development, important transitions under way through devolution of federal responsibilities, and the national government's high-profile stance on Arctic sovereignty and northern issues generally – ensured that federal financial support remained strong. This was, after all, the era of the Government of Canada's "use it or lose it!" mantra on its Arctic responsibilities, highlighted by Prime Minister Stephen Harper's annual summer visit to the Arctic, with a series of promising announcements about Arctic port development, a high Arctic research station at Cambridge Bay, new national parks, and continued national emphasis on northern resource development.

MANAGING THE ECONOMIC DOWNTURN

The Government of the Northwest Territories faced significant challenges as soon as the downturn of the resource economy took hold. The combination of exploration and production in the mineral and oil and gas sectors dominated the territorial economy and had become steadily more important in the Aboriginal communities as well. From the outset, the government focused its spending on the inevitable social assistance required to offset economic decline and a variety of pump-priming activities designed to compensate for the rapid drop off in private-sector spending. The GNWT had spent cautiously in the years immediately preceding 2008 and ensured itself of some fiscal flexibility in the years before the recession. After the recession hit, the GNWT lacked the resources – either from the Government of Canada or from major territorial resource revenues – to make substantial investments or policy changes.

What the Government of the Northwest Territories could and did do was to reposition its expenditures to employment-related activities, to accelerate planned public infrastructure investments, and to prepare the territory for the anticipated recovery of the northern resource economy. The age of national austerity did not unleash a Keynesian-type public investment initiative (although several major projects were moved forward in time) or a comprehensive social assistance reform. Instead, and in keeping with a conservative approach to fiscal management, the government maintained its focus on the financial vitality of Aboriginal communities and governments.

The GNWT managed its affairs cautiously, commencing with the 2008–09 budget and continuing as the recession took hold. Early in 2008, the government indicated potential spending cuts of up to 10% of the territorial budgets. Controversially, the government opted for a smaller $60 million budget reduction, with half of it slated for the 2008–09 fiscal year. Critics challenged the government's assumptions,

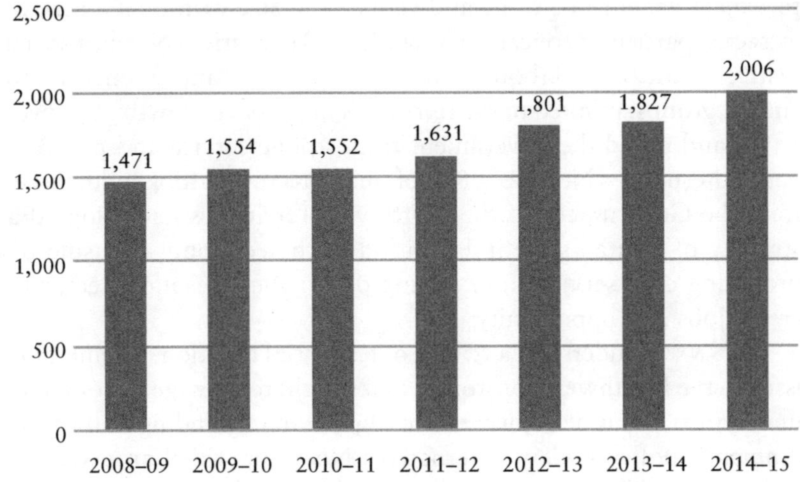

Figure 12.7 NWT territorial revenue, millions of dollars

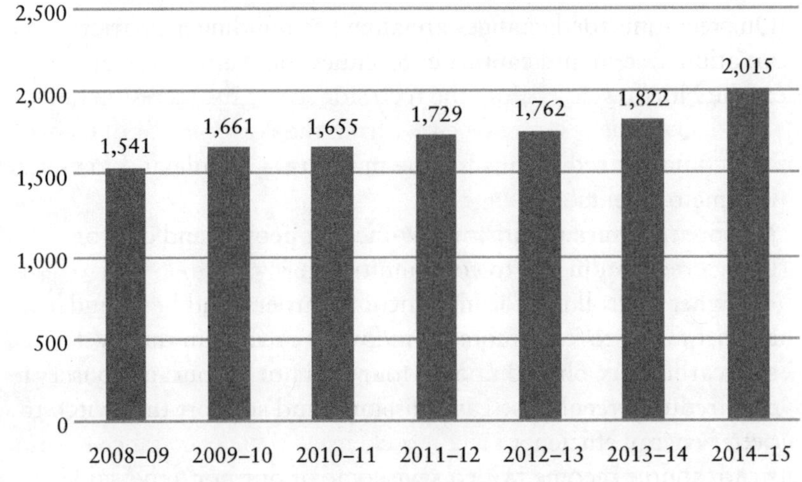

Figure 12.8 NWT territorial expenditures, millions of dollars

pointing to a pattern of under-forecasting surpluses, and urged the government to consider raising additional revenues and spending more aggressively to maintain economic activity. The critics also wondered why the government did not have a formal program review and evaluation process in place. The government's pre-recession plan to cancel vacant positions and reduce the size of the civil service attracted particular concern. The study by Alternatives North, a social justice coalition of labour union, anti-poverty, and women's and church groups, pointed to the territory's impressive growth rate (over 13%) and urged the government to postpone service and program cuts (Alternatives North 2008). Before the recession took hold, therefore, the Government of the Northwest Territories had adopted a strategy of limited state intervention in the economy, focusing on providing core services and relying on a robust resource sector to create jobs and opportunity.

The GNWT undertook a review of territorial taxation, an emerging issue in the Northwest Territories, as it sought to manage its resources under an evolving self-government regime. In responding to the government's policy review, Alternatives North provided an extensive commentary. Their proposals did not address recession-based issues, but focused instead on longer-term, structural issues within the NWT (Alternatives North and Status of Women Council c. 2009, 1):

> Our recommended changes are aimed at building a smarter taxation system and capturing revenues that should be coming to the North.
>
> • Income tax reductions for the majority – middle and low-income residents
> • More income support for low-income people, and cost of living credits adjusted to community levels
> • Higher payroll tax for high income earners, and hotel and airport taxes, to keep more fly-in/fly-out income in the NWT
> • A carbon tax phased in over four years to encourage conservation, reduce greenhouse gas emissions, and support the switch to better energy efficiency
> • A resource income tax, to save some of our non-renewable resource wealth for the future and to help develop a long-term Trust Fund
>
> A good package. Some taxes go up and some go down. A shift in taxes from individuals to big business and to those who can afford to pay. Overall, a smarter tax system.

The onset of the recession and the rapid decline in the resource economy caused immediate concern and forced the Government of the Northwest Territories to reconsider its plans. In the February 2009 budget speech, Minister of Finance Michael Miltenberger tabled a budgetary response (Miltenberger 2009, 1). As he observed,

> We are gathered here in a time of unprecedented global economic turmoil that continues to worsen daily. Our collective task in the NWT is to work together during these difficult times, to meet the many challenges and seize the opportunities as they present themselves. Last year's budget noted the storm warnings on the economic horizon and cautioned that we needed to put the GNWT on a sound fiscal footing. That storm has struck, and the NWT economy has not escaped its effects. The global economic crisis has caused everyone to review their fiscal and economic assumptions and to re-evaluate their plans. The GNWT is no different.

Miltenberger promised to make "investments in our economy, in our environment, and in our people" (ibid., 2). He resisted suggestions of tax increases, slowed the planned reduction in budget cuts, and promised to avoid a territorial deficit. The main features of the budget included substantial capital investments, particularly on highways, schools, airports, hospitals, and parks. There were sizeable commitments to new energy systems (particularly wood pellet boilers designed to capitalize on the territory's considerable forest resources). The territory contributed to federal commitments to northern housing and expanded investments in regional entrepreneurship, Aboriginal and northern skills development, and funding for major resource project acceleration. The rest of the budget included a variety of commitments to social initiatives such as elder care and support for social economy organizations. On the revenue side, the GNWT increased tobacco and liquor taxes, started a review of territorial fees, and increased property tax rates on resource projects.

Two years later, in February 2011, Miltenberger rose again in the house, this time to introduce the 2011–12 GNWT budget. He started by reinforcing the government's long-standing commitment to "live within its means," which meant the avoidance of rapid expenditure growth (Miltenberger 2011, 1). As he noted,

> The global economic upheaval required governments everywhere to take dramatic action. The GNWT was no different. Even when times were better, this government was thinking ahead and

> planning for more turbulent times. When the recession hit we had the fiscal room to respond – we implemented fiscal policies that maintained spending levels, deferred major tax increases, and injected over $865 million in infrastructure investment into the NWT economy over two years. We adopted a fiscal plan in 2009 that would see our economy through the downturn and return us to the path of fiscal sustainability. (Ibid.)

The 2011 statement identified small but significant improvements in the resource economy and the promise presented by the devolution of natural resources to the GNWT. The government continued its pattern of investing in infrastructure development, both to keep the trades and technical workforce busy in anticipation of the improvement in the resource sector, limiting debt, and moderating expenditure growth. The Minister also described a review of government programs and the search for continued efficiencies. After compiling a short-term deficit, the government forecast a small surplus for fiscal 2011–12 and drew attention to its reliance on self-financing government debt, particularly the toll bridge over the Mackenzie River (started in 2008 and completed in 2012).

The bulk of the budget was given over to small interventions in such fields as rural employment, affordable housing, educational programing, preventative health care, initiatives to address the high cost of living, environment protection, and infrastructure improvements, particularly at the community level. Maintaining a multi-year pattern, the minister spoke to the need to "improve the way we manage our resources – whether human, financial or physical, to ensure that we are getting the best value for the dollars we spend" (Miltenberger 2011, 11). The budget also allocated over $170 million (including federal spending) for infrastructure and housing projects. The government avoided tax increases but launched a consultation process with territorial residents to identify opportunities for improvements in the tax regime.

Territorial activists, led by Alternatives North, worked hard to make poverty an issue in the 2011 territorial election. They developed anti-poverty mobilization strategies and called on community members to ask local candidates to commit themselves to anti-poverty initiatives and make the attack on poverty a territorial priority. The Government of the Northwest Territories responded by conducting an anti-poverty survey of its own. The issue did not take hold in a major way and,

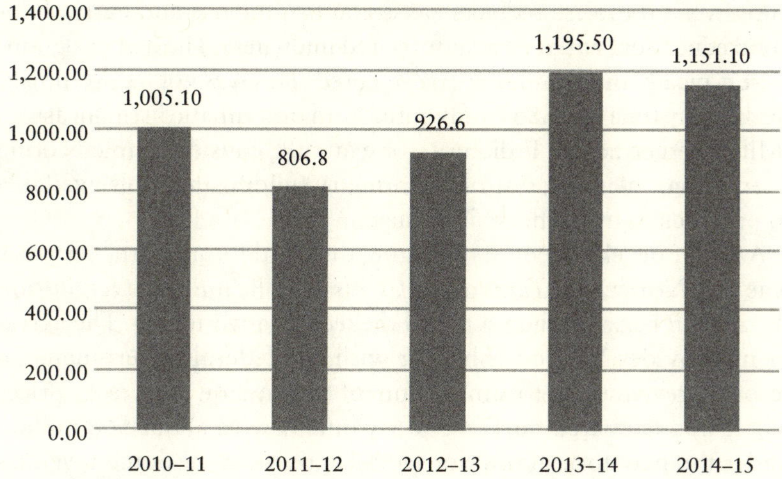

Figure 12.9 NWT capital expenditures, millions of dollars

while significant in some communities, did not attract urgent attention across the territory. Importantly, activists focused on the systemic and large-term foundations of poverty rather than tying poverty to the particular economic and social changes associated with the global recession (Alternatives North 2011a; 2011b).

By 2013, the worst effects of the recession had passed, although the Northwest Territories had not returned quickly to the economic strength of the pre-2008 period. The fiscal caution of the government and the territory came through in Minister Miltenberger's February 2013 address, where he told the legislature that citizens participating in consultations "wanted us to address immediate needs through prevention, fix current programs by doing things better or more efficiently, put more resources into infrastructure, and take full advantage of economic opportunities in an environmental sustainable way" (Miltenberger 2013, 1). The government's strategy remained much as it had been from 2007 on: limited new spending, a focus on core services, concern for administrative efficiencies, and infrastructure investments that either paid their own way or promoted economic growth. As the minister observed, "Nearly 60¢ of every dollar is budgeted for education, health care, social services, housing, policing and corrections programs" (ibid., 4). As before, the GNWT did not expand taxes and focused on economic growth. The budget supported initiatives on topics as diverse as domestic violence and early childhood education, antipoverty efforts and midwifery. The new programs were typically small and narrowly focused. This was not a government that, at any time after 2007, favoured bold or dramatic fiscal measures (Miltenberger 2013). It did not, for example, consider implementing a territorial sales tax, one of the primary fundraising tools available to provincial governments in Canada.

A major development in managing the fiscal future of the territory was the *Northwest Territories Lands and Resources Devolution Agreement* between the NWT and the federal government. The agreement provides for 50% sharing with the federal government on resource revenues up to a maximum of $76 million (before oil prices fell, it was estimated that the NWT would receive about $60 million under the new formula). Prior to the agreement, resource revenues went directly to the federal government. Importantly, the territorial government is the not only beneficiary of the new fiscal arrangement. Within the territory, the territorial government has agreed to share 25% of its amount with Aboriginal governments that have signed onto the devolution agreement.

Learning from the lessons of other resource-based economies to manage through turbulent times, preparing to manage its own share of resource revenue, and aiming to ensure stability in government resources for future generations, the territorial government pursued the idea of creating a sovereign wealth fund, along the lines of the Alaska Permanent Fund and the Alberta Heritage Savings Trust Fund (Northwest Territories Department of Finance 2010). The territorial government considered several options on how a sovereign wealth fund might be structured and what the rules might be to manage it. As we have discussed, however, the territory faced multiple pressures to use resource revenues to meet immediate needs. The Northwest Territories has enormous transportation, communications, social, educational, and health services deficits. The other pressing issue is the territorial public debt. Following the public consultation process on the initiative, however, in 2012 the government enacted legislation to establish the NWT Heritage Fund.

The legislation allows for discretion on the amount that the government can contribute in any given year, but the maximum that can be withdrawn is 5% of the principal (Wohlberg 2014). Interestingly, although the minister of finance first announced that 5% of nonrenewable resource revenues would be deposited into the Heritage

Fund to meet pressing territorial needs, the announcement was met with considerable criticism (Wohlberg 2013). Residents demonstrating forethought and fiscal prudence felt more resource revenue should be saved. Accordingly, the government revised its position and made the decision to put 25% of non-renewable resource revenues into the fund, starting 2015–16 (Wohlberg 2014). The government confirmed that the percentage contributed to the fund could grow over time as territorial needs and the public debt were successfully addressed. Very noteworthy is that the government has made the legislative commitment not to make any withdrawals on the fund for twenty years, enabling the fund with maximum compounded growth.

Nevertheless, the Government of the Northwest Territories entered and exited the great recession in much the same way: they were committed to fiscal responsibility, cautious investments, community-based programming, and support for the natural resource economy. The government tinkered with its budget rather than engaging in dramatic gestures and new initiatives. Because of the nature of the social, economic, and cultural challenges across the territories, but particularly in the smaller communities, the GNWT emphasized preventative programs, capacity building, and the provision of basic services. The government had invested substantially in infrastructure, counting on these expenditures to offset the rapid decline in private-sector investments in the resource sector. The GNWT remained confident in the future, even when coping with major global challenges to economic stability, and counted on the devolution of natural resources and lands to provide the territory with the tools it needed to rebuild the regional economy over the medium to long term. Put more directly, the Government of the Northwest Territories had neither the resources, nor the inclination to engage in programmatic or fiscal experimentation as a means to recover from the recession.

In national terms, the Government of the Northwest Territories is a small fiscal player. With its population widely scattered and with an obligation to maintain basic services for a population facing high levels of unemployment, significant social challenges, and major infrastructure needs, the government lacked the flexibility to undertake significant or transformative changes. The greatest initiative – the Deh Cho (Mackenzie River) Bridge – had been planned over many years and was launched before the recession started. The next major project, the construction of a highway to link Inuvik to Tuktoyuktuk, was a significant focus for political debate and got the Government of

Canada's attention and money, with construction launched in 2014 for a 2018 completion. The government retained its focus on fiscal prudence, in large measure because of the availability of substantial federal transfers that obviated the need to raise funds regionally for territorial programs.

The financial focus through the 2007 to 2013 period remained on program and administrative efficiency, the cautious management of public-sector staff, and the avoidance of dramatic initiatives. Tax increases (beyond the standard "sin" taxes) were discussed and, in the main, rejected. Secondary processes beyond territorial control – including land claims agreements, impact and benefit accords (community–corporate agreements to address duty to consult and accommodate requirements), and self-government arrangements – provided substantial transfers to Aboriginal and community authorities, reducing the need for the territorial government to emphasize activities in this area. The government maintained a watching brief on all of its financial and administrative activities but avoided significant or dramatic changes, in part because of the dominant role the civil service played in NWT public affairs. In his annual reports to the legislature, Minister of Finance Miltenberger commented favourably on the small-scale transitions under way in the public service and in the ongoing review of program effectiveness and service delivery.

The Northwest Territories is, after all, a government-dominated jurisdiction. In 2012, government employees, not including those working for Aboriginal governments, totalled almost 9,000 out of a total territorial population of less than 44,000 people. Of that number, close to 4,800 worked for the territorial government, another 1,250 for the Government of Canada, and some 2,200 for local government and health institutes. Among Canadian sub-national jurisdictions, only in Nunavut and the Yukon were government workers as prominent in the regional workforce as in the NWT, ensuring that politicians and senior administrators alike paid careful attention to the economic, social, and political roles of the public sector. Making major changes was challenging; cuts in employment typically came through attrition and extensive consultations were held before significant programmatic or structural changes. Government employment remained the foundation of the regional and local economies across the Northwest Territories, particularly in the smaller Aboriginal communities where government employment provided almost all of the stable, well-paid

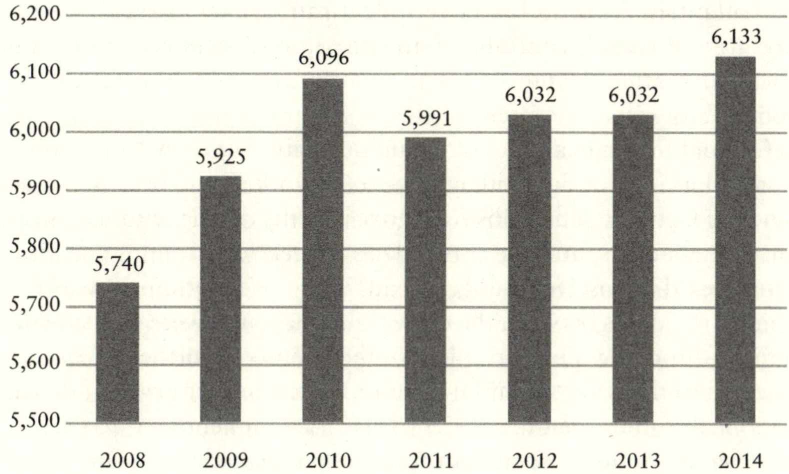

Figure 12.10 NWT public employment (survey of all employment, payrolls, and hours – all levels, annual average, in dollars)

positions in the settlements. Public-sector employment provided security and consistency in an economy that was otherwise vulnerable to fluctuations in global prices and demand. With the federal financial transfer arrangements providing an assurance of substantial annual payments not tied to the success of the territorial economy, government funding was secure and, by extension, so was government employment.

Through the austerity period, social and related programs in the Northwest Territories continued without major changes. The government arrived in 2008 with a firm commitment to "living within our means" and retained that determination throughout. The government relaxed its anti-deficit stance in the face of growing unemployment and reduced economic activity, but without launching major government-driven interventions. It was not that the GNWT was afraid to review, evaluate, and change existing programs. In fact, the government examined its expenditures on a regular basis and undertook, program by program, significant reforms. At the same time, the systemic nature of the social, cultural, and economic challenges facing the Indigenous communities in particular ensured a high level of need. The Government of Canada had obligations to address many of these needs, including Indigenous health, water quality, and policing, sometimes exercised through self-governing Aboriginal communities. As the NWT government ramped up its recession-era investments and programs, many small and localized initiatives emerged relating to housing, Aboriginal education, public health, and community infrastructure.

One of the best examples of the unique nature of GNWT operations rested in its relationship with public-sector workers and unions. Across much of Canada, deficit-obsessed governments coping with recession, austerity budgets, and the contradictory need for stimulus spending often found themselves at loggerheads with the government workers' unions. Relations between the GNWT and the union were occasionally intense – Todd Parsons, president of the Union of Northern Workers, referred to the GNWT's initial offer in 2012 contract negotiations as "an insult to our members" (*Hay River Hub*, 8 February 2012, 15). The deputy minister of human resources indicated that "Our initial proposal is conservative. We're mindful of sustaining the public service ... but we're also mindful that we've got a job to do in delivering quality programs and service within this tight fiscal environment." Parsons shot back: "That is reason for concern. [...] We don't accept that as an acceptable argument not to compensate the territorial public sector fairly" (Wilson 2012, para. 8).

By April 2012, the Union of Northern Workers and the GNWT announced a four-year agreement, with increases of 1%, 1.4%, 2.5%, and 3.3%, covering more than 4,000 employees of the GNWT and the Workers' Safety and Compensation Commission. The two sides congratulated each other on the long-term accord: "I'm happy that both teams showed such strong commitment to find solutions to the complexity of the issues. I look forward to the opportunity to rebuild our working relationship," said Parsons (Government of the Northwest Territories 2012, para. 3). "We are very pleased that an agreement has been reached," said Sheila Bassi-Kellett, deputy minister of human resources (Government of the Northwest Territories 2012, para. 4). She added, "The UNW and the GNWT have collaborated to address the interests of both parties, despite the challenges of the current fiscal environment" (Government of the Northwest Territories 2012, para. 4). A four-year deal was also signed with the teachers the same year. Averting a strike and finding a balance between union and government priorities was no small feat in the midst of the national recession, but it demonstrated the willingness of the union to compromise and the willingness of the GNWT to agree to significant salary increases (Rodan 2012).

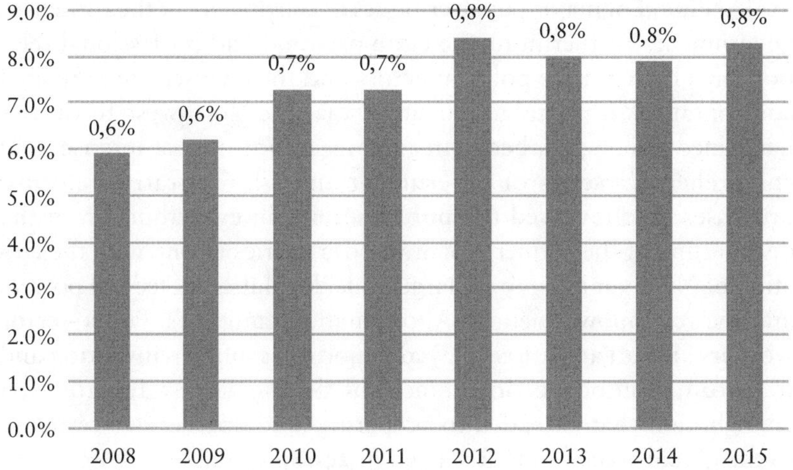

Figure 12.11 NWT unemployment rate

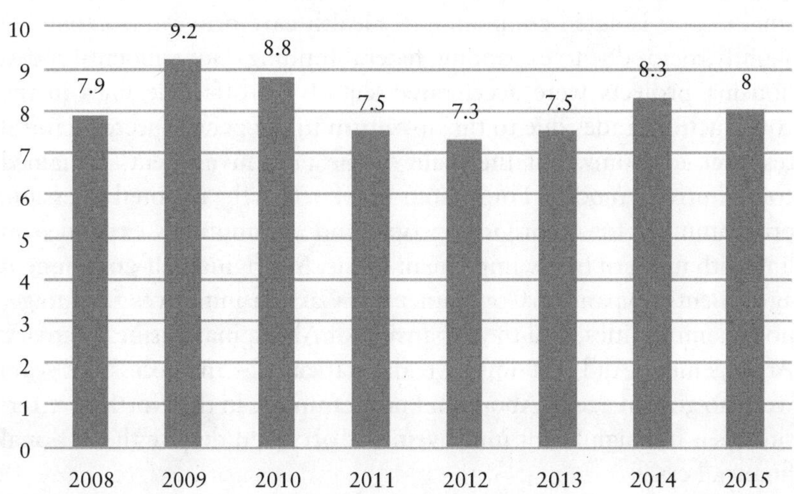

Figure 12.12 NWT not-in-labour force, thousands of people

Invariably, questions emerged about the government's approach to fighting the recession. The obvious and dramatic impact of the global crisis on the northern resource economy created a financial challenge that the territory's citizens could not legitimately lay at the feet of the GNWT. The absence of partisan politics and political parties limited the likelihood of major public critiques of the policies of the consensus government. Furthermore, the close personal and professional relationships between the political actors and the civil service mitigated confrontation. It is vital to remember that the Northwest Territories has, since the 1970s, been engaged in a continuous, intense, and comprehensive series of government and administrative reforms, processes that involved the public service in everything from the dismantling of the former Northwest Territories (along with the creation of Nunavut in 1999) to large-scale devolution of federal powers and the re-empowerment of Aboriginal communities. Public-sector workers and organizations played major roles in the reinvention and transformation of the Government of the Northwest Territories, a contribution that extended to preparing a comprehensive response to the global recession that started in 2008.

Because of the stability of federal transfers and therefore territorial revenues, the GNWT did not make major shifts in social welfare programs, many of which provided the socio-economic foundation of the smaller and isolated communities. Health care provisions expanded slightly, again due to expanding federal funding. Government-funded housing projects were accelerated slightly to offset declines in the construction trades due to the downturn in the private-sector natural resource economy, but the scale of the new investments remained comparatively modest. For reasons unrelated to the national recession, programming for Aboriginal people and communities expanded in line with modern treaty implementations, Aboriginal self-government agreements, expanded Government of Canada initiatives for Indigenous communities, and the expansion of Aboriginal business activity. Arrangements did not improve dramatically – the recession years were no golden age of Aboriginal programming in the Northwest Territories – but significant improvements occurred despite the national financial crisis.

TERRITORIAL RECOVERY FROM THE NATIONAL RECESSION

The situation in the Northwest Territories bears little resemblance to the recession-caused challenges facing provincial governments. The Territorial Formula Funding arrangement is the most generous regional financing scheme in Canada and provides an assurance of financing that is much better than that provided to provincial governments. The recession caused real hardship across the NWT, particularly through sharp reductions in resource activity. The resource sector's reliance on fly-in/fly-out workers, with large and short-term migrations of employees from southern centres and the companies' ability to cut its workforce without disrupting northern communities directly, allowed the mining and oil and gas industries to reduce operations swiftly. Government, in contrast, relied on long-term, locally based employees, making labour force adjustments more difficult and politically sensitive. The core operations of the Government of the Northwest Territories remained largely intact, not experiencing dramatic cuts or major expansions during the period of global uncertainty. The recession reinforced the GNWT's cautious nature, with the government favouring minor program reform and experimentation, careful investments, and constraints on tax increases. In the end, the GNWT worked its way carefully through the austerity years largely because of continued federal largesse, bidding time until the business cycles brought investment and activity back to the northern resource sector.

The Government of the Northwest Territories had been wedded to a fiscally conservative and cautious approach to public affairs. Through the global and national recession, and buttressed by generous and continuing subsidies from the Government of Canada, the GNWT was able to stay in a fiscal surplus despite the downturn in the territorial resource economy. While the federal and provincial governments, with a few exceptions, accepted the inevitability of deficit budgets and the need for fiscal stimulus, the GNWT was able to stay the course. Small diversions of spending into accelerated capital projects kept private-sector operations in business during the resource downturn, but there was little expansion of social programming and job-creating investments.

The Northwest Territories deviated from the national pattern during the years of the recession. Growth slowed but did not stop. Fiscal conditions became more precarious without crossing into dangerous territory. Private-sector activity declined dramatically in response to global market forces, but the reliance on fly-in/fly-out workers from "outside" limited the dislocations within the territory. With a small increase in capital investments, and without increasing territorial debt as southern jurisdictions were forced to do, the GNWT was able to moderate the economic decline and avoid a wide swing in unemployment rates. The government also did not rush to fill the employment

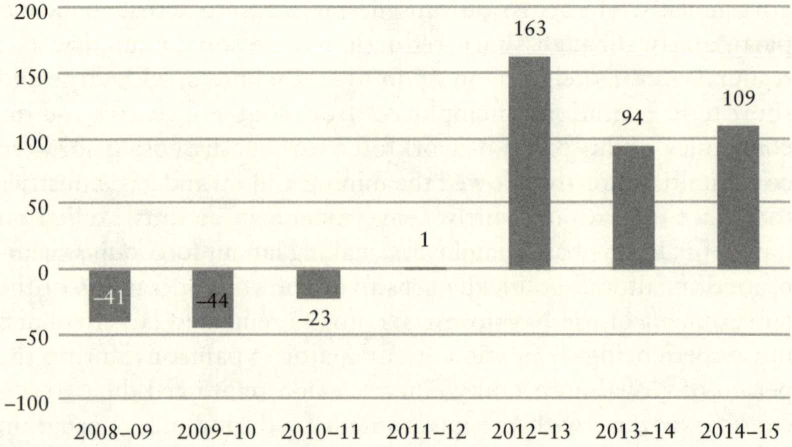

Figure 12.13 NWT territorial surplus/deficit, millions of dollars

gap by hiring additional public-sector workers and took particular care to avoid over-expenditure. The GNWT provided, in effect, fiscally conservative governance without austerity, largely because of the reliability of Government of Canada funding. The NWT had the benefit of state subsidization and was able to use that security to pursue a fiscally conservative governance system. By national standards, GNWT workers coped with extraordinary high costs of living but also enjoyed comparatively high wages, generous benefits, and a high level of public services relative to the size of the population. Government unions pressed hard for their members and secured long-term agreements with significant increases that eluded many public-sector unions in the South.

There was some debate in the Northwest Territories about different approaches, an effort led by a coalition of church and anti-poverty forces organized by Alternatives North. Critiques of government policy were more matters of scale than basic structure. Critics offered fairly standard demands for greater taxation for wealthy individuals and corporations and greater attention to environmental protection. In fact, the "real" opposition and the most concerted demands for changes in policy came through Aboriginal organizations. The Indigenous organizations in the NWT, working with territorial and federal governments on a large set of self-government and land claims agreements, were the strongest counterpoint to the NWT government. By definition, the Indigenous groups focused on community and regional priorities, seeking to draw additional resources and administrative/political autonomy to their governments.

With no official opposition in the NWT legislature – a popular artifact of the territory's consensus-style government – there was no focal political point for criticism of government policy. Political uprisings against the premier and cabinet – culminating in a 2009 non-confidence motion against Premier Roland and his Cabinet colleagues, largely over matters of information sharing and secrecy – were tied to personal rather than ideological or even programmatic reasons. The focus of the motion was on shifts to health benefits, a large loan to Discovery Air, financing for the controversial Deh Cho bridge across the Mackenzie River, and the proposed creation of regional public school and services boards (*CBC News* 2009). Premier Roland his six-member cabinet survived by a vote of ten to eight, hardly a resounding endorsement but far from a condemnation of territorial social and economic policy.

Looked at differently, the recession that started in 2008 provided the first substantial test of the newly autonomous and self-governing Government of the Northwest Territories. Although major elements – natural resources and lands – remained outstanding until 2014, devolution gave the GNWT the financial means, the political authority, and the civil service personnel necessary to exercise considerable control over its future. While the austerity years provided few examples of dramatic or transformation experimentation, this era demonstrated that the Government of the Northwest Territories was fully prepared for large-scale crisis management and for the implementation of "made-in-the-North" solutions to financial challenges that started far from the territory and demonstrated the vulnerability of the North to global economic influences.

The Northwest Territories has struggled financially in subsequent years. The oil and gas sector remained depressed and global mineral prices suppressed exploration and development activity. The diamond industry enjoyed continued prosperity, and small industries like Asian Northern Lights tourism expanded significantly. But government revenues remain depressed, contributing to both a substantial tightening of government spending, albeit with continued emphasis on pump-priming investments on infrastructure. The government of Premier Bob McLeod, selected by his colleagues in 2011, maintained a strong emphasis on budgetary restraint and the promotion of the resource sector. The budget challenges combined with demographic decline, which restricted federal transfers under Territorial Formula Financing, to create sustained political tension in the territory over government spending. In the short term, the Government of the NWT convinced most residents that careful control over spending and the avoidance of substantial debt was in the territory's best interests. As the recession in the resource sector stretched on, with ever-mounting demands for increased social and health spending across the North, political resistance to general austerity and limited investment increased, although the renewal of Premier McLeod in 2015 suggested that the established approach has retained considerable support.

The authors wish to thank Paola Chistie and the research team at the International Centre for Northern Governance and Development, particularly Joelena Leader.

REFERENCES

Alternatives North. 2008. "Government of the Northwest Territories 2008–2009 Budget Cuts: A Review." *Alternatives North*. Yellowknife. 11 June. https://anotheralt.files.wordpress.com/2016/02/2008-06-11-gnwt-budget-analysis.pdf.

– 2011a. "Alternatives North Responses to the GNWT Poverty Survey, March 2011." *Alternatives North*. Yellowknife. 13 January. https://anotheralt.files.wordpress.com/2016/02/2011-03-01-response-to-anti-poverty-survey.pdf.

– 2011b. "No Place for Poverty, Anti-Poverty, Election 2011: Poverty as an Election Tool Kit." *Alternatives North*. Yellowknife. 16 August. https://anotheralt.files.wordpress.com/2016/02/2011-08-16-anti-poverty-election-tool-kit1.pdf.

Alternatives North and Status of Women Council. c. 2009. "More Revenues, Smarter Taxes, and Better Public Services." *Alternatives North and Status of Women Council*.

CBC News. 2009. "N.W.T. Premier, Cabinet Survive Non-confidence Motion." 6 February. http://www.cbc.ca/news/canada/north/n-w-t-premier-cabinet-survive-no-confidence-motion-1.813058.

Coates, Ken S., P. Whitney Lackenbauer, William R. Morrison, and Greg Poelzer. 2008. *Arctic Front: Defending Canada in the Far North*. Toronto: Thomas Allen Publishers.

Government of the Northwest Territories. 2012. "GNWT and UNW Reach Tentative Agreement." Yellowknife: Government of the Northwest Territories, 16 April. http://beta.gov.nt.ca/newsroom/gnwt-and-unw-reach-tentative-agreement.

Irlbacher-Fox, Stephanie, and Stephen J. Mills. 2007. "Devolution and Resource Revenue Sharing in the Canadian North: Achieving Fairness across Generations." Walter and Duncan Gordon Foundation.

Miltenberger, J. Michael. 2009. *Budget Address 2009–2010, Northwest Territories*. Yellowknife: Government of the Northwest Territories, 3rd session of the 16th Legislative Assembly, 5 February. http://www.fin.gov.nt.ca/sites/default/files/2009-10%20Budget%20Address%20and%20Papers.pdf.

– 2011. *Budget Address 2011–2012, Northwest Territories*. Yellowknife: Government of the Northwest Territories, 5th session of the 16th Legislative Assembly, 3 February. http://www.fin.gov.nt.ca/sites/default/files/documents/2011-12_budget_address.pdf.

– 2013. *Budget Address 2013–2014, Northwest Territories*. Yellowknife: Government of the Northwest Territories, 4th session of the 17th Legislative Assembly, 7 February. http://www.fin.gov.nt.ca/sites/default/files/documents/2013-14-budgetaddress_001.pdf.

Northwest Territories. Department of Finance. 2010. "Today's Resources, Tomorrow's Legacy: NWT Heritage Fund Public Consultation." Yellowknife: Government of the Northwest Territories, February. http://www.fin.gov.nt.ca/sites/default/files/documents/todays_resources_tomorrows_legacy_2010.pdf.

Rodan, Galit. 2012. "Union, GNWT Avert Potential Strike." *Northern News Service*, 18 April.

Slowey, A. Gabrielle. 2015. "The Northwest Territories: A New Day?" In *Transforming Provincial Politics: The Political Economy of Canada's Provinces and Territories in the Neoliberal Age*, edited by Bryan Evans and Charles Smith, 367–83. Toronto: University of Toronto Press.

Wilson, Sarah. 2012. "Counter-Offer an 'Insult': UNW." *Northern News Service*, 3 February.

Wohlberg, Meagan. 2013. "NWT Residents Demand More Money for Heritage Fund." *The Northern Journal*, 21 October. http://norj.ca/2013/10/nwt-residents-demand-more-money-for-heritage-fund/.

– 2014. "Heritage Fund Contributions Upped to 25 Per Cent." *The Northern Journal*, 17 February. http://norj.ca/2014/02/heritage-fund-contributions-upped-to-25-per-cent/.

CHAPTER THIRTEEN

Fiscal Outlier: Yukon in an Austere Age

JERALD SABIN

With a healthy balance sheet and, until recently, a roaring economy, Yukon is a fiscal outlier in Canada. The territory is the country's second-smallest economy, after Nunavut, with a gross domestic product (GDP) of about $2.2 billion in 2015 (Yukon Bureau of Statistics 2016). Operating in a high-cost, high-wage, and low-demand environment, its economy is dominated by both the public sector and resource-extractive industries. Despite its reliance on public-sector spending, Yukon has managed to double its revenues and post only one budget deficit in the past decade. The territory has no public debt. At the same time, it has avoided the divisive politics of austerity that have marred other parts of Canada since the global financial crisis. In contrast, Yukon's political discourse has been dominated by debates over capital and service investments rather than cuts. Since 2004, Yukon's economy has grown at over double the median annual rate of the Canadian economy, with striking results.[1] In 2009, for example, Canada's GDP contracted by 3%, while Yukon's grew by 6.2%. As a result, in the midst of widespread distress over national and provincial finances, Yukon has sailed through the decade's economic turmoil almost untouched.

This chapter asks two key questions about Yukon's relatively unique position in confederation: What accounts for its economic and fiscal strength, and how has the territory avoided the politics of austerity seen elsewhere in Canada? In response to the first question, I argue that a confluence of factors explains Yukon's healthy fiscal position and its growing economy. These include strong commodity prices throughout the 2000s and reforms to the structure of territorial financing. Sound fiscal management by Yukon's territorial government may have been a factor to the extent that the territory spent within its means, although this is disputed (Busby and Robson 2014). Over the past decade, Yukon's revenues have grown by 63%, while its growth in expenditures has kept pace at 40%. Yukon has captured the benefits of its booming economy and grown its tax revenues by 95% since 2005–06 and has benefited from an astounding 73% increase in federal transfer payments over the same decade (Canada Department of Finance 2015; Yukon Department of Finance 2007; 2015).

It would be too easy, however, to argue that the absence of austerity in Yukon is just a function of its fiscal health. Indeed, the answer to my second question must be understood within the particular history of political and economic development in Yukon. While the territory is fundamentally dependent on federal transfers to build and maintain its infrastructure and services – its income from taxes still only accounts for 13% of its revenues, while federal transfers account for 71% – its political focus rests almost entirely on the development of its natural resource base.

Following almost a century of political struggle, Yukon gained control over its public lands and non-natural resources in April 2003 (Morrison 1968; Alcantara et al. 2012). The transfer coincided with the start of the 2000s commodities boom, politically intertwining economic expansion with the territory's fiscal health while masking a larger truth; while Yukon's economy may be growing, so too is its dependence on federal transfers in terms of absolute numbers and as a percentage of its revenues. This ongoing revenue growth has enabled Yukon's political class to avoid any real discussion about the sustainability of its programs, services, and capital obligations, or about its reliance on transfers from Ottawa.[2] Yukoners have had the privilege of blithely ignoring the politics of austerity because the federal government, in short, is paying the bills. Unfortunately for governments elsewhere in Canada (see, for instance, Graefe and Ouimet as well as Brownsey in this volume), this model of austerity avoidance is neither exportable, nor sustainable.

YUKON'S FISCAL FRAMEWORK

Beyond what the Government of Yukon has itself produced, almost nothing has been written analyzing Yukon's capitalist economy.[3] There are small literatures examining the operation of Indigenous traditional economies and their relationships to the larger market economy

(Coates 1988; 1991; Nadasdy 2003), the structure of Yukon's fiscal and economic governance (Alcantara 2013; Alcantara et al. 2012; Staples et al. 2013), and the fiscal and economic structure of the territories as a whole (Abele and Prince 2009; Abele et al. 2009; Feehan 2009; Gladstone et al. 2014). The latter literature tends to focus heavily on Nunavut (see Hicks in this volume) and the Northwest Territories (see Coates and Poelzer in this volume), reflecting where much of the scholarly attention has rested in the past two decades (White 2011).

While we can glean some important insights into Yukon's fiscal framework from these studies – particularly the significance of the resource sector politically, environmentally, and in the context of Indigenous claims processes – they tend to overemphasize the importance of devolution to Yukon's economy. The implications of devolution for the territory's finances has been marginal at best and costly at worst, with its greatest impact appearing in the political realm. To illustrate, Yukon reported that it only collected $405,000 in resource leases and royalties during the 2014–15 budget year, or 0.0003% of its total revenues (Yukon Department of Finance 2016). By contrast, motor vehicle licensing fees bring the territory $4.47 million or 0.4% of revenues; this in a jurisdiction with only 52,000 registered vehicles (Statistics Canada 2014). In this chapter, I hope to rebalance the ledger and argue that, while devolution may have been a political coup for the territory, it has not been an economic one. Indeed, long-term trends suggest that Yukon may become more dependent on the federal government, not less.

This is not to say that Yukon's government operates without funding pressures. Yukon has the second-smallest population of any public government in Canada, just ahead of Nunavut, with 37,343 residents spread unevenly across 482,443 thousand square kilometres. All but one of the territory's communities are connected by road, but business and living costs remain significantly higher than elsewhere in Canada (Gladstone et al. 2014). As Abele and Prince (2009, 85) argue, governments in Northern Canada face "the highest per capita costs to build infrastructure and deliver programs, a consequence of their sparse, dispersed and relatively young populations, relatively cold climates, and ... the high cost of transportation of virtually all goods." These costs are also borne by industry and residents, creating an environment that has necessitated the government to offer fulsome incentives encouraging business investment. The Government of Yukon spends more per capita than any other jurisdiction in Canada on direct incentives to the exploration and mining sectors. High costs also discourage the permanent relocation of labour to the territory (Herkes et al. 2013).

Overseeing this unique economy is Yukon's public territorial government. The territory's politics are centrist, although socially progressive, and usually led by a right-leaning government. The Yukon Party, in power from 2002 to 2016 and occupying the centre-right of the territory's political spectrum, has pursued a number of expansionary policies since it came to power. Despite the Yukon Party's conservative roots, under its leadership the territorial public sector grew in absolute terms, negotiated wages have increased, and public services expanded, including the creation of a much-heralded anti-poverty strategy. In the period under study (2007–15), the size of the public sector has grown by almost $100 million, and its percentage share of territorial GDP has fallen from 38.9% to 36.2% (Yukon Department of Economic Development 2015). The distribution of these services is uneven across the territory, although all communities have benefited from the increase in expenditures.

Yukoners have not been completely spared the effects of austerity seen elsewhere in the country (see, for example, Evans and Fanelli as well as Clancy in this volume). Spending on federal public administration in Yukon, as a share of GDP, has remained relatively flat since 2007, with significant cuts to regional offices of federal departments and Crown corporations like Parks Canada and Canada Post. The effects of these cuts were marginal in terms of public expenditures in Yukon, but in the wake of their announcement in 2011 they were, nonetheless, highly political. At the same time, federal spending on major infrastructure projects was increased significantly under *Canada's Economic Action Plan* and the *Build Canada Plan* to an announced amount of $242.91 million (Gladstone et al. 2014, 14). This funding was set to run its course by 2014, and it is unclear at the time of writing to what extent it will be replaced, though the election of a new Liberal federal government in 2015 may result in additional funding for infrastructure projects.

This governance and fiscal framework in Yukon is further complicated by the presence of constitutionally entrenched Aboriginal governments, with their own distinct relationships and funding agreements with the federal government. There are currently eleven self-governing nations in Yukon, each with its own jurisdictional responsibilities and policy priorities.[4] As these self-governments have come online, spending on Aboriginal public administration has slowly increased and now sits at about $70.5 million (Canada Department of Finance 2015). As many of these governments' multi-year financial agreements with Ottawa have expired, Aboriginal leaders have run into difficult negotiations with federal bureaucrats, including threats of funding freezes and transfer reductions. The motivations for these cuts remain unclear, although explanations range from reining in federal spending to the assertion of control over Aboriginal governments by federal officials. While more study is needed in the funding of Aboriginal self-governments to fully capture the dynamics of Aboriginal–federal funding agreements, the ongoing tussle over financing for Aboriginal governments only serves to further highlight the dependence of all northern governments on federal support.

YUKON'S CHANGING ECONOMIC LANDSCAPE

Change may on the horizon for Yukon. Falling commodity prices have led to a significant slowdown in the economy. Yukon fell into recession in 2015 with a negative growth rate of –7.9%. The mining sector has been hit particularly hard. According to the Bank of Canada's (2015) *Commodity Price Index*, the composite price of metals and minerals has declined from an all-time high of USD $787.68 in 2011 to USD $532.12 in 2015 – a decline of 32.0%. Yukon rode a wave of incredible growth in the minerals sector, as index prices rose from USD $271.58 in 2003, just as the territory received devolved control of its public lands and mineral resources. By the end of 2015, only one of Yukon's three mines was fully operational, as declining mineral prices necessitated shutdowns or the scaling back of operations.[5] In addition, according the Department of Economic Development, Yukon's last remaining operation mine in operation, Minto, temporarily closed in 2017 in response to global commodity prices, leading to an estimated 5.7% contraction in GDP. Declines in economic activity in associated sectors, such as construction, will also affect the territory's revenues and economic growth.

To address these declines, in its 2014–15 budget Yukon's government introduced its largest capital budget in history. Estimated at $293 million, the capital budget included projects as diverse as a new secondary school in Whitehorse to $85 million in new transportation construction spending. As Premier Darrell Pasloski put it in his 2014 budget address, "At a time when the private sector is facing economic challenges, this is the time for the Yukon government to step up to the plate and invest in infrastructure that will facilitate and stimulate the private sector" (Yukon Legislative Assembly 2014, Hansard, 3870). The language of government officials avoided such loaded terms as "stimulus" to describe these measures. Fortunately for the finances of Yukon, increasing its capital expenditures by over $100 million in three years is possible because of its growing revenues – driven in good measure by transfers from Ottawa – but this cannot make up for the estimated declines in the mining sector and its connected industries.

The remainder of this chapter is presented in three parts. The next section considers the structure of Yukon's economy and public finances in their historical context, including the devolution of control over natural resources and the structure of fiscal transfers from the federal government. I then take a closer look at Yukon's economy for the period 2007–15 and consider the territory's finances during this period. The final section examines the dynamics of austerity in the territory and austerity's general absence from political discourse and decision making. Here, I examine the growth of the territory's public sector and the nature of federal cuts in Yukon.

YUKON'S ECONOMY IN HISTORICAL CONTEXT

As a territory, Yukon owes its existence to gold. At the height of the Klondike Gold Rush in 1898, when the population of Yukon soared to an estimated 40,000 to 50,000 people, the Canadian government carved out an administrative jurisdiction in the far northwest of the country. Several explanations have been proposed for the creation of the territory, from the need to consolidate Canadian sovereign control over the region to streamlining local administration (Thomas 1956; Zaslow 1988). While both are plausible, each could have been accomplished through the already existing – and rather advanced – governance structures of the old North-West Territories, whose government was located in Regina. In my opinion, the most convincing explanation for Yukon's creation was put forward by C.E.S. Franks (1967): a dispute over the collection of liquor tariffs in the Yukon by the Government of the North-West Territories at Regina led the federal government to assert its control over the territory and to collect these revenues itself (the federal government was already assured any royalties from placer mining). The creation of Yukon was essentially a federal tax measure. Whatever the case, Yukon's place as a site of natural resource wealth – and potential source of revenue for the federal government – was established early in Canada's history.

In the decade following the gold rush, limited administrative control was devolved to the territory, including the creation of a legislative assembly in 1909 (Johnson 2009). As Yukon's population and economic fortunes fell in the lead up to the First World War, driven largely by poor returns on investment, control over territorial affairs reverted to the federal government. Yukon was a virtual fief of the federal government. By 1931, only about 4,000 people remained in the territory, about 2,600 of whom were settlers (Canada Bureau of Statistics 1931). The economy itself rested on four pillars: the traditional Indigenous economy and fur trade, placer mining in the Klondike, prospecting, and a small service sector to support these activities. This early period reflects the first iteration of Yukon's prevailing economic pattern as a boom–bust economy – a pattern that would repeat itself several times over the coming century. As Dacks (1981, 16) describes it, because "the North can itself sustain little economic activity – that it is a high-cost and low-demand economy – explains why the waxing and waning of the South's economic needs have created a boom-and-bust cycle in the North." This pattern has been tempered somewhat by the introduction of welfare-state institutions and growth in the public sector after the Second World War.

For private industry, Yukon's economic luck really changed during the Second World War and, later, with the onset of the Cold War. Across the North, an "initial pulse of federal infrastructure spending in the three decades after the Second World War was oriented toward developing population service centres, satisfying military needs, and supporting the resource extraction sector" (Gladstone et al. 2014, 162). These investments would serve as the basis for economic development – and government service delivery – for decades to come.

In Yukon, this took the form of transportation infrastructure. In an effort to create a secure supply chain to Alaska, the US government built the Alaska Highway. The highway had three significant effects on the territory's economic structure and lead the territory down a particular path of development. First, it opened up the territory by road to the rest of the continent. The road significantly reduced transportation costs and opened new areas of the region to mineral exploration and development. Second, the road brought upwards of 42,000 American military personnel into the territory, kicking off a services boom as an adventurous and entrepreneurial merchant class followed them into Yukon. These early service providers later formed the basis of an independent, small-business class that would be the backbone of Yukon politics throughout the rest of the century. Finally, the road reoriented the traditional economies of Indigenous peoples away from historical spatial and productive patterns and toward the highway. In combination with colonial resettlement programs, the collapse of fur prices, and residential schools, the construction of the Alaska Highway looms as one of the most disruptive forces on Indigenous society in the territory.

Like in many other parts of the Subarctic over the following decades, strong commodity prices, government incentives, and reduced transportation costs combined to produce a boom in the resource sector during the 1960s and 1970s. New mines and communities were built in places such as Clinton Creek and Faro. By 1971, Yukon's population had grown by almost 80% to 18,390. This growth was largely driven by the mineral sector, which by that time had six operating mines – three open-pit and three underground operations, producing 3.8 million tonnes of ore. The mining workforce was mostly resident, unlike today, and was numbered at about 1,900 workers, representing 23.7% of Yukon's labour force. The territory estimated that an additional 25% of employment in service and allied industries was indirectly supported by the mining sector (Yukon Office of the Commissioner 1971, 54). The federal government controlled the minerals sector, so while some benefit of this activity accrued to the territorial government through income taxes and other revenue streams, all royalties were paid to Ottawa.

The mining sector remained strong throughout the early 1970s, with the Cypress-Anvil zinc and lead mine at Faro serving as the "backbone of the Yukon economy" (Coates and Morrison 2005, 278). However, fortunes changed beginning with the high-profile closure of the Clinton Creek asbestos mine in 1977, followed closely in succession by the closure of copper mines at Whitehorse and, most devastating for the Yukon economy, Cypress-Anvil in 1981 (Coates and Morrison 2005). The period 1981–85 has been described as a depression, characterized by massive and entrenched out-migration from the territory that ultimately raised questions about the economic viability of a territory whose economy was subject to such wild fluctuations (Coates and Morrison 2005). For the remainder of the century, and into the early 2000s, the territory's economy was subject to bouts of volatility as each mine opening or closing had an outsized effect on the territory's economic growth. For example, Yukon's economy grew by 57% between 1985 and 1987 because of the reopening of the mine at Faro, while it contracted by 17% in 1993 when the same mine closed permanently (Statistics Canada 1996).

THE EVOLUTION OF FISCAL MANAGEMENT IN YUKON

Stepping into this volatile economy was Yukon's public sector, which provided a stabilizing baseline for economic expenditure. The public sector has always represented a large share of the economy, both to act as an economic anchor, but also because so little private industry exists in the territory.[6] In 1995, for example, the broader public sector made up 39% of the labour force, compared to 24% in the rest of Canada (Grenon 1997, 22). The public sector has played an outsized role in all northern economies in Canada, not only as the largest employer, but also by shaping migration and settlement patterns in the absence of industry. As such, for a resource economy, Yukon's population has become surprisingly concentrated in Whitehorse.[7] With the expansion of the welfare state in the postwar period, alongside the growth in population in the 1970s, managing the public sector was a key priority for Yukon's government.

A fulsome history of territorial fiscal management is beyond the scope of this chapter, but a few key details are pertinent here to understand the recent fiscal structure of Yukon. Prior to 1960, all financial decisions of the Yukon Territorial Government (as it was then known) were made by the Department of Northern Affairs and Natural Resources – usually in the form of a federally appointed commissioner and his staff (Johnson 2009; Yukon Office of the Commissioner 1974). Responsible government, or cabinet government, was not introduced to Yukon until 1979 (Dacks 1981).

In 1960, the *Yukon Act* was amended to introduce an Advisory Committee on Finance, which enabled three elected territorial councillors to discuss financial planning and priorities for the territory with federal bureaucrats. Increased financial oversight was devolved to the territory over the late 1960s and 1970s, until it assumed complete control in 1979. In 1985, the budgeting process for the territorial government became more predictable with the introduction of the Territorial Formula Financing Agreement, a "multi-year formula based upon actual past expenditures and eventually, past expenditures, rising public sector expenditures in the rest of Canada, and population" (Abele and Prince 2009, 86). Predictability enabled longer-term planning, increasing the financial autonomy of the territory.

Two key changes to Yukon's fiscal framework have been made in the past ten years. The first was the devolution of control over public lands and natural resources in 2003. As argued above, devolution represents more of a political success for Yukon – particularly for its settler population who saw it as an important step on the road to full autonomy from the federal government – than for its public finances. Far more significant for Yukon's bottom line has been reforms to Canada's Territorial Formula Financing agreements with the territories. I consider devolution first, before turning to a discussion of the reform of Yukon's fiscal transfer agreements with the federal government.

DEVOLUTION

Control over public lands and natural resources was devolved from the federal government to Yukon in April 2003, joining the management of oil and gas which had been devolved a decade earlier in 1993. In marking the transfer, then-premier Dennis Fentie declared that after "years of negotiation, we are finally masters in our own home" (Yukon Executive Council Office 2003). Devolution held great promise for Yukon, not least of which was the expectation of new revenue streams from natural resource exploration, permitting, and extraction royalties. As the benefits of devolution were realized, the government foresaw improved services for Yukoners. The extent of these benefits when compared to devolution's costs, however, remains unclear.

Devolution fulfilled the long-term political aspirations of Yukon's settler population who had, over the course of forty years, fought for institutional recognition, political autonomy, and control over the territory's economic future (Sabin 2014). While political recognition of the settler community was achieved relatively early in this struggle – in 1979, with the granting of responsible government – economic control was a source of continuing frustration until the late 1990s. Several factors disinclined the federal government from granting the territory these powers earlier. Most prominent among them was the contention that the territorial government had not sufficiently matured, lacking the capacity to adequately oversee its public lands. Another factor was the general reluctance on the part of federal officials to see resource revenues disappear from the federal treasury. Equally, Yukon did not want to see its federal transfers clawed back as a result of increasing resource revenues. These barriers were overcome in the final devolution agreement, which saw certain revenues exempted from federal clawbacks.

The other significant impediment was the need to settle First Nations' claims in Yukon. Indigenous peoples were reluctant to support the transfer without "assurances that the [territorial governments] would agree to resource transfers and resource revenue sharing on a basis that would be acceptable in future settlements" (McArthur 2009, 215). An important step toward removing this barrier was the signing of the 1993 *Umbrella Final Agreement* between the federal government, Yukon First Nations, and the territorial government. The agreement laid out conditions for land claim negotiations and "other substantive matters, including self-government, financial compensation, traditional land use, and resource management" (Feehan 2009, 348). This reassured Yukon First Nations about the equity of any potential devolution agreement and, in fact, some First Nations have benefited immensely from mineral resource development on their lands.[8]

Two principal revenue streams flow directly from devolution to territorial coffers: first, revenues from the staking, registration, and renewal of claims, and second, royalties from resource extraction and output. Until 2012, revenues from the oil and gas sector and all other natural resources, such as mineral and forestry industries, were handled under separate devolution agreements with the federal government. Under the 1993 *Canada Yukon Oil and Gas Accord*, Yukon could keep up to $3 million in revenues without any clawback on its annual federal transfer. Similarly, under the 2001 *Yukon Northern Affairs Program Devolution Agreement* that governed all other resources, Yukon would receive a "net fiscal benefit" with no clawbacks on the first $3 million in collected revenues (Irlbacher-Fox and Mills 2007). These exemptions were combined in 2012, increasing the total exempted revenues to $6 million.[9]

Yukon has yet to approach its exemption cap from resource activities, which were estimated to be about $3.3 million for 2014–15. Most of that comes from exploration activities. There were 244,633 active claims and leases in Yukon in 2013–14, the last year for which data was available. Income from leases and royalties amounted to an estimated $233,000 in 2014–15 and has remained relatively flat since 2005–06 when it was $209,000 (Yukon Department of Finance 2008;

2014). This amount is shockingly low for a sector that contributed 19% to the territory's GDP in 2013. One plausible explanation for the disconnect between GDP figures and territorial revenues is that Yukon does not collect royalties for mines on First Nations land, such as the Minto Mine near Pelly Crossing in central Yukon, currently Yukon's only operating large scale mine.

The more significant reason for low royalty returns, however, is that royalty rates are incredibly low. The government has set placer mining (gold) rates at 2.5% of the value of an ounce of gold. That value is set by regulation, not by the open market, at USD$15 per troy ounce, which results in a royalty payment of 37.5¢ per troy ounce. In 2013–14, approximately 58,700 troy ounces of gold were produced through placer mining, resulting in total revenues for the government of just $22,023 (Yukon Department of Finance 2014). At a market price of $1,336 – the price of gold at the end of fiscal year 2013–14 – royalties could have amounted to almost $2 million. Royalty rates are not as low for quartz mining, but with lower than expected output, returns to the government have been minuscule or nonexistent. Indeed, as both the Bellekeno and Wolverine mines had suspended operations as of January 2015, and future mine closures on the way, revenues could be even lower than expected in future budgets given the multiplier effect of mining in the territorial economy.

But what about the costs associated with devolution? Beyond the administrative costs – the budget of the Department of Energy, Mining, and Resources was $6 million in 2014–15 – are the various incentive programs designed to encourage investment in the resources sector. These include such programs as the Strategic Industries Development Fund to support growth in key industries with awards of up to $500,000. The Yukon Mining Incentives Program, designed to promote exploration and prospecting, had a $770,000 budget in 2013. There are also gas tax exemptions for authorized off-road commercial vehicles, as well as exemptions on royalties for mines during their first year of production. No total estimate exists for the government expenditures on these incentives, but they far outweigh current or projected revenues from natural resources.

Despite these costs, Yukon has benefited politically from devolution. It has enabled Yukoners to make decisions about the pace of development, the type and tenor of corporate incentives, and how to invest resource revenues. Devolution affirmed the economic autonomy of settler Yukoners and offered a frame for almost all political debate in the territory over the past decade. Indigenous–settler relations, environmental protection, taxes, post-secondary education, housing, and poverty have all been framed as issues that are exacerbated by or beneficial to the resources industry. It is clear, however, that these devolution-framed discussions have masked more fundamental conversations about the long-term prospects of Yukon's economy during the period under study.

Devolution has not always been politically positive for the government. Following the 2014–15 budget release – which did not use the term "stimulus" to describe its historic capital expenditures – the government focused its comments on growing expenditures, rather than acknowledging its rapidly changing economic environment. In her response to the budget, NDP opposition leader Liz Hanson stated that "the Premier has said the government is focused on growing the economy, but with the growth rate for last year down at one percent" – it has since been revised to −7.9% – "the government is clearly not succeeding. One of the reasons for this is they have failed to take any serious measures to diversify the economy" (Yukon Legislative Assembly 2014, 3921). Even in the opposition's remarks, the focus was on spending priorities rather than shifting economic fundamentals. Hanson continued, "with significant and steadily rising amounts coming to the territory from Ottawa from the federal government since devolution, the Yukon should, on all indices, be in an enviable position relative to other provinces and territories. With no public debt or deficit, the Yukon has the opportunity to do what many provinces across the country can only dream of" (ibid.).

The boosterish position of Yukon's government toward mineral development has also added to the political distraction, as conflict with Yukon First Nations over development in the Peel Watershed has resulted in protracted and costly litigation.[10] In 2011, for example, the Peel Watershed Planning Commission, working independently on behalf of the Yukon Government and four First Nation governments, released its final recommendations on the development of natural resources in the Peel Watershed region of Northern Yukon.[11] The region – about 67,000 square kilometres in size – is one of the last intact ecosystems remaining in North America, but sits on top of mineral reserves whose estimated worth is hundreds of billions of dollars (Royal Bank of Canada 2014).

While the Planning Commission recommended protecting 80% of the region from mining, the Yukon government decided in January

2014 to only set aside 29% of the land as protected areas. In reaction, First Nations and environmental groups have filed a lawsuit with the Yukon Supreme Court over what Thomas R. Berger (*Northbeat* 2013) has called a "complete rewrite" of the Commission's plan – an alleged breach of the *Umbrella Final Agreement*. Ed Champion, Chief of the Na-Cha Nyak Dun First Nation, argues that the government's position "does not recognize all of the work that has gone into negotiating these final agreements and the last twenty years of implementing them, meaning that the Yukon Government with this unilateral decision has undermined that whole process. So, First Nations cannot ignore this, because it means that our final agreements may not be worth the paper they're written on if we allow the Yukon Government to go down this road" (CBC *North* 2013). The Yukon Government, in its decision to ignore the Commission's recommendations, has continued to signal its general orientation toward international investment and mining activity in Yukon (Dixon 2013). As such, environmental groups and First Nations argue that settler institutions have privileged the global commodities market over treaty obligations. Demonstrating the Yukon government's commitment to the devolution frame, Premier Pasloski summed up his position in January 2015 the following way: "When it comes to public land, it should be the publicly, democratically elected government that should be able to have the final say" (CBC *North* 2015). Regardless of the material and political cost, devolution is Yukon's sacred cow.

TERRITORIAL FORMULA FINANCING

If Yukon's economic fundamentals are teetering like elsewhere in Canada, and the government has failed to acknowledge this fundamental shift, then what is enabling the territory's revenues to continue growing? In short, rapid growth in federal transfers to the territory since the 2007–08 federal budget have enabled Yukon's revenue growth, primarily located with the Territorial Formula Financing (TFF) component of federal transfers in a program similar to the provincial equalization program. While the Canada Health Transfer has grown by 33% over the past decade, the Canada Social Transfer has remained relatively constant (see table 13.1). The TFF, by contrast, has grown by 43%, from $501 million in 2005–06 to $874 in 2015–16. According to government of Canada figures, the TFF made up 59% of Yukon's budget in 2006–07; in 2015–16 it stands at 67%.

Table 13.1
Major federal transfers to Yukon, dollars

	Total federal support[1]	*Territorial Formula Financing (TFF)*	*Percentage growth in TFF (%)*	*Canada Health Transfer*	*Canada Social Transfer*
2005–06	533,000,000	501,000,000		22,000,000	10,000,000
2006–07	549,000,000	517,000,000	3.0	22,000,000	10,000,000
2007–08	576,000,000	544,000,000	5.0	23,000,000	9,000,000
2008–09	598,000,000	564,000,000	3.5	23,000,000	10,000,000
2009–10	649,000,000	612,000,000	7.8	26,000,000	11,000,000
2010–11	690,000,000	653,000,000	6.3	26,000,000	11,000,000
2011–12	744,000,000	705,000,000	7.5	27,000,000	12,000,000
2012–13	809,000,000	767,000,000	8.0	29,000,000	12,000,000
2013–14	861,000,000	817,000,000	6.1	32,000,000	13,000,000
2014–15	898,000,000	851,000,000	4.0	33,000,000	13,000,000
2015–16	923,000,000	874,000,000	2.6	35,000,000	14,000,000
2016–17	947,000,000	895,000,000	2.3	38,000,000	14,000,000

Note:
1 Equal to Territorial Formula Financing, Canada Health Transfer, and Canada Social Transfer.
Source: Department of Finance Canada 2015.

By 2015–16, all three federal transfers combined represented 70.8% of Yukon's budget.

Changes in the 2007–08 federal budget have resulted in this growth in revenues. The TFF is an annual unconditional transfer from the federal government, much like equalization, that is determined by formula and enshrined in statute. The unconditionality is important, according to Abele and Prince (2009, 89), as it maximizes "the territorial governments's potential to initiate policy dialogue and make policy choices important to local residents and communities." The transfer is based on the difference between Yukon's gross expenditure base and its revenues (with certain exemptions such as those found in the devolution agreement). To encourage economic development, and presumably to lessen each territory's dependence on the TFF, the federal government also included "incentives for the territories to increase their own revenues and development their economies by excluding 30% of territories' measured revenue capacity from the calculation" (Canada Department of Finance 2015). While commodity prices are out of the hands of Yukon's government, the growth in territorial reliance on federal transfers remains very much, if uncomfortably, within the territory's control.

As the TFF has grown, so too have Yukon's expenditures. This growth has not resulted in budget deficits, however, as the government has kept spending in line with expanding revenues. The accuracy with which Yukon has estimated these expenditures has been recently questioned. A recent C.D. Howe Institute report demonstrates that Yukon, along with Nunavut, present the least accurate budgets in the federation when comparing their estimated versus actual revenues and expenditures (Busby and Robson 2014). Concerns over spending have also been raised by Canada's Auditor General and local media, and ongoing audit information of capital projects is difficult to obtain (Winter 2013). While devolution has become the political focus of territorial politics, it is the TFF and other federal transfers that are enabling territorial spending. The economic boom of the 2000s and expectations of a return to these conditions, along with growing federally sourced monies, have discouraged a political of austerity at the territorial level.

YUKON'S ECONOMY 2007–15

Yukon has seen considerable population and economic growth over the past decade. Since 2007, the population of Yukon has grown by about 5,500 people or by 15.1%. Much of this growth has been through in-migration, although the territory's Indigenous population also continues to grow at rates surpassing the general population. Yukon has the lowest proportion of Indigenous residents in the territories at 20.9%, most of whom live in Yukon's small dispersed communities. Meanwhile, Yukon's large settler population is largely concentrated in Whitehorse, where 76% of the population lives (Yukon Bureau of Statistics 2014).

Significantly, for our purposes, is the rate of growth in the economy. Table 13.2 presents general economic indicators for the territory, including population, annual GDP growth, and the rate of unemployment. Over the past decade, Yukon's economy has grown by 34.4%, and consistently faster than the national economy. While this is an impressive rate, the small size of Yukon's economy lends itself to large swings in positive or negative GDP growth. The construction and

Table 13.2
General economic indicators

	Population	*Yukon GDP (% increase)*	*Canada GDP (% increase)*	*Yukon unemployment rate*
2006	32,678	5.5	2.6	4.6
2007	32,171	5.6	2.1	4.8
2008	33,225	9.7	1.0	5.0
2009	34,108	6.2	-3.0	6.9
2010	34,836	4.3	3.1	7.2
2011	35,203	4.9	3.1	5.3
2012	35,883	4.0	1.7	7.0
2013	36,626	1.5	2.2	5.8
2014	36,701	0.6	2.5	4.2
2015	37,343	-7.9	1.1	6.1

Source: Yukon Bureau of Statistics 2016, 2017; Statistics Canada 2016b.

opening of a single mine, for example, can bump GDP considerably, as seen in the period 2007–09 when the Minto Mine was being constructed. Yukon's unemployment rate spiked in 2009, but territorial economists believe this reflects the economic downturn elsewhere in Canada rather than reflecting an underlying weakness in the territorial economy (Yukon Bureau of Statistics 2010). More recent economic indicators suggest a difficult road ahead for Yukon, as commodity prices remain depressed. In 2015, GDP declined 7.9%, while the annualized unemployment rate rose to 6.1%.

Delving deeper into Yukon's GDP, we see that the economy surpassed the $2 billion mark in 2009–10. While the rest of the country was experiencing a recession, Yukon's economy continued to expand, due largely to the strength of both the mineral and construction sectors. Table 13.3 presents Yukon GDP figures for select sectors. Since 2007, Yukon's public sector has seen both an increase in terms of dollar expenditures – from $668.8 million in 2007 to $789 million in 2015, an increase of 18% – and an overall decline in its share of territorial GDP. The sector represented 38.5% of GDP in 2007 but fell to 36.2% by 2015. This decline reflects growth in both the natural resources and construction sectors. The falling share of the natural resources sector between 2009 and 2011 reflects declines in the oil

Table 13.3
Yukon GDP and select industries, millions of chained (2007) dollars

	Gross domestic product	*Public sector*[1] *(% of GDP)*	*Mining, quarrying, and oil and gas extraction (% of GDP)*	*Construction (% of GDP)*
2007	1,737.0	668.8 (38.5)	119.1 (6.9)	173.8 (10.0)
2008	1,905.0	685.0 (36.0)	256.5 (13.5)	151.4 (7.9)
2009	2,203.6	721.6 (35.7)	331.2 (16.4)	171.8 (8.5)
2010	2,111.6	734.0 (34.8)	329.2 (15.6)	218.2 (10.3)
2011	2,214.8	748.2 (33.8)	330.21 (14.9)	249.0 (11.2)
2012	2,302.9	757.7 (32.9)	517.1 (22.5)	169.6 (11.7)
2013	2,283.5	768.1 (33.6)	489.7 (21.4)	167.3 (7.3)
2014	2,264.3	779.4 (34.4)	437.1 (19.3)	173.1 (7.6)
2015	2,177.3	789.4 (36.2)	248.9 (11.4)	181.9 (8.3)

Note
1 Represents a composite of Public Administration, Educational Services, and Health Care and Social Assistance industry indicators.
Sources: Yukon Bureau of Statistics 2016; Statistics Canada 2016.

and gas sector in particular (an amount that now rests at $0). At the same time, construction grew from 8.5% to 11.2% of the economy as the Wolverine and Bellekeno mines were built.

The sharp fall in construction after 2011 reflects the absence of large scale construction projects in the territory, hence the emphasis in capital expenditures in Yukon's 2014–15 budget. Construction appears to be a leading indicator in Yukon of future output in the natural resources sector. While that sector's output remained relatively stable between 2012 and 2015, this is likely to decline starting in 2016. With both the Bellekeno and Wolverine mines no longer actively producing, and the Minto Mine set to temporarily close in 2017, GDP is likely to continue its decline.

Yukon's fiscal position reflects both its expanding economy and federal transfers. Since the 2007–08 budget year, the territory's revenues have grown 52.2%, along with its expenditures by 52.2%. Yukon saw its first billion-dollar budget in 2009–10, but also its first budget deficit in almost a decade. While the deficit was a modest

Table 13.4
Yukon budget, thousands of dollars

	Total revenue	*Total expenditures*	*Budget surplus (deficit)*	*Net surplus*	*Accumulated surplus*
2007–08	854,449	829,346	34,555	165,084	577,209
2008–09	882,174	890,075	1,368	135,544	547,247
2009–10	934,973	1,006,617	(25,675)	67,467	521,572
2010–11	1,025,697	977,520	49,163	166,911	1,339,367[2]
2011–12	1,079,462	1,007,561	72,930	183,968	1,407,932
2012–13	1,175,325	1,059,796	119,092	281,112	1,539,128
2013–14	1,216,457	1,130,789	91,668	345,689	1,628,622
2014–15	1,244,605	1,152,974	94,533	389,088	1,723,121
2015–16[1]	1,303,131	1,265,398	37,733	284,724	1,734,614

Notes
1 Estimated values presented in Yukon's 2016–17 Budget Financial Information.
2 The Public Sector Accounting Board issued new accounting standards which came into effect for the fiscal year 2012–13. The accounting changes were applied retroactively to the 2010–11 fiscal year. The new standard added the unamortized balance of Yukon's deferred capital contributions, more than doubling the territory's accumulated surplus.
Sources: Department of Finance, Government of Yukon 2005, 2006, 2007, 2008, 2009, 2010, 2011, 2012, 2013, 2014, 2015.

$25.6 million, it was accompanied by declines in both its net and accumulated surpluses.[12] Table 13.4 present's Yukon's budgetary figures from 2007–16. The 2015–16 budget sits as $1.265 billion, with a projected $37.7 million surplus. Yukon has no public debt and an estimated accumulated surplus of $1.73 billion in 2015–16. This surplus is significant, particularly given the overall size of Yukon's economy, and is greater than total expenditures for the territory.

Table 13.5 presents an overview of Yukon's revenues, along with specific figures from federal transfers and taxes and general revenues. Yukon's revenues have grown, driven largely by growth in federal transfers. Taxes and general revenues have grown over the period, from $104.5 million in 2007–08 to an estimated $171 million in 2015–16, or by 38.8%. The share of Yukon's revenues from taxes and general revenues, however, has not. They have remained relatively stable over the period, growing between 2011–13, but settling around the 12% to 13% mark in the 2014–15 and 2015–16 budgets.

Table 13.5 Yukon revenues

	Total revenue[1] *(thousands of dollars)*	*Government of Canada transfers*[2] *(thousands of dollars)*	*Government of Canada transfers (%)*	*Taxes and general revenues (thousands of dollars)*	*Taxes and general revenues (%)*
2007–08	854,449	576,000	67.4	104,486	12.2
2008–09	882,174	598,000	68.5	114,110	12.9
2009–10	934,973	649,000	69.3	116,426	12.4
2010–11	1,025,697	690,000	71.1	120,195	12.7
2011–12	1,079,462	744,000	71.3	144,976	14.1
2012–13	1,175,325	809,000	71.2	161,481	14.2
2013–14	1,216,457	861,000	70.8	175,653	14.4
2014–15	1,244,605	898,000	72.2	155,005	12.5
2015–16[3]	1,303,131	923,000	70.8	171,368	13.2

Notes
1 Includes transfers from Canada, taxes and general revenues, recoveries from Canada and third parties, funding and service agreements with other parties, and income from investment in government business enterprises (i.e. Yukon Development Corporation, Yukon Liquor Commission).
2 Includes the Canada Health Transfer, the Canada Social Transfer, and Territorial Formula Financing.
3 Estimated values presented in Yukon's 2016–17 Budget Financial Information and by the Department of Finance Canada.
Sources: Department of Finance, Government of Yukon 2005, 2006, 2007, 2008, 2009, 2010, 2011, 2012, 2013, 2014, 2015; Department of Finance Canada 2015.

Yukon's fiscal position remains healthy. This has allowed the territorial government to make investment decisions rather than decisions about cuts, like in other parts of the country. This fiscal health, however, has been largely driven by growth in federal transfers, a fact that has been masked by concurrent growth in the economy. This economic growth has contributed to territorial coffers, but not at a rate rapid enough to surpass the increasingly large share of Yukon's budget supplied by federal cash.

YUKON AND THE POLITICS OF AUSTERITY

The purpose of this section is to examine what, if any, have been the consequences of austerity for Yukon's public sector and, in particular, its public-sector workers. In short, they have been marginal, except at the federal level, where there have been some layoffs in regional offices located in Yukon. As stated above, Yukon's broader public sector represented the largest portion of its economy at 36.2% of GDP in 2015. Since 2007, public employment in Yukon has grown from 6,600 full-time equivalent employees (FTES) to 7,900 FTES in 2014. These FTES are not only located in the territorial government, but also with Aboriginal, municipal, and federal levels of government.

Data is no longer available that provides a breakdown of separate figures for each level of government, but GDP data does shed some light on growth in the public sector since 2007. Federal expenditures on public administration in the territory remained stagnant between 2007 and 2014, averaging $69 million per year. By contrast, territorial expenditures, as a proportion of GDP, grew by 14.2% over the same period, while expenditures on Aboriginal public administration grew by 18.6% to $76.4 million in 2013. The rise in Aboriginal public administration reflects the implementation of Aboriginal self-government in the territory over the past decade.

The increase in territorial public-sector expenditures is the result of both hiring and negotiated wage increases. Table 13.6 presents public-sector wage increases from 2009 to 2015 for the Public Service Alliance of Canada (PSAC), which represented territorial public servants, and the Yukon Teachers Association (YTA). In the midst of the global financial crisis, PSAC was able to negotiate a 12.25% wage increase over six years, while the YTA was able to negotiate a similar 12.25% increase over a similar period.

At the federal level, there were high-profile cuts, and this is where we see something approaching austerity in the territory. While personally difficult for the employees involved, these cuts did not slow overall growth in the territory's public sector. In 2012, the federal government announced the elimination of sixty-four Parks Canada positions in Northern Canada, thirty of them in Yukon. This resulted in the closing of some tourist sites and reductions in service offerings in the territory. The impact on Yukon's broader tourism sector from these cuts is unclear, but Yukon's arts, entertainment, and recreation sector did shrink by 32% between 2007 and 2014, reflecting declines in North American tourism generally.

CONCLUSION: WILL YUKON'S FISCAL FORTUNES HOLD?

The period 2003 to 2012 may represent an extraordinary run for a territory whose primary sectors are in natural resources and public

Table 13.6
Public-sector negotiated wage increases

	Public Service Alliance of Canada (%)	*Yukon Teachers Association (%)*
2009		2
2010	2	2.25
2011	2.25	2.25
2012	2.25	2
2013	2	1.75
2014	2	2
2015	1.75	

Sources: Public Service Alliance of Canada 2010, 2013; Yukon Teachers Association 2009, 2012.

service delivery. Since 2013, however, Yukon's economic environment has been rapidly shifting. Declines in global mineral, oil and gas, and other commodity prices have begun to effect Yukon's economic output. The shuttering of all three of the territory's mines, along with a general slowdown in construction, will not help. While the territorial government continues to promote its mineral sector – most recently on a high-profile trip by former premier Pasloski to Toronto in February 2015 to speak with business leaders and the media, and to ring the opening bell at the Toronto Stock Exchange – its growing reliance on federal transfers has yet to become a general political concern. Moreover, while Yukon has benefited from these transfers and avoided anything approaching austerity, there are few lessons here for other parts of Canada when it comes to battling their own fiscal troubles.

NOTES

1 Between 2006 and 2015, Yukon's GDP grew a median of 4.6 % and a cumulative 34.4 % over the decade. Canada's GDP, by contrast, grew by 2.2 % or a cumulative 16.4 % (Statistics Canada 2015).

2 A fundamental critique that has always followed calls for Yukon provincehood, especially in the 1970s and 1980s, has been the inability of the jurisdiction to get anywhere near becoming financially self-sufficient with its current tax base (Dacks 1981; Sabin 2014).

3 The last major studies of the Yukon economy were conducted in the late 1960s by University of Toronto political economist Kenneth Rea (1968),

and a study by D.W. Carr & Associates (1968) commissioned by the federal government as a substitute for a more fulsome investigation like the Advisory Commission on the Development of Government in the Northwest Territories. Historical accounts of economic development, including the history of resource extraction, can be found in Zaslow (1988) and Coates and Morrison (2005).

4 There are fourteen Yukon First Nations, but only eleven have settled their final self-government agreements.

5 Operations at the Bellekeno mine were suspended in September 2013 due to falling silver prices, while the Wolverine zinc mine was shuttered in January 2015.

6 There is no manufacturing base, for example, and small craft and tourism are only recently increasing as shares of the economy.

7 This concentration does not appear in either the Northwest Territories or Nunavut, where their capitals represented 45% and 21% of the population respectively in 2006 (Feehan 2009: 360).

8 In 2013, for example, the Minto Mine paid $1.77 million in royalties, almost all of that going to the Selkirk First Nation. Meanwhile, the development of the Minto Mine benefited from subsidies and incentives from the Yukon government, which sees almost no direct revenue from the mine.

9 Oil and gas used to provide Yukon with steady revenues, amounting to $4.2 million in 2005–06. This amount has fallen to $0 as there were no active oil and gas wells in Yukon as of 2013. The combination of the two exemption schemes was advantageous to Yukon, as one press release put it, because "in 2010 our revenue from mineral, forestry, water, and land resources was $4.7 million which meant that Yukon's grant from Canada was reduced by $1.7 million because of the $3 million cap. This new agreement means we would have kept that $1.7 million in the territory" (Yukon 2012).

10 In late 2014, the Yukon Supreme Court ruled that the government had failed to respect the consultation process with Yukon First Nations when drawing up its land use plan for the Peel, ordering the government to return to First Nations for further consultations.

11 These First Nations governments include the Na-cho Nyak Dun, the Gwich'in Tribal Council, the Vuntut Gwitchin First Nation, and the Tr'ondëk Hwëch'in First Nation.

12 Net surplus refers to "the difference between financial assets and liabilities," while the accumulated surplus is a more expansive measure of a jurisdiction's assets. The accumulated surplus includes "the combined

amount of net financial resources and non-financial assets … It is the cumulative excess of revenues over expenses. Since non-financial assets, including tangible capital assets, provide resources that the Government of Yukon can use in the future to accomplish its objectives, non-financial assets form part of the accumulated surplus" (Yukon Department of Finance 2016).

REFERENCES

Abele, Frances, Thomas J. Courchene, F. Leslie Siedle, and France St-Hilaire, eds. 2009. *Northern Exposure: Peoples, Powers and Prospects in Canada's North*. Montreal: Institute for Research on Public Policy.

Abele, Frances, and Michael J. Prince. 2009. "A Little Imagination Required: How Canada Funds Territorial and Northern Aboriginal Governments." In *How Ottawa Spends 2008–09: A More Orderly Federalism?*, edited by Allan Maslove, 82–109. Montreal and Kingston: McGill-Queen's University Press.

Alcantara, Christopher. 2013. "Preferences, Perceptions, and Veto Players: Explaining Devolution Negotiation Outcomes in the Canadian Territorial North." *Polar Record* 49 (2): 167–79.

Alcantara, Christopher, Kirk Cameron, and Steven Kennedy. 2012. "Assessing Devolution in the Canadian North: A Case Study of the Yukon Territory." *Arctic* 65 (3): 328–38.

Bezeau, M.V. 1985. "The Realities of Strategic Planning: The Decision to Build the Alaska Highway." In *The Alaska Highway: Papers of the 40th Anniversary Symposium*, edited by Kenneth Coates, 25–37. Vancouver: UBC Press.

Busby, Colin, and William B.P. Robson. 2014. *Credibility on the (Bottom) Line: The Fiscal Accountability of Canada's Senior Governments*. Toronto: C.D. Howe Institute.

Canada. Bureau of Statistics. 1931. *Census of Canada*. Ottawa: J.O. Patenaude, King's Printer.

Canada. Statistics Canada. 1972. *Census of Canada*. Ottawa, ON.

– 1996. *Yukon's GDP at 1986 Prices*. Ottawa, ON. http://www.statcan.gc.ca/daily-quotidien/960513/c960513k.gif.

– 2011. *Focus on Geography Series, 2011 Census, Yukon*. Ottawa, ON. http://www12.statcan.gc.ca/census-recensement/2011/as-sa/fogs-spg/Facts-PR-eng.cfm?LANG=Eng&GK=PR&GC=60.

– 2014. *Table 405-0004 – Motor Vehicle Registrations by Province and Territory (Yukon, Northwest Territories, and Nunavut)*. CANSIM (database). https://www.statcan.gc.ca/tables-tableaux/sum-som/101/cst01/trade14d-eng.htm.

– 2016a. *Table 282-0100 – Labour Force Survey Estimates (LFS), by Territories, Sex and Age Group, Three-Month Moving Average, Seasonally Adjusted and Unadjusted*, CANSIM (database). http://www5.statcan.gc.ca/cansim/a26?lang=eng&id=2820100.

– 2016b. *Table 384-0038 – Gross Domestic Product, Expenditure-Based, Provincial and Territorial, Annual*, CANSIM (database). http://www5.statcan.gc.ca/cansim/a26?lang=eng&id=3840038.

– 2016c. *Table 380-0101 – Gross National Income and Gross Domestic Income, Annual*, CANSIM (database). http://www5.statcan.gc.ca/cansim/a26?lang=eng&id=3800101.

Canada. Bank of Canada. 2015. *Commodity Price Index – Annual.* Ottawa, ON. www.bankofcanada.ca/rates/price-indexes/bcpi/commodity-price-index-annual.

Canada. Department of Finance. 2015. *Federal Support to Provinces and Territories.*

CBC North. 2013. *Northbeat.* 22 January.

– 2015. "Peel Watershed: Darrell Pasloski Explains Reasons for Appeal." 13 January.

Carr, D.W., and Associates. 1968. *The Yukon Economy: Its Potential for Growth and Continuity.* Ottawa: Queen's Printer.

Coates, Kenneth. 1988. "On the Outside in Their Homeland: Native People and the Evolution of the Yukon Economy." *The Northern Review* 1 (Summer): 73–89.

– 1991. *Best Left as Indians: Native-White Relations and the Yukon Territory.* Montreal and Kingston: McGill-Queen's University Press.

Coates, Kenneth, and William R. Morrison. 2005. *Land of the Midnight Sun: A History of Yukon.* Montreal and Kingston: McGill-Queen's University Press.

Cruikshank, Julie. 1977. "Myths and Futures in the Yukon Territory: The Inquiry as a Social Dragnet." *Canadian Issues* 2 (2): 53–69.

Dacks, Gurston. 1981. *A Choice of Futures: Politics in the Canadian North.* Toronto: Methuen.

Dixon, Currie. 2013. "Yukon & the Arctic Council." *Northern Public Affairs* 2(1): 48–51.

Feehan, J.P. 2009. "Natural Resource Devolution in the Territories: Current Status and Unresolved Issues." In *Northern Exposure: Peoples, Powers and Prospects in Canada's North*, edited by F. Abele, T.J.

Courchene, F.L. Seidle, and F. St-Hilare. The Art of the State, vol. 4. Montreal: Institute for Research on Public Policy.

Franks, C.E.S. 1967. "How the Sabbath Came to Yukon." *Canadian Public Administration* 10(1): 123–35.

Gladstone, Joshua, Sheena Kennedy, and Frances Abele. 2014. "Promises to Keep: Federal Spending on Communications and Transportation Infrastructure in the Territorial North." In *How Ottawa Spends 2013–2014*, edited by Christopher Stoney and Bruce Doern, 159–71. Montreal and Kingston: McGill-Queen's University Press.

Grenon, Lee. 1997. "Employment and Industrial Development in the North." *Perspectives* 6 (1): 18–27.

Herkes, Jennifer, James Mooney, and Holly Smith. 2013. *Exploring Residency in Yukon*. Whitehorse: ECOFOR.

Irlbacher-Fox, Stephanie, and Stephen Mills. 2007. *Devolution and Resource Revenue Sharing in the Canadian North: Achieving Fairness across Generations*. Toronto: Walter and Duncan Gordon Foundation.

Johnson, Linda. 2009. *With the People Who Live Here: The History of the Yukon Legislature, 1909–1961*. Whitehorse: Legislative Assembly of Yukon.

– 2012. *At the Heart of Gold: The Yukon Commissioner's Office 1898–2010*. Whitehorse: Legislative Assembly of Yukon.

McArthur, D. 2009. "The Changing Architecture of Governance in Yukon and the Northwest Territories." In *Northern Exposure: Peoples, Powers and Prospects in Canada's North*, edited by F. Abele, T.J. Courchene, F.L. Seidle, and F. St-Hilare. The Art of the State, vol. 4. Montreal: Institute for Research on Public Policy.

Morrison, David R. 1968. *The Politics of the Yukon Territory, 1898–1909*. Toronto: University of Toronto Press.

Nadasdy, Paul. 2003. *Hunters and Bureaucrats: Power, Knowledge, and Aboriginal-State Relations in the Southwest Yukon*. Vancouver: UBC Press.

Northwest Territories. Department of Finance. 2014. *Main Estimates 2014–2015*. Yellowknife, NWT.

Nunavut. Department of Finance. 2014. *Main Estimates 2014–2015*. Iqaluit, Nunavut.

Public Service Alliance of Canada. 2010. *Collective Agreement between Government of Yukon and the Public Service Alliance of Canada Effective January 1, 2010 to December 31, 2012*.

– 2013. *Collective Agreement between Government of Yukon and the Public Service Alliance of Canada Effective January 1, 2013 to December 31, 2015.*

Rea, Kenneth. 1968. *The Political Economy of the Canadian North: An Interpretation of the Course of Development in the Northern Territories of Canada to the Early 1960s.* Toronto: University of Toronto Press.

Royal Bank of Canada. 2014. *Canadian Federal and Provincial Fiscal Tables.* Toronto, ON.

Sabin, Jerald. 2014. "Contested Colonialism: Responsible Government and Political Development in Yukon." *Canadian Journal of Political Science* 47 (2): 375–96.

Staples, K., M. Chávez-Ortiz, M.J. Barrett, and D.A. Clark. 2013. "Fixing Land Use Planning in the Yukon before It Really Breaks: A Case Study of the Peel Watershed." Northern Review 37: 143–65.

Thomas, Lewis Herbert. 1956. *The Struggle for Responsible Government in the North-West Territories: 1870–1897.* Toronto: University of Toronto Press.

Winter, Jesse. 2013. "Auditor General Slams Hospital Spending." *Yukon News*, 27 February.

White, Graham. 2011. "Go North, Young Scholar, Go North." *Canadian Journal of Political Science* 44 (4): 747–68.

Yukon. Office of the Commissioner. 1971. *Yukon Territory: Annual Report of the Commissioner April 1st, 1970 to March 31st 1971.* Whitehorse, YK.

– 1974. *Short History of the Council of the Yukon Territory.* Whitehorse: Queen's Printer.

Yukon. Executive Council Office. 2003. *Devolution Marks Historic Day for the Yukon.* Whitehorse: Government of Yukon. https://web.archive.org/web/20050109235302/http://www.gov.yk.ca:80/news/2003/apr/03-059.pdf.

Yukon. Department of Finance. 2005. *2005–06 Financial Information.* Whitehorse: Government of Yukon. http://www.finance.gov.yk.ca/pdf/budget/2005_2006_fininfo.pdf.

– 2006. *2006–07 Financial Information.* Whitehorse: Government of Yukon. http://www.finance.gov.yk.ca/pdf/budget/2006_2007_fininfo.pdf.

– 2007. *2007–08 Financial Information.* Whitehorse: Government of Yukon. http://www.finance.gov.yk.ca/pdf/budget/2007_08_fininfo_e.pdf.

– 2008. *2008–09 Financial Information.* Whitehorse: Government of Yukon. http://www.finance.gov.yk.ca/pdf/budget/2008_09_fininfo_e.pdf.

– 2009. *2009–10 Financial Information.* Whitehorse: Government of Yukon. http://www.finance.gov.yk.ca/pdf/budget/2009_10_fininfo_e.pdf.

– 2010. *2010–11 Financial Information.* Whitehorse: Government of Yukon. http://www.finance.gov.yk.ca/pdf/budget/English_-_Financial_Information_2010-2011.pdf.
– 2011. *2011–12 Financial Information.* Whitehorse: Government of Yukon. http://www.finance.gov.yk.ca/pdf/budget/2011_12_fininfo_e.pdf.
– 2012. *2012–13 Financial Information.* Whitehorse: Government of Yukon. http://www.finance.gov.yk.ca/pdf/budget/2012_2013_fininfo_e.pdf.
– 2013. *2013–14 Financial Information.* Whitehorse: Government of Yukon. http://www.finance.gov.yk.ca/pdf/budget/2013-14_fininfo_e.pdf.
– 2014. *2014–15 Financial Information.* Whitehorse: Government of Yukon. http://www.finance.gov.yk.ca/pdf/budget/2014-15budget_Financial_Information_e.pdf.
– 2015. *2015–16 Financial Information.* Whitehorse: Government of Yukon. http://www.finance.gov.yk.ca/pdf/budget/Financial_information.pdf.
– 2016. *2016–17 Financial Information.* Whitehorse: Government of Yukon.
Yukon. Legislative Assembly. 2014. (Hon. Mr. Pasloski). *Hansard.* Whitehorse: 3870, 25 March.
Yukon. Yukon Bureau of Statistics. 2010. *Yukon Statistical Review: 2010 Annual Review.* Whitehorse: Government of Yukon.
– 2014. *Population Report – September 2014.* Whitehorse: Government of Yukon. http://www.eco.gov.yk.ca/pdf/populationSep_2014.pdf.
– 2016. *Yukon Employment Annual Review.* Whitehorse: Government of Yukon.
– 2017. *Gross Domestic Product (GDP) by Industry at Basic Prices 2014.* Whitehorse: Government of Yukon. http://www.eco.gov.yk.ca/pdf/mr_jan2016.pdf.
Yukon. Department of Economic Development. 2015. *Yukon Economic Outlook – January 2015.* Whitehorse: Government of Yukon.
– 2016. *Yukon Economic Outlook – May 2016.* Whitehorse: Government of Yukon. http://www.finance.gov.yk.ca/pdf/YukonEconomicOutlook_May2016.pdf.
Yukon. Department of Energy, Mines and Resources. 2014. *Minerals Management Yearly Activity Report, 2013–14.* Whitehorse: Government of Yukon.
Yukon Teachers' Association. 2009. *Collective Agreement between the Government of Yukon and the Yukon Teachers' Association Effective July 1, 2009 to June 30, 2012.*

– 2012. *Collective Agreement between the Government of Yukon and the Yukon Teachers' Association Effective July 1, 2012 to June 30, 2015.*
Zaslow, Morris. 1971. *The Opening of the Canadian North.* Toronto: McClelland and Stewart.
– 1988. *The Northward Expansion of Canada, 1914–1967.* Toronto: McClelland and Stewart.

Contributors

KEITH BROWNSEY is professor at Mount Royal University's Department of Economics, Justice, and Policy Studies. Dr Brownsey's academic interests include Alberta and Canadian politics and the politics of oil and gas as well as related environmental issues. He is the co-author (with Michael Howlett) of *The Provincial State: Politics in Canada's Provinces and Territories,* as well as co-editor (with Luc Bernier and Micheal Howlett) of *Executive Styles in Canada: Cabinet Structures and Leadership Practices in Canadian Government.*

DAVID CAMFIELD teaches labour studies and sociology at the University of Manitoba. He is the author of *Canadian Labour in Crisis: Reinventing the Workers' Movement* and *We Can Do Better: Ideas for Changing Society.*

PETER CLANCY is a senior research professor at St Francis Xavier University. Dr Clancy's work centres on the interplay of economic and political interests in a variety of settings, including business politics and resource industries. He is the author of *Freshwater Politics in Canada* and *Offshore Petroleum Politics: Regulation and Risk in the Scotian Basin.*

KEN COATES is a professor and Canada Research Chair in Regional Innovation in the Johnson-Shoyama Graduate School of Public Policy. He is also the Macdonald-Laurier Institute's Senior Policy Fellow in Aboriginal and Northern Canadian Issues. He has previously published on such topics as Arctic sovereignty, Aboriginal rights in the Maritimes, northern treaty and land claims processes, regional economic development, and government strategies for working with Indigenous peoples in Canada. He is the author of *A Global History of Indigenous Peoples: Struggle and Survival*, and co-author (with Greg Poelzer) of *From Treaty Peoples to Treaty Nation*.

PATRICIA ANN CONRAD holds a PhD from the Institute of Health Policy, Management and Evaluation at the University of Toronto. Her doctoral research was a comparative cross-case study of provincial regionalization models implemented in the Maritime provinces that analyzed outcomes of reallocating resources to home care. She is the former executive director of the Newfoundland and Labrador Health Boards Association and is currently practising as an independent consultant in Nova Scotia concentrating on health policy and systems research projects.

BRYAN EVANS is full professor in the Department of Politics and Public Administration at Ryerson University. He is the co-author (with John Shields) of *Shrinking the State: Globalization and Public Administration Reform*, and co-editor (with Stephen McBride) of *The Austerity State*, as well as *Austerity: The Lived Experience*.

CARLO FANELLI is assistant professor of work and labour studies in the Department of Social Science and appointed to the graduate program in sociology at York University. He is the author of *Megacity Malaise: Neoliberalism, Public Services and Labour in Toronto*, and co-editor (with Ingo Schmidt) of *Reading Capital Today: Marx after 150 Years*. Since 2010, he has been editor-in-chief of *Alternate Routes: A Journal of Critical Social Research*.

JAMIE GILLIES is assistant professor of journalism and communication at St Thomas University. A political scientist by training, his academic work is focused on political communications and public policy, in particular American presidents and Anglo-American executive leadership, US White House advisers, and the personalization of political leadership.

PETER GRAEFE is associate professor in the Department of Political Science at McMaster University. He is interested in Canadian political economy and public policy, social and economic development policies in Quebec and Ontario, provincial social assistance policies, and federal and provincial intergovernmental relations strategies. He is the co-editor (with Julie M. Simmons and Linda A. White) of *Overpromising and Underperforming: Understanding and Evaluating New Intergovernmental Accountability Regimes.*

JACK HICKS helped develop the Nunavut Suicide Prevention Strategy and is a suicide prevention researcher and practitioner. He is adjunct professor in the Department of Community Health and Epidemiology at the University of Saskatchewan, and co-author (with Graham White) of *Made in Nunavut: An Experiment in Decentralized Government.*

GREG POELZER is professor in the School of Environment and Sustainability at the University of Saskatchewan. His research is focused on comparative politics and policy as it relates to Aboriginal-state relations, energy and resource development in the circumpolar north, capacity building in northern regions, and northern development. He has written extensively on the historical and contemporary aspects of communities located in the circumpolar north and the Canadian sub-arctic, focusing on Aboriginal development, the development of regional infrastructure, and the mining sector. He is the co-author (with Ken Coates and P. Whitney Lackenbauer) of *Arctic Front: Defending Canada in the Far North* and (with Ken Coates) of *From Treaty Peoples to Treaty Nation.*

HUBERT RIOUX OUIMET holds a PhD in political science with a concentration in comparative public policy from McMaster University. He is a Banting Postdoctoral Fellow at the École nationale d'administration publique in Quebec City, Canada.

JERALD SABIN is a SSHRC postdoctoral fellow in the Department of Political Science at Western University and a research associate with the Carleton Centre for Community Innovation at Carleton University. He is a publisher and journalist, serving as founding and managing editor of *Northern Public Affairs*, and co-author (with David Rayside and Paul Thomas) of *Religion and Party Politics.*

CHARLES W. SMITH is associate professor in the Department of Political Science at St Thomas More College, University of Saskatchewan. His research interests include Canadian and International political economy, public law, labour unions, and federal and provincial public policy. He is the co-editor (with Bryan Evans) of *Transforming Provincial Politics*, co-author (with Larry Savage) of *Unions in Court: Organized Labour and the Charter of Rights and Freedoms*, and co-editor of *Labour/Le Travail*.

ROBERT C.H. SWEENY is professor of history at Memorial University. He is the author of *Why Did We Choose to Industrialize? Montreal, 1819–1849*, recipient of the 2016 Governor General's History Award for Scholarly Research: The Sir John A. Macdonald Prize.

HEATHER WHITESIDE is assistant professor of political science at the University of Waterloo. Dr Whiteside studies the political economy of privatization, financialization, and fiscal austerity. She is the author of *About Canada: Public-Private Partnerships*, *Purchase for Profit: Public-Private Partnerships and Canada's Public Health Care System*, and *Private Affluence, Public Austerity: Economic Crisis and Democratic Malaise in Canada* (with Stephen McBride).

Index